Teaching An Introduction to Literature
Fiction / Poetry / Drama

Tenth Edition

Sylvan Barnet
Morton Berman
William Burto

 HarperCollins*CollegePublishers*

TEACHING AN INTRODUCTION TO LITERATURE:
Fiction/Poetry/Drama
by Sylvan Barnet, Morton Berman, and William Burto

Copyright © 1993 HarperCollins College Publishers

ISBN: 0-673-54058-8

93 94 95 96 9 8 7 6 5 4 3 2 1

PREFACE

What follows is something close to a slightly organized card file. In the course of writing and then of teaching *An Introduction to Literature*, we have amassed jottings of various sorts, and these may be of some use to others as well as to ourselves. Perhaps most useful will be the references to critical articles and books from which we have profited. We have plowed through a fair amount of material and tried to call attention to some of the best. We have also offered suggestions for theme assignments, but many of the questions printed at the ends of sections in *An Introduction to Literature* are suitable topics for writing. We have offered, too, relatively detailed comment on some of the stories, poems, and plays. (Most of the comments on *Oedipus* and *Death of a Salesman* are drawn from our *Types of Drama*.) These may serve, especially if they seem wrongheaded, to give an instructor a jumping-off place.

Contents

The First Meeting

The night before the first class, every teacher knows the truth of Byron's observation: "Nothing so difficult as a beginning." What to do in the first meeting is always worrisome. Students will not, of course, have prepared anything, and you can't say, "Let's open the book to page such-and-such," because half of them won't have the book. How, then, can one use the time profitably? A friend of ours (Marcia Stubbs, of Wellesley College) offers a suggestion. We have tried it and we know it works, so we suggest that you consider it, too, if you are looking for an interesting beginning.

Begin reading the Japanese anecdote (text, 29) aloud, stopping after "A heavy rain was still falling." Then ask, "What do you think will happen now?" Someone is bound to volunteer, "They'll meet someone." Whom will they meet? (It may be necessary to say at this point that Tanzan and Ekido are both men.) You will certainly be informed that if two men meet someone, it will be a woman. Continue reading, "Coming around the bend they met a lovely girl. . . ." After "unable to cross the intersection," ask again what will happen, and entertain answers until you get an appropriate response. Read again, and pause after "temple." Who are Tanzan and Ekido? The temple may suggest to someone that they are monks; if not, provide the information. Continue reading, up through "Why did you do that?" Now inform the class that the story ends with one more line of print, and ask them to supply the brief ending. The students will then see the perfect rightness of it.

The point of the exercise: First a story sets up expectations, partly by *excluding* possibilities. (A relevant remark by Robert Frost appears on 456 of the text, but it can be effectively introduced at the first meeting. A work of literature—Frost is talking about a poem, but we can generalize—"assumes direction with the first line laid down.") After the first line or so, the possibilities are finite. The story must go on to fulfill the expectations set up. At the same time, a story, to be entertaining, must surprise us by taking us beyond what we have imagined and expect. But the fulfillment and the surprise must be coherent or the storyteller will appear arbitrary and the story, no matter how entertaining, trivial. (Notice E.M. Forster's pertinent comment, quoted on 37: "Shock, followed by the feeling, 'Oh, that's all right,' is a sign that all is well with the plot.")

By satisfying expectations, literature confirms the truth of our own experience, teaching us that we are not alone, not singular; our perceptions, including moral perceptions (e.g., cause leads to effect, guilt leads to punishment or retribution) are shared by other human beings, people who may not even be of our own century or culture. Something along these lines can be suggested at the first meeting; subsequent meetings can be devoted to showing that literature, by exceeding and yet not violating our expectations, can also expand our powers of observation, imagination, and judgment.

The first chapter ("Reading and Responding to Literature") is fairly short; it can be given as the first reading assignment, and since it includes very short poems (both called "Immigrants") and two very short prose narrative (The Prodigal Son, and Grace Paley's "Samuel"), the discussion in class can hardly flag.

If, however, you prefer to skip the first chapter and you plan to spend the first few weeks on fiction, you may want to begin with Chapter 2, which includes Hemingway's "Cat in the Rain," along with comments about annotating and keeping a journal. If none of this pedagogical material appeals to you, you may want to give as the first assignment, that is, the reading for the next meeting, Poe's "The Cask of Amontillado" (text, 158). The story is short and arresting, and it is familiar to many students. There will almost certainly be ample discussion in class, yet even students who come to class thinking they know the story well will probably leave class having learned new things about it. And in any case, an instructor who wishes to follow up on the lessons of "Muddy Road"—not the theme of the story but the lessons about plot and characterization—can examine Poe's story with an eye toward the way one episode follows another, arousing curiosity and then satisfying it. Shirley Jackson's "The Lottery" (text, 266), another high-school favorite, can be used in a similar fashion.

Chapter 1

Reading and Responding to Literature

This chapter begins with two very short poems. If you want to begin by teaching fiction, you may want to skip this chapter and start with the next chapter (Hemingway's "Cat in the Rain"). On the other hand, we think these two poems make a good introduction to literature, and in any case, since they are closely followed by two short works of prose, The Parable of the Prodigal Son and Grace Paley's "Samuel," you can use the chapter even if you devote the first third of the course to fiction.

Robert Frost "Immigrants" (p. 2) and Pat Mora "Immigrants" (p. 6)

These two poems are discussed at some length in the text. Those words may sound ominous, even deadly, but we are sure you will find that much remains to be done in class. Enough questions are raised in the text to stimulate lots of discussion.

The text makes the point that Frost's poem was written for an anniversary celebration of the arrival of the Mayflower, and that is really all that students need to know about the background, but instructors may be interested in a bit more. The lines originally were the fourth stanza of a long poem that Frost wrote in 1920, "The Return of the Pilgrims," for *The Pilgrim Spirit—A Pageant in Celebration of the Landing of the Pilgrims at Plymouth, Massachusetts, December 21, 1620*, organized by George Pierce Baker. The literary aspects of the pageant were published (under the title just given) in 1921, but Frost never again reprinted the entire poem. Instead, he extracted only this one stanza from his poem, called it "Immigrants," and printed it in *West-Running Brook* (1928) and in many of his later volumes.

In the text in our discussion of Frost we ignore one large matter— the speaking voice. We omitted this issue because we felt we had talked enough (maybe more than enough) about the poem, and because the matter of voice is fairly subtle, but instructors may want to ask several students to read the poem aloud, and then to discuss the voice. Briefly, it seems to us that in this poem we get an authoritative voice—a voice which is by no means offensive but which is highly confident and indeed by its confidence (and its mastery of form) inspires confidence or faith in its assertion.

Pat Mora's voice in her "Immigrants" is marvelously different— for one thing, we get (as our comment in the text tries to suggest) *several* voices in her poem. Where Frost gives us the voice of the poet as an assured elder statesman (though he was only 46 at the time), Mora gives us the voices of the uneasy immigrants as well as the voice of the ironic commentator.

At least three voices are head in Mora's poem: the voice of the immigrant, hoping that his or her child will resemble Americans (WASPS, that is); the voice of the immigrant, fearful that the child will not be liked because the child will not seem sufficiently American; and the ironic voice of the poet expressing skepticism about the hopes for assimilation to an Anglo-American model.

The almost comic glimpse of imperfect pronunciation given in line 8 ("hallo, babee, hallo")—the speaker of the poem here seems to have a somewhat superior attitude—disappears in the last three lines which, though written in English, sympathetically represent the fear that is thought "in Spanish or Polish." If you discuss these lines, you may want to invite students to express their opinions about why "american" is not capitalized in the last two lines, even though it is capitalized in the first ("the American flag"), and "Spanish" and "Polish" are capitalized. We take it that by not capitalizing "american" in the last two lines the poet implies that it's not all that wonderful to become an "american," indeed there may be a loss in changing from "Spanish" or "Polish" to "american."

Put it this way: the poem shifts from the eager activity of immigrant parents (presented almost comically in lines 1–7) to a more sympathetic presentation of deep fears in lines 8–14, but the whole is complicated by the author's implied criticism (chiefly through "american") of the immigrants' understandable but mistaken activity.

In short, we think that if you ask several students to read both of the poems aloud, the class will enjoy what Frost in a letter called "the sound of sense," and they will also see that works of literature have an almost palpable sensuous appeal. They will see, too, that Mora's poem is able to hold its own in the company of Frost's. We confess that we are unable to think of a more effective way than this if one wants to introduce students to the idea of "multiculturalism."

One last word about this part of the chapter, specifically about Frost's poem. A reader of our manuscript objected that Frost offered an offensive mythic view of America (the land of freedom and opportunity) and that in our commentary we had bought this myth. He suggested that many immigrants—especially the Asian laborers in the nineteenth century—had been imported as cheap labor, and existed virtually as chattel. And before the Asians came, thousands of English, for instance, had come as indentured servants, obliged to work for years before they could be free. Still, it seems evident that even for these people life in America promised opportunities that were unavailable in the Old Country. Similarly, for those Asians who came here, life in this country (or Hawaii)—however grinding—must have seemed preferable to life in China or Japan or the Philippines. For instance, the Japanese who worked in the sugar plantations of Hawaii (beginning in 1868) endured terrible conditions, but the prospects were better for them than was life in Japan, and at the end of their contractual period most of them elected *not* to return to Japan. In time, of course, many of these people migrated to the mainland. Our own instinct is *not* to go into this issue in discussing Frost's poem, partly because we do not find his view offensive, but chiefly because we want to talk about literature, not about history.

Luke "The Parable of the Prodigal Son" (p. 7)

A bibliographic note about parables may be useful. In the *Encyclopedia Britannica*, in a relatively long article entitled "Fable, Parable, Allegory," fable and parable are defined as "short, simple forms of naive allegory," and yet a few paragraphs later it reads "The rhetorical appeal of a parable is directed primarily toward an elite, in that a final core of its truth is known only to an inner circle, however simple its narrative may appear on the surface. . . ." Perhaps, then, a parable is not a "naive allegory." Two other passages from the article are especially interesting: "The Aesopian fables emphasize the social interaction of human beings," whereas "parables do not analyze social systems so much as they remind the listener of his beliefs." That may not always be true, but it is worth thinking about.

The traditional title of this story is unfortunate, since it makes the second half of the story (the father's dealings with the older brother) superfluous. Joachim Jeremias, in *The Parables of Jesus,* suggests that the work should be called "The Parable of the Father's Love."

Here is a way to provoke thoughtful discussion of the parable. Roger Seamon, in "The Story of the Moral: The Function of Thematizing in Literary Criticism," [*Journal of Aesthetics and Art Criticism* 47 (1989): 229–236], offers an unusual way of thinking about this parable. He summarizes his approach as follows:

> I want to reverse the traditional and common sense view that stories convey, illustrate, prove or emotionally support themes. Morals and themes, I argue, convey to audiences what story is to be made out of sentences.

The story flows, so to speak, from theme, rather than the theme following from the story.[p. 230]

He goes on to suggest an experiment. "Imagine," he says, that instead of reading a story that traditionally is called "The Prodigal Son,"

> We were to find the same set of sentences in another book under the title "The Prodigal Father," and at the end we found the following moral: "Waste not your heart on the unworthy, lest you lose the love of the righteous." We now go back and re-read the sentences, and we find that *we are now reading a different story*. In the new story the father's giving the son money is wrong.

Seamon goes on to say that in *this* story the son's confession is "a way of evading responsibility for his error," and that the father is as prodigal with his love as he was with his property." In this version (remember: the sentences are identical, but the title is different), Seamon claims, "The story concludes with the father happily returning to his error. The absence of poetic justice at the end is meant to arouse our indignation" (p. 232).

It's interesting to hear students respond to this view. Of course Seamon's title, "The Prodigal Father," is merely his own invention, but the conventional title ("The Prodigal Son") has no compelling authority. The question is this: Once we apply Seamon's title, do we read the story the way he suggests—that is, do we see the father as blameworthy and the stay-at-home son as justified? If not, why not? Again, Seamon's point is that although the common-sense view holds that the story yields a moral, in fact the reverse is true: the moral (i.e. the theme we have in mind) yields the story. For Seamon, "A thematic statement conveys information about how the critic constructs the *nature and motivations of the characters*, [and] *the value of their actions . . .*" p. 233). True, but can't we add that the skilled critic, i.e., reader, is in large measure guided by the author who knows (again, at least in large measure) how to control the reader's response? Seamon apparently takes a different view, for he holds that "the sentences used to project the events are not, in themselves, sufficient to tell us how we are to characterize or evaluate what is going on." Our response to Seamon is of no importance; what *is* important is to get students to think about why they do or do not accept the view that the story might be entitled "The Prodigal Father."

We spend some time in class teaching this parable because we find the artistry admirable—and also because the story is profound. One small but telling artistic detail may be noted here, a detail mentioned by Joachim Jeremias, who points out that the elder son, speaking to his father, "omits the address"; we had never noticed this, but now it seems obvious and surely it is revealing that when the younger son addresses his father he says, "Father," and that when the father addresses the older son he says, "Son." The older son's lack of address, then, speaks volumes: he refuses to see himself as bound by family ties of love—a position evident also when, talking to his father, he identifies the prodigal not as "my brother" but as, "this thy son." The story is (among many other things) an admirable example of work in which a storyteller guides an audience into having certain responses.

It's also worthwhile in class to spend some time cautioning against a too-vigorous attempt to find meaning in every detail. (Professionals as well as students sometimes don't know when to leave well enough alone. For instance, a writer in *Studies in Short Fiction* 23[1986], talking about Updike's "A & P," says that Queenie's *pink* bathing suit "suggests the emerging desires competing with chastity." But come to think of it, this statement isn't surprising, considering what has been said about the pink ribbon in "Young Goodman Brown." One writer, for instance, says it symbolizes feminine passion, and another says it symbolizes a state between the scarlet of total depravity and the white of innocence.)

To illustrate the danger of pressing too hard, you might mention medieval allegorizations of the story. The gist of these is this: the older brother represents the Pharisees and teachers who resented the conversion of the Gentiles. Thus the fact that the older brother was in the fields when the prodigal returned was taken as standing for the remoteness of the Pharisees and the teachers from the grace of God. The younger brother, according to medieval interpretations, represents the Gentiles, who wandered in illusions and who served the devil (the owner of the swine) by tending the devil's demons (the swine). The pods that the prodigal ate represent either the vices (which cannot satisfy) or pagan literature (again, unsatisfying). The father represents God the Father; his going forth to meet the prodigal stands for the Incarnation; his falling on the neck of the prodigal stands for the mild yoke that Christ places on the neck of his followers (Matthew 11:29–30). The music which the older brother hears represents the praise of God, and the feast of the fatted calf represents the Eucharist. A great deal more of this sort of thing can be found in Stephen L. Wailes, *Medieval Allegories of Jesus' Parables* (pp. 236–245). The point should already be clear. On the other hand, it's also worth mentioning that the medieval interpreters of the parable at least paid it the compliment of taking it seriously. Odd as the interpretations now seem, they were the result of an admirable love of the word, and surely such an excess is preferable to indifference.

Is the parable an allegory? No, and yes. Certainly it does not have the detailed system of correspondences that one associates with allegory. Moreover, since the prodigal says, "Father, I have sinned against heaven and . . . thee," the father cannot be said to represent heaven, i.e,, God. And yet, as Jeremias says (p. 131):

> The parable describes with touching simplicity what God is like, his goodness, his grace, his boundless mercy, his abounding love.

Need a reader believe in God or in the divinity of Jesus in order to value this story? The point is surely worth discussing in class. Most students will agree that such belief is not necessary, and from here one can go on to discuss stories as ways of imaginatively entering alien worlds.

Grace Paley "Samuel" (p. 11)

"All those ballsy American stories," Grace Paley has said of much of the American canon, "had nothing to say to me." Is she, then, a feminist writer? She denies it, insisting that she is something rather different, "a feminist and a writer." Some instructors may wish to have a class consider in what ways, if any, "Samuel" is the work of a feminist.

There is a particularly female insight in the last two paragraphs of "Samuel," which (though the second of these mentions Samuel's father) focus on Samuel's mother. The first of these paragraphs emphasizes the mother's agony when she learns of her son's death; the final paragraph, describing a later time, emphasizes a grief that is less visible or audible but that is perhaps even more painful, for this grief is stimulated by the sight of her newborn baby: "Never again will a boy exactly like Samuel be known."

Interestingly, the narrator (can we say the female author?) conveys a good deal of enthusiasm for what some people might regard as offensive *macho* displays of jiggling on the subway, riding the tail of a speeding truck, and hopping on the tops of trucks. Paley makes these actions sympathetic partly by implying that they take real skill, partly by implying that the show-off performing kids usually turn out to be very decent guys (one dare-devil has graduated from high school, is married, holds a responsible job, and is going to night school), and partly by mildly discrediting those who oppose them. Thus one lady who disapproves of the jigglers thinks, "Their mothers never know where they are," but the narrator immediately assures us that the mothers of these boys *did* know where they were, and, moreover, the boys had been engaged in the thoroughly respectable activity of visiting a "missile exhibit on Fourteenth Street."

Like this woman, the man who pulls the alarm cord is somewhat discredited: he is "one of the men whose boyhood had been more watchful than brave." Although it's no disgrace for a boy to be "watchful," the sentence probably guides most readers to feel some scorn for the man who (so to speak) was never a boy. Many readers will feel that although the man "walked in a citizenly way" to pull the cord, he is motivated less by an impulse of good citizenship than (though probably he doesn't know it) by resentment, by irritation that these children are experiencing a joy that he never experienced in his childhood. On the other hand, Paley does not present him as a villain, and the story is not chiefly concerned with his guilt. By the end of the story, readers are probably so taken up with the mother's grief that they scarcely remember the man.

Although "Samuel" resembles a fable in that it is fairly brief, is narrated in an apparently simple manner, and concludes with a message, it differs significantly from a fable. Most obviously, it does not use the beasts, gods, and inanimate objects that fables commonly use. In fact, these are not essential in fables. More significantly, the characters in "Samuel" are more complicated, since the noisy boys are treated sympathetically and the apparently respectable adults are treated ironically. Finally, where the fable traditionally utters or implies a hard-headed, worldly-wise (and often faintly cynical) message, the message uttered at the end of "Samuel" arouses the reader's deepest sympathy.

Additional Topics for Writing

1. If you had been on the train, would you have pulled the emergency cord? Why, or why not?
2. Write a journalist's account (250–300 words of the accidental death of a boy named Samuel. Use whatever details Paley provides, but feel free to invent what you need for an authentic news story.

Chapter 2

A First Approach to Fiction

Ernest Hemingway "Cat in the Rain" (p. 19)

To the best of our knowledge "Cat in the Rain" has not been anthologized in college textbooks of this sort, but we think that it ought to be better known, and we find that it provokes lively discussion when used as an introduction to fiction.

The best published discussion is David Lodge's "Analysis and Interpretation of the Realist Text," *Poetics Today* 1 (1980), 5–19, conveniently reprinted in Lodge's *Working with Structuralism* (1981). Lodge begins by summarizing Carlos Baker's discussion, in which Baker (in *Ernest Hemingway: The Writer as Artist* [1952]) assumed that the cat at the end is the cat at the beginning. As Lodge puts it, in this reading

> [T]he appearance of the maid with a cat is the main reversal, in Aristotelian terms, in the narrative. If it is indeed the cat she went to look for, then the reversal is a happy one for her, and confirms her sense that the hotel keeper appreciated her as a woman more than her husband.

On the other hand, Lodge points out, if the cat is not the same cat,

> We might infer that the padrone, trying to humour a client, sends up the first cat he can lay hands on, which is in fact quite inappropriate to the wife's needs. This would make the reversal an ironic one at the wife's expense, emphasising the social and cultural abyss that separates her from the padrone, and revealing her quasi-erotic response to his professional attentiveness as a delusion.

Lodge goes on to discuss a very different interpretation by John Hagopian, published in *College English* 24 (Dec 1962), 220–22, in which Hagopian argued that the story is about "a crisis in the marriage . . . involving the lack of fertility, which is symbolically foreshadowed by the public garden (fertility) dominated by the war monument (death)." For Hagopian, the rubber cape worn by the man in the rain "is a protection from rain, and rain is a fundamental necessity for fertility and fertility is precisely what is lacking in the American wife's marriage." Put bluntly, Hagopian sees the rubber cape as a condom. Lodge correctly points out that although rain often stands for fertility, in this story the rainy weather is contrasted with "good weather." What the rubber cape does is to emphasize the bad weather, and thus to emphasize the padrone's thoughtfulness (and the husband's indifference).

Lodge's careful and profound article can't be adequately summarized, but we'll give a few more of his points. Near the end of the story, when we read that "George shifted his position in the bed," a reader may feel that George will put down the book and make love to his wife, but this possibility disappears when George says, "Oh, shut up and get something to read."

Taking Seymour Chatman's distinction between stories of *resolution* (we get the answer to "What happened next?") and stories of *revelation* (events are not resolved, but a state of affairs is revealed) Lodge suggests that this story

> seems to share characteristics of both: it is, one might say, a plot of revelation (the relationship between husband and wife) disguised as a plot of resolution (the quest for the cat). The ambiguity of the ending is therefore crucial. By refusing to resolve the issue of whether the wife gets the cat she wants, the implied author indicates that this is not the point of the story.

On point of view, Lodge demonstrates that Hemingway's story is written from the point of view of the American couple, and from the wife's point of view rather than the husband's. (Of course he doesn't mean that the entire story is seen from her point of view. He means only that we get into her mind to a greater degree—e.g., "The cat would be round to the right. Perhaps she could go along under the eaves"—than into the minds of any of the other characters.) Lodge's argument is this: at the end, when the maid appears, "the narration adopts the husband's perspective at this crucial point," and so that's why we are told that the maid held *a* cat rather than *the* cat. After all, the man had not seen the cat in the rain, so he can't know if the maid's cat it is the same cat.

Finally, another discussion of interest is Warren Bennett, "The Poor Kitty . . . in 'Cat in the Rain,'" *Hemingway Review* 8 (Fall 1988) 26–36. Bennett reviews Lodge's discussion of Baker and Hagopian, and insists that the wife is not pregnant (Lodge had suggested, in arguing against Hagopian, that the wife *may* be pregnant). Bennett says that

> [T]he girl's feelings as she thinks of the padrone pass through three stages, tight inside, important, and of momentary supreme importance, and these stages reflect a correspondence to the sensations of desire, intercourse, and orgasm.

Not all readers will agree, though probably we can all agree with Bennett when he says that "The wife's recognition of the padrone's extraordinary character suggests that her husband, George, lacks the qualities which the wife finds so attractive in the padrone. George has neither dignity, nor will, nor commitment."

In any case, Bennett suggests that when the wife returns to the room "her sexual feelings are transferred to George. She goes over to George and tries to express her desire for closeness by sitting down 'on the bed.'"

Bennett's article makes too many points to be summarized here, but one other point should be mentioned. He says that female tortoise-shell cats do not reproduce tortoise-shells, and that males are sterile. Since he identifies the woman with the cat, he says that the woman's "destiny is that of a barren wandering soul with no place and no purpose in the futility of the wasteland *In Our Time.*"

An audio cassette of Ernest Hemingway reading is available from HarperCollins.

Chapter 3

Stories and Meanings

Anton Chekhov "Misery" (p. 30)

Like all good stories, this one can be taught in many ways. Since we teach it at the beginning of the course, we tend to emphasize two things: the artistry of the story and the reader's response, especially the reader's response to the ending. But first we want to mention that plot is given little emphasis. The cabman encounters several passengers, but these encounters do not generate happenings—actions—in the obvious or usual sense, though of course they are in fact carefully arranged and lead to the final action when Iona speaks to the mare. Second, we want to mention that we believe that writers usually express their values in the whole of the story, not in a detachable quotation or in a statement that a reader may formulate as a theme. Chekhov himself made a relevant comment to an editor: "You rebuke me for objectivity, calling it indifference to good and evil, absence of ideals and ideas, etc. You would have me say, in depicting horse thieves, that stealing horses is evil. But then, that has been known for a long while, even without me. Let jurors judge them, for my business is only to show them as they are."

By "the artistry," we mean chiefly the restrained presentation of what could be a highly sentimental action. Chekhov does not turn Iona into a saint, and he does not turn the other characters into villains. The passengers are unsympathetic, true, but chiefly they are busy with their own affairs, or they are drunk. (One of the drunks is a hunchback, and although we feel that he behaves badly toward Iona, we feel also that nature has behaved badly toward him.) Second, Chekhov does not simply tell us that the world is indifferent to Iona; rather, he takes care to *show* us the indifference before we get the explicit statement that Iona searched in vain for a sympathetic hearer. Third, it seems to us that the episodes are carefully arranged. First we get the officer, who, despite his initial brusqueness, makes a little joke, and it is this joke that apparently encourages Iona to speak. The officer displays polite interest–he asks of what the boy died–and Iona turns to respond, but the passenger immediately (and not totally unreasonably) prefers the driver to keep his eyes on the road. Next we get the drunks, who can hardly be expected to comprehend Iona's suffering. All of this precedes the first explicit statement that Iona searches the crowd for a single listener. Next, in an extremely brief episode (we don't need much of a scene, since we are already convinced that Iona cannot find an audience) the house-porter dismisses him, and finally, again in a very brief scene, even a fellow cabman—presumably exhausted from work—falls asleep while Iona is talking. But again Chekhov refrains from comment and simply shows us Iona going to tend his horse. At this point Iona does not intend to speak to the animal, but the sight of the horse provokes a bit of friendly talk ("Are you munching?"), and this naturally leads to a further bit of talk, now about the son, couched in terms suited to that horse—and this, in turn, opens the floodgates.

So far as responses go, all readers will have their own, but for what it's worth, we want to report that we find the ending not so much painful as comforting. The tension is relieved; Iona finds an audience after all, and if the thought of a man telling his grief to his horse has pathos, it also has its warmth. It seems to us to be especially satisfying, but we will have to explain our position somewhat indirectly. First, we will talk about attempts to state the theme of the story.

On pages 37-38 in the text we give the attempts of three students to state the theme. Of the three, we find the third ("Suffering is incommunicable, but the sufferer must find an outlet") the closest to our response. That is, we are inclined to think that the reason Iona cannot tell his story to the officer or to any other person is that grief of this sort cannot be communicated. It isolates the grief-stricken person. One notices in the story how much physical effort goes into Iona's early efforts to communicate with people. As a cabman, of course, he is in front of his passengers, and he has to turn to address his audience. At first his lips move but words do not come out, and when he does speak, it is "with an effort." Near the end of "Misery," just before he goes to the stable. Iona thinks about how the story of his son's death must be told:

> He wants to talk of it properly, with deliberation. He wants to tell how his sone was taken ill, how he suffered, what he said before he died, how he died. . . . He wants to describe the funeral, and how he went to the hospital to get his son's clothes. He still has his daughter Anisya in the country . . . . And he wants to talk about her too. . . . Yes, he has plenty to talk about.

Now we are all decent people—not at all like the brusque officer or the drunken passengers or the indifferent house-porter or the sleepy young cabman—but which of us could endure to hear Iona's story? Which of us really could provide the audience that he needs? Which of us could refrain from interrupting him with well-intended but inadequate mutterings of sympathy, reassurances, and facile piety? Iona's grief is so deeply felt that it isolates him from other human beings, just as the indifference of other beings isolates them from him. Overpowering grief of this sort sets one apart from others. We hope we are not showing our insensitivity when we say that the mare is the only audience that can let Iona tell his story, in all its detail, exactly as he needs to tell it. And that is why we think that, in a way, this deeply moving story has a happy ending.

For another (and very different) story about a father grieving for his son see Chekhov's "Enemies," reprinted in the text, and discussed later in this manual.

Kate Chopin "Ripe Figs" (p. 39)

This story teaches marvelously. Some stories supposedly teach well because the instructor can have the pleasure of showing students all sorts of things that they missed, but of course stories of that kind may, by convincing students that literature has deep meanings that they don't see, turn students away from literature. "Ripe Figs" teaches well because it is a first-rate piece that is easily accessible.

Elaine Gardiner discusses it fully in an essay in *Modern Fiction Studies* [28:3 (1982)], reprinted in Harold Bloom's collection of essays, *Kate Chopin* (1987, pp. 83–87). Gardiner's essay is admirable, but instructors will be interested to find that their students will make pretty much the same points that Gardiner makes. Gardiner emphasizes three of Chopin's techniques: her use of *contrasts, natural imagery,* and *cyclical plotting.*

The chief contrast is between Maman-Nainaine and Babette, that is, age versus youth, patience versus impatience, experience versus innocence, staidness versus exuberance. Thus, Chopin tells us that "Maman-Nainaine sat down in her stately way," whereas Babette is "restless as a hummingbird," and dances. Other contrasts are spring and summer, summer and fall, figs and chrysanthemums.

Speaking of natural imagery, Gardiner says, "Not only are journeys planned according to when figs ripen and chrysanthemums bloom, but places are defined by what they produce; thus, Bayou-Lafourche, for Maman-Nainaine, is the place 'where the sugar cane grows.'" Gardiner calls attention to the references to the leaves, the rain, and the branches of the fig tree, but of course she emphasizes the ripening of the figs (from "little hard, green marbles" to "purple figs, fringed around with their rich green leaves") and the flowering of the chrysanthemums. The contrasts in natural imagery, Gardiner says, "ultimately convey and emphasize continuity and stability."

Turning to cyclical plotting—common in Chopin—Gardiner says, "With the ripening of the figs in the summertime begins the next period of waiting, the continuance of the cycle, both of nature and of the characters' lives. . . . The reader finishes the sketch anticipating the movements to follow–movements directed by the seasons, by natural happenings, by the cyclical patterns of these people's lives."

Kate Chopin "The Story of an Hour" (p. 210)

The first sentence of the story, of course, proves to be essential to the end, though during the middle of the story the initial care to protect Mrs. Mallard from the "sad message" seem almost comic. Students may assume, too easily, that Mrs. Mallard's "storm of grief" is hypocritical. They may not notice that the renewal after the first shock is stimulated by the renewal of life around her ("the tops of trees . . . were all aquiver with the new spring of life") and that before she achieves a new life, Mrs. Mallard first goes through a sort of death and then tries to resist renewal: Her expression "indicated a suspension of intelligent thought," she felt something "creeping out of the sky," and she tried to "beat it back with her will," but she soon finds herself "drinking the elixir of life through that open widow," and her thoughts turn to "spring days, and summer days."

Implicit in the story is the idea that her life as a wife—which she had thought was happy—was in fact a life of repression or subjugation, and the awareness comes to her only at this late stage. The story has two surprises: the change from grief to joy proves not to be the whole story, for we get the second surprise, the husband's return and Mrs. Mallard's death. The last line ("the doctors . . . said she had died . . . of joy that kills") is doubly ironic: The doctors wrongly assume that she was overjoyed to find that her husband was alive, but they were not wholly wrong in guessing that her last day of life brought her great joy.

In a sense, moreover, the doctors are right (though not in the sense they mean) in saying that she "died of heart disease." That is, if we take the "heart" in a metaphorical sense to refer to love and marriage, we can say that the loss of her new freedom from her marriage is unbearable. This is not to say (though many students do say it) that her marriage was miserable. The text explicitly says "she had loved him–sometimes." The previous paragraph in the story nicely calls attention to certain aspects of love—a satisfying giving of the self—and yet also to a most unpleasant yielding to force: "There would be no one to live for her during those coming years; she would live for herself. There would be no powerful will bending her in that blind persistence with which men and women believe they have a right to impose a private will upon a fellow-creature."

A biographical observation: Chopin's husband died in 1882, and her mother died in 1885. In 1894 in an entry in her diary she connected the two losses with her growth. "If it were possible for my husband and my mother to come back to earth, I feel that I would unhesitatingly give up every thing that has come into my life since they left it and join my existence again with theirs. To do that, I would have to forget the past ten years of my growth–my real growth."

Note: the chapter includes two other works by Chopin, "Ripe Figs" and "The Storm."

Additional Topic for Discussion or Writing

Chopin does not tell us if Mrs. Mallard's death is due to joy at seeing her husband alive, guilt for feeling "free," shock at the awareness that her freedom is lost, or something else. Should the author have made the matter clear? Why, or why not?

Kate Chopin "The Storm" (p. 42)

Chopin wrote this story in 1898 but never tried to publish it, presumably because she knew it would be unacceptable to the taste of the age. "The Storm" uses the same characters as an earlier story, "The 'Cadian Ball," in which Alcée is about to run away with Calixta when Clarisse captures him as a husband.

Here are our tentative responses to the topics for discussion and writing in the text.

1,2. (On the characters of Calixta and Bobinôt.) In Part I, Bobinôt buys a can of shrimp because Calixta is fond of shrimp. Our own impression is that this detail is provided chiefly to show Bobinôt's interest in pleasing his wife, but Per Seyersted, in *Kate Chopin*, finds a darker meaning. Seyersted suggests (p. 223) that shrimp "may represent a conscious allusion to the potency often denoted by sea foods." (To the best of our knowledge, this potency is attributed only to oysters, but perhaps we lead sheltered lives.) At the beginning of Part II Calixta is "sewing furiously on a sewing machine," and so readers gather that she is a highly industrious woman, presumably a more-than-usually diligent housekeeper.

The excuses Bobinôt frames on the way home (Part III) suggest that he is somewhat intimidated by his "overscrupulous housewife." Calixta is genuinely concerned about the welfare of her somewhat simple husband and of her child. The affair with Alcée by no means indicates that she is promiscuous or, for that matter, unhappy with her family. We don't think her expressions of solicitude for the somewhat childlike Bobinôt are insincere. We are even inclined to think that perhaps her encounter with Alcée has heightened her concern for her husband. (At least, to use the language of reader-response criticism, this is the way we "naturalize"—make sense out of— the gap or blank in the narrative.)

3. Alcée's letter to his wife suggests that he thinks his affair with Calixta may go on for a while, but we take it that the affair is, like the storm (which gives its title to the story), a passing affair. It comes about unexpectedly and "naturally": Alcée at first takes refuge on the gallery, with no thought of entering the house, but because the gallery does not afford shelter, Calixta invites him in, and then a lightning bolt drives her (backward) into his arms. The experience is thoroughly satisfying, and it engenders no regrets, but presumably it will be treasured rather than repeated, despite Alcée's thoughts when he writes his letter.

4. By telling us, in Part V, that Clarisse is delighted at the thought of staying a month longer in Biloxi, Chopin diminishes any blame that a reader might attach to Alcée. That is, although Alcée is unfaithful to his wife, we see that his wife doesn't regret his absence: "Their intimate conjugal life was something which she was more than willing to forego for a while."

5. Is the story cynical? We don't think so, since cynicism involves a mocking or sneering attitude, whereas in this story Chopin regards her characters affectionately. Blame is diminished not only by Clarisse's letter but by other means. We learn that at an earlier time, when Calixta was a virgin, Alcée's "honor forbade him to prevail." And, again, by associating the affair with the storm, Chopin implies that this moment of passion is in accord with nature. Notice also that the language becomes metaphoric during the scene of passion. For instance, Calixta's "lips were as red and as moist as pomegranate seed," and her "passion . . . was like a white flame," suggesting that the characters are transported to a strange (though natural) world. There is, of course, the implication that people are less virtuous than they seem to be, but again, Chopin scarcely seems to gloat over this fact. Rather,

she suggests that the world is a fairly pleasant place in which there is enough happiness to go all around. "So the storm passed and everyone was happy." There is no need to imagine further episodes in which, for instance, Calixta and Alcée deceive Bobinôt; nor is there any need to imagine further episodes in which Calixta and Alcée regret their moment of passion.

Two additional points can be made. First, there seems to be a suggestion of class distinction between Calixta and Alcée, though both are Creoles. Calixta uses some French terms, and her speech includes such expressions as "An' Bibi? he ain't wet? Ain't hurt?" Similarly Bobinôt's language, though it does not include any French terms, departs from Standard English. On the other hand, Alcée speaks only Standard English. Possibly, however, the distinctions in language are also based, at least partly based, on gender as well as class; Calixta speaks the language of an uneducated woman largely confined to her home, whereas Alcée–a man who presumably deals with men in a larger society–speaks the language of the Anglo world. But if gender is relevant, how can one account for the fact that Bobinôt's language resembles Calixta's, and Clarisse's resembles Alcée's? A tentative answer: Bobinôt, like Calixta, lives in a very limited world, whereas Clarisse is a woman of the world. We see Clarisse only at the end of the story, and there we hear her only through the voice of the narrator, but an expression such as "The society was agreeable" suggests that her language (as might be expected from a woman rich enough to take a long vacation) resembles her husband's, not Calixta's.

Chapter 4

Narrative Point of View

A good deal of critical discussion about point of view is in Wayne Booth, *The Rhetoric of Fiction;* for a thorough history and analysis of the concept, consult Norman Friedman, "Point of View in Fiction," *PMLA* 70 (December 1955): 1160–1184. Also of interest is Patrick Cruttwell, "Makers and Persons," *Hudson Review* 12 (Winter 1959–1960): 487–507.

Among relatively easy stories in other chapters that go well with discussions of point of view are Poe's "The Cask of Amontillado," Frank O'Connor's "Guests of the Nation," Alice Walker's "Everyday Use," Toni Cade Bambara's "The Lesson," and Amy Tan's "Two Kinds"—all first-person stories. (More difficult first-person stories are Gilman's "The Yellow Wallpaper" and Joyce's "Araby.")

Many third-person stories in the book are fairly easily accessible to students (e.g., Flannery O'Connor's "Revelation"), but since the three stories in the previous chapter are told from the third person ("Misery," "The Story of an Hour," and "The Storm"), one need hardly assign a third-person story now even if one wishes to take a story with a different point of view, one can hardly do better than to assign Porter's "The Jilting of Granny Weatherall" (stream of consciousness). Then, for the next assignment, partly to avoid seeming to plod through the book mechanically, we would teach some additional stories from Chapter 8 ("A Collection of Short Fiction"), choosing them partly according to issues that arose in class while teaching this chapter on point of view.

John Updike "A & P" (p. 53)

It may be useful for students to characterize the narrator and see if occasionally Updike slips. Is "crescent," in the third sentence too apt a word for a speaker who a moment later says, "She gives me a little snort," and "If she'd been born at the right time they would have burned her over in Salem"? If this is a slip, it is more than compensated for by the numerous expressions that are just right.

Like Frank O'Connor's "Guests of the Nation," "A & P" is a first-person story, and in its way is also about growing up. Invite students to characterize the narrator as precisely as possible. Many will notice his hope that the girls will observe his heroic pose, and some will notice, too, his admission that he doesn't want to hurt his parents. His belief (echoing Lengel's) that he will "feel this for the rest of his life" is also adolescent. But his assertion of the girls' innocence is attractive and brave.

Some readers have wondered why Sammy quits. Nothing in the story suggests that he is a political rebel, or that he is a troubled adolescent who uses the episode in the A & P as a cover for some sort of adolescent emotional problem. An extremely odd article in *Studies in Short Fiction* [23 (1986): 321–323], which seeks to connect Updike's story with Hawthorne's "Young Goodman Brown," says that "Sammy's sudden quitting is not only a way of attracting the girls' attention but also a way of punishing himself for lustful thoughts." Surely this is nonsense, even further off the mark than the same author's assertion that Queenie's pink bathing suit "suggests the emerging desires competing with chastity" (p. 322). Sammy quits because he wants to make a gesture on behalf of these pretty girls, in appearance and in spirit (when challenged, they assert themselves), are superior to the "sheep" and to the tedious Lengel. Of course Sammy hopes his gesture will be noticed, but in any case the gesture is sincere.

What sort of fellow is Sammy? Is he a male chauvinist pig? An idealist? A self-satisfied deluded adolescent? Someone who thinks he is knowledgeable but who is too quick to judge some people as sheep? Maybe all of the above, in varying degrees. Certainly his remark that the mind of a girl is "a little buzz, like a bee in a glass jar," is outrageous—but later he empathizes with the girls, seeing them not as mindless and not as mere sex objects but as human beings who are being bullied. If we smile a bit at his self-dramatization ("I felt how hard this world was going to be to me hereafter"), we nevertheless find him endowed with a sensitivity that is noticeably absent in Lengel.

Additional Topics for Discussion or Writing

1. Sammy: comic yet heroic?
2. What kind of person does Sammy think he is? What kind of person do you think he is?
3. Updike has said what he things stories should do:

> I want stories to startle and engage me within the first few sentence, and in their middle to widen or deepen or sharpen my knowledge of human activity, and to end by giving me a sense of completed statement.

In your opinion does "A & P" meet his criteria? Explain.

John Updike "The Rumor" (p. 59)

One might almost have thought that the emergence of the gay liberation movement had put an end to all talk about "latent" homosexuality, but it hasn't; indeed, although sexual identity is much talked
about, it remains as mysterious as ever.

One of the interesting things about "The Rumor" is that it is about
sex and yet it has very little sexual action in it. We hear that Sharon had
had sex with Frank when she was sixteen, that they "made love just two
nights ago," that Frank had had a "flurry of adulterous womanizing,"
and (about a third of the way through the story) that Frank, after the
rumor has changed everything, engages in "pushing more brusquely
than was his style at her increasing sexual unwillingness," but that's
pretty much it, as far as sexual activity goes. Yet the story glances at a
wide spectrum of sexual activity. We can begin with heterosexuality:

1. Frank and Sharon married partly as a way of getting out of Cincinnati. ("Their early sex had been difficult for her; she had sub-
   mitted to his advances out of a larger, more social, rather idealistic
   attraction. She knew that together they would have the strength
   to get out of Cincinnati and, singly or married to others, they
   would stay.")
2. Frank has had adulterous heterosexual affairs—but after the
   rumor has reached his ears, he wonders if these were not really a
   manifestation of his homosexuality.

As for his homosexuality, there is

1. The unambiguous homosexuality of Walton Fuller and Jojo, and
   of others who make up "the queer side" of the art world;
2. the part of Frank's nature that, as he now sees it, is homosexual.
   Here too we find a spectrum. Probably some of Frank's specula-
   tions strikes a reader as tenuous (e.g., his belief that his attraction
   to "stoical men" had a homosexual component). The passage
   about the golfing trip in Bermuda, however, is more convincing;
   Frank "had felt his heart make many curious motions, among
   them the heaving, all-but-impossible effort women's hearts
   make in overcoming men's heavy grayness and achieving—a
   rainbow born of drizzle—love." Finally, at the end of the story, it
   seems clear that Frank's interest in Jojo, which he characterizes as
   "Hellenic friendship," is a mixture of the physical ("that silvery
   line of a scar, . . . lean long muscles, . . . white skin.") and the in-

tellectual and paternal (Jojo now seems unexpectedly intelligent," and someone who "needed direction").

Is Frank a homosexual? Any answer would of course have to say what homosexuality is, or, more precisely, would have to say what it means to *be* a homosexual. It's our sense of the story that as the rumor persists, Frank finds in himself things that seem to confirm it, that is, he beings to take his identity from the identity ascribed to him. He now looks back on various episodes and sees in them a homosexual slant which cannot quite be disproven, though it cannot be proven either, for example, the idea that his adulterous affairs were an attempt to deny his essential homosexuality.

The first half of the story pretty clearly establishes Frank—or seems to establish him—as heterosexual, though even here there are some ambiguous notes. For instance, when he first denies that he has a lover, he does so "too calmly." We take the comment to reflect Sharon's perception, but it comes from the omniscient narrator and therefore can at least be conceived as an authoritative comment. Similarly, Frank's hostile comment about gays—"You know how gays are. Malicious. Mischievous"—sounds like the unambiguous comment of a straight male, yet of course it can be taken as a reflection of Frank's insecurity, a disparaging comment made by someone unsure of his own masculinity. (By the way, the comment is *Frank's*, not—as some students may think—Updike's.)

The idea that gays are "malicious" probably is fairly common among straight men; what is especially interesting in this story is that Updike goes on to use the words "malice" and "maliciousness" in connection with Frank's behavior: "Frank sensed her discomfort and took a certain malicious pleasure in it," and Sharon's belief in the rumor "justified a certain maliciousness" on Frank's part. So, again, we get Frank taking his identity from society's view; if (at least in Frank's view) gays are malicious, Frank—now rumored to be gay— will be malicious. In any case, the first half of the story is largely devoted to setting forth the rumor and to giving evidence of Frank's heterosexuality, and the second half of the story is largely devoted to Frank's perception (creation?) of himself as a homosexual. Whereas in the first half of the story, his denial increased his wife's belief in the truth of the rumor, and indeed the very "outrageousness" of the rumor paradoxically served to confirm her suspicions, now, in the second half we find a new belief (Frank's) based, it may seem to most readers, on evidence almost equally insubstantial. In the first half she spied on him, looking for tiny clues (e.g., his response to a waiter) and interpreting them in one way, and in the second half he spies on himself, equally attentive to tiny clues, and equally seeing the evidence only one way.

Does Updike take a stand on the nature/nurture argument about gender identity? We don't think so (and we certainly don't think a writer of fiction need do so), but he does force the issue into a reader's mind. Frank himself sometimes seems to incline to the "nature" view, for instance when he thinks of himself as someone likely to be a homosexual because he is a man with "a slight build, with artistic interests," but at other times he senses that what he is depends on what is around him: "Depending on which man he was standing with, Frank felt large and straight and sonorous, or, as with Wes, gracile and flighty."

A word about some of the questions we ask in the text. Question 1: The point of view in the first paragraph is omniscient (we are told about the feelings of both characters). Question 2: as we have already said, in "Frank said, too calmly," the reader enters into Sharon's mind, that is, here (and in some other passages early in the story) the "central intelligence" is Sharon. Question 3: here (and in much of the second half of the story) we get into Frank's mind, "annoyingly, infuriatingly" (his response to her action).

Chapter 5

Allegory and Symbolism

"Allegory" and "symbolism" have accumulated a good many meanings. Among the references to consult are Edwin Honig, *The Dark Conceit;* C.S. Lewis, *The Allegory of Love;* and Dorothy Sayers, *The Poetry of Search.*

Among highly symbolic stories in the book are Kafka's "The Metamorphosis" and Viramontes's "The Moths," but of course less evident symbols appear in almost all stories. "Araby" is a good story to focus on if one wants to get into a discussion of how far to press details for symbolic meanings.

In our discussion of the Parable of the Prodigal Son (in this manual, Chapter 1), we have already talked about pressing a work very hard in an effort to make it an allegory, and we have also mentioned that some readers put an awful lot of weight on details. How much emphasis should one put on the fact that a girl's bathing suit is pink (in Updike's "A & P"), or on the rusty bicycle pump in "Araby"? Different readers will have different answers. (Our own answer is that much depends on the amount of weight that the author gives to the details.)

Nathaniel Hawthorne "Young Goodman Brown" (p. 73)

Lea B. V. Newman's *A Reader's Guide to the Short Stories of Nathaniel Hawthorne* (1979) provides a valuable survey of the immense body of criticism that "Young Goodman Brown" has engendered. (By 1979 it had been discussed in print at least five hundred times.) We can begin by quoting Newman's remark that the three chief questions are these: "Why does Brown go into the forest? What happens to him there? Why does he emerge a permanently embittered man?"

Newman grants that there is a good deal of "ambivalence" in the story, but she finds most convincing the view that Brown is a victim, a man who "is deluded into accepting spectral evidence as conclusive proof of his neighbors' depravity." Newman also finds convincing another version of the "victim" theory, this one offered by psychologists who hold that "Brown is a sick man with a diseased mind who cannot help what he sees in the forest or his reaction to it." But her survey, of course, also includes references to critics who see Brown "as an evil man who is solely responsible for all that happens to him" (pp. 342–344).

Various critics—it almost goes without saying—press various details very hard. For instance, one critic says that Faith's pink ribbons symbolize Brown's "insubstantial, pastel-like faith." (Instructors expect to encounter this sort of reductive reading in essays by first-year students, but it is disappointing to find it in print.) How detailed, one might ask, is the allegory? Probably most readers will agree on some aspects: the village—a world of daylight and community—stands (or seems to stand) for good, whereas the forest—a dark, threatening place—stands (or seems to stand) for evil. The old man—"he of the serpent"—is the devil. But, again, as Newman's survey of criticism shows, even these interpretations have been debated.

The journey into the forest at night (away from the town and away from the daylight) suggests, of course, a journey into the dark regions of the self. The many ambiguities have engendered much comment in learned journals, some of which has been reprinted in a casebook of the story, *Nathaniel Hawthorne: Young Goodman Brown*, ed. Thomas E. Connolly. Is the story—as David Levin argues in *American Literature* [34 (1962):344–352]—one about a man who is tricked by the devil, who conjures up specters who look like Brown's neighbors in order to win him a damnable melancholy? Does Faith resist the tempter? Does Goodman (i.e., Mister) Brown make a journey or only dream that he makes a journey? Is the story about awareness of evil, or is it about the crushing weight of needlessly assumed guilt? That is, is the story about a loss of faith (Austin Warren, in *Nathaniel Hawthorne*, says it is about "the devastating effect of moral skepticism"), or is it about a religious faith that kills one's joy in life? And, of course, the story may be about loss of faith not in Christ but in human beings; young Goodman Brown perceives his own corruption and loses faith in mankind.

With a little warning the student can be helped to see that the characters and experiences cannot be neatly pigeonholed. For example, it is not certain whether or not Faith yields to "the wicked one"; indeed, it is not certain that Brown actually journeyed into the wood. Richard H. Fogle points out [*New England Quarterly* 18 (Dec. 19454): 448–465, reprinted in his *Hawthorne's Fiction*] that "ambiguity is the very essence of Hawthorne's tale." Among other interesting critical pieces on the story are Marius Bewley, *The Complex Fate*; Thomas Connolly, "Hawthorne's 'Young Goodman Brown': An Attack on Puritanic Calvinism" [*American Literature* 28 (November 1956): 370–375]; and Frederick C. Crews, *The Sins of the Fathers: Hawthorne's Psychological Themes*. Connolly argues that Brown does not lose his faith, but rather that his faith is purified by his loss of belief that he is of the elect. Before the journey into the woods, he believes that man is depraved, but that he himself is of the elect and will be saved. In the forest he sees "a black mass of cloud" hide "the brightening stars," and (according to Connolly) his faith is purified, for he comes to see that he is not different from the rest of the congregation.

On the other hand, one can point out (as J. L. Capps does, in *Explicator*, Spring 1982), that only once in the story does Hawthorne use the word "hope" ("'But where is Faith' thought Goodman Brown; and as hope came into his heart, he trembled"), and the word "charity" never appears, indicating that Brown lacks the quality that would have enabled him to survive despair.

Speaking a bit broadly, we can say that critics fall into two camps: those who believe that Goodman Brown falls into delusion (i.e., misled by the devil, he destroys himself morally by falling into misanthropy), and those who believe that he is initiated into reality. Thus, for readers who hold the first view, Brown's guide into the forest is the devil, who calls up "figures" or "forms" of Brown's acquaintances, and it is Brown (not the narrator) who mistakenly takes the figures for real people. Even what Brown takes to be Faith's pink ribbon is for the narrator merely "*something* [that] fluttered lightly down through the air, and caught on the branch of a tree." In this view, (1) the fact that Faith later wears the ribbon is proof that Brown has yielded to a delusion, and (2) we are to judge Brown by recalling the narrator's objective perceptions. For instance, Brown's guide says that "evil is the nature of mankind," and Brown believes him, but the narrator (who is to be trusted) speaks of "the good old minister" and of "that excellent Christian," Goody Cloyse. There is much to be said for this view (indeed much *has* been said in journals), but against it one can recall some words by Frederick Crews: "The richness of Hawthorne's irony is such that, when Brown turns to a Gulliver-like misanthropy and spends the rest of his days shrinking from wife and neighbors, we cannot quite dismiss his attitude as unfounded" (*The Sins of the Fathers*, p. 106).

Additional Topics for Discussion and Writing

1. Ambiguity in "Young Goodman Brown"
2. What are the strengths and weaknesses of the view that Brown is tricked by the devil, who stages a show of specters impersonating Brown's neighbors, in order to destroy Brown's religious faith?
3. Brown's guide says, "Evil is the nature of mankind," but does the *story* say it?

4. Is the story sexist, showing Brown more horrified by his wife's sexuality than his own?

5. Retell the story using a modern setting. Make whatever changes you wish, but retain the motif of the temptation of a man and a woman by evil.

6. What do you think Hawthorne gains (or loses) by the last sentence?

Eudora Welty "Livvie" (p. 84)

In Welty's story, Livvie has been carried away on the Old Natchez Trace into the deep country, but on the first day of spring Cash rescues her from this death-in-life with old Solomon, who, for all of his piety, represents an attempt to impose a lifeless order on nature. Notice that the pieces of furniture—and even the mousetraps—are symmetrically arranged. Best of all is the yard—"a clean dirt yard with every vestige of grass patiently removed." Solomon seeks also to control time (hence the emphasis on his watch); even in his sleep he is said to keep track of time. When Livvie drops the watch, she becomes free from Solomon.

Among the many details that set forth the contrast between Cash (life, renewal, resurrection) and Solomon (old age, death) are the following: Cash is associated with spring, Solomon with winter; Cash is a field-hand, dressed in "leaf-green" and brown (vegetation and soil), Solomon (living in a house whose yard has not a blade of grass) has a black hat; Cash is young, Solomon old; Cash shatters the bottles that confine spirits, Solomon has placed the bottles on the trees.

Other details suggesting that Cash and Livvie represent life or re-birth are: Livvie's name, Cash's name (suggestive of material things, and of power), Cash's statement that he is "ready for Easter," Cash's three jumps (possibly a suggestion of the three days Christ spent in the underworld before the Resurrection), Cash's appearance "like a vision," and his face that is "so black it was bright." The Easter setting is further emphasized by the references to eggs, the white horse and the white mule, the golden lipstick case and the purple lipstick, etc. All these details are ways of showing that reality is a mystery (see question 1 in the text).

Question 5 in the text can make a good essay, especially if it is restated thus: What is the function of Miss Baby Marie? We confess some puzzlement. The abundant biblical echoes (Solomon's bed is like King Solomon's throne, Livvie thinks of figs and of a man fishing) suggest a biblical reference here. There is of course the contrast of Miss

Baby Marie's artificial youth and Livvie's genuine youth, that is, a false promise of vitality versus the new young life that Livvie will soon experience, but is there also a suggestion of Mary Magdalene? And does Miss Baby Marie's sniffy comment, "It is not Christian or sanitary to put feathers in a vase," combined with the "little patty-cake of white between the wrinkles of her upper lip" suggest that she is a Pharisee, a whited sepulcher?

Chapter 7

A Fiction Writer in Depth:
Flannery O'Connor

Flannery O'Connor "A Good Man Is Hard To Find" (p. 103)

In the early part of this story the grandmother is quite as hateful as the rest of the family—though students do not always see at first that her vapid comments, her moral clichés, and her desire to be thought "a lady" are offensive in their own way. Her comment, "People are certainly not nice like they used to be" can be used to convince students of her mindlessness and lack of charity.

The Misfit, like Jesus, was "buried alive"; he believes that "Jesus thrown everything off balance," and he finds no satisfaction in life (i.e., his life without grace). Life is either a meaningless thing in which all pleasure is lawful (and, ironically, all pleasure turns to ashes), or it derives its only meaning from following Jesus. The Misfit, though he does not follow Jesus, at least sees that the materialistic view of life is deficient. Confronted by the suffering of The Misfit, the nagging and shallow grandmother suddenly achieves a breakthrough and is moved by love. She had earlier recognized The Misfit ("'You're The Misfit! she said. 'I recognized you at once'"), and now she has a further recognition of him as "one of her own children," that is, a suffering fellow human. Faced with death, she suddenly becomes aware of her responsibility: her head clears for an instant and she says, "You're one of my own children." This statement is not merely an attempt to dissuade The Misfit from killing her; contrast it with her earlier attempts, when, for example, she says, "I know you come from nice people! Pray! Jesus, you ought not to shoot a lady. I'll give you all the money I've got." Rather, at last her head is "cleared." This moment of grace transfigures her and causes her death. The Misfit is right when he says, "She would of been a good woman if it had been somebody there to shoot her every minute of her life."

On the "moment of grace" in O'Connor's fiction, see *College English* [27, December 1965): 235–239], and R. M. Vande Kiefte in *Sewanee Review* [76 (1968): 337–356]. Vande Kiefte notes that the description of the dead grandmother ("her legs crossed under her like a child's and her face smiling up at the cloudless sky") suggests that death has jolted the grandmother out of her mere secular decency into the truth of eternal reality. See also Martha Stephens, *The Question of Flannery O'Connor*.

For Flannery O'Connor's comments on this story, see our text, p. 153. In her collected letters, entitled *The Habit of Being*, O'Connor says (letter to John Hawkes, Dec. 26, 1959) that she is interested in "the moment when you know that Grace has been offered and accepted—

such as the moment when the Grandmother realizes The Misfit is one of her own children" (p. 367).

Topics for Discussion an Writing

1. Explain the significance of the title.
2. Interpret and evaluate The Misfit's comment on the grandmother: "She would of been a good woman if it had been somebody there to shoot her every minute of her life."
3. O'Connor reported that once, when she read aloud "A Good Man Is Hard to Find," one of her hearers said that "it was a shame someone with so much talent should look on life as a horror story." Two questions: What evidence of O'Connor's "talent" do you see in the story, and does the story suggest that O'Connor looked on life as a horror story?
4. What are the values of the members of the family?
5. Flannery O'Connor, a Roman Catholic, wrote, "I see from the standpoint of Christian orthodoxy. This means that for me the meaning of life is centered in our Redemption by Christ and what I see in the world I see in relation to that." In the light of this statement, and drawing on "A Good Man Is Hard to Find," explain what O'Connor saw in the world.

Flannery O'Connor "Revelation" (p. 115)

This story, like "A Good Man Is Hard To Find," is concerned with a moment of grace, which most obviously begins when Mary Grace hurls a book at Mrs. Turpin—an action somewhat parallel to The Misfit's assault on the grandmother. The doctor's office contains a collection of wretched human beings whose physical illnesses mirror their spiritual condition. There is abundant comedy ("The nurse ran in, then out, then in again"), but these people are treated sympathetically too. Mrs. Turpin's pitiful snobbery—especially her desperate effort to rank people in the eyes of God—is comic and horrible, but it at least reveals an uneasiness beneath her complacency, an uneasiness that finally compares well with the monumental hatred that characterizes Mary Grace. Yet Mary Grace, a pimply girl, is a messenger of grace. And so when the blow comes (from a book nicely called *Human Development*), it is not in vain. The girl's accusation ("Go back to hell where you came from, you old wart hog") strikes home, and later, among the pigs that Mrs. Turpin so solicitously cleans, the message produces a revelation, a revelation that forces upon her an awareness of the inadequacy of "virtue" (her horrible concept of respectability) as she has known it. Virtue is of as little value to fallen humanity as a hosing-down is to a pig; in her vision she sees that even virtue or respectability is burned away in the movement toward heaven.

On the one hand, some students have difficulty seeing that Mrs. Turpin is not simply a stuffy hypocrite; on the other, some students have difficulty seeing that her respectability is woefully inadequate and must be replaced by a deeper sympathy. But perhaps students have the greatest difficulty in reconciling the comic aspects of the story with its spiritual depth, and here the instructor can probably not do much more than read some passages and hope for the best.

In O'Connor's writings the sun is a common symbol for God. Here, the light of the sun transforms the hogs, so that they appear to "pant with a secret life," a parallel to the infusion of grace into Mrs. Turpin, which causes her to see the worthlessness of her earlier "respectable" values.

The story is deeply indebted to the Book of Revelation, traditionally attributed to St. John the Evangelist and probably written at the end of the first century A.D. (A revelation is, etymologically, an "unveiling," just as an apocalypse is, in Greek, an unveiling. What is unveiled in the Book of Revelation is the future.) Numerous details in O'Connor's story pick up details in the biblical account: O'Connor's "red glow" in the sky echoes the fiery heaven of Revelation; the "watery snake" that briefly appears in the air echoes the water-spewing "serpent" of Revelation (12:15), and even the "seven long-snouted bristling shoats" echo the numerous references to seven (angels, churches, seals, stars) in Revelation. But the details should not be pressed too hard; what matters most is the apocalyptic vision of the oppressed rejoicing and shouting hallelujah at the throne of God.

The story is not difficult, and no published discussions of it are essential reading, though it is of course discussed in books on O'Connor and in general comments on her work, such A. R. Coulthard, "From Sermon to Parable: Four Conversion Stories by Flannery O'Connor" [*American Literature* 55 (1983): 55–71]. Two essays devoted entirely to "Revelation" are "'Revelation' and the Book of Job" by Diane Rolmedo [*Renascence* 30 (1978): 78–90], and Larue Love Slone's "The Rhetoric of the Seer: Eye Imagery in Flannery O'Connor's 'Revelation'" [*Studies in Short Fiction* 25 (1988): 135–145].

Topics for Discussion and Writing

1. Why does Mary Grace attack Mrs. Turpin?
2. Characterize Mrs. Turpin before her revelation. Did your attitude toward her change at the end of the story?
3. The two chief settings are a doctor's waiting room and a "pig parlor." Can these settings reasonably be called "symbolic?" If so, symbolic of what?
4. When Mrs. Turpin goes toward the pig parlor, she has "the look of a woman going single-handed, weaponless, into battle." One there, she dismisses Claud, uses the hose as a weapon against the pigs, and talks to herself "in a low fierce voice." What is she battling, besides the pigs?

Flannery O'Connor "Parker's Back" (p. 132)

This is O'Connor's last story. Much of it was written in the hospital a few weeks before her death.

Like many of her other stories, and especially like "Revelation" (written at almost the same time as "Parker's Back"), this story is about conversion, which is literally a "turning" or "returning," that is, toward God. And as in many of her other stories, the turning is brought about through a violent act of grace.

Parker, earlier "as ordinary as a loaf of bread" discovers "wonder" at a sideshow, when he sees a tattooed man:

> The man, who was small and sturdy, moved about on the platform, flexing his muscles so that the arabesque of men and beasts and flowers on his skin appeared to have a subtle motion of its own. Parker was filled with emotion, lifted up as some people are when the flag passes.
>
> Parker had never before felt the least motion of wonder in himself. Until he saw the man at the fair, it did not enter his head that there was anything out of the ordinary about the fact that he existed. Even then it did not enter his head, but a peculiar unease settled in him. It was if a blind boy had been turned [here we get a clear reference to conversion] so gently in a different direction that he did not know his destination had been change.

This "unease," which alters Parker's direction, proves to be of the sort, we can surely say, that St. Augustine spoke of when he said, "Restless I am until I rest in Thee."

So Parker begins his quest for tattoos. Each new tattoo, however, brings him only brief comfort; he is driven to seek another, and another, and still he is dissatisfied:

> The effect was not of one intricate arabesque of colors but of something haphazard and botched. A huge dissatisfaction would come over him and he would go off and find another tattooist and have another space filled up.

He is, apparently, trying to transform his body, but it is his soul that needs to be transformed. (It may be noted parenthetically that the impulse to acquire a tattoo presumably arises from a discontent with the natural body; this discontent—however grotesque tattooing may seem as an image of the human craving for a higher life—is the basis of O'Connor's story.)

Parker's second great perception occurs when he cries out, "God above," drives his tractor into a tree, sets the tree afire, and is knocked out of his shoes. Perhaps this episode is meant to remind us of Moses and the burning, in Exodus 32:1–6, where God appears in a burning bush and tells Moses to remove his shoes, "for the place whereon thou standest is holy ground." A passage from the New Testament is also relevant; although Parker himself says, "God above," the conjunction of sudden light and the words Parker utters may put a reader in mind of St. Paul's conversion, which was accompanied by a blinding light and by voices in heaven. Even without associating the episode of the tractor with any particular episode in the Bible, we must feel that when he is knocked out of his shoes, Parker—now barefoot—is reborn:

> Parker did not allow himself to think on the way to the city. He only knew that there had been a great change in his life, a leap forward into a worse unknown, and that there was nothing he could do about it. It was for all intents accomplished.

Given the decisiveness of this experience, it may not be fanciful to suggest that the words "It was for all intents accomplished" deliberately echo *Consummatum est*, the words of Christ on the Cross (see John 19:30). (The usual translation is "It is finished," or "It is fulfilled.")

At the tattooist's office Parker looks through a book with the images of God. Because the tattooist tells him that "The up-to-date ones are in the back," he begins at the back, where he encounters images of the Good Shepherd, the Smiling Jesus, and Jesus the Physician's Friend—that is, sentimental images that suit modern taste. These cozy images are of a God who demands nothing, and they are therefore of no interest to Parker, who, as he moves toward the front of the book, encounters pictures that are "less and less reassuring," old-fashioned images of a God almost forgotten today. A pair of "all-demanding eyes" (the Byzantine Christ) arrests his attention.

His back adorned with the tattoo of Christ—with, we might say, Christ not merely on his back but literally under his skin—Parker nevertheless denies to the tattooist and later to his cronies in the pool hall that he has "gone and got religion." He is still resisting the workings of grace. An allusion to Jonah (the pool hall from which Parker is ejected is compared to "the ship from which Jonah had been cast into the sea") emphasizes the idea that Parker is a man struggling (unsuccessfully, like Jonah) to evade God's demand of total obedience. "Examining his soul" in the alley behind the pool hall, Parker sees that "the eyes that were now forever on his back were eyes to be obeyed."

The emphasis on Christ's eyes reminds a reader of the emphasis on Sarah Ruth's "icepick eyes." In the first paragraph of the story, for instance, we are told that her eyes were "sharp like the points of two icepicks." Though Parker's marriage to Sarah Ruth remains something of a mystery, it's safe to assert that he marries her partly because of these eyes; she is mysterious, demanding, different from himself. She humiliates him, and thus is an agent of grace. Now, when Parker returns to her, hoping to gain her approval, she further humiliates him, alleging that she does not know him. O'Connor emphasizes the immense importance of this moment by giving us a mysteriously illuminated landscape:

> The sky had lightened slightly and there were two or three streaks of yellow floating above the horizon. Then as he stood there, a tree of light burst over the skyline.

The next sentence in the story, a paragraph by itself, is especially important:

> Parker fell back against the door as if had been pinned there by a lance.

Surely this passage is meant to remind us of the Crucifixion. Sarah Ruth persists in asking Parker who he is, until he finally whispers "Obadiah." And at this moment

> he felt the light pouring through him, turning his spider web soul into a perfect arabesque of colors, a garden of trees and birds and beasts.

We recall that the tattooed man at the fair wore an "arabesque of men and beasts and flowers on his skin," but Parker's "arabesque," O'Connor specifies, is not of the skin but of the "soul." At this moment, when perhaps the idea of Eden flits through a reader's mind, Parker whispers the Biblical name (Obadiah Elihue) that he has long disguised by using only his initials.

What does one make of the ending, when Sarah Ruth beats Obadiah with a broom, just as she had done when she first met him. There is something comic, of course, in such a line as "She stamped the broom two or three times on the floor and went to the window and shook it out to get the taint of him off it," but there is more. When she thrashes Obadiah across the shoulders, and raises "large welts . . . on the face of the tattooed Christ," surely we see a repetition of the Crucifixion. Which is not to say that Parker is Christ. Of course he is not. He is Parker, the broken man, "crying like a baby" (the last words of the story)—and therefore at last (one may guess) he is fully humiliated and capable of salvation.

The fullest discussion of the story is Preston Browning, Jr., "'Parker's Back': Flannery O'Connor's Iconography of Salvation and Profanity," *Studies in Short Fiction* 6 (1968–69): 525–35.

Topics for Discussion and Writing

1. What is the meaning of the title? (Three points come to mind. First, of course, one thinks of that part of Parker's body on which the image of Christ is tattooed, or perhaps of the image itself. Second, one may think of Parker's return to God: his early vague dissatisfaction leads him ultimately not simply to acquire an image of Christ but to admit his Biblical name, and to accept a scourging by the world. He is, so to speak, back with God.)
2. Why does Parker keep adding tattoos?
3. Why does Parker, who had promised himself never to get "caught," marry, and marry a woman whose values are so different from his own?
4. Putting aside the problem of the "meaning" of the story, are there characters or actions of episodes that you especially enjoyed reading about? If so, cite two or three, and explain what you found especially engaging about them.
5. Do you think "Parker's Back" is saying something about idolatry and about religion? If so, what?

Chapter 8

A Collection of Short Fiction

Edgar Allan Poe "The Cask of Amontillado" (p. 158)

Because many students will have read this story in high school, it can be used effectively as the first assignment: They will start with some ideas about it, and at the end of the class discussion they will probably see that they didn't know everything about the story. It may be well to begin a class discussion by asking the students to characterize the narrator. The opening paragraph itself, if read aloud in class, ought to provide enough for them to see that the speaker is probably paranoid and given to a monstrous sort of reasoning, though, of course, at the start of the story we cannot be absolutely certain that Fortunato has not indeed heaped a "thousand injuries" on him. (In this paragraph, notice too the word "impunity," which we later learn is part of the family motto.) When we meet Fortunato, we are convinced that though the narrator's enemy is something of a fool, he is not the monster that the narrator thinks he is. And so the words at the end of the story, fifty years later, must have an ironic tone, for though *in pace requiescat* can apply to Fortunato, they cannot apply to the speaker, who is still talking (on his deathbed, to a priest?) of his vengeance on the unfortunate Fortunato.

The story is full of other little ironies, conscious on the part of Montresor, unconscious on the part of Fortunato:

The narrator is courteous but murderous;
The time is one of festivity, but a murder is being planned;
The festival of disguise corresponds to the narrator's disguise of his feelings;
Fortunato thinks he is festively disguised as a fool, but he *is* a fool;
He says he will not die of a cough, and the narrator assures him that he is right;
Fortunato is a Freemason, and when he asks the narrator for the secret sign of a brother, the narrator boldly, playfully, outrageously shows him the mason's trowel that he will soon use to wall Fortunato up.

But what to make of all this? It has been the fashion, for at least a few decades, to say that Poe's situations and themes speak to our anxieties, our fear of being buried alive, our fear of disintegration of the self, and so on. Maybe. Maybe, too, there is something to Marie Bonaparte's interpretation: She sees the journey through the tunnel to the crypt as an entry into the womb; the narrator is killing his father (Fortunato) and possessing his mother. And maybe, too there is something to Daniel Hoffman's assertion in *Poe Poe Poe Poe Poe Poe Poe* (p. 223) that Montresor and Fortunato are doubles: "When Montresor leads Fortunato down into the farthest vault of his family's wine-cellar, into a catacomb of human bones, is he not . . . conducting his double thither? My treasure, my fortune, down into the bowels of the earth, a charnel-house of bones." Maybe.

A video cassette of Edgar Allan Poe's "The Cask of Amontillado" is available from HarperCollins. An audio cassette of Basil Rathbone reading Edgar Allan Poe's "The Cask of Amontillado" and "The Pit and the Pendulum" is also available from HarperCollins.

Guy de Maupassant "Mademoiselle" (p. 164)

Anthologists who want to include a story by Maupassant surely have a duty to find something other than the grotesquely over-anthologized "Necklace." We browsed through his stories and came upon "Mademoiselle," a story that we find both moving and puzzling. To the best of our knowledge this story about gender-identity has not been anthologized in any book comparable to *An Introduction to Literature*.

What do we make of the story? We are inclined to think that the chief point is this: society (beginning with the boy's mother) has made him into what at first sight might seem to be a cross-dresser. That is, the family has dressed this delicate, weak boy in girl's clothing, and the rest of society follows, giving him approval in this guise. The boy accepts the role, perhaps partly because he is simple, but chiefly, we imagine, because the role provides him with the warmth (approval and affection) that he needs. He accepts this role, and so does society (the family, and the whole village). Why does society accept it? The boy is mentally and perhaps physically unusual for a male, and society therefore finds it convenient to treat him as something other than a male. Those around him give him a feminine identity, and, to repeat, he responds by acting out a feminine gender role. Notice, however, that in the middle of the story we are told that "he thought more of his nickname than he did of his dress." The story clearly is *not* about someone who is sexually excited by wearing clothes of the opposite sex, but rather is (up to this point) about a young man who finds apparent satisfaction in a role society creates for him.

By accepting the role that society has given to him, he gets the warmth that a human being requires. When, however, he dresses like a boy, society rejects him. His use of male clothing

> created quite a disturbance in the neighborhood, for the people who had been in the habit of smiling at him kindly when he was dressed as a woman, looked at him in astonishment and almost in fear, while the indulgent could not help laughing, and visibly making fun of him.

The distress of the community when it sees male clothing on a female-like person is paralleled by the distress of the boy: "Suppose that, after all, I am a girl?" The boy knew before that he was not a girl, and that he was "in disguise," but he did not fully understand what the disguise consisted of. He thought it was a matter only of clothing, yet when he wears male clothing the disguise does not end: "He had totally lost all masculine looks and ways."

Later in the story he makes a second attempt to assert his maleness this time when he tries to have sex with Josephine. She screams (understandably), and he is seized (again understandably). Society for a second time will not let him assert or express his masculinity. And in fact, this attempt to confirm his sex is no more successful than was the exchange of female clothes for male clothes. Each of his attempts to declare his biological nature encounters difficulty: Society is angry when he prances in male garb, and society is angry when he attacks Josephine. Both events imply a tragic side to the old collusion between the boy and the world around him, to call him "Mademoiselle." That is, it robbed him of the ability to bring his behavior in line with his biological nature.

In our view, the story is largely about the way in which society establishes gender (masculine or feminine behavior). Gender usually corresponds with external genitals, but in this case society has (for its own reasons) preferred to see the boy as feminine, and the boy for a while has acquiesced. After he finds (by observing couples, and in the encounter with Josephine) his erotic orientation, he learns that he is locked into the wrong gender.

We offer this reading with some hesitancy (and only after we have modified it in line with discussions with Professor Donald Stone, a specialist in French literature), since we don't quite know what to make of certain passages in the story. For instance, although the boy says that he dresses like a girl "only . . . for a joke," he also says, "But if I dress like a lad, I shall no longer be a girl; and then, *I am a girl*" (our italics). Still, although we find a contradiction between these passages, we think that the statement (already quoted) that he values his nick-name more than his dress clearly indicates that the dress itself is of only minor importance to him; it does not in itself give him pleasure, but it is the means whereby he gets approval from the community.

The story ends with the boy asserting his maleness. It does not tell us what happened thereafter, that is, whether (for example) from that time onward he refused to wear female clothing, or (again, for example) whether society continued to treat him as a girl. Donald Stone finds the dark irony thoroughly in Maupassant's vein. He points out that there is even a similarity with Maupassant's "Necklace," in which a woman, eager to shine (see also the boy's quest for affection), borrows a dia-mond necklace, loses it, spends much of the rest of her life in efforts to pay for it, and at last finds out that the necklace was of no value.

Students might be invited to write a paragraph to be added to the ending, or to write an essay explaining why the present ending is preferable.

Anton Chekhov "Enemies" (p. 168)

A videotape of this story, and an interview with the adaptor, Jamaica Kincaid, is available from HarperCollins. (For information, please consult your sales representative.)

Like Chekhov's "Misery," in Chapter 3, this story deals with a father's grief for his son, but the stories are very different.

The following discussion is indebted to Beverly Hahn, *Chekhov* (1977). In "Enemies" Chekhov juxtaposes two characters, Dr. Kirilov and Abogin. The first paragraph tells us that just when the doctor lost his son, a stranger came to the door. In the first few paragraphs we learn about the doctor only of his loss and (in the second paragraph) something of the numbing effect of the loss on him: his waistcoat is unbuttoned, and he does not wipe his wet face or his "hands which were scalded with carbolic." Actually we learn one additional thing, something that confirms the conclusions a reader probably draws from the description of physical details; he speaks rather abruptly to the stranger ("I am at home . . . . What do you want?") Presumably a reader understands this brusqueness to be the effect of the doctor's grief. On the other hand, the stranger, who knows nothing of Kirilov's loss, appears rather voluble:

> I am very . . . very glad! We are acquainted. My name is Abogin and I had the honour of meeting you in the summer at Gnutchev's. I am very glad

to have found you at home. . . . For God's sake don't refuse to come back
with me at once. . . . My wife has been dangerously ill. . . . And the carriage is waiting.

It is entirely appropriate for Abogin to introduce himself, to mention
that he and the doctor have met, and to express his great relief that the
doctor is at home, but somehow even in these few paragraphs Chekhov seems to have set up two rather different people, the withdrawn
doctor and the effusive Abogin.

Probably during the first two-thirds of the story most readers find
Kirilov the more sympathetic of the two. After all, he has suffered a
great loss, and yet he sets out—with great reluctance of course, but,
still, he sets out—to minister to Abogin's ill wife. When Abogin appeals to the doctor "For the love of humanity!" the doctor rightly says,
"Humanity—that cuts both ways," and he explains why he should
not be asked to go on an assignment at this time. But he does go, numb
as he is, and, further, he leaves behind his grief-stricken wife, a point
that emphasizes his dedication to his calling as a physician. When the
carriage crosses a river—that is, when he has, so to speak, left his own
realm and entered Abogin's—he again seeks, very humanly, to be ex-
cused ("let me go"), but he nevertheless continues on his journey, true
to the ethics of his calling.

While it would be wrong to say that Abogin seems contempt-
ible, he does seem, in the earlier part of the story, less impressive
than Kirilov. We are told that in his initial remarks to the doctor
"there was a note of unaffected sincerity and childish alarm in
his voice," and that (like a person who is "frightened and
overwhelmed"), he "spoke in brief, jerky sentences and uttered
a great many unnecessary, irrelevant words." Nothing to be
ashamed of, but, still, not the way Kirilov would behave, we
feel, and good deal less dignified. Later, when Abogin is at home,
we get a fairly full description of him, partly by means of a
contrast with the doctor. The doctor, we are told, was "stooped,
was untidily dressed and not good looking," and he had "an
unpleasantly harsh, morose, and unfriendly look," whereas Abogin
(we quote only part of a fairly long passage)

presented a very different appearance. He was a thick-set, sturdy-look-
ing, fair man with a big head and large, soft features; he was elegantly
dressed in the very latest fashion. In his carriage, his closely buttoned
coat, his long hair, and his face there was a suggestion of something generous, leonine.

If the first part of this description makes him seem a bit unmanly ("soft features," "elegantly dressed in the very latest fashion"), the later part of the description puts a favorable interpretation on the words ("generous, leonine"). The whole of the passage should be read carefully, and notice should be taken of how the slightly or potentially negative comments ("there was a shade of refined almost feminine elegance in the manner in which he took off his scarf and smoothed his hair") are diminished ("these things did not detract from his dignity"). In short, Abogin begins to rise in a reader's estimation.

Abogin's dwelling, too, makes a contrast to Kirilov's. In the luxurious drawing-room Kirilov sees a violoncello case (something will be made of this in a moment) and "a stuffed wolf as substantial and sleek-looking as Abogin himself." In a moment the elegance and refinement disappear, and Abogin is hysterical as he reports the trick that his wife has played. At this point a reader probably sees him as the stock figure (the cuckold) in a farce—and that is what Kirilov takes the situation to be:

> And here I am forced to play a part in some vulgar farce, to play the part of a stage property.

Notice, however, that Kirilov sees not Abogin but *himself* as a figure in this farce. Of course, a reader may see Abogin too as farcical—again, the cuckold is a stock figure in farce—but Chekhov now seems concerned to make Abogin more sympathetic, and to make Kirilov less sympathetic. We get a passage that is fairly unusual in Chekhov, in which the narrator moralizes, in effect telling us that the doctor behaved badly and implying that *we* ought to behave differently:

> With tears in his eyes, trembling all over, Abogin opened his heart to the doctor with perfect sincerity. He spoke warmly, pressing both hands on his heart, exposing the secrets of his private life without the faintest hesitation, and even seemed to be glad that at last these secrets were no longer pent up in his breast. If head talked this way for an hour or two, and opened his heart, he would undoubtedly have felt better. Who knows, if the doctor had listened to him and had sympathized with him like a friend, he might perhaps, as often happens, have reconciled himself to his trouble without protest, without doing anything needless and absurd. . .
> But what happened was quite different.

The doctor, we are told, shifts from "indifference and wonder" to "bitter resentment, indignation, and anger." Given the death of the doctor's son, and the somewhat farcical nature of the situation at Abogin's house, these moods are certainly understandable, but Chekhov pretty clearly implies that a more humane person would have responded differently. The doctor's bitterness is revealed directly and fully, in the most obvious terms, but we can't resist calling attention to a subtle touch in which Chekhov reveals the doctor's contempt (and his limitations): "Make a display of humane ideas, play (the doctor looked sideways at the violoncello case) play the bassoon and the trombone, grow as fat as capons, but don't dare to insult personal dignity." The contemptuous reference to playing a musical instrument—and the preposterously wrong instrument, at that—is fully revealing. And so too, for that matter, is the doctor's comment about his "personal dignity," and his rejection of a fee: "How dare you offer me money?"

We do not mean to say that the doctor is finally perceived as a villain. Far from it; he is nearly a hero when, exhausted and grief-struck, he leaves his wife and sets out on a journey "to save a human life," and his exasperation is entirely understandable. But Chekhov finally gives us a picture of a man who, though true to the ideas of his profession, is warped by his sense of "personal dignity." We often hear that suffering humanizes, and we can almost imagine a scene in which the doctor comforts Abogin, but in this story we see a man who can see no grief but his own. Admittedly we cannot take Abogin's loss as equivalent to the doctor's, but we probably hope that we and those around us will be able, even in moments of great stress, to enter imaginatively into the sufferings of others, and this the doctor cannot do. Chekhov does not blame him, but merely observes, "Unhappiness does not bring people together but draws them apart." Ironically, so great is the power of unhappiness that—in the doctor's case, of unhappiness rooted in a sense of injured pride—it even manages (in the next-to-last paragraph) to make the grieving doctor forget about his wife and dead son.

Charlotte Perkins Gilman "The Yellow Wallpaper" (p. 178)

In this story the wife apparently is suffering from postpartum depression, and her physician-husband prescribes as a cure the things that apparently have caused her depression: isolation and inactivity. Victorian medical theory that held that women—more emotional, more nervous, more fanciful than men—needed special protection if they were to combat lunacy. As Gilman tells us in her autobiography, *The Living of Charlotte Perkins Gilman* (1935), the story (published in (1892) is rooted in the author's experience: After the birth of her child, Gilman became depressed and consulted Dr. S. Weir Mitchell (physician and novelist, named in the story), who prescribed a rest cure: "Live as domestic a life as possible, Have your child with you all the time. Lie down an hour after each meal. Have but two hours intellectual life a day. And never touch pen, brush or pencil as long as you live." Gilman in fact tried this routine for a month, then took a trip to California, where she began writing, and recovered nicely. Thinking about Mitchell's plan later, Gilman concluded that such a way of life would have driven her crazy.

Although the prescribed treatment in the story is not exactly Mitchell's, it does seem clear enough that the smug husband's well-intended treatment is responsible for the wife's hallucinations of a woman struggling behind the wallpaper. The narrator is mad (to this degree the story resembles some of Poe's), but she is remarkably sane compared to her well-meaning husband and the others who care for her. Elaine R. Hedges, in the afterword to the edition of *The Yellow Wallpaper* published by the Feminist Press (1973) comments on the narrator:

> At the end of the story the narrator both does and does not identify with the creeping women who surround her in her hallucinations. The women creep through the arbors and lanes along the roads outside the house. Women must creep. The narrator knows this. She has fought as best she could against creeping. In her perceptivity and in her resistance lie her heroism (or heroineism). But at the end of the story, on her last day in the house, as she peels off yards and yards of wallpaper and creeps around the floor, she has been defeated. She is totally mad. But in her mad-sane way she has seen the situation of women for what it is. [p.53]

Judith Fetterley offers a thoughtful interpretation of Gilman's story in "Reading about Reading" in *Gender and Reading: Essays on Readers, Texts, and Contexts,* edited by Elizabeth A. Flynn and Patrocinio P. Schwieckart (1986, pp. 147–164). Here (in direct quotation) are some of Fetterley's points, but the entire essay should be consulted:

> Forced to read men's texts [i.e. to interpret experience in the way men do], women are forced to become characters in those texts. And since the stories men tell assert as fact what women know to be fiction, not only do women lose the power that comes from authoring: more significantly,

they are forced to deny their own reality and to commit in effect a kind of psychic suicide. [p. 159]

The nameless narrator of Gilman's story has two choices. She can accept her husband's definition of reality [that his version is sane and that her version is mad] . . . or she can refuse to read his text, refuse to become a character in it, and insist on writing her own, behavior for which John will define and treat her as mad. . . . [p. 160]

Despite the narrator's final claim that she has, like the woman in the paper, "got out," she does not in fact escape the patriarchal text. Her choice of literal madness may be as good as or better than the "sanity" prescribed for her by John, but in going mad she fulfills his script and becomes a character in his text. Still, going mad gives the narrator temporary sanity. It enables her to articulate her perception of reality and, in particular, to cut through the fiction of John's love. [p. 163]

The narrator's solution finally validates John's fiction. In his text, female madness results from work that engages the mind and will; from the recognition and expression of feelings, and particularly of anger; in a word, from the existence of a subjectivity capable of generating a different version of reality from his own. [pp. 164–165]

More insidious still, through her madness the narrator does not simply become the character John already imagines her to be as part of his definition of feminine nature; she becomes a version of John himself. Mad, the narrator is manipulative, secretive, dishonest; she learns to lie, obscure, and distort. [p. 164]

This desire to duplicate John's text but with the roles reversed determines the narrator's choice of an ending. Wishing to drive John mad, she selects a denouement that will reduce him to a woman seized by a hysterical fainting fit. Temporary success, however, exacts an enormous price, for when John recovers from his faint he will put her in a prison from which there will be no escape. [p. 164]

Of the many feminist readings of the story, perhaps the most widely known is that of Sandra M. Gilbert and Susan Gubar, *The Madwoman in the Attic* (1979). For Gubar and Gilbert, the wallpaper represents "the oppressive structures of the society in which [the narrator] finds herself" (p. 90). The figure behind the wallpaper is the narrator's double, trying to break through. But Jeanette King and Pam Morris, in "On Not Reading Between the Lines: Models of Reading in 'The Yellow Wallpaper'" [*Studies in /Short Fiction* 26(1989): 23–32], raise questions about this interpretation. Their essay, influenced by Lacan, is not easy reading (one finds such terms as "decentered subject," "signified and signifier," "a polysemic potential"), but they present some impressive evidence against the widespread view that the woman behind the paper is "the essential inner psyche which has been trapped by repressive social structures" (p. 25). First, they argue that if the woman indeed is the essential inner psyche, "the breaking free, even if only in the hallucination of madness, ought surely to indicate a more positive movement than the chilling conclusion of the tale suggests" (p. 25). They point out that the wallpaper is *not* described in terms of "a controlling order"; rather, the narrator says it has "sprawling flamboyant patterns," and it resembles "great slanting waves" that "plunge off at outrageous angles . . . in unheard-of contradictions." For King and Morris, the wallpaper's "energy and fertility are anarchic and lawless, at times aggressive. It displays, that is, an assertive creativity and originality that have no place in the wifely ideal constructed by patriarchal ideology" (p. 29). They therefore interpret it not as a metaphor of a repressive society but as a metaphor of the "forbidden self" (p. 29), "the repressed other" (p. 30). The narrator, seeking to comply with the male ideals, is thus threatened by the wallpaper, and her "attempts to tear down this obdurate wallpaper are not intended . . . to free her from male repression . . . but to eliminate the rebellious self which is preventing her from achieving ego-ideal." p. 30). That is, she wishes to remove the paper (the image of her secret self, which she strives to repress) in order to gain John's approval. "When the woman behind the paper 'gets out,' therefore, this is an image not of liberation but of the victory of the social idea." We get a "grotesque, shameful caricature of female helplessness and submissiveness—a creeping woman." Nevertheless, King and Morris argue, the narrator does indeed have "a desperate triumph . . . : she crawls over her husband" (p. 31).

King and Morris assume that "Jane" (mentioned only near the end of the story) is the narrator, but, like most earlier critics, they do not greatly concern themselves with arguing this point. William Veeder, in "Who Is Jane?" [*Arizona Quarterly* 44(1988): 41–79], does argue the point at length. He writes "By defining a context beyond Poesque horror and clinical case-study, Kolodny, Nedges, and others have convincingly described the heroine's confrontation with patriarchy. What remains to be examined is another source of the heroine's victimization. Herself" (p. 41). Veeder discusses Gilman's difficult childhood (an absent father and a "strict and anxious mother"), and, drawing on Freud and Melanie Klein, argues that the history is not only about a repressive marriage but also about "the traumas wrought by inadequate nurturing in childhood" (p. 71). To escape bondage to men, "Jane moves not forward to the egalitarian utopia of *Herland* but back into the repressive serenity of the maternal womb" (p. 67).

Topic for Discussion or Writing

In the next-to-last paragraph the narrator says, "I've got out at last." What does she mean, and in what way (if any) does it make sense?

James Joyce "Araby" (p. 191)

Probably the best discussion of "Araby" remains one of the earliest, that of Cleanth Brooks and Robert Penn Warren in *Understanding Fiction*. Among more recent discussions, L. J. Morrissey, "Joyce's Narrative Strategies in 'Araby'" [*Modern Fiction Studies* 28 (1982): 45–52], is especially good.

Students have difficulty with the story largely because they do not read it carefully enough. They scan it for what happens (who goes where) and do not pay enough attention to passages in which (they think) "nothing is happening." But when students read passages aloud in class, for instance the first three paragraphs, they *do* see what is going on (that is, they come to understand the boy's mind) and enjoy the story very much. To help them hear the romantic boy who lives in what is (from an adult point of view) an unromantic society it is especially useful to have students read aloud passages written in different styles. Compare, for instance, "At night in my bedroom and by day in the classroom her image came between me and the page I strove to read" with "I asked for leave to go to the bazaar on Saturday night. My aunt was surprised and hoped it was not some Freemason affair."

That the narrator is no longer a boy is indicated by such passages as the following:

[h]er name was like a summons to all my foolish blood.

Her name sprang to my lips at moments in strange prayers and praise which I myself did not understand. My eyes were often full of tears (I could not tell why).

What innumerable follies laid waste my waking and sleeping thoughts. . . .

Morrissey points out that in addition to distancing himself from his past actions by such words as "foolish" and "follies" (and, at the end of the story, "vanity"), the narrator distances himself from the boy he was by the words "imagined" and "seemed," words indicating that his present view differs from his earlier view.

The narrator recounts a story of disillusionment. The first two paragraphs clearly establish the complacent middle-class world into which he is born—the houses "conscious of decent lives within them" gase with "imperturbable faces." This idea of decency is made concrete by the comment in the second paragraph that the priest's charity is evident in his will: He left all of his money to institutions and his furniture to his sister. (Probably even the sister was so decent that she too thought this was the right thing to do.) Morrissey, interpreting the passage about the priest's will differently, takes the line to be the boy's innocent report of "what must have been an ironic comment by adults."

As a boy he lived in a sterile atmosphere, a sort of fallen world:

> The house is in a "blind" or dead-end street.
> The rooms are musty.
> The priest had died (religion is no longer vital?).
> A bicycle pump, once a useful device, now lies rusty and unused under a bush in the garden.
> An apple tree in the center of the garden in this fallen world.
> Nearby are the odors of stable and garbage dumps.

Nevertheless the boy is quickened by various things, for instance by the yellow pages of an old book, but especially by Mangan's sister (who remains unnamed, perhaps to suggest that the boy's love is spiritual). He promises to visit "Araby" (a bazaar) and to return with a gift for her.

The boy for a while moves through a romantic, religious world:

> He sees her "image".
> He imagines that he carries a "chalice."
> He hears the "litanies" and "chanting" of vendors. He utters "strange prayers."

Delayed by his uncle, whose inebriation is indicated by the uncle's "talking to himself" and by "the hall-stand rocking" (his parents seem not to be living; notice the emphasis on the boy's isolation throughout the story, e.g. his ride alone in the car of the train), he hears the clerks counting the days' receipts—moneychangers in the temple.

"The light was out. The upper part of the hall was now completely dark." The darkness and the preceding trivial conversations of a girl and two young women reveal (Joyce might have said epiphanize) the emptiness of the world. The boy has journeyed to a rich, exotic (religious?) world created by his imagination and has found it cold and trivial, as dead as the neighborhood he lives in.

The boy's entry through the shilling entrance rather than through the sixpenny (children's) entrance presumably signals his coming of age.

This brief discussion of "Araby" of course seems reasonable to its writer, even the remarks that the rusty bicycle pump suggests a diminished world, and that the entry through the shilling entrance rather than the sixpenny entrance suggests, implies, or even—through one hesitates to use word—symbolizes (along with many other details) his initiation into an adult view. But how far can (or should) one press the details? An article in *James Joyce Quarterly* [4(1967): 85–86] suggests that the pump under the bushes stands for the serpent in the garden. Is there a difference between saying that the rusty pump—in the context of the story—puts a reader in mind of a diminished (deflated) world, and saying that it stands for the serpent? Is one interpretation relevant, and the other not? Students might be invited to offer their own views on how far to look for "meaning" or "symbols" in this story, or in any other story. They might also be advised to read—but not necessarily to swallow—the brief discussions of symbolism in the text and in the glossary.

An audio cassette of James Joyce reading is available from HarperCollins.

Franz Kafka "The Metamorphosis" (p. 196)

If we call something Shakespearean, the something is likely to be a passage of poetry; if we call something Shavian, the something is likely to be a play. But if we call something Kafkaesque, the something is not likely to be literature, but an experience—a maddening encounter with bureaucracy or a supremely banal moment of horror.

Horror fiction used to deal with misshapen people and strange instruments of torture, but Kafka, probably more than any other literary figure, changed all that and gave us a literature of commonplace horror: encounters with bewildering officials, dreamlike efforts of ordinary people to clear up petty things, incomprehensible interruptions in our routines, a sense of isolation from one's fellows and even from oneself. These experiences are set forth in a matter-of-fact style that serves, by its passionless recording of precise details, to relate them convincingly to the reader's daily life. *The Metamorphosis* is somewhat unusual in its fantastic premise, but even this story about a man who has turned into an insect is told with no sense of wonder.

No writer on Kafka fails to point out this deep sense of isolation or exile that is Kafka's recurrent theme; he was a Jew in a Gentile world, a German speaker in Prague, a victim of tuberculosis, neurotically estranged from his domineering father, and a literary man in a bourgeois society. An entry in his diary, where he imagines himself as some sort of impotent winged creature, is of special interest to readers of "The Metamorphosis," and it may help to reveal the sense of isolation that he felt his literary gift had imposed on him:

> What will be my fate as a writer is very simple. My talent for portraying my dreamlike inner life has thrust all other matters into the background; my life has dwindled dreadfully, nor will it cease to dwindle. . . . I waver, continually fly to the summit of the mountain, but then fall back in a moment.

His "Letter to His Father," a lucid account of the sense of inferiority that his authoritarian father instilled in him, also has some images that connect interestingly with *The Metamorphosis:* Kafka's friends are, in his father's words, "vermin" and "fleas," and Kafka imagines his father replying to the letter by calling Kafka a kind of "vermin" that "sucks blood in order to sustain its own life." But what is especially important for us, since we are interested in Kafka's novel rather than in his life, is a passage in which he describes a moment of intense humiliation and then—astoundingly—adds, "I was frantic with desperation and at such moments all my bad experiences in all spheres fitted magnificently together." "Magnificently" is the astounding word: the chaos and traumas sometimes cohered and he was able to make them into something magnificent.

Exactly what this magnificent thing in front of us, *The Metamorphosis,* is can be much debated, but debate tends to reduce it to simple formulas such as our unconscious feeling of guilt, the Jew in a Gentile society, the writer in a bourgeois society, or the writer's inability to communicate his vision. Probably something of all these interpretations, and a good many more, is in the novel, but surely, as we read it, we respond, rather than interpret, and we respond at least partly because the emotions described in the story are recognizably our own. The first two or three pages, for instance, carefully record normal responses on awakening: "What about sleeping a little longer?" "What an exhausting job I've picked," "A man needs his sleep," "Well, supposing he were to say he was sick." Of course, in addition to the astounding premise of a man who changes into a bug, there are strange dreamlike passages, such as those concerning the three lodgers, and Gregor's father's insistence on wearing his uniform even when off duty. But on the whole the story holds us not by its fantasy but by its realism, its patient recounting of familiar states of mind and its patient description of the insect.

These states of mind, doubtless occasionally felt in all ages, seems especially modern, and it is highly appropriate that Kafka chose for his hero, or antihero, a traveling salesman, for the salesman's profession necessarily imposes rootlessness and discontinuity upon him. One is tempted to say that Kafka depicts alienation, the individual's sense that he is separated from his "real self" and forced to adopt a role that does not involve the "real self." But Gregor, at the start, is only intermittently aware that the life he leads is alien to his true self; he grumbles, of course, but he also takes pleasure in being the support of his family, and he is almost wholly devoted to his work. We are told that he does not go out of the house during the evenings but spends his time reading newspapers and railway timetables, and the only suggestions of a life other than his life of drudgery are his interest in fretwork and the pinup girl on the wall. Spineless, he is not so much a man who feels he is forced into the role of a bug as he is a bug itself, which is why the story begins, rather than ends, with Gregor's metamorphosis. (But we cannot easily feel superior to Gregor; we somehow recognize that Kafka's image of human feelings within an insect's body is a brilliant representation of our dual nature.)

The remainder, and bulk, of the story, recounts society's rejection of this drudge, and his perception that he is utterly unloved, a perception that causes him to cease to hang onto life. (This is Gregor's most notable perception, but in the story there are a few other passages indicating, curiously, that as a bug Gregor occasionally is more perceptive than has been earlier. The description of his response to his sister's music is especially suggestive.) His family feels an enormous relief when this bug dies, and Kafka takes some pains to let the reader share in this relief, for the story—even while it ends with the parents plotting to marry off the daughter to some suitable husband—concludes with references to "the open country" (the story began inside a bedroom, on a rainy and overcast day), "vivacity," and the daughter rising and stretching. It is almost as though the metamorphosis at the beginning is balanced by another—this one of the entire family. In his diaries, Kafka refers cryptically to the "unreadable ending" of *The Metamorphosis,* but he did not suggest an alternative; he was too honest to suggest that Gregor's death could be anything other than a relief to Gregor and to all who knew him or heard his story.

For an extremely interesting feminist interpretation, see Nina Pelikan Straus, "Transforming Franz Kafka's 'Metamorphosis'" [*Signs* 14 (1989): 651–667]. The gist of the essay is that the story is less about "a father-son conflict" than it is about "brother-sister or gender-based relationships" (p. 653). Because Straus's essay is moderately long and very closely reasoned, a summary cannot do justice to it, but a few quotations may serve to indicate something of her argument.

> The story of Gregor is a parabolic reflection of Kafka's own self-exposure and self-entombment. . . . For him exposure is both liberating, because writing releases the repressed, and dehumanizing, because language can describe the human as nonhuman. This pattern of simultaneous liberation an dehumanization is repeated when Grete is pried loose from her social role and liberated at the end of the story, and, like Gregor, she must pay a dehumanizing price for her liberation. If Grete is a symbol of anything, it is the indeterminacy of gender roles, the irony of self-liberation. Grete's role as a woman unfolds as Gregor's life as a man collapses into itself. [p. 653]

> As a gigantic insect, Gregor exchanges responsibility for dependency, while Grete exchanges dependency for the burdensome efficiency and independence that Gregor formerly displayed. . . . [The] deepest resonances [of the metamorphosis] involve the relations of men and women, of the man's wish to be a woman, the woman's wish to be a man. [p. 655]

> The sentence "In this manner Gregor was fed" highlights, even in its grammar, his passive, dependent relation to [Grete] and indicates the moment in the text when Gregor's degradation and gradual disappearance are finally exchanged for Grete's social upgrading and visibility. . . . As she withdraws her service from him, her female voice begins to rise independently in the text, alongside the conflated voice of narrator and male character. [p. 664]

> Having passed through stages of submission and sympathy, through the burden of symbolically mothering a being that resembles a sickly and degenerate child, and having replicated her brother's stages of maturation and professionalism (for she now has a job), Grete initiates her liberation. Like Gregor, who had wanted to "tell his chief exactly what I think of him," Grete feels repressed and exploited at work. . . . Her decision that

Gregor "must go" . . . dehumanizes her ethically as it inspires the bloom of her body and confidence. [p. 665]

The tale is not merely an oedipal fantasy but more broadly a fantasy about a man who does so that a woman may empower herself. Her self-empowering, the transference of a woman into a position where a man used to be, does not transform the social system, however, but merely perpetuates it. When women become as men are, Kafka seems to be saying, there is no progress. Such metamorphoses merely exchange one delusive solution for another. . . . It is Grete who will now sell and be sold, who will perpetuate the system of exchanges and debts that was formerly Gregor's business. [p. 637]

Katherine Anne Porter "The Jilting of Granny Weatherall" (p. 233)

Students do not always understand that there are two narratives here: one of a woman's dying hour and another of the past that floods her mind. The old lady, a tough Southerner or Southwesterner with an intense love of life, has "weathered all," even a jilting; she had expected a groom, George, and was publicly disappointed when he failed to show up. Now, at her death, again a priest is in the house, and again she is disappointed or "jilted": the Bridegroom (Christ) fails to appear. (It surely is worthwhile to call attention to the parable of the wise and foolish virgins, in Matthew 25:1–13, where the bridegroom does appear, but the foolish virgins miss him.) The first jilting could in some measure be overcome, but the second is unendurable.

Porter gives us the stream of Granny's consciousness, and if we are not always perfectly clear about details (did Hapsy die in childbirth?) we are nevertheless grateful for the revelation of an unfamiliar state of consciousness.

Exactly who is Hapsy? We assume that Hapsy was her last child, "the one she really wanted," and that is why Hapsy plays such an important role in Granny's consciousness. Presumably she had at last come to love her husband. (On this point, it is relevant to mention, too, that one of her sons is named George—presumably for the man who jilted her—and the other son is not named John, for his father, but Jimmy.) But other readers interpret Hapsy differently. Among the interpretations that we find farfetched are (1) Hapsy was a black friend and midwife who secretly delivered Ellen of an illegitimate child, but George learned of this and therefore jilted Ellen, and (2) Hapsy was

Ellen's illegitimate child, fathered by George, and George then jilted her.

Also, who is the "he" who, at the first jilting, "cursed like a sailor's parrot and said, I'll kill him for you"? Among the answers usually given are: her father, a brother, the man she later married. Probably the question can't be answered authoritatively. And who is the driver of the cart, whom she recognizes by "his hands"?

These details probably do not affect the overall interpretation of the story. To return to a large matter, what interpretation of the story makes the most sense? What happens if we consider the story chiefly in the light of the Parable of the Ten Virgins? "The Jilting of Granny Weatherall" has engendered considerable comment in books on Porter, in journals, and especially in the instructors' manuals that accompany textbooks, but it is probably fair to say that the story is usually interpreted as setting forth the picture of an admirable—even heroic—woman who finds, at the end of her life, that there is no God, or, more specifically, that Christ the Bridegroom does not come to her. That is, putting aside the matter of the author's own beliefs (and putting the whole matter rather crudely) the story shows us an energetic woman who at the end of her life learns that she lives in a godless world.

This is the way we have long seen the story, and we still have a strong attachment to that view, but a rereading of the parable (Matthew 25:1–13), may raise some doubt:

1. Then shall the kingdom of heaven be likened unto ten virgins, which took their lamps, and went forth to meet the bridegroom.
2. And five of them were wise, and five were foolish.
3. They that were foolish took their lamps, and took no oil with them.
4. But the wise took oil in their vessels with their lamps.
5. While the bridegroom tarried, they all slumbered and slept.
6. And at midnight there was a cry made, Behold, the bridegroom cometh; go ye out to meet him.
7. Then all those virgins arose, and trimmed their lamps.
8. And the foolish said unto the wise, Give us of your oil; for our lamps are gone out.
9. But the wise answered, saying, Not so; lest there be not enough for us and you: but go ye rather to them that sell, and buy for yourselves.
10. And while they went to buy, the bridegroom came; and they that were ready went in with him to the marriage: and the door was shut.

11. Afterward came also the other virgins, saying, Lord, Lord, open to us.
12. But he answered and said, Verily I say unto you, I know you not.
13. Watch therefore, for ye know neither the day nor the hour wherein the son of man cometh.

Before we learned (chiefly from Wimsatt and Beardsley) of "the Intentional Fallacy," we might have studied Porter's letters, prefaces, and other stories in an effort to ascertain her view of the parable—we still might try to do so, but if we do we will be frustrated since Porter apparently did not comment on the parable, except in this story. Nor does the fact that she had a Catholic education tell us much about what she made of the parable. It appears that to understand the story we can do nothing more than read the story, and perhaps read the parable.

Matthew's final line, "Watch [i.e. remain awake] therefore, for ye know neither the day nor the hour wherein the son of man cometh," somewhat confuses the point of the parable, since the wise virgins as well as the foolish virgins slept, but the point nevertheless is very clear: the foolish virgins—foolish because they were short-sighted—overlooked the possibility of the Bridegroom's delay. The Bridegroom came unexpectedly.

Can one (or should one) interpret the story in the light of the evident meaning of the parable? If one interprets it thus, the point or theme might be roughly stated along these lines: Granny, despite all her apparently commendable worldly activity—ministering to the sick, keeping the farm in good repair, and so on—is (in a spiritual sense) improvident. The second Bridegroom does not appear at the moment that she expects him, and she therefore despairs and abandons her belief:

> For the second time there was no sign. Again no bridegroom and the priest in the house. She could not remember any other sorrow because the grief wiped them all away. Oh, no, there's nothing more cruel than this—I'll never forgive it. She stretched herself with a deep breath and blew out the light.

One might also say Granny Weatherall is guilty of the sort of hubris shown by some of Flannery O'Connor's characters, who think (for example) that because they wear clean clothing (the grandmother in "A Good Man Is Hard to Find") or hose down their pigs (Mrs. Turpin in "Revelation") they will be saved. Some support for this reading can be found in this passage:

> Granny felt easy about her soul. . . . She had her secret comfortable understanding with a few favored saints.

However, another way of looking at the story is to emphasize the point that, although at the end she is deeply disappointed, she remains active; she blows out the light. Against this, David C. Estes argues [*Studies in Short Fiction* 22 (1953)], "Her final act . . . reveals the ironic futility of all that has kept her so busy."

The interpretation that she is hubristic is offered very tentatively, and certainly not as one that gives *the* meaning of the story. But a reading of the parable is bound to call into question the usual view that "The Jilting of Granny Weatherall" is a story about a strong woman's perception that her faith is delusive.

A video cassette of Katherine Anne Porter's "The Jilting of Granny Weatherall" is available from HarperCollins.

Topics for Discussion and Writing

1. The meaning of the title, "The Jilting of Granny Weatherall."
2. The reader's developing response to Ellen Weatherall.
3. Religious imagery in "The Jilting of Granny Weatherall."
4. The meaning of "duty" in "The Jilting of Granny Weatherall."
5. The two narratives of "The Jilting of Granny Weatherall."
6. The imagery of darkness and light in "The Jilting of Granny Weatherall."

William Faulkner "A Rose for Emily" (p. 240)

The chronology of the story—not very clear on first reading—has been worked out by several writers. Five chronologies are given in M. Thomas Inge, *William Faulkner: "A Rose for Emily"*; a sixth is given in Cleanth Brooks, *William Faulkner: Toward Yoknapatawpha and Beyond* (pp. 382–384). Brooks conjectures that Miss Emily is born in 1852, her father dies around 1884, Homer Barron appears in 1884 or 1885, dies in 1885 or 1886, the delegation calls on Miss Emily about the smell in 1885/86.–In 1901 or 1904 or 1905, Miss Emily gives up the lessons in china-painting. Colonel Sartoris dies in 1906 or 1907, the delegation calls on her about the taxes in 1916, and Miss Emily dies in 1926.

The plot, of course, is gothic fiction: a decaying mansion, a mysteriously silent servant, a corpse, necrophilia. And one doesn't want to discard the plot in a search for what it symbolizes, but it is also clear that the story is not only "about" Emily Grierson but also about the South's pride in its past (including its Emily-like effort to hold on to what is dead) and the guilt as well as the grandeur of the past. Inevitably much classroom discussion centers on Miss Emily's character, but a proper discussion of her character entails a discussion of the narrator.

(This paragraph summarizes an essay on this topic by John Daremo, originally printed in S. Barnet, *A Short Guide to Writing about Literature*.) The unnamed narrator is never precisely identified. Sometimes he seems to be an innocent eye, a recorder of a story whose implications escape him. Sometimes he seems to be coarse: He mentions "old lady Wyatt, the crazy woman," he talks easily of "niggers," and he confesses that because he and other townspeople felt that Miss Emily's family "held themselves a little too high for what they really were," the townspeople "were not pleased exactly, but vindicated" when at thirty she was still unmarried. But if his feelings are those of common humanity (e.g. racist and smug), he at least knows what these feelings are and thus helps us to know ourselves. We therefore pay him respectful attention, and we notice that on the whole he is compassionate (note especially his sympathetic understanding of Miss Emily's insistence for three days that her father is not dead). True, Miss Emily earns our respect by her aloofness and her strength of purpose (e.g., when she publicly appears in the buggy with Homer Barron, and when she cows the druggist and the alderman), but if we speak of her aloofness and her strength of purpose rather than of her arrogance and madness, it is because the narrator's imaginative sympathy guides us. And the narrator is the key to the apparently curious title: Presumably the telling of this tale is itself the rose, the community's tribute (for the narrator insistently speaks of himself as "we") to the intelligible humanity in a woman whose unhappy life might seem monstrous to less sympathetic observers. Another meaning, however, may be offered (very tentatively) for the title. In the story Faulkner emphasizes Miss Emily's attempts to hold on to the past: her insistence, for example, that her father is not dead, and that she has no taxes to pay. Is it possible that Homer Barron's corpse serves as a source of pressed or preserved will, a reminder of a past experience of love? If so, the title refers to him.

For a feminist reading, sees Judith Fetterley, in *The Resisting*

Reader: A Feminist Approach to American Fiction (1978), reprinted in *Literary Theories in Praxis*, edited by Shirley F. Staton (1987). Fetterley sees the story as revealing the "sexual conflict" within patriarchy (whether of the South or the North, the old order or the new). Emily's confinement by her father represents the confinement of women by patriarchy, and the remission of her taxes reveals the dependence of women on men. Emily has been turned into a "Miss," a lady, by a chivalric attitude that is "simply a subtler and more dishonest version of her father's horsewhip." The narrator represents a subtle form of this patriarchy. According to Fetterley, the narrator sees her as "'dear, inescapable, impervious, tranquil, and perverse'; indeed, anything and everything but human."

Fetterley—the "resisting reader" of her title, that is the reader who refuses to accept that text—argues that the story exposes "the violence done to a woman by making her a lady; it also explains the particular form of power the victim gains from this position and can use on those who enact their violence. . . . Like Ellison's invisible man, nobody sees *Emily*. And because nobody sees *her*, she can literally get away with murder."

An audio cassette of William Faulkner reading is available from HarperCollins.

Topics for Discussion or Writing

1. How valid is the view that the story is an indictment of the decadent values of the aristocratic Old South? Or a defense of these values (embodied in Emily) against the callousness (embodied in Homer Barron) of the North?
2. Suppose Faulkner had decided to tell the story from Miss Emily's point of view. Write the first 200 or 300 words of such a version.
3. Characterize the narrator.

Zora Neale Hurston "Sweat" (p. 247)

Zora Neale Hurston was not simply a black writer, or a woman writer; she was a black woman writer, and much of her fiction comes from this perspective. (Bell Hooks, in *Ain't I a Woman*, interestingly discusses black women and feminism.)

The contrast between the two chief characters is boldly drawn—clearly Delia is good and Sykes is bad—but it is not without complexity. After all, Delia does allow Sykes to die, and Sykes, though a brute, obviously suffers (despite his boasting and his bullying) from a sense of inferiority which apparently is heightened by the sight of his wife engaged in a menial task for white people: "Ah done tole you time and again to keep them white folks' clothes outa dis house." Though Hurston does not explicitly make the point that black men had a harder time than black women in finding employment, a reader presumably is aware of the fact that an oppressive white society made black men feel unmanly, and that they sometimes compensated by brutal expressions of what they took to be manliness. When Sykes deliberately steps on the white clothes, we understand that he is expressing not only a cruel contempt for his wife but also hostility toward white society.

Still, that Sykes is a brute cannot be doubted; the other black men in the story testify to this effect. This is the intent of question 2 in the text. Notice especially the longish speech to the effect that some men abuse women simply because the men are bad:

> Taint no law on earth dat kin make a man be decent if it aint in 'im. . . . Dey knows whut dey is doin' while dey is at it, an' hates theirselvs fuh it but they keeps on hangin' after huh tell she's empty. Den dey hates huh fuh bein' a cane-chew an' in de way.

Further, even before Sykes came to hate his wife, he never loved her but only lusted after her.

> She had brought love to the union and he had brought a longing for the flesh.

In this respect, however, he apparently is not much different from the other men in the story, who seem to regard an attractive woman only as a commodity, not as a person with ideas and feelings. Thus one of them, commenting on Delia's good looks in her earlier days, says, "Ah'd uh mah'ied huh mahself if he hadn'ter beat me to it." It does not occur to him that she might have had a say in the choice of her husband.

Classroom discussion will probably focus on Delia, especially on the question of whether a woman as devout as Delia would stand by and allow even the worst of husbands to die. (Question 3 approaches this point.) But "stand by" is misleading, since Hurston takes pains to emphasize not only the suffering that Delia has undergone at Sykes's hands but also the helplessness she experiences when the snake bites him. She becomes "ill," and we are told that "Delia could not move— her legs were gone flabby." Seeing him in agony, she experiences "a surge of pity," but "Orlando with its doctors was too far." All of these statements extenuate—indeed, eliminate—any blame that otherwise a reader might conceivably attach to Delia.

Further, Sykes is responsible for his own death since he malevolently introduces the snake into the house, and it is presumably Sykes who has transferred the snake from the box to the laundry basket, in an effort to murder Delia. He is thus justly punished, undone by his own hand. Interestingly, a passage in Ecclesiastes (10: 8–9) uses the image of a snake:

> He that diggeth a pit shall fall into it; and whoso breaketh an hedge, a serpent shall bite him.
>
> Whoso removeth stones shall be hurt therewith; and he that cleaveth wood shall be endangered thereby.

We are thus in a world of tragedy, where a person aiming at good (doubtless in his brutal mind Sykes thinks that it will be good—for him—to eliminate Delia) destroys himself. With the passage from Ecclesiastes in mind, one can almost speak of the physics of the world: for every action, there is an equal and opposite reaction. Delia, one notices, tells Sykes that she now hates him as much as she used to love him, and he counters that his hatred form her equals her hatred for him. At the start of the story he torments Delia by terrifying her with what seems to be a snake, and at the end of the story he is terrified by a snake. He puts the snake in her laundry basket, but the snake crawls into his bed—where Sykes is bitten. A final comment on the reciprocal structure or geometry of the story: "Sweat" begins late at night, and ends with "the red dawn," which gradually changes into full light, as "the sun crept on up." The image of daylight implies a new day, a new life for Delia, though of course nothing can bring back her youth or her love.

Topics for Discussion and Writing

1. Summarize the relationship of Delia and Sykes before the time of the story.
2. What function, if any, do the men on Joe Clark's porch serve?
3. Do you think Delia's action at the end of the story is immoral? Why, or why not?

Frank O'Connor "Guests of the Nation" (p. 257)

We once began teaching this story by asking, "What is this story about?" The first answer, "War," brought the reply, "Yes, but what about war? Is it, for example, about the heroism, that war sometimes stimulates?" Another student replied, "No, it's about the cruelty of war." The point: Though it is obvious to all instructors that the story is Bonaparte's, specifically about his growing up or initiation or movement from innocence to experience, this movement is not so evident to inexperienced readers.

This is not to say, of course, that it is not also about the conflict between the ideas of society and the ideals of the individuals. Jeremiah Donovan, though he thinks of himself as experienced, seems never to have gown up, never to have come to any sorrowful awareness of man's loneliness. The bickering between Noble and Hawkins is, however, not a sign of enmity but a sort of bond. They may quarrel, but at least they share a relationship. Hawkins's offer to join the Irish cause indicates not so much his cowardice as his intuitive awareness that life and fellowship are more important than blind nationalism that excuses murder by an appeal to "duty."

Question 4, below, lends itself well to a theme. The old woman is a "simple . . . countrywoman," but she knows (as the narrator finds out) that "nothing but sorrow and want can follow the people that disturb the hidden powers." An interview with O'Connor in *Writers at Work*, edited by Malcolm Cowley, reveals some of O'Connor's ideas about fiction. Asked why he chose the short story as his medium, O'Connor said, "Because it's the nearest thing I know of to lyric poetry. . . . A novel actually requires far more logic and far more knowledge of circumstances, whereas a short story can have the sort of detachment from circumstances that lyric poetry has." O'Connor's ideas about the short story are expressed at some length in his book on the topic, *The Lonely Voice*.

Topics for Discussion and Writing

1. Although the narrator, Noble, and Donovan are all patriotic Irishmen, Donovan's attitude toward the English prisoners is quite different from that of the other two. How does that difference in attitude help point up the story's theme?

2. When he hears he is about to be shot, Hawkins, to save his life,

volunteers to join the Irish cause. Is his turnabout simply evidence of his cowardice and hypocrisy? Explain.

3. Throughout most of the story Belcher is shy and speaks little; just before his execution, however, he suddenly becomes quite loquacious. Is he trying to stall for time? Would it have been more in character for Belcher to have remained stoically taciturn to the end, or do the narrator's remarks about Belcher's change make it plausible?

4. Does the old woman's presence in the story merely furnish local color or picturesqueness? If so, is it necessary or desirable? Or does her presence further contribute to the story's meaning? If so, how?

5. The following is the last paragraph of an earlier version. Which is the more effective conclusion?

> So then, by God, she fell on her two knees by the door, and began telling her beads, and after a minute or two Noble went on his knees by the fireplace, so I pushed my way past her, and stood at the door, watching the stars and listening to the damned shrieking of the birds. It is so strange what you feel at such moments, and not to be written afterwards. Noble says he felt he seen everything ten times as big, perceiving nothing around him but the little patch of black bog with the two Englishmen stiffening in it; but with me it was the other way, as though the patch of bog where the two Englishmen were was a thousand miles away from me, and even Noble mumbling just behind me and the old woman and the birds and the bloody stars were all far away, and I was somehow very small and lonely. And nothing that ever happened to me after I never felt the same about again.

6. How does the point of view help to emphasize the narrator's development from innocence to awareness? If the story had been told in the third person, how would it have effected the story's impact?

Shirley Jackson "The Lottery" (p. 266)

This story is based on fertility rituals of the sort described in Sir James Frazer's *The Golden Bough*: a community is purged of its evil, and fertility is ensured, by the sacrifice of an individual, that is, by killing a scapegoat. "Lottery in June, corn be heavy soon," Old Man Warner says. In "The Lottery," the method of execution is stoning, which Frazer reports was a method used in ancient Athens.

Until the last six paragraphs we think we are reading a realistic story about decent small-town life. Probably on rereading we notice that, despite all the realism, the time and the place are never specified; we may feel we are reading about a twentieth-century New England town, but we cannot document this feeling. On rereading, too, we pay more attention to the early references to stones, and to the general nervousness, and of course we see the importance of Tessie Hutchinson's outburst. [Consult Helen E. Nebeker, "'The Lottery': Symbolic Tour de Force," *American Literature* 46 (1974): 100–107.] With the last six paragraphs the horror comes, and it is described in the same matter-of-fact, objective tone used in the earlier part of the story.

Inevitably a discussion turns to the question, "Does the story have any meaning for a modern society?" Students in the 1990s may have to be reminded that a lottery was used as recently as the Vietnam War to pick the people who would be subject to slaughter.

In *Come Along with Me*, Shirley Jackson discusses the furor "The Lottery" evoked after its original publication in the *New Yorker* in 1948. Lenemaja Friedman, in *Shirley Jackson* (1975) reports that Jackson said of the theme: "Explaining just what I hoped the story to say is very difficult. I suppose I hoped, by setting a particularly brutal ancient rite in the present and in my own village, to shock the story's readers with a graphic demonstration of the pointless violence and general inhumanity in their own lives." On the other hand, Jack O'Shaughnessy in *The New York Times Book Review* (August 18, 1988, p. 34), said that after reading the story in the *New Yorker* he wrote to Jackson, asking, "What does it mean?" He says that Jackson replied, on a postcard, "I wish I knew. Shirley Jackson."

Perhaps this story should not be pressed for its meaning or theme. Formulations such as "Society engages in ritualized slaughter," or "Society disguises its cruelty, even from itself," or "Even decent people seek scapegoats" do not quite seem to fit. Isn't it possible that the story is an effective shocker, signifying nothing? As many people have pointed out, much of the effect of the story depends on the contrast between the objective narration and the horrifying subject. The story is clever, a carefully wrought thriller, but whether it is an allegory—something about the cruelty of humanity, a cruelty which is invisible to us because it is justified by tradition—is a matter that may be reasonably debated.

The date of the story is significant, June 27, close to the summer solstice, and the season for planting. Some of the names, too, are obviously significant: the ritual is presided over by Mr. Summers, the first man to draw a lot is Mr. Adams, and conservative warnings are uttered by Mr. Warner. Note, too, that the leaders of the attack on Mrs. Hutchinson are Adams (the first sinner) and Graves (the result of sin was death).

One last point about the ritual: Clyde Dunbar, at home with a broken leg, does not participate. Why? Because a sacrificial victim must be unblemished.

Topics for Discussion and Writing

1. Is "The Lottery" more than a shocker?
2. What is the community's attitude toward tradition?
3. Doubtless a good writer could tell this story effectively from the point of view of a participant, but Jackson chose a nonparticipant point of view. What does she gain?
4. Let's say you were writing this story, and you had decided to write it from Tessie's point of view. What would your first paragraph, or your first 250 words, be?
5. Suppose someone claimed that the story is an attack on religious orthodoxy. What might be your response? (Whether you agree or disagree, set forth your reasons.)

Hisaye Yamamoto "Yoneko's Earthquake" (p. 273)

Despite the title, the story can be thought of primarily as the mother's story, rather than as Yoneko's; that is why the questions in the text concentrate on the mother.

On the other hand, it is entirely right that classroom discussion consider Yoneko in some detail. Strictly speaking, the story is not told from her point of view, but we nevertheless learn of the events as she sees them. Students might be invited to discuss her character in an effort to help them see that part of a reader's interest in the story depends on perceiving the gap between what Yoneko sees (she is a sort of innocent eye) and what the reader understands to have happened—first between Mrs. Hosoume and Marpo (they have had an affair, and Mrs. Hosoume has become pregnant), then to Mrs. Hosoume (she has an abortion, and when Seigo dies she takes his death as a punishment visited upon her by God for having taken the life of the fetus), and finally to Mr. Hosoume (he seeks to comfort his wife). One might say, perhaps a bit too simply, that Yoneko's loss of Christian faith is ironically contrasted with Mrs. Hosoume's acquisition of Christian faith, and with Mr. Hosoume's ultimate Christian (charitable) behavior. But this way of putting things makes the story sound too solemn: it is largely Yoneko's engaging character that gives the reader immediate pleasure. The story is in many ways warm and even humorous.

If the title refers to Yoneko's loss of faith in God—a powerful experience—it also puts us in mind of the "earthquake"—the disastrous event—that the girl does *not* perceive. Is Yoneko to be regarded as conspicuously imperceptive? Surely not. She is an engaging child, genial, affectionate (despite her teasing of her brother), and in some ways thoughtful, as when she wonders if Jesus was exempted "from stinging eyes when he shampooed that long, naturally wavy hair of his." But, not unnaturally, she is more concerned with the pretty ring than with wondering about where it came from, and when (in the last two paragraphs) she perceives that her mother is examining "with peculiarly intent eyes," her distress at having lost the ring preoccupies her.

The domestic tragedy—how Mr. Hosoume's incapacitation leads to Mrs. Hosoume's increasing dependence on Marpo, and then to Mr. Hosoume's perception that his role has been (in one way or another) usurped—is perceived only dimly by Yoneko, who is "thunderstruck" when her father slaps her mother, but who does not understand the implications. None of this should lead a reader to think that Yoneko is in any way slow, though perhaps today, when the issue of abortion is aired daily on television, the unstated happenings of the story might seem evident even to a youngster.

Topics for Discussion and Writing

1. Why does Mrs. Hosoume tell Yoneko not to tell Mr. Hosoume where the ring came from?
2. Why does Mrs. Hosoume strike his wife?
3. Why does Marpo disappear on the same day that Mrs. Hosoume goes to the hospital?
4. Why does Mrs. Hosoume say—out of the blue, so far as Yoneko is concerned—"Never kill a person, Yoneko."

Gabriel García Márquez "A Very Old Man with Enormous Wings" (p. 283)

A neighbor is the first to call the winged man an angel, and then other characters call him an angel—maybe he is, but maybe he is just a winged old man. That is, despite the references to an angel, and even to the somewhat biblical-sounding start with its "third day," its torrent of rain (in the Old Testament such a torrent is symbolic of God's power), and its "newborn child," we need not assume that the story is about the human response to the divine.

Most of our students, like most of our colleagues, argue that the story satirizes the inability of people to perceive the spiritual. Thus the angel attracts attention only briefly and is, when not abused, finally neglected. All of this, in the common view, constitutes a satire on humanity, an attack that suggests we are like those contemporaries of Jesus who saw in him only a troublemaker.

But this is to assume that Garcia Márquez, like Flannery O'Connor, subscribes to a Christian view of reality. Such an assumption is highly doubtful. Moreover, the assumption that in this story Garcia Márquez is talking about our inability to perceive and revere the miraculous neglects the fact that he deals in fantasy or, perhaps more precisely, that he employs fantasy in order to write about the individual's isolation in an unintelligible world. Such worlds as he gives us in his stories and novels are, he would say, projections of his mind rather than pictures of objective reality.

In short, we doubt that the story is about the ways in which human beings ignore, domesticate, or in other ways maltreat the divine. Of course, there is some satire of churchgoers and of the church: the old lady who thinks angels live on meatballs, the inappropriate miracles, and especially the correspondence with the authorities in Rome and the business about the priest who suspects that the winged man is an impostor because he doesn't speak Latin. But satire in this story is directed less at religious faith than at exploitative capitalism—selfishness, gullibility, etc.

To say that the story is satiric is to say also that it is comic. One ought not to be so concerned with creating a religious allegory that one fails to see the humor, for instance, in the comments on the priest, the mail from Rome, and the "lesson" taught by the spider-woman. (In this last we hear a jibe at the conventional morality of fairy tales and of bourgeois standards.) As in other satire, the vision of human stupidity and cruelty is as unnerving as it is amusing. And what perhaps is especially unnerving is the fact that Pelayo and Elisenda are, at least when they discover the man, not particularly villainous. "They did not have the heart to club him to death," and so they at first (kindly, by their standards) plan to set him adrift on a raft for three days and "leave him to his fate on the high seas." Such is the depth, or rather the shallowness, of decency.

For a good discussion of the story, sees John Gerlach, "The Loss of Wings," in *Bridges to Fantasy* [ed. George E. Slusser et al. (1982)]. Rejecting the fairly common view that the story of a feeble old flyer is meant to explode our taste for antiquated myths, Gerlach points out that many passages are puzzling. For instance, a line such as "He answered in an incomprehensible dialect with a strong sailor's voice" makes the careful reader wonder what a "sailor's voice" is. Or take, for instance, the last sentence of the story, which says that the old man "was no longer an annoyance in [Elisenda's] life, but an imaginary dot on the horizon of the sea." First, there is the odd contrast between an "annoyance" (an abstraction) and a "dot" (something barely visible); Gerlach calls the sentence grammatically uncomfortable. Second, Gerlach points out that an "imaginary dot" is strange; Elisenda is simultaneously seeing and imagining. Briefly, Gerlach's gist is that although the world of myth seems to be demeaned by this story about a winged old man who looked "like a huge decrepit hen," the story gives us a world of mystery, partly in the almost miraculous patience of the old man and partly in its puzzling statements. One mystery is that the mysterious, winged old man seems more real (in his behavior) than the others in the story. Drawing heavily on Tzvetan Todorov's *The Fantastic,* Gerlach's overall point is that this story, like other works of fantasy, evokes "hesitation" (we'd say uncertainty). In Todorov's view, fantasy is not simply a matter of improbable happenings. The happenings in an allegory are usually improbably, but allegories are not fantasies, Todorov, says, because the supernatural events can be interpreted on a naturalistic level. But in "A Very Old Man," there remains a strong sense of uncertainty, an uncertainty that survives such an allegorical interpretation as "There is a winged aspect of man that can fly despite the lack of appreciation of others."

Topics for Discussion and Writing

1. The subtitle is "A Tale for Children." Do you think that the story is more suited to children than to adults? What in the story do you think children would especially like, or dislike?
2. Is the story chiefly about the inability of adults to perceive and respect the miraculous world?
3. Characterize the narrator of the story.
4. Characterize Pelayo, Elisenda, their son, and the man with wings.

Alice Munro "How I Met My Husband" (p. 288)

One way of teaching this story is to approach it as a delightful semi-comic version of the usually portentous (and usually male) story of initiation, or of the movement from innocence to experience. The narrator, Edie, is now mature, but she is reporting (like, say, the narrator of Joyce's "Araby") an early experience.

"I was fifteen and way from home for the first time"—such words suggest considerable naiveté, and indeed in the course of the story we learn that Edie was inexperienced in all sorts of ways, especially in the ways of young men. We learn too that she was not much of a student (she left high school after one year), that she is childish enough to put on Mrs. Peebles's makeup and one of her dresses, etc. If you ask a student to read the opening paragraph aloud in class, students will probably hear a fairly naive voice in "We heard . . . and we were sure . . . so we all ran out . . . the first close-up plane I ever saw." (On the other hand, it is Mrs. Peebles, not the narrator, who screams.) The title of the story itself has a naive (or at least matter-of-fact) tone to it, and one can argue that the story reveals the narrator's naiveté, since it tells the reader what caused her to smile while she waited for the mailman, and how her smile charmed the man who did become her husband.

If Edie is in some ways naive, she is also endowed with lots of native smarts. Of course, strictly speaking, one can't be sure that what she now reports is what she felt when she was 15 years old, but the reader gets the feeling that much of the report, though delivered by a mature woman, accurately conveys Edie's original perception. Since some passages are explicitly said to be later interpretations (e.g., "I wasn't even old enough then to realize how out of the common it [was] . . . for a man to say a world like *beautiful*"), we naturally take the rest of the story to be a fairly accurate report of her original responses. For instance:

> Dessert was never anything to write home about, at their place. A dish of Jell-O or sliced bananas or fruit out of a tin. "Have a house without a pie, be ashamed until you die," my mother used to say, but Mrs. Peebles operated differently.

Although the expression "Mrs. Peebles operated differently" has the wryness of maturity, the earlier words expressing scorn for desserts that are not home-made presumably represent the view she held at the time.

Readers who are familiar both with Jell-O and with home-made pies will not be quick to call Edie naive. As one reads the story one keeps encountering an inexperienced girl who nevertheless is extremely perceptive, for instance about human ways (Dr. Peebles "had a calming way of talking, like any doctor"), and especially about class distinctions. ("Dr. Peebles was only an animal doctor"). The comments on the behavior of the others reveal a quick mind. Example: "Asking people to stay, just like that, is certainly a country thing, and maybe seemed natural to [Dr. Peebles] now, but not to Mrs. Peebles, from the way she said, oh yes, we have plenty of room." Edie also is an adept housekeeper, and she shows an awareness of professional responsibility: "I was scared, but I never admitted that, especially in front of the children I was taking care of." Her naiveté is chiefly confined to sex and to the belief that Chris Watters will send her a letter.

Most important, Edie is a very *good* person. For instance, she excuses Mrs. Peebles's unthinking remark about gawking farmers: "She didn't say that to hurt my feelings. It never occurred to her." Somewhat similarly, she tells Chris that his sign is attractive, and, more important, she continued to smile at the mailman because he was "counting on it, and he didn't have an easy life, with the winter driving ahead." In the last line of the story she explicitly says that she likes people to be happy, but the line gains its force from what we have seen earlier.

Her desire that people be happy does not extend to the dreadful Alice Kelling. Students might be invited to discuss their attitude toward Edie's lie. Almost all will probably excuse Edie, on various grounds: (1) Edie admits that lying is wrong; (2) Edie lies in part to protect someone else; (3) Alice is awful. By the way, it's interesting to notice that although Edie lies to Alice *before* Alice reveals her full loathesomeness, even the few readers who are uneasy about Edie lying tend to excuse Edie retroactively, so to speak, after Alice unleashes a torrent of abuse. Another point about Alice, or about Alice and Edie: Edie does not do much in the way of offering negative comments about Alice. Munro lets us form an opinion on our own, and thus preserves Edie from speaking harshly.

One way of teaching this story is to compare it with a stories of male initiation (e.g. Joyce's "Araby").

Topics for Discussion and Writing

1. Since Edie tells the story, we know about the other characters only as much as she tells us. Do you think her view of Mrs. Peebles and of Loretta Bird is accurate? On what do you base your answer?

2. Edie offers explicit comments about Mrs. Peebles and Loretta Bird, but not about Alice Kelling, or at least not to the same degree. Why?
3. Characterize Edie.
4. What do you think of the title? Why?

Joyce Carol Oates "Where Are You Going, Where Have You Been?" (p. 302)

The title seems to be derived from Judges 19:17 ("So the old man said, 'Where are you going, and where do you come from?"), a point made in a rather strained discussion of the story in *Explicator* (Summer 1982).

Tom Quirk, in *Studies in Short Fiction* [18 (1981): 413–419], pointed out that the story derives from newspaper and magazine accounts (especially one in *Life*, Mar. 4, 1966) of the activities of a psychopath known as "The Red Piper of Tucson," who drove a gold-colored car and seduced and sometimes murdered teenage girls in the Tucson area. Because he was short, he stuffed his boots with rags and flattened tin cans, which caused him to walk unsteadily. Oates herself has confirmed, on various occasions, her use of this material (e.g., *New York Times*, Mar. 23, 1986).

According to Oates, in an early draft of her story "Death and the Maiden" (she is fond of a type of fiction that she calls "realistic allegory"), "the story was minutely detailed yet clearly an allegory of the fatal attractions of death (or the devil). An innocent young girl is seduced by way of her own vanity: she mistakes death for erotic romance of a particularly American/trashy sort." The story went through several drafts. Oates has said she was especially influenced by Bob Dylan's song, "It's All Over Now, Baby Blue." One line of Dylan's song ("The vagabond who's standing at your door") is clearly related to the story, and note that in the story itself Connie wishes "it were all over."

In speaking of the revisions, Oates writes that "the charismatic mass murderer drops into the background and his innocent victim, a 15-year-old, moves into the foreground. She becomes the true protagonist of the tale. . . . There is no suggestion in the published story that Arnold Friend has seduced and murdered other young girls, or even that he necessarily intends to murder Connie." Oats goes on to explain that her interest is chiefly in Connie, who "is shallow, vain, silly, hopeful, doomed—perhaps as I saw, and still see, myself?—but capable nonetheless of an unexpected gesture of heroism at the story's end. . . . We don't know the nature of her sacrifice [to protect her family from Arnold], only that she is generous enough to make it." Instructors who are interested in discussing the intentional fallacy (and is it a fallacy?) will find, if they use this passage, that students have strong feelings on the topic.

The story has abundant affinities with the anonymous ballad called "The Demon Lover". The demon lover has "music on every hand," and Connie "was hearing music in her head"; later, Arnold and Ellie listen to the same radio station in the car that Connie listens to in the house; the demon lover's ship has "masts o' the beaten gold," and Arnold's car is "painted gold."

The first sentence tells us that Connie "had a quick nervous giggling habit of craning her neck to glance into mirrors." Her mother attributes it to vanity, and indeed Connie does think she is pretty, but a more important cause is insecurity. Connie's fear that she has no identity sometimes issues in her a wish that "she herself were dead and it were all over with." "Everything about her had two sides," which again suggests an incoherent personality.

Arnold Friend has a hawklike nose, thick black lashes, an ability to see what is gong on in remote places, a curious (lame) foot, a taste for strange bargains, incantatory speech, an enchanted subordinate, and a charismatic personality; all in all he is a sort of diabolical figure who can possess Connie, partly because he shows her an enormous concern that no one else has shown her. (The possession—"I'll come inside you, where it's all secret"—is possession of her mind as well as of her body.) Notice, too, that like a traditional evil spirit, Arnold Friend cannot cross the threshold uninvited.

The dedication to Dylan has provoked considerable comment. Marie Urbanski, in *Studies in Short Fiction* [15 (1978): 200–203], thinks it is pejorative, arguing that Dylan made music "almost religious in dimension among youth." Tom Quirk, on the other hand, says it is "honorific because the history and effect of Bob Dylan's music had been to draw youth away from the romantic promises and frantic strains of a brand of music sung by Buddy Holly, Chuck Berry, Elvis Presley, and others." A. H. Petry [*Studies in Short Fiction* 25 (1988), 155–157] follows Quirk, and goes on to argue that Ellie is meant to suggest Elvis Presley (lock of hair on forehead, sideburns, etc.) According to Petry, Oates is seeking "to warn against the dangerous illusions and vacuousness" generated by Elvis's music, in contrast to Bob Dylan's.

Perhaps the most astounding comment is by Mike Tierce and John

Michael Crafton [*Studies in Short Fiction* 22 (1985): 219–224], reprinted in our text. Tierce and Crafton argue that Arnold Friend, the mysterious visitor, is not satanic but rather a savior, and that he is (as his hair, hawklike nose, unshaved face, and short stature suggest) an image of Bob Dylan. Arnold's visit, in their view, is a fantasy of Connie's "overheated imagination," and it enables her to free herself "from the sense of confinement she feels in her father's house. . . . She broadens her horizons to include the 'vast sunlit reaches of the land' all around her."

Many readers find resemblances between the fiction of Oates and Flannery O'Connor, but in an interview in *Commonweal* (Dec. 5, 1969), Oates said that although she at first thought her fiction was indebted to Flannery O'Connor, she came to see that in O'Connor there is always a religious dimension whereas in her own fiction "there is only the natural world."

The story has been made into a film called *Smooth Talk* (Spectra Films, 1986). The essay in *The New York Times* in which Oates discusses the film is reprinted in a volume of her essays entitled *(Woman)Writer*, and reprinted in our text.

Topics for Discussion and Writing

1. Characterize Connie. Do you think the early characterization of Connie prepares us for her later behavior?
2. Is Arnold Friend clairvoyant—definitely, definitely not, maybe? Explain.
3. Evaluate the view that Arnold Friend is both Satan and the incarnation of Connie's erotic desires.
4. What do you make of the fact that Oates dedicated the story to Bob Dylan? Is she perhaps contrasting Dylan's music with the escapist (or in some other way unwholesome) music of othe popular singers?
5. If you have read Flannery O'Connor's "A Good Man is Hard to Find" (text), compare and contrast Arnold Friend and the Misfit.

Raymond Carver "Cathedral" (p. 316)

You might begin by asking students to indicate what sort of impression the narrator makes on them in the first paragraphs. (You may want to assign a short writing requirement of this sort along with the story. If students come to class with a paragraph or two on the topic, the discussion is usually good.)

Probably no single word adequately describes the narrator at this stage, but among the words that students have suggested in their paragraphs are "mean," "cynical," "bitter," "sullen," (this seems especially apt), "unfeeling," "cold," and "cruel"; all of these words are relevant. He is also (though fewer students see this at first) jealous, jealous both of the blind man and of the officer who was his wife's first husband. His jealousy of the officer emerges in his wry reference to "this man who'd first enjoyed her favors." (Later in the story his hostility to the officer is more open, for instance, in this passage: "Her officer—why should he have a name? he was the childhood sweetheart, and what more does he want?—came home from somewhere, found her, and called the ambulance.")

With the blind man, too, the narrator's characteristic form of aggression is the ironic or mocking comment, as when he tells his wife that he will take the blind man bowling. His jealousy of the affectionate relationship between his wife and Robert is understandable if unattractive, and equally unattractive is the way in which he at last reveals that he does not fear this intruder into his house, when he flips open her robe, thus "exposing a juicy thigh." Still, this action is a step toward his accepting Robert and ultimately responding to Robert's influence. One other characteristically aggressive response also should be mentioned: Only rarely does he call Robert by his name. In speaking about him, as early as the first sentence of the story but pretty much throughout the story, he usually calls him "the blind man," a way of keeping him at a distance. (Not surprisingly, we soon learn that the narrator has no friends.) Late in the story, when Robert asks the narrator if he is "in any way religious," the narrator replies, "I guess I don't believe in it. In anything." This reply is not surprising; all of his behavior has shown that he doesn't believe "in anything."

The narrator seems to me, until near the end, to be a thoroughly unattractive figure. His irony is scarcely witty enough to make us deeply interested in him, so why do we continue reading the story after we have read the first few paragraphs? Mark A. R. Facknitz interestingly suggests in *Studies in Short Fiction* (Summer 1986) that "perhaps what pushes one into the story is a fear of the harm [the narrator] may do to his wife and her blind friend" (p. 293).

Despite the narrator's evident aggressiveness, fairly early in the story he does profess some sympathy for Robert and especially for Robert's late wife, who died without her husband

> having ever seen what the goddamned woman looked like. It was beyond my understanding. Hearing this, I felt sorry for the blind man for a little bit. And then I found myself thinking what a pitiful life this woman must have led. . . . A woman whose husband could never read the expression on her face, be it misery or something better. Someone who could wear makeup or not—what difference to him? . . . And then to slip off into death, the blind man's hand on her hand, his blind eyes streaming tears—I'm imagining now—her last thought maybe this: that he never even knew what she looked like, and she on the express to the grave. Robert was left with a small insurance policy and half of a twenty-peso Mexican coin. The other half of the coin went into the box with her. Pathetic.

But to say that the narrator displays "sympathy" here is, obviously, to use the word too loosely. What is displayed, again, is his bitterness, cynicism, and (despite his "imagining") his utter inability to understand the feelings of others. (Later, when the blind man's hand rests on the narrator's as the narrator draws a box—like his house—that turns into a cathedral, he will presumably come close to the experience that here he so ineptly imagines.)

Almost by chance the blind man enters into the narrator's life and thaws the ice frozen around his heart, or better, the blind man enables the narrator to see. As Facknitz puts it,

> Carver redeems the narrator by releasing him from the figurative blindness that results in a lack of insight into his own condition and which leads him to trivialize human feelings and needs. Indeed, so complete is his misperception that the blind man gives him a faculty of sight that he is not even aware that he lacks.[p. 293]

The narrator so dominates the story that there is a danger in class that no other matters will get considered, but it's worth asking students to characterize the wife and also Robert. Carver has taken care not to make Robert too saintly a fellow, full of wisdom and goodness and all that. True, Robert does have an uncanny sense of the difference between a black-and-white television set and a color set, but Carver nicely does not dwell on this; he just sort of lets it drop. Further, Robert's use of "bub" is maddening, and his confidence that he has "a lot of friends" in "Guam, in the Philippines, in Alaska, and even in Tahiti" suggests that he takes quite a bit for granted. It is easy, in fact, to imagine that one wouldn't much like Robert. The man who brings the narrator to a new consciousness is not sentimentalized or etherealized.

The story also invites comparison with Flannery O'Connor's "Revelation," which is about unearned grace, although the word "grace" should be used metaphorically when talking about Carver, whereas O'Connor was literally concerned with the working of the Holy Spirit. Talking of several of Carver's stories (including "Cathedral"), Facknitz puts the matter thus:

> Grace, Carver says, is bestowed upon us by other mortals, and it comes suddenly, arising in circumstances as mundane as a visit to the barber shop, and in the midst of feelings as ignoble or quotidian as jealousy, anger, loneliness, and grief. It can be represented in incidental physical contact, and the deliverer is not necessarily aware of his role. Not Grace in the Christian sense at all, it is what grace becomes in a godless world— a deep and creative connection between humans that reveals to Carver's alienated and diminished creatures that there can be contact in a world they supposed was empty of sense or love. Calm is given in a touch, a small, good thing is the food we get from others, and in the cathedrals we draw together, we create large spaces for the spirit. [pp. 295–296]

One last point: Obviously a cathedral is a more appropriate and richer symbol for what Carver is getting at than is, say, a gas station or shopping mall. Notice, too, that in the television program about cathedrals there is an episode in which devils attack monks; that is an assault is made on the soul. Presumably the narrator is unaware of morality plays, but some readers will understand that this scene introduces the possibility of a sort of spiritual change. A little later the inner change is further prepared for by the narrator's comments about a change in physical sensation. When he goes upstairs to get a pen so that he can draw a cathedral, he says, "My legs felt like they didn't have any strength in them. They felt like they did after I'd done some running."

Topics for Discussion and Writing

1. What was your impression of the narrator after reading the first five paragraphs?
2. Why does the narrator feel threatened by the blind man? Has he any reason to feel threatened?
3. What attitude does the narrator reveal in the following passage:

She'd turned so that her robe slipped away from her legs, exposing a
juicy thigh. I reached to draw her robe back over her and it was then
that I glanced at the blind man. What the hell! I flipped the robe open
again.

4. Why does the narrator not open his eyes at the end of the story?
5. The television program happens to be about cathedrals, but if the
   point is to get the narrator to draw something while the blind
   man's hand rests on the narrator's, the program could have been
   about some other topic, for example, about skyscrapers or about
   the Statue of Liberty. Do you think that a cathedral is a better
   choice, for Carver's purposes, than these other subjects? Why?
6. In what ways does Carver prepare us for the narrator's final state
   of mind?

Toni Cade Bambara "The Lesson" (p. 328)

It would be hard to find a less strident or more delightful story preach-
ing revolution. At its heart "The Lesson" calls attention to the enormous inequity in the distribution of wealth in America, and it suggests
that black people ought to start thinking about "what kind of society it
is in which some people can spend on a toy what it would cost to feed a
family of six or seven" for a year. That the young narrator does not quite
get the point of Miss Moore's lesson—and indeed steals Miss Moore's
money— is no sure sign that the lesson has failed. (Presumably Miss
Moore doesn't much care about the loss of her money; the money is well
lost if it helps the narrator, who plans to spend it, to see the power of
money.) In any case, the narrator has been made sufficiently uneasy ("I
sure want to punch somebody in the mouth") so that we sense she will
later get the point: "I'm goin . . . to think this day through." The last line
of the story seems to refer to her race to a bakery, but it has larger implications: "Ain't nobody gonna beat me at nuthin."

The difference between Sylvia's response and Sugar's response to
Miss Moore's lesson is worth discussing in class. As Malcolm Clark, of
Solano Community College, puts it, "The obvious question of the
story is, 'What is the lesson?' . . . It's clear that Miss Moore is trying to
teach these children a lesson in economic inequity. . . . Sugar learns
this lesson, as her comments to Miss Moore indicate. However, Sylvia
has also learned this lesson, though she does not reveal her understanding to Miss Moore." As Clark goes on to point out, Miss Moore's
lesson is not simply that some people are rich and others are not. She

wants to bring the children to a state where they will demand their share of the pie. "And it is in learning this part of the lesson that Sylvia and Sugar part company. Despite Sugar's obvious understanding of the lesson and her momentary flash of anger—strong enough to make her push Sylvia away—her condition is only temporary.

At the end of the story she is unchanged from the little girl she was at the beginning. It is she who wants to go to Hascomb's bakery and spend the money on food, essentially the same thing they intended to do with the money before the lesson began. . . . Sylvia, however, is greatly changed. She does not intend to spend the money with Sugar; instead, she plans to go over to the river and reflect upon the lesson further."

Topics for Discussion and Writing

1. In a paragraph or two, characterize the narrator.
2. Let's suppose Bambara had decided to tell the story through the eyes of Miss Moore. Write the first 250 words of such a story.
3. What is the point of Miss Moore's lesson? Why does Sylvia resist it?
4. Describe the relationship between Sugar and Sylvia. What is Sugar's function in the story?
5. Miss Moore says, "Imagine for a minute what kind of society it is in which some people can spend on a toy what it would cost to feed a family of six or seven. What do you think?" In an essay of 500 words, tell a reader what you think about this issue.

Margaret Atwood "Rape Fantasies" (p. 334)

Responses to this story will of course vary—from the view that rape is not a fit subject for humor, or that the story is not at all humorous, to the view that the story is humorous and a great deal more. In any case, most readers do find amusing the would-be rapist whose zipper gets stuck, and the would-be rapist who talks funny because he has a cold. It's worth asking those who find the story funny *why* they think it is funny. Among the points that probably will come up are these:

1. The rapists whom Estelle describes are all—as she describes them—weak and unthreatening; in fact, none of the fantasies end with rape. (Again, one thinks of the man whose zipper is stuck, and of the man who has a bad cold; earlier in the story there is the

man who politely holds the junk from her bag until she finds the plastic lemon with which to squirt him.)

2. The rapists are not only unthreatening, they are in varying degrees sympathetic and pathetic. The last of them, for instance, is imagined as having leukemia.

3. They are sympathetic—that is, we regard them with some sympathy—because the narrator regards them thus. Of course in fiction the reader does not always see things the way the narrator does, but in this story, where the narrator is frankly inventing stories (fantasies), and is not an innocent eye recounting what the reader is supposed to take to be a real event, the narrator is rather like an author, that is, is an inventor of stories, and probably we do in large measure regard her fantasies the way in which she regards them. And since she is a decent person—superficially tough, but fundamentally kind—we don't have a great deal of trouble accepting her point of view. Her fantasies chiefly describe scenes not of violence but of vulnerability and, in response to this awareness of vulnerability, a sense of fellowship and support.

4. Another reason that the story is not fundamentally disturbing, despite the title, is that the rape fantasies of Estelle's friends (at the beginning of the story) are not, as Estelle sharply points out, rape fantasies. "I mean, you aren't getting *raped*, it's just some guy you haven't met formally."

Under the apparently playful story of fantasies that reveal human kinship, is there in fact, however, a darker story? Is the narrator talking to a man, and, if so, are to assume that this man may later rape her, at least try to rape her?

The sexual identity of the hearer is never clearly established. Some students focus on two passages that, they say, sound as though Estelle must be talking to a man. The first occurs two-thirds through the story:

I'm telling you, I was really lonely when I first came here; I thought it was going to be such a big adventure and all, but it's a lot harder to meet people in a city. But I guess it's different for a guy.

The second occurs in the fourth paragraph from the end:

But maybe it's different for a guy.

These two passages, in which Estelle conjectures that men may hold a different view, are sometimes taken to indicate that Estelle is chatting with a man and is in some degree sounding him out. Other readers disagree. It's worth asking a student to read the passages aloud in class, and then discussing them.

The sex of the auditor is a matter of importance if, as some readers suggest, we are to understand that the rape fantasies may be replaced by a real rape, or at least by an attempted rape. For these readers, the story is essentially ironic; Estelle is chatting away about rape fantasies that are, first, amusing, and, second, rather sad in that they reveal pitiful creatures, but we are given clues that her auditor will seek to rape her. To say that we are given clues, however, is something of an overstatement. The evidence adduced is (1) the passages already indicated that are said to suggest that the listener is a male, and (2) the next-to-last paragraph, which begins thus:

> The funny thing about these fantasies is that the man is always someone I don't know, and the statistics in the magazines, well, most of them anyway, they say it's often someone you do know, at least a little bit....

Toward the end of this paragraph Estelle says

> I don't know why I'm telling you all this, except I think it helps you get to know a person, especially at first, hearing some of the things they think about. At work they call me the office worry wart, but it isn't so much worrying, it's more like figuring out what you should do in an emergency, like I said before.

Are we being told that Estelle will soon find herself confronted by an "emergency?" None of the passages already quoted will convince a skeptic that the story is about an attempt at rape that takes place after the last sentence of the story, but there can be no doubt that the exuberant comedy of the rape fantasies is no longer present in the last two paragraphs.

Topics for Discussion and Writing

1. In the next-to-last paragraph we learn that the narrator is speaking to someone in a bar, but we don't know—at least not for sure—the sex of the listener. Do you assume the listener is a man? If so, why do you make this assumption, and does it color your view of the narrator?

2. Do you assume that the fantasies reported by the narrator's

friends are indeed their fantasies, or are these reports inventions meant to interest the listener?

3. Did you find the story, ar at least parts of it, funny? If so, what is funny, and why?

Garrison Keillor "The Tip-Top Club" (p. 341)

One way of approaching this easy and engaging story is to introduce a discussion of two rather different kinds of comedy, wit and humor. Put briefly, the witty speaker amuses us with satiric barbs, whereas the humorist amuses us by showing the genial eccentricities of our fellows—including those of the humorist. The satirist, it is often said, jokes in earnest, whereas the humorist is content to be playful, spoofing even his or her own eccentricities.

It is not quite accurate to say (as sometimes is said) that the satirist is conscious whereas the humorist is unconscious, since the successful humorist of course knows what he or she is doing. It is better to make the distinction this way: The satirist laughs derisively *at* the objects of satire, and the humorist laughs affectionately *with* the objects of humor.

Does Keillor possess the "savage indignation" (Swift's words) of the satirist, or does he delight in the spectacle that he sets before us? Answers will vary with readers, of course, but our own response is this: Keillor, far from being indignant with the inanity of the hosts of talk shows, delights in them. It's our guess that he enjoys Bud and Wayne equally, and wouldn't have them any other way.

Certainly the chief characters in the story are in the old tradition of "humor characters," that is, they are Jonsonian one-dimensional figures whose uncomplicated personalities entertain us. This is true not only of Bud (utterly self-effacing) and of Wayne (the gasbag), but also of Roy Elmore, Jr. (the fusspot) and of Harlan (the lovable curmudgeon). A single example of Harlan's talk will suffice: "I hit the button and they die like rats." If you have students read a few speeches in class, the strong distinctions between the characters will become pretty clear, although some students may not immediately see Wayne's fatuousness since his sort of gibberish is such common currency today:

> There's a lot of anger and violence out there—and I don't say people shouldn't feel that way, but I do feel people should be willing to change. Life is change.

One student, who perhaps had too closely read the letters of Keats, saw Bud as an example of one kind of artist, Keats's poet who possesses "negative capability," and Wayne as an example of another kind, the poet who embodies what Keats called "the egotistical sublime." (Keats was talking about Wordsworth.) This is going pretty far and seems to miss much of the fun of the story. We prefer to see "The Tip-Top Club" as more or less in the tradition of the tall tale, where the deadpan narrator amuses us by recounting—with a straight face—an engaging anecdote about odd people whom we can't take seriously. Still the student at least paid the story the compliment of reading it closely, and, after all, the student's interpretation *is* one way of looking at "The Tip-Top Club."

Topics for Discussion and Writing

1. Compare Bud and Wayne. Why is Bud a successful host and Wayne a failure?
2. We are told that Bud's "approach offended a few listeners ('the *New York Times* crowd,' he called them.") What sort of people were offended by Bud's approach? And why do you suppose "the few nuts who called in" preferred talking to Alice rather than to Bud?
3. Moving from the story to real life, do you think that Keillor is making a valid point about talk-show hosts and audiences? Can you support your view with reference to real talk shows? Is Keillor making a serious point, or is he just kidding around? Or a little of each?

José Armas "El Tonto del Barrio" (p. 351)

If you have any Spanish-speaking students in your class, or even students whose acquaintance with Spanish does not go beyond a few years of high school study, you might ask them how they would translate the title. We thought of glossing "El Tonto" as "The Fool" or "The Idiot," but "Fool" is a bit old-fashioned and "Idiot"—as Armas suggested to us—is too strong. Armas's own suggestion, "Dummy," strikes us as exactly right.

While one is reading the story, say through the first one-third, it may seem to be chiefly a character sketch of Romero and a sketch of the community in which he lives, but then come two sentences that mark a turning point:

> Romero kept the sidewalks clean and the barrio looked after him. It was a contract that worked well for a long time.

"Worked well *for a long time*" implies that something happened that broke the contract, and we are promptly introduced to the disruptive element:

> Then, when Seferino, Barelas' oldest son, graduated from high school he went to work in the barber shop for the summer. Seferino was a conscientious and sensitive young man and it wasn't long before he took notice of Romero and came to feel sorry for him.

In the light of what happens next, some readers may think that the narrator (or the author?) is being ironic, even sarcastic, when he characterizes Seferino as "conscientious and sensitive," but Seferino really *is* conscientious and sensitive. He just isn't mature, wise in the ways of the barrio and (an important point) isn't able to understand that not everyone feels as he does. Thus, when he argues with his father he says, "How would you like to do what he does and be treated in the same way?" That's a reasonable position (we all know that we should do unto others as we would have others do unto us)—but Barelas's answer is wiser than Seferino's question: "I'm not Romero." Further, and this may seem to be a paradox, Barelas is not only wise enough to know that he is not Romero, but he is also wise enough to know (as Seferino does not) *why* Romero sweeps the sidewalks: "He sweeps the sidewalks because he wants something to do, not because he wants money."

Although the conflict between Seferino and Romero is the obvious conflict, the conflict (though that is almost too strong a word) between Seferino and Barelas is worth discussing in class. (The question in the text about Barelas's character is one way of approaching it.) This conflict is amusingly resolved when the well-meaning Seferino disappears into Harvard, thus sparing us a potentially embarrassing or painful scene in which the boy acknowledges his error. Indeed, instead of emphasizing the conflict between Barelas and his son, we get a scene in which Barelas—whose son has caused Romero to misbehave—is pitted against the rest of the community, which now seeks to confine Romero. And although Barelas again is on the right side, in one tiny detail he reveals that he too has been rattled, we might even say corrupted by his son's well-intentioned plan. When one of the men of the barrio says, "What if [Romero] hurts . . . ," Barelas interrupts: "He's not going to hurt anyone." Tino replies: "No, Barelas, I was going to say, what if he hurts himself?" It's a lovely touch, showing that Barelas (who is right about so much) can be mistaken, and, more important, showing that even though the community wants to lock Romero up, it is concerned chiefly for Romero's well being.

These comments are obvious, and perhaps a bit too solemn, since the story has a good deal of delightful humor in it. (One can ask the class what it finds *amusing* in the story.) A favorite passage is the bit recounting how Romero, after breaking with Seferino, at first simply skipped the barber shop in his sweeping, but then refined his action and pushed all of the trash from elsewhere in front of the barber shop.

Topics for Discussion and Writing

1. What sort of man do you think Barelas is? In your response take account of the fact that the townspeople "sort of want" Barelas 'to start off the list" of petitioners seeking to commit Romero.
2. The narrator, introducing the reader to Seferino, tells us that "Seferino was a conscientious and sensitive young man." Do you agree? Why, or why not?
3. What do you make of the last line of the story?
4. Do you think this story could take place in almost any community? If you did not grow up in a barrio, could it take place in your community?
5. The story is about Romero, but almost as interestingly it is about Seferino. We can fairly easily guess what will happen to Romero in the next few years. What would you guess will happen to Seferino? Will his Harvard education lead to his increasing alienation from his community? (Our own response is yes, in the short run, but—since he is a bright and sensitive youth and he has a wise father—we can hope that in the long run he will learn to appreciate and to cherish the ways of the Barrio.)

Alice Walker "Everyday Use" (p. 357)

The title of this story, like most other titles, is significant, though the significance appears only gradually. Its importance, of course, is not limited to the fact that Dee believes that Maggie will use the quilts for "everyday use"; on reflection we see the love, in daily use, between the narrator and Maggie, and we contrast it with Dee's visit—a special occurrence—as well as with Dee's idea that the quilts should not be put to everyday use. The real black achievement, then, is not the creation of works of art that are kept apart from daily life; rather, it is the everyday craftsmanship and the everyday love shared by people who cherish and sustain each other. That Dee stands apart from this achievement is clear (at least on rereading) from the first paragraph, and her pretensions are suggested as early as the fourth paragraph, where we are told that she thinks "orchids are tacky flowers." (Notice that in the fifth paragraph, when the narrator is imagining herself as Dee would like her to be on a television show, she has glistening hair—presumably because the hair has been straightened—and she appears thinner and lighter-skinned than in fact she is.) Her lack of any real connection with her heritage is made explicit (even before the nonsense about using the churn top as a centerpiece) as early as the paragraph in which she asks if Uncle Buddy whittled the dasher, and Maggie quietly says that Henry whittled it. Still, Dee is confident that she can "think of something artistic to do with the dasher." Soon we learn that she sees the quilts not as useful objects, but only as decorative works; Maggie, however, will use the quilts, and she even knows how to make them. Dee talks about black "heritage" but Maggie and the narrator embody this heritage and they experience a degree of contentment that eludes Dee.

Many white students today are scarcely aware of the Black Muslim movement, which was especially important in the 1960s, and they therefore pass over the Muslim names taken by Dee and her companion, the reference to pork (not be eaten by Muslims), and so on. That is, they miss the fact that Walker is suggesting that the valuable heritage of American blacks is not to be dropped in favor of an attempt to adopt an essentially remote heritage. It is worth asking students to do a little work in the library and to report on the Black Muslim movement.

Houston A. Baker, Jr. and Charlotte Pierce-Baker discuss the story in *Southern Review* [new series 21(Summer 1985)], in an issue that was later published as a book with the title *Afro-American Writing Today* [ed. James Olney (1989)]. Their essay is worth reading, but it is rather overheated. Sample:

> Maggie is the arisen goddess of Walker's story; she is the sacred figure who bears the scarifications of experience and knows how to convert patches into robustly patterned and beautifully quilted wholes. As an earth-rooted and quotidian goddess, she stands in dramatic contrast to the stylishly fiery and other-oriented Wangero. [p. 131]

The essay is especially valuable, however, because it reproduces several photographs (in black and white only, unfortunately) of quilts and their makers. Lots of books on American folk art have better reproductions of quilts, but few show the works with the artists who made them. It's worth bringing to class some pictures of quilts, whether from the essay by the Bakers or from another source. Even better, of course, is (if possible) to bring some quilts to class.

Topics for Discussion and Writing

1. "Everyday Use" is by a black woman. Would your response to the story be the same if you knew it were written by a white woman? Or by a man? Explain.
2. How does the narrator's dram about her appearance on the television program foreshadow the later conflict?
3. Compare "Everyday Use" with Bambara's "The Lesson" (p. 328). Consider the following suggestions: Characterize the narrator of each story and compare them. Compare the settings and how they function in each story. What is Miss Moore trying to teach the children in "The Lesson?" Why does Sylvia resist learning it? In "Everyday Use" what does Dee try to teach her mother and sister? Why do they resist her lesson? How are objects (such as quilts, toys) used in each story? How in each story does the first-person narration enlist and direct our sympathies?

Tim O'Brien "The Things They Carried" (p. 364)

A few words should be said about the movement away from the highly anecdotal story of, say, the Middle Ages and even of the late nineteenth century (e.g., Maupassant)—a movement toward what has been called the lyric style of, say, Chekhov and Joyce.

Most stories, even those of the twentieth century, retain something of the anecdotal plot, a fairly strong element of conflict and reversal. Howard Nemerov offers a satirical summary in *Poetry and Fiction* (1963):

> Short stories amount for the most part to parlor tricks, party favors with built-in snappers, gadgets for inducing recognitions and reversals; a small pump serves to build up the pressure, a tiny trigger releases it, there follows a puff and a flash as freedom and necessity combine; finally a

celluloid doll drops from the muzzle and descends by parachute to the floor. These things happen, but they happen to no-one in particular.

Some writers, however, have all but eliminated plot, and it's not unusual for twentieth-century writers of stories to disparage narrative (especially the novel) and to claim some affinity with poets. Frank O'Connor, in an interview in *Paris Review* (reprinted in *Writers at Work*, edited by Malcolm Cowley), said that the short story was his favorite form

> because it's the nearest thing I know to lyric poetry—I wrote lyric poetry for a long time, then discovered that God had not intended me to be a lyric poet, and the nearest thing to that is the short story. A novel actually requires far more logic and far more knowledge of circumstances, whereas a short story can have the sort of detachment from circumstances that lyric poetry has.

In his book on the short story, *The Lonely Voice,* O'Connor amplifies this point.

Faulkner makes pretty much the same point in another *Paris Review* interview that is reprinted in the same collection. Faulkner says

> I'm a failed poet. Maybe every novelist wants to write poetry first, finds he can't, and then tries the short story, which is the most demanding form after poetry. And failing at that, only then does he take up novel writing.

Doubtless Faulkner is being at least somewhat facetious, but we can't quite dismiss his implication that the short story is allied to the poem—by which he must mean the lyric.

If the course is being taught chronologically, students probably have already encountered Chekhov, Joyce, and Hemingway; if, for instance, they have read "Araby" they have read a story in which (many of them think) "nothing happens." In the "lyric story" (if there is such a species) the emphasis is not on telling about a change of fortune, marked by a decisive ending, but rather is on conveying (and perhaps inducing in the reader) an emotion—perhaps the emotion of the narrator. There is very little emphasis on plot, that is, on "What happened next?" (Chekhov said, "I think that when one has finished writing a short story one should delete the beginning and the end"), though of course there is a good deal of interest in the subtle changes or modulations of the emotion.

Certainly in "The Things They Carried"—a story set in a combat zone—there is none of the suspense and catastrophic action that one would expect in a war story of the nineteenth century, say a story by Ambrose Bierce or Stephen Crane. In "The Things They Carried" we learn fairly early that Ted Lavender got killed; because no one else gets killed, an inexperienced reader may conclude that nothing much happens in the story.

Of course, as far as plot is concerned, what "happens" is that Lieutenant Cross, feeling that his thoughts of Martha have led him to relax discipline with the result that one of his men has been killed, determines to pay attention to his job as a military leader and he therefore burns Martha's letters and photographs. But this narrative could scarcely sustain a story of this length; or, to put it another way, if *that's* what the story is about, much of the story seems irrelevant.

Even inexperienced readers usually see that "The Things They Carried" is not to be judged on its plot, any more than is (say) "Born in the U.S.A." If some passages are read aloud in class, even the least experienced readers—who may miss almost all of the subtleties when they read the story by themselves—will see and hear that O'Brien interestingly varies "the things they carried," from physical objects (chewing gum, and the latest gear for killing) to thoughts and emotions. In short, he uses verbal repetition (which creates rhythm) and metaphor to a degree rarely if ever found in the novel.

Not least of "the things they carried" are themselves and their minds. "For the most part they carried themselves with poise, a kind of dignity." "For the most part" is important. O'Brien doesn't sentimentalize the soldiers; they can be afraid and they can be wantonly destructive. He tells us, fairly late in the story, that "They shot chickens and dogs, they trashed the village well." He tells us, too, that "They carried the soldier's greatest fear, which was a fear of blushing." "They carried all the emotional baggage of men who might die." "They carried shameful memories." This insistent repetition, rather like the incremental repetition in the old popular ballads (e.g. "Edward," "Lord Randall," "Barbara Allen"), serves less to record a sequence of events than to deepen our understanding of a state of mind.

Still, there is, as has already been said, something of the traditional narrative here: Lieutenant Cross at last *does* something overt (burns Martha's letters and photographs). He thus "carries" less, literally, since the first line of the story is "First Lieutenant Jimmy Cross carried letters from a girl named Martha." Whether by burning the letters and photos he will in fact lighten his load—his guilt—is something about which readers may have different opinions. He may indeed impose stricter discipline, but it's hard to imagine that he will think less of Ted Lavender. Cross himself seems skeptical. "Lavender was dead. You couldn't burn the blame." One may lighten one's load by shooting off fingers and toes, and thus gain release from combat, and one can dream of flying away ("the weights fell off; there was nothing to bear"), but a reader may doubt that when Cross lightens his physical load he will find that the weights will fall off, and that he will have nothing, or only a little, to bear. He will still be a participant in a war where "men killed and died, because they were embarrassed not to." One may wonder, too, if Cross will be able to forget about Martha, or, so to speak, to keep her in her place. He thinks he will be able to do so, but the matter is left unresolved:

> Henceforth, when he thought about Martha, it would be only to think that she belonged elsewhere. He would shut down the daydreams. This was not Mount Sebastian, it was another world, where there were no pretty poems or midterm exams, a place where men died because of careless-ness and gross stupidity. Kiowa was right. Boom-down, and you were dead, never partly dead.

This quotation, however, raises yet another question, and perhaps a central question if one takes the story to be about Cross rather than about the soldiers as a group. Cross here seems to assume that death comes only to those who are careless or stupid. He thinks, presumably, that it is his job as an officer to prevent the carelessness and the stupid-ity of his men from getting them killed. But of course we know that in war even the careful and the bright may get killed. Further, nothing in the story tells us that Lavender was careless or stupid. He was killed while urinating, but even the careful and the bright must urinate. We are told that he was shot in the head, and perhaps we are to under-stand that, contrary to standard operating procedure, he was not wearing his helmet, but the point is not emphasized. When we first hear of Lavender's death we are told that Cross "felt the pain" and that "he blamed himself," although the reader does not know exactly why the lieutenant is blameworthy. Later perhaps a reader concludes (though again, this is not made explicit) that it was Cross's job to insist that the men wear their helmets. In any case, the reader is probably much easier on Cross than Cross is on himself.

To the extent that the story is about Cross's isolation—and, as Kiowa knows, Cross *is* isolated—it fits Frank O'Connor's remark (in *The Lonely Voice*) that a short story is "by its very nature remote from the community—romantic, individualistic, and intransigent." But, to repeat, it's probably fair to say that O'Brien is as much concerned with celebrating the state of mind of all the "legs or grunts" as he is with recording the sequence of actions that constitutes Lieutenant Cross's attempts to deal with his sense of guilt.

This story has been reprinted in a book called *The Things They Carried*, where it is one of twenty-two related but discontinuous pieces ranging from 2 to 20 pages. The book is dedicated to "the men of Alpha Company," and the names in the dedication correspond to the names in the stories. Further, in the book the narrator identifies himself as Tim O'Brien. A question thus arises: Is *The Things They Carried* a collection of stories, or is it biography, history, or whatever? Perhaps one's first thought, given the dedication and the name of the narrator, is that the book reports what O'Brien experienced—and yet in an interview in *Publisher's Weekly* O'Brien said, "My own experience has virtually nothing to do with the content of the book." He claims he used his own name for that of the narrator merely because he thought it would be "neat." (In another interview, he said the use of his own name was "just one more literary device.") If we believe what he told the interviewer, the book is fiction. But perhaps O'Brien is toying with the interviewer. Or perhaps he is behaving in accordance with a point made in the book: "In war you lose your sense of the definite, hence your sense of truth itself, and therefore it's safe to say that in a true war story nothing is ever absolutely true." Has O'Brien been infected by the "fact-or-fiction?" game of much recent writing? If so, should someone tell him that what we value in his writing is his ability to bring the Vietnam War home to us, rather than his philosophizing?

Topics for Discussion and Writing

1. What is the point of the insistent repetition of the words "the things they carried?" What sorts of things does Lieutenant Cross carry?
2. We are told that "Kiowa admired Lieutenant Cross's capacity for grief." But we are also told that although Kiowa "wanted to share the other man's pain," he could think only of "Boom-down" and of "the pleasure of having his boots off and the fog curling in around him and the damp soil and the Bible smells and the plush comfort of night." What might account for the different responses of the two men?
3. Near the end of the story, Lieutenant Cross "burned the two photographs." Why does he do this?

Leslie Marmon Silko "The Man to Send Rain Clouds (p. 137)

The church—especially perhaps the Roman Catholic Church—has often adapted itself to the old ways and beliefs of new converts, sometimes by retaining the old holidays and holy places but adapting them and dedicating them to the new religion. For instance, although the date of birth of Jesus is not known, from the fourth century it was celebrated late in December, displacing pagan festivals of new birth (e.g., the Roman *Saturnalia*, which celebrated the sowing of the crops on December 15–17, and the feast of the *Natalis Solis Invicti*, celebrating the renewal of the sun a week later).

Practices of this sort have facilitated conversion, but from the church's point of view the danger may be that the new believers retain too much faith in the old beliefs. In Silko's story the priest has every reason to doubt that his parishioners have fully accepted Christianity. The unnamed priest—he's just "the priest" or "the young priest," not anyone with a personal identity, so far as the other characters in the story are concerned—is kind and well-meaning, and he is even willing to bend the rules a bit, but he knows that he does not have the confidence of the people. He is disturbed that they didn't think the Last Rites and a funeral Mass were necessary, and he is not at all certain that they have given up their pagan ways: He looked at the red blanket, not sure that Teofilo was so small, wondering if it wasn't some perverse Indian trick—something they did in March to ensure a good harvest. . . ." He is wrong in suspecting that Teofilo (the name means "loving God," from the Greek *theos* = God, and *philos* = loving) is not in front of him, but he is right in suspecting that a "trick" is being played, since the reader knows that the holy water is wanted not to assist Teofilo to get to the Christian heaven but to bring rain for the crops. In Part One we heard Leon say, "Send us rain clouds, Grandfather"; in Part Three we heard Louise express the hope that the priest would sprinkle water so Teofilo "won't be thirsty"; and at the very end of the story we hear that Leon "felt good because it was finished, and he was happy about the sprinkling of the holy water; now the old man could send them big thunderclouds for sure."

We aren't quite sure about what to make of Paragraph 35, in which the water, disappearing as soon as it is sprinkled on the grave, "reminded" the priest of something, but the passage is given some emphasis and surely it is important. Our sense is that the priest vaguely intuits an archetypal mystery, something older and more inclusive than the Roman Catholic ritual he engages in.

During most of the story the narrator neither editorializes nor enters the minds of the characters; we are not told that the characters are reverential, and (for the most part) we are not allowed to hear their thoughts. Rather, we see them perform ceremonies with dignity, and, because the point of view is chiefly objective, we draw our own conclusions. Possibly, too, by keeping outside of the minds of the characters the narrator helps to convey the traditional paleface idea that Native Americans are inscrutable people, people of few words. Certainly Leon hoards words when, responding to the priest's admonition not to let Teofilo stay at the sheep camp alone, he says, "No, he won't do that any more now." But we do get into the priest's mind, notably in the passage in which he suspects trickery, and we get into Leon's mind at the end of the story when, in what almost seems like a thunderstorm of information, we are told his thoughts about the water.

Because the narrator, like the characters, is taciturn, some readers may think that Leon and his companions are callous. "After all," one student said, "don't they first round up the sheep before attending to the burial rites? And why don't they weep?" Class discussion can usually bring out the dignity of the proceedings here, and some students may be able to provide specific details about burial customs unfamiliar to other members of the class.

We do not know if the different colors of paint—white, blue, yellow, and green—have specific meanings, but perhaps blue suggests the sky and the water, yellow suggests corn meal, and green suggests vegetation. White is a fairly widespread sign of purity, gut we have not been able to find out how Pueblo people regard it. (If you know about these things, we'll be most appreciative if you write to us, in care of the publisher.)

Topics for Discussion and Writing

1. How would you describe the response of Leon, Ken, Louise, and Teresa to Teofilo's death? To what degree does it resemble or differ from responses to death that you are familiar with?
2. How do the funeral rites resemble or differ from those of your community?
3. How well does Leon understand the priest? How well does the priest understand Leon?

4. At the end of the story we are told that Leon "felt good." Do you assume that the priest also felt good? Why, or why not?
5. From what point of view is the story told? Mark the passages where the narrator enters a character's mind, and then explain what, in your opinion, Silko gains (or loses?) by doing so.

Jamaica Kincaid "Girl" (p. 382)

Jamaica Kincaid, like her fictional heroine Annie John, lived in Antigua, a much doted on only child, until she was seventeen, when she came to the United States to continue her education. In an interview in the *New York Times Book Review* (April 7, 1985, p. 6), she said, "I did sort of go to college but it was such a dismal failure. I just educated myself, if that's possible." She has published two collections of short stories based on her life in the West Indies.

In this story we meet a girl in her early adolescence, under the constant tutelage of her mother for her coming role as a woman. The mother is a powerful presence, shrewd and spirited as well as overprotective and anxious about her daughter's burgeoning sexuality. The girl is attentive to her mother, and mostly submissive; we sense that it is through her reverie that we hear her mother's monologue, which the daughter twice interrupts briefly. But the repetition of instruction and correction in the monologue, especially of the incessant "this is how to," suggests the tension between the two that we know, from our own experience, will lead to a confrontation that will permanently alter the relationship. Despite the references to the Island culture, which provide the story's rich, exotic texture, the central drama of coming of age could be happening anywhere.

A good way to teach the story is to read it aloud in class. It's short, humorous, and in passages pleasantly rhythmical. The students will hear the shift in voices, and will want to discuss the characters and the conflict.

A video cassette of Jamaica Kincaid reading "Girl" is available from HarperCollins.

Topics for Discussion or Writing

1. What is the conflict in this story?
2. Is the girl naive? Explain.
3. Taking "Girl" as a model, write a piece about someone—perhaps

a relative, teacher, or friend—who has given you more advice than you wanted.

Amy Tan "Two Kinds" (p. 384)

It's not a bad idea to ask a student to read the first two paragraphs aloud, and then to invite the class to comment. What, you might ask them, do they hear besides some information about the mother's beliefs? Probably they will hear at least two other things: (1) the voice of a narrator who does not quite share her mother's opinion, and (2) a comic tone. You may, then, want to spend some time in class examining *what the writer has done* that lets a reader draw these inferences. On the first point, it may be enough to begin by noticing that when someone says, "My mother believed," we are almost sure to feel some difference between the speaker and the reported belief. Here the belief is further distanced by the fivefold repetition of "You could." The comedy—perhaps better characterized as mild humor—is evident in the naiveté or simplicity of ambitions: open a restaurant, work for the government, retire, buy a house with almost no money down, become famous. Many readers may feel superior (as the daughter herself does) to this mother, who apparently thinks that in America money and fame and even genius are readily available to all who apply themselves—but many readers may also wish that their mother was as enthusiastic.

The second paragraph adds a sort of comic topper. After all, when the mother said, in the first paragraph, "you could be anything you wanted to be in America," the ambitions that she specified were not impossible, but when in the second paragraph she says, "you can be prodigy too," and "you can be best anything," we realized that we are listening to an obsessed parent, a woman ferociously possessive of her daughter. (In another story in Tan's *Joy Luck Club* a mother says of her daughter, "How can she be her own person? When did I give her up?") Obsessions of course can be the stuff of tragedy—some students will be quick to talk about Macbeth's ambition, Brutus's self-confidence, and so forth—but obsessions are also the stuff of comedy; witness the lover who writes sonnets to his mistress's eyebrow. Harpo Marx in pursuit of a blonde, the pedant, and all sorts of other monomaniacs whose monomania (at least as it is represented in the work of art) is not dangerous to others.

The third paragraph, with its references to the terrible losses in

China, darkens the tone, but the fourth restores the comedy, with its vision of "a Chinese Shirley Temple." The fifth paragraph is perhaps the most obviously funny so far: when Shirley Temple cries, the narrator's mother says to her daughter: "You already know how. Don't need talent for crying."

There's no need here to belabor the obvious, but students—accustomed to thinking that everything in a textbook is deadly serious— easily miss the humor. They will definitely grasp the absurdity of the thought that "Nairobi" might be one way of pronouncing Helsinki, but they may miss the delightful comedy of Auntie Lindo pretending that Waverly's abundant chess trophies are a nuisance ("all day I have no time do nothing but dust off her winnings"), and even a deaf piano teacher may not strike them as comic. (Of course in "real life" we probably would find pathos rather than comedy in a deaf piano teacher— and that's a point worth discussing in class.) So the point to make, probably, is that the story is comic (for example, in the mother's single-mindedness, and in the daughter's absurd hope that the recital may be going all right, even though she is hitting all the wrong notes) but is also serious (the conflict between the mother and the daughter, the mother's passionate love, the daughter's rebelliousness, and the daughter's later recognition that her mother loved her deeply). It is serious, too, in the way it shows us (especially in the passage about the "old Chinese silk dresses") the narrator's deepening perception of her Chinese heritage.

As a child, she at first shares her mother's desire that she be a "prodigy," but she soon becomes determined to be herself. In the mirror she sees herself as "ordinary" but also as "angry, powerful"; she is an independent creature, not an imitation of Shirley Temple. The question is, Can a young person achieve independence without shattering a fiercely possessive parent? Or, for that matter, without shattering herself? We can understand the narrator's need to defy her mother ("I now felt stronger, as if my true self had finally emerged"), but the devastating effect when she speaks of her mother's dead babies seems almost too great a price to pay. Surely the reader will be pleased to learn that the narrator and her mother became more or less reconciled, even though the mother continued to feel that the narrator just didn't try hard enough to be a genius. It's worth reading aloud the passage about the mother's offer of the piano:

And after that, every time I saw it in my parents' living room, standing in front of the bay window, it made me feel proud, as if it were a shiny trophy that I had won back.

As a mature woman, the narrator comes to see that "Pleading Child" (which might almost be the title of her early history) is complemented by "Perfectly Contented." Of course, just as we have to interpret "Pleading Child" a bit freely—let's say as "Agitated Child"—so "Perfectly Contented" must be interpreted freely as, say, "Maturity Achieved." We get (to quote the title of the story) "two kinds" of experience and "two kinds" of daughter, in one.

Topics for Discussion and Writing

1. Try to recall your responses when you had finished reading the first three paragraphs. At that point, how did the mother strike you? Now that you have read the entire story, is your view of her different? If so, in what way(s)?
2. When the narrator looks in the mirror, she discovers "the prodigy side," a face she "had never seen before." What do you think she is discovering?
3. If you enjoyed the story, point out two or three passages that you found particularly engaging, and briefly explain why they appeal to you.
4. Do you think this story is interesting only because it may give a glimpse of life in a Chinese-American family? Or do you find it interesting for additional reasons? Explain.

Sandra Cisneros "One Holy Night" (p. 393)

Some readers may feel that not much happens in this story; others may feel that there is indeed a sort of O. Henry story here, with an ironic ending (the boyfriend turns out to be a murderer), but it seems to us that the special pleasure of the story is in the narrator's voice, or, rather, voices, since the narrator lets us hear Chaq Uxmal Paloquin.

Take the epigraph. It is colloquial, almost Holden Caulfieldish in its diction ("About the truth, if you . . . ") and at the same time it is powerfully resonant in its content. Similarly, the first paragraph of the story consists of rather simple assertions("He said. . . . That's what he told me. He was . . . This is what Boy Baby said"), but the content is richly evocative ("Chaq Uxmal Paloquin," "ancient line of Mayan kings," "Yucatán, the ancient cities"). Later we learn that Boy Baby is associated with mystery, with ancient rites—but the voice that tells us about these things, and about "the moon, the pale moon with its one yellow eye, the moon of Tikal, and Tulum, and Chichén," also tells us that the moon "stared through the pink plastic curtains."

In short, it seems to us that the story catches both the common-places of life (think, for instance, of the delightful bit about how "Abuelita chased [Boy Baby] away with the broom") and something of the mysteries of life. Thus, the sexual experience with Boy Baby was exotic ("So I was initiated beneath an ancient sky by a great and mighty heir—Chaq Uxmal Paloquin. I, Ixchel, his queen") and yet, "The truth is, it wasn't any big deal at all." Something of this multiple or paradoxical presentation given by a girl who has become a woman is evident in the comment that Boy Baby "seemed boy and baby and man all at once," and especially in the last three paragraphs, where we get three versions of what love is like. Students might be invited to try to put into other words these three versions of love.

Students might also be asked what they make of the title. Our own sense is that a reader is likely to begin with the expectation that the story will in some way be related to a Christian experience—maybe it will take place on a Christian holiday, or perhaps, given the early reference to Abuelita rubbing the speaker's "belly with jade," it will tell of some non-Christian ritual. The reader soon realizes, however, that what is holy is the mystery of ordinary existence.

What we have just said strikes even our ears as pretentious, false to the colloquial quality and the humor of the story (Abuelita wielding her broom, the lie about the pushcart, the frank appraisal that the sexual experience "wasn't a big deal"). The trick in teaching the story, we think, is to help the students see and enjoy Cisneros's skill in presenting mystery in an ordinary-seeming way.

Helena Maria Viramontes "The Moths" (p. 399)

Like most other stories with fantastic elements, "The Moths" has a good deal of highly realistic detail. Thus, for instance, the narrator is very specific when she tells us that she planted flowers, grasses, and vines in "red Hills Brothers coffee cans." Presumably humble details such as this help to establish the credibility of the narrator and thus serve to make the fantastic elements convincing.

Another way of making the fantastic acceptable is to cast doubt on it explicitly, that is to say what the reader presumably thinks, and then to confirm the fantastic; thus the girl tells us that she was skeptical of the powers of Abuelita's potato slices, but they nevertheless seem to have cured her of scarlet fever: "You're still alive, aren't you?" Further, Viramontes begins with a relatively acceptable bit of fantasy, since most readers probably entertain the idea that folk medicines may (sometimes) work. Thus the improbable yet possible business about the potato slices helps to prepare us for the next (and much greater) improbability, Abuelita's shaping of the girl's hands by means of a balm of dried moth wings and Vicks. And this in turn helps to prepare us for the moths at the end of the story.

On the other hand, a skeptic can argue that the girl is an unreliable narrator: the death of her grandmother is so traumatic that the narrator imagines seeing the moths that her grandmother had told her "lay within the soul and slowly eat the spirit up." It's hard to argue against this view, though it seems excessively literal or materialistic in a story that is pretty clearly fantastic and symbolic.

Putting aside the moths, what are some of the other symbols? Perhaps the most obvious are the roots that "would burst out of the rusted coffee cans and search for a place to connect." During a discussion in class, students can relate these searching roots to the girl, who is not "pretty or nice" like her older sisters, and who finds little sympathy at home, where (doubtless partly because she is not "respectful") she is teased by her sisters and threatened by her father. She is also separated from the church, which she describes as cold and furnished with "frozen statues with blank eyes." However, she is connected to her grandmother, Abuelita, whose house provides a refuge from the "quarrels and beatings" of her own house. In short, the narrator is isolated from her immediate family, with which her harsh father is allied.

A second fairly obvious symbol is the sun, which in one paragraph is related to death and rebirth:

> . . . [T]here comes an illumination when the sun and earth meet, a final burst of burning red orange fury reminding us that although endings are inevitable, they are necessary for rebirths, and when that time came, just when I switched on the light in the kitchen to open Abuelita's can of soup, it was probably then that she died.

The passage is fairly dense and complex; it's worth asking a student to read it aloud in class before discussing it.

Death and birth also meet in the bath, which is both a ritual cleansing of the dead grandmother and a baptism or rebirth of the girl. (Notice that the girl does not deposit the grandmother in the tub; rather, she enters the tub holding the grandmother.) In the tub, the girl is mother to the old lady ("There, there, Abuelita, I said, cradling her"); even as she sobs like a child she becomes a woman.

Finally, there are the moths. There is possibly some connection here with the butterfly, which in antiquity was a symbol of the soul leaving the body at death, and in early Christian art was a symbol of the resurrected soul. However, in the last paragraph we are explicitly informed that Abuelita had told the narrator "about the moths that lay within the soul and slowly eat the spirit up." The appearance of the moths at the end thus suggests that Abuelita is at last free (in death) from the pressures that consume the spirit of a human being (specifically from the types of oppression that we have seen operate in the narrator, an unconventional female in a highly traditional society that severely limits the role of women). The loss of Abuelita reduces the narrator to tears and to infancy ("I wanted to return to the waters of the womb with her"), but it also serves to make clear that she is now, more than ever before, alone. We are not told that the experience liberates her, but perhaps we can assume that this rebellious girl, who knew how to use a brick in a sock, knows that her life will not be easy.

Topics for Discussion and Writing

1. The narrator says that she was not "pretty or nice," could not "do ... girl things," and was not "respectful." But what can she do, and what is she? How, in short, would you characterize her?
2. Elements of the fantastic are evident, notably in the moths at the end. What efforts, if any, does the author exert in order to make the fantastic elements plausible or at least partly acceptable.?
3. Why do you suppose the author included the rather extended passages about the sprouting plants and (later) the sun?
4. We can say, on the basis of the description of the bathing of Abuelita in the final paragraph, that the narrator is loving, caring, and grief-stricken. What else, if anything, does this paragraph reveal about the narrator?

Chapter 9

Observations on the Novel

It sometimes seems that books about the novel (or books including some discussion of the novel) are as numerous as novels. Among the commentaries of the last few decades that we have found valuable are the following:

Robert Martin Adams, *Strains of Discord*
Robert Alter, *Partial Magic: The Novel as a Self-Conscious Genre*
Miriam Allott, *Novelists on the Novel*
Wayne C. Booth, *The Rhetoric of Fiction*
William H. Gass, *Fiction and the Figures of Life*
Barbara Hardy, *The Appropriate Form*
W. J. Harvey, *Character and the Novel*
Robert Liddell, *Robert Liddell on the Novel* (a combined edition of *A Treatise on the Novel* and *Some Principles of Fiction*)
David Lodge, *The Language of Fiction*
Mary McCarthy, *On the Contrary*
Robert Scholes and Robert Kellogg, *The Nature of Narrative*
Philip Stevick, ed., *The Theory of the Novel*

But this is mere stalling. The question is, What novel to teach? The only time we experience any success in teaching a novel in an introductory course is when the novel is fairly short. Which means that we have failed miserably with *Portrait of a Lady*, *Bleak House*, and *The Brothers Karamazov* and even with *Crime and Punishment*. Our moderate successes are limited to traditional favorites of freshman English, things like the following:

The Great Gatsby
Hard Times
Heart of Darkness
Miss Lonelyhearts
Notes from the Underground
A Portrait of the Artist as a Young Man
The Stranger

Among more recent titles that work well are the following:

Chinua Achebe, *Things Fall Apart*
Anthony Burgess, *A Clockwork Orange*
Evan S. Connell, Jr., *Mrs. Bridge*
Graham Greene, *The Human Factor*

Brian Moore, *The Lonely Passion of Judith Hearne*
Sylvia Plath, *The Bell Jar*
Philip Roth, *The Ghost Writer*
Anne Tyler, *A Slipping Down Life*
Alice Walker, *The Color Purple*

Experienced teachers do not need us to suggest these titles; inexperienced teachers will perhaps do best if they choose a short novel that they read and enjoyed when they were freshmen or sophomores.

Chapter 10

A First Approach to Poetry

Langston Hughes "Harlem" (p. 412)

In the eight lines enclosed within the frame (that is, between the first and next-to-last lines) we get four possibilities: The Dream may "dry up," "fester," "crust and sugar over," or "sag." Each of these is set forth with a simile, for example, "dry up / like a raisin in the sun." By the way, the third of these, "crust up and sugar over—like a syrupy sweet," probably describes a dream that has turned into smiling Uncle Tomism. Similes can be effective, and these *are* effective, but in the final line Hughes states the last possibility ("Or does it explode?") directly and briefly, without an amplification. The effect is, more or less, to suggest that the fancy (or pretty) talk stops. The explosion is too serious to be treated in a literary way. But, of course, the word "explode," applied to a dream, it itself figurative. That is, the last line is as "literary" or "poetical" as the earlier lines, but it is a slightly different sort of poetry.

A word about the rhymes: Notice that although the poem does use rhyme, it does not use a couplet until the last two lines. The effect of the couplet (load / explode) is that the poem ends with a bang. Of course, when one reads the poem in a book, one sees where the poem ends—though a reader may be surprised to find the forceful rhyme— but an audience hearing the poem recited is surely taken off-guard. The explosion is unexpected (especially in the context of the two previous lines about a sagging, heavy load), and powerful.

Topic for Discussion and Writing

One might keep the first line where it is, and then rearrange the other stanzas—for instance, putting lines 2–8 after 9–11. Which version (Hughes's or the one just mentioned) do you prefer? Why?

A "Voices and Visions" video cassette of Langston Hughes is available from HarperCollins.

Chapter 11

Lyric Poetry

One can engage in more profitable activities than in fretting about whether a given poem is a narrative poem or a lyric, but the topic is worth at least a little thought. Something, of course, depends on the way in which the text is rendered. Spirituals, for instance, often have considerable narrative content, and yet one feels that their affinities are with the lyric and that the story is subordinate to the state of mind. This sense of lyrical meditation is, of course, heightened by the refrains—repetitions that do not advance the story and that help to communicate and to induce a visionary state. An instructor who wants to pursue this topic may want to discuss such works as "Didn't My Lord Deliver Daniel," "Go Down, Moses," and "Joshua Fit the Battle of Jericho."

There is much fascinating material about the theory of nineteenth-century lyric poetry in M. H. Abrams, *The Mirror and the Lamp*. See also C. Day Lewis, *The Lyric Impulse,* and W. R. Johnson, *The Idea of the Lyric: Lyric Modes in Ancient and Modern Poetry.*

Versions of "Michael" were in print in the 1870s, and the song is still popular. Among effective recordings is one by Pete Seeger on Columbia (CS9717). "Careless Love" easily leads to a discussion of the blues. Here is a brief part of Ralph Ellison's comment on the genre in an essay on Richard Wright in Ellison's *Shadow and Act:* "Their attraction lies in this, that they at once express both the agony of life and the possibility of conquering it through sheer toughness of spirit. They fall short of tragedy only in that they provide no solution, offer no scapegoat but the self."

In the chapter on "Rhythm," we quote a remark by Ezra Pound that an instructor may wish to use in connection with "Michael," "Careless Love," or "The Colorado Trail." Pound says, "Poetry withers and dries out when it leaves music, or at least imagined music, too far behind it. Poets who are not interested in music are, or become, bad poets." In "Colorado Trail," surely the repetitions of sounds help to make the poem singable and memorable. Ask students if they find "Blow winds blow" as attractive to the ear (as well as to the mind) as the poem's "Wail winds wail," or "all along the length of" as attractive as the poem's "all along, along, along." One can also try to account for the difference between, say, "Annie was a pretty girl," and "Laura was a pretty girl." Our own feeling is that the liquids in Laura (*l, r*) go better with the other liquids in the line ("pretty girl"), but other ears may hear something different.

127

Anonymous "Western Wind" (p. 421)

"Western Wind" has been much discussed. Probably most readers will find R. P. Warren's suggestion (*Kenyon Review*, 1943, 5) that the grieving lover seeks relief for the absence of his beloved in "the sympathetic manifestation of nature." But how do you feel about Patric M. Sweeney's view (*Explicator*, October 1955) that the speaker asserts that "he will come to life only when the dead woman returns, and her love, like rain, renews him"? In short, in this view the speaker "cries out to the one person who conquered death, who knows that the dead, returning to life, give life to those who loved them." We find this reading of the poem hard to take, but (like many readings) it is virtually impossible to *dis*prove.

One other point. Some readers have asked why other readers assume that the speaker is a male. A hard question to answer.

Li-Young Lee "I Ask My Mother to Sing" (p. 422)

Singing is infectious; the speaker asks his mother to sing, and his grandmother joins her. The reference to the deceased father—who would have joined in too if he had been there—adds a note of pathos and thus anticipates the second stanza, where we learn that the song is about the land of the speaker's ancestors, a land he has never seen.

The song apparently is joyful (picknickers—though admittedly the picnic is dispelled by rain), but since it is about a lost world it is also sorrowful (the women begin to cry). yet singing even about sorrow provides the singer with joy, or, we might say, the making of a work of art (here, singing a song) is pleasurable even when the content is sorrowful. One way of mastering sorrow, of course, is to turn it into art.

Langston Hughes "Evenin' Air Blues" (p. 423)

Though perhaps when we first think of blues we think of songs of disappointed love, blues include songs concerned with other kinds of loneliness, and some at least implicitly relate this loneliness to an oppressive society that is built on segregation and that engenders wandering and alienation. Hughes' "Evenin' Air "Blues," then, is genuinely related to the blues tradition, though not surprisingly the note of social protest is a little more evident.

The last stanza, chiefly by virtue of its first line, seems to make a natural conclusion, but as in most blues, the stanzas can pretty much stand independently; perhaps less blueslike is the perfection of the rhyme (one almost feels that the single near-rhyme [by the standards of standard English] *fine:mind* in the first stanza is a conscious imitation of such blues rhymes as *ride:by* or *dime:mine*). The blues often uses a three-line stanza, in which the second line repeats the first; Hughes's six-line stanza, in which the fourth line repeats the second, is a variation on the usual form.

A "Voices and Visions" video cassette of Langston Hughes is available from HarperCollins.

Langston Hughes "Negro" (p. 423)

Although the speaker identifies himself in the first line by saying, "I am a Negro," he might equally well have said, "I am the Negro," since the poem gives a brief history of blacks (not just of Africans or of African-Americans), rather than the emotion of a particular speaker in a particular situation.

The poem moves chronologically from ancient times ("Caesar") to the present, that is 1926 ("They lynch me still in Mississippi"), but it ends with a stanza that repeats the first stanza. That is, fundamentally the poem is lyric, not narrative, the expression of emotion rather than the telling of a story.

A "Voices and Visions" video cassette of Langston Hughes is available from HarperCollins.

John Lennon and Paul McCartney "Eleanor Rigby" (p. 425)

We aren't explicitly told what Eleanor Rigby is waiting for, but presumably it is for a handsome man who will rescue her from loneliness, such being the ideal of a materialistic male-dominated society. But Father McKenzie is also lonely, a spiritual figure in a materialistic world. The two are brought together at Eleanor Rigby's funeral (to which nobody comes), and this perhaps arouses thoughts of his own funeral, about which no one will care.

The Beatles' version of the song is in their album *Revolver* (Capitol Records ST76).

Topics for Discussion and Writing

1. Do you think that the poem is chiefly about Eleanor Rigby? How do you account for Father McKenzie?
2. What do you make of "wearing the face that she keeps in a jar by the door" (7)? Is the sermon (14) only a sermon, or are there further implications?

Edna St. Vincent Millay "The Spring and the Fall" (p. 426)

We begin with the rhyme scheme of the poem.

year	*a* (with internal *a*)
dear	*a*
wet	*b*
year	*a* (with internal *b*)
peach	*c*
reach	*c*
year	*a* (with internal *a*)
dear	*a*
trill	*d*
year	*a* (with internal *d*)
praise	*e*
ways	*e*
falling	*f* (with an internal *f*, but as an off-rhyme)
calling	*f*
hear	*a*
year	*a* (with internal *d*)
days	*e*
ways	*e*

Obviously there's lots of rhyme here; this is a highly lyrical lyric, close to song. In addition to the repetition of sound gained through rhyme, there are other repetitions—not only in the form of alliteration (e.g., "bough . . . blossoming," "rooks . . . raucous") and consonance (e.g. "trees . . . see") but also in the form of entire words: the first half of the first line is repeated verbatim in the second half of the line; "In the spring of the year" (1.1) becomes "In the fall of the year" (1.7), words repeated verbatim in the second half of the line, and in the third stanza the two phrases about the seasons are joined in 1.16, but with a significant change: "the" year becomes "a" year.

Many highly lyrical poems employ what can be called a repetitive or perhaps an intensifying structure, each stanza going over the same ground, deepening the feeling but not advancing a narrative, even a narrative of the progress of a feeling. "The Spring and the Fall," however, is a lyric that includes a narrative, a progression, as a reader probably suspects immediately from the title. The first stanza deals with spring, the second with fall. Further, in the first stanza the lovers are physically and emotionally united (they walk together, and he obligingly—lovingly—presents her with "a bough of the blossoming peach"); in the second stanza the lovers are together only physically, not emotionally: "He laughed at all I dared to praise". Instead of giving her a gift, he laughs at (not with) her, and we hear of rooks making a "raucous" sound. The last line of the second stanza explicitly announces the break: "And broke my heart, in little ways." (The word "way," incidentally, was introduced in the first stanza—the peach-bough he gave her a sign of his love, "was out of the way and hard to reach." And in the last stanza "ways" appears again, in the last line, where we are told that when love went it "went in little ways.")

Another notable difference between the first two stanzas; ordinarily the stanzas in a lyric poem repeat a metrical pattern, but in this poem the last two lines of the second stanza are shorter than the last two lines of the first two stanza, thus conveying a sense of something cut short. The difference is made especially evident by the fact that the change is unanticipated; the first two lines of the second stanza closely resemble (as one expects) the first two lines of the first stanza.

The narrative, then, in effect is completed at the end of the second stanza. Or nearly so: although at the end of the second stanza we learn that the speaker's heart was broken "in little ways," we don't learn until the last two lines of the third stanza that what especially hurts is that love went "in little ways." The third stanza, as has already been mentioned, brings the two seasons together; its first four lines seem joyous and loving, but its last two lines comment on the end of this love affair. The third stanza differs from the first two in several technical details. For example, as we have already mentioned, the first line of the first stanza, like the first line of the second stanza, repeats a phrase ("In the spring of the year, in the spring of the year," "In the fall of the year, in the fall of the year"). The third stanza, however, reflecting a different state of mind, begins with a different form of repetition: "Year be springing or year be falling." Another difference, admittedly small, is that the third stanza is the only stanza to use a feminine rhyme ("falling . . . calling).

Wilfred Owen "Anthem for Doomed Youth" (p. 427)

Here are our responses to the questions we put in the text:

1. An anthem is (a) a hymn of praise or loyalty or (b) a sacred composition set to words of the Bible. In Owen's poem, "orisons," "prayers," "save," "choirs," "flowers," "holy glimmers," and even "die" and "pall" might be found in an anthem, but among the unexpected words and phrases are "die as cattle," "stuttering rifles' . . . rattle," "mockeries," "demented," and perhaps "blinds." (One might, or might not, want to talk about the onomatopoeia in "stuttering rifles' rapid rattle.")

2. This question anticipates the next chapter, "The speaking Tone of Voice," but we see no reason not to anticipate it. We'd characterize the tone thus: The first line asks a pained question, but in "monstrous anger" (2) we begin to hear indignation, and in line 3 ("stuttering rifles' rapid rattle") bitterness. In this poem the word "mockeries" is not unexpected; the speaker is not, of course, mocking the dead, but his pain and indignation seem to find an outlet in mockery. For instance, in calling his poem an "anthem" he mocks traditional praises of the glory of dying in war. (Owen's "Dulce et Decorum Est" [text, 596] pretty decisively sums up Owen's view not only of the First World War, but of all wars, but a different poet might have mocked not war in general but only a specific war. That is, a satiric poet might use the word "anthem" ironically, mocking a specific war precisely because it is base in comparison with those wars for which anthems might fittingly be composed.) He finds some comfort, however, in the "holy glimmers of good-byes" which shine in the soldiers' eyes, in the "pallor of girls' eyes," which are the pall, and in the "tenderness of patient minds," which serves as "flowers" (a floral tribute more worthy than wreathes accompanied by conventional funeral oratory). What sad comfort there is, then, is provided by those who die and their loved ones, not by church and state. By the last line the indignation has quieted, though the sadness remains.

The poem can be taught effectively in conjunction with "Dulce et Decorum Est" (text 596).

It is interesting to compare the final version with the first draft of the poem, printed in Owen's *Collected Poems* and in John Stallworthy's

Wilfred Owen. The first version, untitled and chiefly unrhymed, goes
thus:

> What minute bells for these who die so fast?
> > Only the monstrous anger of our guns.
> Let the majestic insults of their iron mouths
> > Be as the priest-words of their burials.
> Of choristers and holy music, none;
> > Nor any voice of mourning, save the wail
> The long-drawn wail of high, far-sailing shells.
> > What candles may we hold for these lost souls?
> Not in the hands of boys, but in their eyes
> Shall many candles shine, and [?] light them.
> Women's wide-spreaded arms shall be their wreathes,
> Their flowers, the tenderness of all men's minds,
> And every dusk, a drawing-down of blinds.

Owen showed the draft to Siegfried Sassoon, who suggested
some changes and who also suggested a title, "Anthem for Dead
Youth." Owen accepted the changes and the title and wrote at least
three more versions, facsimiles of which can be found in Stallworthy.
When Owen showed the final version to Sassoon, Sassoon suggested
changing the title to "Anthem for Doomed Youth."

Walt Whitman "A Noiseless Patient Spider" (p. 428)

Whitman's "A Noiseless Patient Spider" is in free verse, a form discussed later in the text in connection with Whitman's "When I Heard
the Learn'd Astronomer," but most instructors find it appropriate to
say a few words about the form at this stage. In fact, of course, the
poem is not terribly "free"; each stanza has five lines, helping to establish the similitude of spider and soul, and the first line of each stanza
is relatively short, the other lines being longer to help establish the
idea of "venturing, throwing." The near-rhyme at the end helps to tie
up the poem, as though finally the bridge is at least tentatively
"form'd," the "anchor" holding, but the fact that the action is not yet
complete, the soul is not yet anchored. A discussion of this poem will
also necessarily get into Whitman's use of figurative language. Implicitly the speaker's soul is a noiseless, patient spider, "ceaselessly
musing, ceaselessly venturing," building a "bridge" in the vastness

(i.e., uniting the present with eternity. Or are the filaments that the soul flings poems that unite mankind?).

Topics for Discussion and Writing

1. In about 250 words describe some animal, plant, or object that can be taken as a symbol of some aspect of your personality or experience.
2. The text gives Whitman's final version (1871) of "A Noiseless Patient Spider." Here is Whitman's draft, written some ten years earlier. Compare the two poems and evaluate them.

> **The Soul, Reaching, Throwing Out for Love**
>
> The soul, reaching, throwing out for love,
> As the spider, from some little promontory, throwing out filament
>   after filament, tirelessly out of itself, that one at least may catch
>   and form a link, a bridge, a connection
> O I saw one passing along, saying hardly a word—yet full of love I
>   detected him, by certain signs
> O eyes wishfully turning! O silent eyes!
> For then I thought of you o'er the world,
> O latent oceans, fathomless oceans of love!
> O waiting oceans of love! yearning and fervid! and of you sweet
>   souls perhaps in the future. delicious and long:
> But Death, unknown on the earth—ungiven, dark here, unspoken,
>   never born:
> You fathomless latent souls of love—you pent and unknown
>   oceans of love!

A "Voices and Visions" video cassette of Walt Whitman is available from HarperCollins.

John Keats "Ode on a Grecian Urn" (p. 429)

On Keats's "Grecian Urn," see Harvey Leon's casebook, *Keats's Well-Read Urn*. For a microscopic analysis of the poem, see Earl Wasserman, *The Finer Tone*. Among the newer lucid discussions of this poem are those in books on Keats by Walter Jackson Bate, Douglas Bush, Aileen Ward, and Helen Vendler. All these discussions are valuable, but Vendler's long essay (35 pages) is the most penetrating and complete.

E. E. Cummings "anyone lived in a
pretty how town" (p. 430)

It can be useful to ask students to put into the usual order (so far as one can) the words of the first two stanzas, and then to ask students why Cummings's version is more effective. Here are a few rough glosses: 1.4 "danced his did" = lived intensely (versus the "someones" who in 1.18 "did their dance," that is unenthusiastically went through motions that might have been ecstatic); 1.7: "they sowed their isn't they reaped their same" gives us the little-minded or small-minded who, unlike "anyone," are unloving and therefore receiving nothing; 1.8: "sun moon stars rain" = day after day; 1.10: "down they forgot as up they grew" implies a mental diminution that accompanies growing up; 1.17: "someones," that is, adults, people who think they are somebody; 1.25: "anyone died," that is, the child matured, stopped loving (and became dead as the other adults). The last two stanzas imply that although children grown into "Women and men" (1.33) as the seasons continue. (This reading is heavily indebted to R. C. Walsh, *Explicator* 22 no. 9 [May 1964], Item 72. For a more complicated reading, see D. L. Clark, *Lyric Resonance*, pp. 187–94.)

An audio cassette of E. E. Cummings reading is available from HarperCollins.

Chapter 12

The Speaking Tone of Voice

Reuben Brower, in *The Fields of Light*, and also in his books on Pope and on Frost, has written excellently about this topic. Frost himself several times refers to the matter in *Selected Letters*, notably on page 107 ("The living part of a poem is the intonation entangled somehow in the syntax, idiom and meaning of a sentence"), pages 110–111 and page 191.

If you are a bit less squeamish than we are, you may invite your class to comment on the levels of diction in Byron's epitaph for Castlereagh (the much-despised Castlereagh was the foreign secretary from 1812 to 1822):

> Posterity will ne'er survey
> A nobler grave than this;
> Here lie the bones of Castlereagh.
> Stop, traveller, and piss.

Robert Burns "Mary Morison" (p. 434)

"O Mary, at thy window be" is not a remark addressed to an absent beloved person, but rather is a passionate hope that the speaker expresses to himself.

In the first stanza, "smiles and glances," "miser's treasure," "weary slave," "sun to sun," and "rich reward" are stock diction or something close to it, but (perhaps because of the urgency of the first two lines) they are not lifeless expressions. Still, to our ears, the poem becomes more vital in the second stanza. Possibly we feel this way because the diction is fresher. Although "trembling string," "my fancy took its wing," and "the toast of . . . the town" are familiar expressions, at least to American readers, the Scotch words ("gaed," "ha'," "braw," "amang," "a'," "na") add an inviting touch of novelty. Further, the stanza is especially memorable because of the relatively sharply presented flashback that tells us how, when "the dance gaed through the lighted ha'," the speaker could think only of Mary, who was not present.

The first four lines of the third stanza reveal a more self-pitying speaker than we have heard in the first two stanzas. But to our ears, although the next two lines (21–22) call for pity, they are also rather slyly seductive:

> If love for love thou wilt na gie,
> At least be pity to me shown.

One other point about this stanza: Although it seems to us to be less excited and less memorable than the second stanza, its self-pity is not bothersome, and the poem ends (as do the previous stanzas) not with the poet, but with Mary. What strikes us as especially powerful in this final stanza is that the speaker goes beyond praising May simply as an object who attracts him and at last attributes to her a moral quality: "A thought ungentle canna be / The thought o' Mary Morison."

Students might be asked how much the speaker tells us about Mary Morison. In fact, he tells us nothing about her except that he is entranced by her, and that (according to him) she cannot harbor an "ungentle" thought. He does not even claim, for instance, that she is more beautiful than the other women at yesterday's dance. He merely says that none of them was Mary Morison, and that therefore none of them was of any interest to him. We find this method of depicting her—she exists only as a beloved person—fully engaging. There is probably no better way of convincing a reader (one really should say a hearer, for the song should be sung) of Mary's worth than by saying that the speaker can think only of her. Merely to utter her name is, for him, one of the two possible ways of praising Mary. The other way is to say of anyone else, "Ye are na Mary Morison."

Robert Burns "John Anderson my Jo" (p. 434)

We find nothing in the diction that distinguishes the speaker as an old woman, but we value the poem nevertheless. Class discussion may (appropriately) wander from the topic of the chapter and may get into a discussion of whether or not the poem is sentimental. On sentimentality, the best remark we know of is Helen Vendler's comment, in *Part of Nature, Part of Us*:

> There is, of course, no such thing as a sentimental emotion; emotions are felt or not felt, and that is all. It is the language of expression which is or is not sentimental. To find language better than that of greeting-card verse to express the sentiment of love is the poet's task: the rest of us are not equal to it [page 265].

Robert Browning "My Last Duchess" (p. 435)

Robert Langbaum has a good analysis of "My Last Duchess" in *The Poetry of Experience*. On this poem, see also Laurence Perrine, *PMLA* 74 (March 1959): 157–159. W. J. T. Mitchell, in "Representation," in *Critical Terms for Literary Study*, ed. Frank Lentricchia and Thomas McLaughlin, discusses the poem at some length. One of his points is: "Just as the duke seems to hypnotize the envoy, Browning seems to paralyze the reader's normal judgment by his virtuosic representation of villainy. His poem holds us in its grip, condemning in advance all our attempts to control it by interpretation. . . ."

It may be mentioned here that although every poem has a "voice," not every poem needs to be a Browningesque dramatic monologue giving the reader a strong sense of place and audience. No one would criticize Marvell's "To His Coy Mistress" on the grounds that the "lady" addressed in line 2 gives place (in at least some degree) to a larger audience—let us say, a general audience—when we get to "But at my back I always hear / Time's winged chariot hurrying near."

Topic for Writing

You re the envoy, writing to the Count, your master, a 500-word report of your interview with the duke. What do you write? In an essay of 500 to 750 words, describe the duke's attitude toward himself, and then describe your attitude (or attitudes) toward him. In this second part of your essay you may want to indicate that a reader's attitudes are complex and multiple rather than simple and single.

Robert Herrick "To the Virgins, to Make Much of Time" (p. 439)

On Herrick's "To the Virgins," see E. M. W. Tillyard in *The Metaphysicals and Milton;* Tillyard argues effectively that in "To the Virgins," "the trend of the poem is urgency, touched with reflection."

This wonderful lyric seems ideally suited to introduce students to matters of persona and tone. We have found that when asked, "Who is speaking?" most students will answer, "A man." (Possibly some offer this opinion simply because a man wrote this poem.) A few will say that a woman is the speaker, and we have found it interesting to ask them why. (Those who say that a woman is the speaker usually suggest that she is unmarried and is speaking regretfully.) Almost all students hear the voice of an older person, though they cannot always say why. Similarly, although a few students find the speaker aggressively offering unsolicited advice, most hear a friendly voice. True, the first and last stanzas begin with imperatives ("Gather ye rosebuds," "Then be not coy"), but most students hear in "Old Time," "a-flying," and "a-getting" an engaging old-codgerliness. They may hear too even a touch of elderly loquacity in the explanation of a fairly obvious figure: "The glorious lamp of heaven, the sun."

One other point about Herrick's poem: The shift to "you" in the last stanza (from the earlier "ye") gives the moral great emphasis.

The *carpe diem* motif allows the poem to be related easily to Marvell's "Coy Mistress." What is especially interesting, however, is the difference in tone, even though the poems share both a motif and a structure—the logical argument.

Is the poem offensive to women? Some of our students have found it so. Our hope is that readers will be able to read the poem not so much as advice to women to submit passively to marriage as advice (which can apply to males as well as to females) "to make much of time." Against "dying" and "setting," we can "gather," "smile," and "run."

Topic for Discussion and Writing

This seventeenth-century poem suggests that a woman finds fulfillment only in marriage. Can the poem, then, be of any interest to a society in which women may choose careers in preference to marriage?

Thomas Hardy "The Man He Killed" (p. 440)

The speaker's diction is that of a simple, uneducated rustic ("old ancient," "Right many a nipperkin," "list," "off-hand-like"). He tells us (15) that he enlisted because he was out of work and broke, but line 10 reveals that he also responded to customary wartime propaganda and appeals to patriotism. He is still too trusting to reject what he was told about his "foe," but in the third stanza the repetitions, abrupt pauses, and attempts to reassure himself in "of course he was," and "That's clear enough" all indicate his struggle to overcome incipient doubts. The heavy pauses in the fourth stanza show the difficulty a man unused to thinking about large matters has when what he has been taught by his "betters" conflicts with his own feelings. In the fifth stanza he resolves his doubts with a platitude—war is "quaint and curious"—but we feel that he'll be retelling his story at one pub or another and pondering his experience for the rest of his life.

One can have a field day talking about irony here: the ironic distance between poet and speaker and between speaker and reader, the "irony of fate" in which the soldier is trapped, the dramatic irony in the fact that the speaker had to kill a man before he could recognize him as a potential neighbor or friend, a man like himself. And finally, this simple man *is* one of us. Like him, we are mere pawns, trapped between forces whose meaning, though it continues to allude us, we continue to question.

Topic for Discussion and Writing

What state of mind would you have to be in to think of war as "quaint and curious"? To think of a man you killed as a "foe"? *Is* the speaker convinced by the words he utters? Whether your answer is "Yes" or "No," why do you think so?

Michael Drayton "Since There's No Help" (p. 491)

The first quatrain (though joined to the next quatrain by a semicolon) is in effect a complete sentence. The speaker seems resolute, though perhaps in retrospect we feel that the repetition of "glad" in line 3 ("I am glad, yea, glad with all my heart") is a clue that insincerity causes him to protest too much. The second quatrain, which also can stand as a sentence, continues the matter-of-fact tone. But then, after the eighth line, comes the turn, or *volta,* so often found in sonnets. In the third quatrain and couplet—this quatrain cannot stand as a sentence, but passionately overflows into the couplet, and so the quatrain and couplet together can be taken as a sort of sestet—we hear a new breathlessness or sense of urgency that dispels the earlier apparent confidence. The personified abstractions, too, are new (Passion, Faith, et.); they do *not* indicate insincerity or lack of feeling, but, on the contrary, take us into a world of bruised feelings, evident earlier in such an expression as "you get no more of me." Even the shift from "you" in line 2 to the more intimate "thou" in line 13 is significant in establishing the change. The poem ends with a feminine rhyme, probably to keep it from ending too emphatically or, to put the matter a bit differently, to indicate that the speaker is not the master of the situation.

Elizabeth Bishop "Filling Station" (p. 442)

We hope that we are not being sexist pigs (doubtless something that sexist pigs often say) when we say that we hear a woman's voice in "Oh, but it is dirty!" (It's a good idea to ask students to read this line aloud— and, indeed to read the entire poem aloud.) We even hear a woman's voice, though less obviously, in "Be careful with that match!" (One can ask students if they hear a woman's voice. If they do, it can be interesting to ask them to alter the line to something a man might say—perhaps, "Watch out with that match," or some such thing.) Other words that seem to us to indicate a female speaker: "saucy" (describing the sons, in line 10), "all quite thoroughly dirty" (13), "comfy" (20, though here perhaps the speaker is consciously using the diction of the woman who may live at the gas station), "Why, oh why, the doily?" (30), and the knowledgeable remarks about embroidery in lines 30–33.

The somewhat snobbish tone of the first stanza is moderated in the third, when the speaker begins to take an interest in the *life* of this station, and if snobbery continues in the fourth and fifth stanzas (21–30), it is also moderated by the speaker's interest in the technique of the doily. In the last stanza there is a bit of snide humor in "Somebody waters the plant,/ or oils it, maybe," but clearly by now the speaker is won over. However coarse the taste of the owners, they have tried to add a bit of order and a bit of beauty to life—not only to their own lives, but to the lives of passersby. The cans that spell out **ESSO** of course advertise a product, but they speak "softly" (38), their "so-so-so" serving to soothe the drivers of "high-strung automobiles," as a groom might soothe a horse or a mother her fretful baby. "Somebody loves us," the poet ends, referring most obviously to the owners of the filling station, but surely the reference is also larger, perhaps even unobtrusively hinting at the existence of a loving God. The close attention to detail, for which Bishop is widely known, is in fact loaded with moral value. Students might be invited to think of the poem partly in terms of Frost's comment (later in the text, 553) about a poem as "a clarification of life . . . [and] a momentary stay against confusion."

The movement in this poem from the rather prim and disapproving opening line, through the sympathetic union with what she observes—achieved especially when the speaker, taken out of herself by her rapt attention to the embroidery—and finally to the larger or more generous view reminds us of a comment about her poetry in one of Bishop's letters. The arts, Bishop says, begin in observation. "Dreams, works of art, . . . unexpected moments of empathy . . . , catch a peripheral vision of whatever it is one can never really see full-face but that seems enormously important. . . . What one seems to want in art, in experiencing it, is the same thing that is necessary for its creation, a self-forgetful, perfectly useless concentration" (quoted by Helen McNeil in *Voices and Visions*, ed. Helen Vendler, p. 395).

A "Voices and Visions" video cassette of Elizabeth Bishop is available from HarperCollins.

Gerard Manley Hopkins "Spring and Fall: To a Young Child" (p. 443)

In our experience, students will have considerable difficulty if they simply read the poem silently to themselves, but if they read (and re-read) it aloud, it becomes clear—and more important, it becomes something they value.

We begin, then, as we usually do with poems, by having a student rad the poem aloud, and then we invite comments about the title and its connection with the two people in the poem. Students usually see that the poem presents youth and age, that Margaret is associated with spring and the speaker with the fall, and this leads to discussion of the Fall in Christian thought. Many students, however, do not know that in Christian thought the disobedience of Adam and Eve brought consequences that extended to nature, and that the perennial spring of Eden therefore yielded to autumn and winter; that is, "Goldengrove" inherited death. ("Goldengrove," incidentally, might seem to suggest preciousness and eternity, but here the golden leaves are a sign of transience and death.)

In the original version of "Spring and Fall" (1880), line 8 ran, "Though forests low and leafmeal lie." When he revised the poem in 1884, Hopkins changed "Though forests low and" to "Though worlds of wanwood," thus introducing the pallor of "wanwood" and also wonderfully extending the vista from "forests" to "worlds." Margaret's sorrow for the trees stripped of their golden foliage is finally sorrow for the Fall, whose consequences are everywhere. Her mouth cannot formulate any of this, but her spirit has intuited it ("ghost guessed").

On "Spring and Fall," see Paul L. Mariani, *A Commentary on the Complete Poems of Gerard Manley Hopkins,* Marylou Motto, *The Poetry of Gerard Manley Hopkins,* and Peter Milward's essay in Milward and R. V. Schoder, *Landscape and Inscape.* George Starbuck has a modern version ("Translations from the English") in his book of poems, *White Paper.*

Ted Hughes "Hawk Roosting" (p. 444)

Like many of Ted Hughes's other poems, "Hawk Roosting" celebrates the energy of nature, especially its egotistical aggressiveness. (For a different view, arguing that the poem is a satire against aggressive, materialistic men, see Anne Williams in *Explicator* 38[Fall 1979]: 39–

41.) If we compare this poem with Tennyson's "The Eagle" (in Chapter 13), we get an idea of the difference between Victorian and mid-twentieth-century nature poetry. Although in *In Memoriam* Tennyson speaks of "Nature red in tooth and claw," in "The Eagle" he manages to sanitize his rapacious bird. We are told nothing of the prey the eagle seizes, and the emphasis is on the bird's grandeur: The bird lives among "mountain walls," and when he plummets, he is "like a thunderbolt." And although Tennyson uses personification, the bird is not sullied by any close resemblance to man. But Hughes's hawk seems to speak with both the voice of Nature and the voice of rapacious man: "I sit on top of the world"; "I kill where I please"; "No arguments assert my right"; "I am going to keep things like this." If this is menacing, it is also refreshingly honest. Hughes reads this poem on Caedman cassette SWC 1535.

William Blake "The Clod and the Pebble" (p. 445)

Additional Topics for Discussion and Writing

1. What does it mean to say (lines 1–4) that self-sacrificing love "builds a Heaven in Hell's despite"? And (lines 9–12 that selfish love "builds a Hell in Heaven's despite"?
2. What would be the effect of beginning with lines 9–12, and ending with 1–4—and, of course, revising the middle stanza?

Countee Cullen "For a Lady I Know" (p. 445)

Although Cullen sometimes wrote about African-American life he also wrote on other topics and in traditions other than the vernacular tradition employed by Langston Hughes.

"For a Lady I Know" is indeed about white/black relations, but it is in the tradition of the polished epigram of Martial and other Roman satirists and their successors. "Low" diction occurs in "snores, but for the most part the diction is refined, echoing the language that the "lady" might use: "lies late, "poor black cherubs," rise at seven," "celestial chores." The satiric force of the poem comes largely from stating a repulsive idea elegantly.

E. E. Cummings "next to of course god america i" (p. 446)

E. E. Cummings's "next to of course god america i" uses Cummings's characteristic unconventional typography, but here the effect is not so much to break with lifeless convention as it is to emphasize the mindless, unvarying, unstoppable jabbering of politicians.

An audio cassette of E. E. Cummings reading is available from HarperCollins.

John Updike "Youth's Progress" (p. 447)

In our second question we ask what the speaker's attitude toward himself is and what the author's attitude toward the speaker is. If one takes the idea of a speaker terribly seriously, one may find oneself talking about this speaker's naiveté, and about the author's ironic attitude toward the speaker. But surely we should read the poem as light verse; Updike, amused by a line in *Life*, is having fun, and indeed his invented speaker is genial enough, a fellow who (no less than his creator) can look at himself with amused detachment. He recalls that at the age of fourteen he combed his hair "a fancy way" and that he shaved his upper lip even though "nothing much was there." He recites all this in so amiable a way that the object of satire is not so much Dick Schneider as *Life* or the interfraternity ball.

Marge Piercy "Barbie Doll" (p. 448)

The title alerts us to the world of childhood, so we are not surprised in the first line by "This girlchild" (like "This little pig") or by "peepee" in the second line. The stanza ends with the voice of a jeering child. The second stanza drops the kid-talk, adopting in its place the language of social science. (The stanza has much of the sound of Auden's "The Unknown Citizen.") We have not, then, made much progress; the "girlchild" who in the first stanza is treated like a Barbie doll is in the second treated like a healthy specimen, a statistic. The third stanza sounds more intimate, but she is still an object, not a person, and by the end of this stanza, there is a painful explosion. The two preceding stanzas each ended with a voice different from the voice that spoke the earlier lines of the stanza (in 6, "You have a great big nose and fat legs," we hear a jeering child, and in 11, "Everyone saw a fat nose on thick legs," we hear an adolescent imagining how others see her), but the third stanza ends with something of the flatly stated violence of a fairy tale: "So she cut off her nose and her legs / and offered them up." In the fourth and final stanza she is again (or better, still) a doll, lifeless and pretty.

In recent years, in addition to white Barbies there have been African-American, Hispanic and Asian Barbies, but until the fall of 1990 the TV and print ads showed only the fair-skinned blue-eyed version. For additional information about Barbie, see Sydney Ladensonhn Stern and Ted Schoenhaus, *Toyland: The High-Stakes Game of the Toy Industry.* Barbie's wardrobe has changed from flight attendant to astronaut, and from garden-party outfits to workout attire. She has a dress-for-success and a briefcase—but they are pink.

Marge Piercy "What's That Smell in the Kitchen?" (p. 449)

Putting aside the title (in which, at least in retrospect, perhaps we hear the voice of the oafish husband comfortably seated in the TV room), the first words of the first line ("All over America women are") might lead us to expect some sort of feminist/Whitmanesque assertion of glorious unity, or of flourishing individuality, and in a sense we get something like this, but in a comic domestic vein. The burnt dinners are fully explained in the final line, but the reason becomes evident fairly soon in the poem—certainly by line 9, with its punning glance at kitchen utensils in "Anger sputters in her brainpan."

Mitsuye Yamada "To the Lady" (p. 450)

First, some background. In 1942 the entire Japanese and Japanese-American population on America's Pacific coast—about 112,000 people—was incarcerated and relocated. More than two-thirds of the people moved were native-born citizens of the United States. (The 158,000 Japanese residents of the Territory of Hawaii were not affected.)

Immediately after the Japanese attack on Pearl Harbor, many journalists, the general public, Secretary of the Army Henry Stimson, and congressional delegations from California, Oregon, and Washington called for the internment. Although Attorney General Francis Biddle opposed it, on February 19, 1942 President Franklin D. Roosevelt signed Executive Order 9066, allowing military authorities "to prescribe military areas . . . from which any or all persons may be excluded." In practice, no persons of German or Italian heritage were disturbed, but Japanese and Japanese-Americans on the Pacific coast were rounded up (they were allowed to take with them "only that which can be carried") and relocated in camps. Congress, without a dissenting vote, passed legislation supporting the evacuation. A few Japanese-Americans challenged the constitutionality of the proceeding, but with no immediate success.

Many students today may find it difficult to comprehend the intensity of anti-Japanese sentiment that pervaded the 1940s. Here are two samples, provided by David Mura, whose poem about the internment camps appears on page 626. Lt. General John DeWittt, the man in charge of the relocation plan, said:

> The Japanese race is an enemy race and while many second and third generation Japanese born on United States soil, possessed of United States citizenship, have become "Americanized," the racial strains are undiluted. To conclude otherwise is to expect that children born of white parents on Japanese soil sever all racial affinity and become loyal Japanese subjects. . . . Along the vital Pacific Coast over 112,000 enemies, of Japanese extraction, are at large today. There are indications that these are organized and ready for concerted action at a favorable opportunity. The very fact that no sabotage has taken place to date is a disturbing and confirming indication that such action will be taken.

One rubs one's eyes in disbelief at the crazy logic that holds that *because* "no sabotage has taken place," such action "will be taken." The second quotation Mura has called to our attention is a remark made in 1942 by Senator Tom Steward, of Tennessee:

> They [the Japanese] are cowardly and immoral. They are different from Americans in every conceivable way, and no Japanese . . . should have the right to claim American citizenship. . . . A Jap is a Jap anywhere you find him. They do not believe in God and have no respect for an oath of allegiance.

By the way, not a single Japanese-American was found guilty of subversive activity. For two good short accounts, with suggestions for further readings, see the articles entitled "Japanese Americans, wartime relocation of," in *Kodansha Encyclopedia of Japan*, 4:17–18, and "War Relocation Authority," in 8:228.

It may be interesting to read Yamada's poem aloud in class, *without* having assigned it for prior reading, and to ask students for their responses at various stages—after line 4, line 21, and line 36. Lines 1–4 pose a question that perhaps many of us (young and old, and whether of Japanese descent or not) have asked, at least to ourselves. The question, implying a criticism of the victims, shows an insufficient awareness of Japanese or Japanese-American culture of the period. It also shows an insufficient awareness of American racism; by implying that protest by the victims *could* have been effective, it reveals ignorance of the terrific hostility of whites toward persons of Japanese descent.

The first part of the response shows one aspect of the absurdity of the lady's question. Japanese and Japanese-Americans were brought up not to stand out in any way (certainly not to make a fuss), and to place the harmony of the group (whether the family, or society as a whole) above individual expression. Further, there was nothing that these people could effectively do, even if they had shouted as loudly as Kitty Genovese did. For the most part they were poor, they had no political clout, and they were hated and despised as Asians. The absurdity of the view that they could have resisted effectively is comically stated in "should've pulled myself up from my / bra straps" (echoing the red-blooded American ideal of pulling oneself up by one's bootstraps), but of course the comedy is bitter.

Then the speaker turns to "YOU," nominally the "lady" of the title but in effect also the reader, and by ironically saying what we would have done points out what in fact we did not do. (The references to a march on Washington and letters to Congress are clear enough, but most students will not be aware of the tradition that the King of Denmark said that he would wear a Star of David [line 27] if Danish Jews were compelled by Nazis to wear the star.)

Thus far the speaker has put the blame entirely on the white community, especially since lines 5–21 strongly suggest that the Japanese-Americans *couldn't* do anything but submit. Yet the poem ends with a confession that because Japanese-Americans docilely subscribed to "law and order"—especially the outrageous Executive Order 9066— they were in fact partly responsible for the outrage committed against them. The last line of the poem, "All are punished," is exactly what Prince Escalus says at the end of *Romeo and Juliet*. Possibly the echo is accidental, though possibly the reader is meant to be reminded of a play, widely regarded as "a tragedy of fate," in which the innocent are victims of prejudice.

For another poem about the internment, see David Mura's "An Argument: On 1942," on p. 626 of the text.

Louise Erdrich "Dear John Wayne" (p. 452)

The title suggests a fan letter (and therefore a naive, adoring writer-speaker), but the poem turns out to be a witty, vigorous satire, with a good deal of Swiftian *saeva indignatio* under the wit.

The mock heroic diction of "to *vanquish* hordes of mosquitoes" quickly yields to the simplicity of "Nothing works," but the mosquitoes as enemies reappear in "They break through the smoke-screen for blood," where the line also evokes thoughts of cowboys and Indians in battle. Other elevated passages include "There will be no parlance" and "die beautifully," but such terms are mixed with "ICBM missiles" and "this wide screen," so they are undercut; the apparent heroism is Hollywood phoniness, as phony as John Wayne's smile, "a horizon of teeth."

Satire of course is a way of talking seriously, of expressing indignation under a veil of comedy. If the absurdity of what is happening on the screen causes the Indians to laugh and "fall over the hood, / slipping in the hot spilled butter," these lines about Native Americans eating popcorn remind us of the cliché about people slipping in blood during battle, and the cliché reminds us of the reality of the battles in which, finally, the whites took the land from the Native Americans.

Chapter 13

Figurative Language: Simile,
Metaphor, Personification,
Apostrophe

If the idea that metaphors are like riddles is appealing, ask the class why the camel is "the ship of the desert." They will see that the figure goes beyond saying that the camel is a means of transportation, for the figure brings out both the camel's resemblance (at a great distance) to a sail boat and the desert's resemblance to an ocean.

If one wants to get into this business of metaphors as riddles (and we recommend it), one can have great fun in class by assigning Craig Raine's "A Martian Sends a Postcard Home" (text, p.622)

On figurative language, consult Monroe Beardsley, *Aesthetics;* Isabel Hungerland, *Poetic Discourse;* W. K. Wimsatt, Jr., and Cleanth Brooks, *Literary Criticism,* p. 749–750; and Terence Hawkes, *Metaphor.* Probably as good as any statement about figurative language is Shelley's, that the language of poets "is vitally metaphoric; that is, it marks the before unapprehended relations of things and perpetuates their apprehension."

At some point during our classroom discussion of metaphor we usually manage to give students Kenneth Burke's comment on metaphor (from his essay on Marianne Moore): Metaphor is "a device for seeing something *in terms of* something else. It brings out the thisness of a that, or the thatness of a this!"

Robert Burns "A Red, Red Rose" (p. 455)

Probably few instructors will feel the need to discuss this poem in class, but we include it in the book because we like it and because it offers figures that are easily perceived. What do we like about it? Well, we like the figures (even though they are obvious); we like the repetition ("red, red rose" (1), "And I" (7, 11, 15), "Till a' the seas gang dry" (8, 9), "my dear" (9, 11), and especially "luve" (a noun in 1 and 3, referring to the beloved; a noun in 6, referring the speaker's mental state; a verb in 7; a noun in 13 and 15). We like the fact that the poem scarcely advances, but keeps returning to the beloved. Of course, one can find a structure (e.g., the song moves from the local and familiar ("a red, red rose") to the remote ("ten thousand mile"), but chiefly one feels that the poet keeps coming back to his beloved and to his love for her.

David Daiches, in *Robert Burns,* page 312, praises the poem for its "combination of swagger and tender protectiveness." Somehow, this characterization doesn't seem exactly right to us, and you may want to ask your students if his view corresponds to theirs:

Nowhere in literature has that combination of swagger and tender protectiveness so characteristic of the male in love been so perfectly captured, and it is all done by simple similes and simple exaggeration.

Sylvia Plath "Metaphors" (p. 457)

Sylvia Plath's "Metaphors," in nine syllables each, with nine metaphors, is a sort of joking reference to the nine months of pregnancy, which is what this riddling poem is about.

A "Voices and Visions" video cassette and an audio cassette of Sylvia Plath are available from HarperCollins.

Richard Wilbur "A Simile for Her Smile" (p. 458)

The comparison is not of her smile to the approaching riverboat (the "packet," in line 9), but of the pause in the speaker's mind (a pause that follows the "hope, the thought" of her smile) to the pause in traffic when the boat approaches the drawbridge. In the second stanza some of the words describing the life around the speaker can easily be thought to refer also to the woman: "the packet's *smooth* approach," "the *silken* river." Probably the last line, with its rather grand image ("And slow cascading of the paddle wheel"), comes as a pleasant surprise.

There is no need to get into matters of versification (though no harm, either), but you may want to point out that the poem is divided into two sestets, and that the open space between them corresponds to the space made as the drawbridge starts to rise. The space also stands for the silence that comes over the horns and motors.

John Keats "On First Looking into Chapman's Homer" (p. 459)

In "On First Looking into Chapman's Homer," Keats uses figures to communicate to the reader the poet's state of mind. Figures of traveling (appropriate to a poem about the author of *The Iliad* and *The Odyssey*, and also, via "realms of gold" or El Dorado, to the Elizabethans) give way in the sestet to figures of more breathtaking exploration and discovery. (By the way, it is not quite right to say that at line 9 we pass from the octave's images of land to the sestet's images of discovery. An important shift occurs in line 7, with "Yet" no less important than line 9's "Then." "Breathe" in line 7 is probably transitional, linked to the octave's idea of foreign travel and also to the sestet's early reference to the skies.)

It is probably fair to say that the octave (or at least its first six lines as compared with the sestet) has a somewhat mechanical, academic quality. "Realms of gold," "goodly states," "bards in fealty to Apollo," "demesne," etc. all suggest something less than passionate utterance, a tone reinforced by the rather mechanical four pairs of lines, each pair ending with a substantial pause. But in the sestet the language is more concrete, the lines more fluid (it can be argued that only line 10 concludes with a pause), and the meter less regular, giving a sense of new excitement that of course corresponds to the meaning of the poem.

Almost all critics agree that Keats erred in giving Cortez for Balboa, but C. V. Wicker argues in *College English* 17(April 1956):383–387 that Keats meant Cortez, for the point is not the first discovery of something previously unknown, but an individual's discovery for himself of what others have earlier discovered for themselves. Still, it seems evident that Keats slipped, and instructors may want to spend some class time discussing the problem of whether such a factual error weakens the poem.

In line with much contemporary criticism that sees poetry as being reflective discourse concerned with itself, Lawrence Lipking, in *The Life of the Poet*, sees this poem as being about Keats's discovery of Keats. Well, yes, in a way, but surely the poem is also about the discovery of the world's literature, a world other than the self. See also P. McNally, in *JEGP* 79(1980):530–540.

Marge Piercy "A Work of Artifice" (p. 460)

Bonsai is the art of dwarfing trees by pruning the branches and roots and by controlling the fertilization. The grower shapes the tree by wiring the trunk and the branches. The important point, so far as Piercy's poem goes, is that a bonsai (the word can be used of a specimen itself, as well as of the art) is *not* a special hybrid dwarf, but is a tree distorted by the grower. (The somewhat freakish shape of the poem perhaps imitates the miniaturized tree.) Lines 1–8 give students the gist of what they need to know about bonsai. Students will readily see that Piercy's bonsai is a metaphor; the real "work of artifice" that the poet is concerned with is the female shaped by a dominant male society. The metaphor extends through line 16, when it yields to the closely related image of "the bound feet" (footbinding was practiced in China until well into the twentieth century) and then by easy association to "the crippled brain," which in turn yields to "the hair in curlers." Students might be invited to comment on the connection between these last two images: In what way is "hair in curlers" a kind of crippling (not only of the hair, of course, but of the woman's mind, which is persuaded or bullied into distorting itself in order to be acceptable to men)? The last two lines remind us of an advertisement, perhaps for a soap or skin lotion, but we can't identify it. In any case, in "the hair you love to touch" the reader gets the modern American male's version of the gardener who soothingly "croons" (11) to his tree while he maims it.

Edmund Waller "Song" (p. 462)

If the previous chapters have already been read, students will have encountered roses in "To the Virgin to Make Much of Time" and in Burns's "A Red, Red Rose." In the next chapter they will encounter Blake's "The Sick Rose." In line 1, "wastes" is perhaps more potent than many students at first find it, for it implies not simply squandering but destroying, as in, for instance, "to lay waste a city." Thus the idea of death, explicit in lines 16–17, is present almost from the start of the poem.

William Carlos Williams "The Red Wheelbarrow" (p. 464)

Roy Harvey Pearce, in *The Continuity of American Poetry*, p. 339, regards William Carlos Williams's "The Red Wheelbarrow" as sentimental (but of some value), and says that what "depends" is the poet: "He assures himself that he is what he is by virtue of his power to collocate such objects into sharply annotated images like these." Charles Altieri, in *PMLA* 91(1976):111, suggests that although the items are stripped of associations, "No poem in English is more metonymic. Three objects evoke a mode of life in the sparsest, most succinct manner possible. The poverty of detail, like that in the rural paintings of Andrew Wyeth, at once intensifies the starkness of rural life and exemplifies it." Altieri also points out that in each of the last three stanzas, the first line "depends" on the second, for the word that ends each first line is often a noun ("wheel," "rain," White"), but in the poem turns out to be an adjective. Thus the reader's mind "is made to hover over details until its waiting is rewarded, not only within the stanza, but also as each independent stanza emerges to fill out this waiting and to move us beyond details to a complex sense of a total life contained in these objects." John Hollander (*Vision and Resonance*, p. 111) suggests that cutting "wheelbarrow" and "rainwater" (with no hyphens to indicate that "rain" and "white" are parts of the compounds) helps to convey what the poem is about: seeing the constituents of things in the freshness of light after rain.

A "Voices and Visions" video cassette of William Carlos Williams is available from HarperCollins. An audio cassette of William Carlos Williams reading is also available from HarperCollins.

Alfred, Lord Tennyson "The Eagle" (p. 464)

Tennyson's concise account in "The Eagle" seems literal enough, but of course from the first the bird is personified, by being called "He" instead of "it" and by being given "hands" instead of talons. Note also that "his mountain walls" implies that the bird is lord of a fortress. "Wrinkled sea" and "crawls" are other obvious figures, giving us the sea from a man-bird's eye view. The simile "like a thunderbolt he falls" returns us from the eagle's point of view to the observer's. "Ringed with the azure world," we should mention, has been interpreted as expressing the bird's view of the earth spread out in a circle before him, but we assume that "azure" is proof that the description is not of the earth but of the sky around the bird, and so the line is from an observer's point of view.

Robert Graves assaults the poem in *On Poetry: Collected Talks and Essays*, pp. 402–405. Graves suggests that if the eagle's claws are hands, when we are told that the eagle "stands" he must be standing on his wings, and Graves claims that line 3 adds nothing: "Since the eagle perches on his crag close to the sun, a background of blue sky has already been presumed." Graves goes on to complain that "lands" has been chosen for the rhyme with "hands" and "stands", not for the sense, because "the eagle can stand only in one land." And "close to the sun" is objectionable; "What," Graves asks, "are a few hundred feet, compared with 92,000,000 miles!"

In teaching "The Eagle," we have occasionally found that a student too familiar with the ways of English teachers may insist that the bird is symbolic of something or other. Christ has been suggested, on the grounds that the bird descends from heaven ("Close to the sun") to earth, and the word "falls" has been said to contain an allusion to the Fall of Man. (By the way, we *do* include Hopkins's "The Wind-hover" in this book, and the two poems can be compared interestingly with an eye toward degrees of symbolism.) Such a symbolic rendering can be gently but firmly rejected, though perhaps it contains a germ of truth: The bird is presented as an intent watcher of the world beneath it. To this degree perhaps one can say that the bird resembles the keen-eyed poet, though this is not to say that the bird is a symbol for the poet. The bird is a bird, in fact an eagle.

Christina Rossetti "Uphill" (p. 465)

How can one be sure that the poem is metaphorical? This is part of what we are getting at in our first question, in which we ask the student to respond to a reader who assumes the speaker is making inquiries preparatory to a bit of touring. The question is not meant to be frivolous. Instructors know that this is a poem about larger matters, but that's because instructors are used to reading poems and to figurative language. Most students are unfamiliar with the way poems work—which is why they sometimes read too literally and why, on other occasions, they read too freely, ignoring some passages and imposing highly personal readings on others.

Our second question asks, Who is the questioner? The poem is not a Browningesque dramatic monologue, and we think it is enough to say that the questioner is the poet, or the poet as a universal spokesperson. By the way, we don't know exactly what to make of the suggestion of a student that the answerer in "Uphill" is a ghost, that is, someone who has made the journey and therefore answers authoritatively.

As for our final question in the text, we do find the answer (with their dry understatement, as in "You cannot miss that inn," i.e., "Don't worry, you will certainly die") chilling as well as comforting, but we are unconvinced that a reader is supposed to imagine a dialogue between the poet and a revenant. Rather, we believe (guided by Jerome J. McGann's essay on Christina Rossetti in his *The Beauty of Inflections*) that the poet is speaking with what McGann calls "her divine interlocutor" (p. 242). McGann points out that the ending of "Uphill" is easily misinterpreted. Rossetti is not saying that the pilgrimage of the Christian soul ends with an eternal sleep. Rather, she is alluding to the Anabaptist doctrine known as "Soul Sleep" (technically, psychopannychism), which holds that at death the soul is put into a condition of sleep until the millennium. On the Last Day the soul awakens and goes to its final reward. McGann fully discusses the point in his essay.

Randall Jarrell "The Death of the Ball Turret Gunner" (p. 466)

We reprint here a good explication, by a student, of the poem:

Reading the first line aloud, one pauses slightly after "sleep," dividing the line in half. The halves make a sharp contrast. The point of transition in this line is "I fell," a helpless movement from the mother to the State, from sleep to the State. The mother and the State make an evident contrast, and so do "sleep" and "the State," which resemble each other in their first sound and in their position at the end of a half-line but which have such different associations, for sleep is comforting and the State is associated with totalitarianism. ("The country" or "the land" might be comforting and nourishing, but "the State" has no such warm suggestions.) We will soon see in the poem that life in the "belly" of the state is mindless and cold, a death-like life which ends with sudden and terrible death. A mother, even in her "sleep," naturally protects and nourishes the child in her warm womb; the State unnaturally cramps the man in its icy belly. He "hunched in its belly" until his "wet fur froze." We gather from the title that "its" refers not only to the State but also the airplane in whose womb-like ball turret he led his confined existence and died. Given the title, the fur probably literally refers to the fur lining of the jackets that fliers wore in World War II, and it also suggests the animal-like existence he led while confined by this unfeeling foster parent, the State-airplane.

His unnatural existence is further emphasized by the fact that, in the airplane, he was "Six miles from earth." From such an existence, far from the "dream of life" that people hope for, and still hunched in the turret like a baby in the womb, he was born again, that is, he awoke to (or became aware of) not a rich fulfillment of the dream but a horrible reality that is like a nightmare. "Woke to black flak" imitates, in its rattling *k*'s at the end of words, the sound of the gunfire that simultaneously awakened and killed him. His awakening or birth is to nightmarish reality and death. It is not surprising, but it is certainly horrifying, that in this world of an impersonal State that numbs and destroys life, his body is flushed out of the turret with a hose. That this is the third horrible release: the first was from the mother into the State; the second was from the belly of the State into the belly of the airplane; and now in shreds from the belly of the airplane into nothing. This life-history is told flatly, with no note of protest, of course increases the horror. The simplicity of the last line more effectively brings out the horror of the experience than an anguished cry or an angry protest could do.

Jarrell reads and discusses the poem on Caedman cassette SWC1363.

Seamus Heaney "Digging" (p. 466)

The comparison of the pen resting in the hand, "snug as a gun," may especially remind a reader that in Ireland literature has often been closely connected with politics and with war, but of course the idea of the pen as a weapon is widespread, best known in the adage that "The pen is mightier than the sword." Less well known, but in the same vein, is Napoleon's preference of newspapers to battalions.

The image of the weapon is then largely replaced by the lines about the speaker's father digging—now flowerbeds but twenty years ago he dug nourishing potatoes—though such words as "lug," "shaft," and "cool hardness" (though said of potatoes) keep the gun in our midst, at least faintly. Similarly, the emphasis on the father's posture (careful, professional, expert) suggests the discipline of a marksman—and of a writer.

Heaney then goes further back in time, to his grandfather digging not potatoes but turf, the fuel that cooks the potatoes and that heats a home, thus a substance no less necessary to life than food. But the evocation of these pictures of father and grandfather digging serves to remind the poet that he has "no spade to follow them" (24). What, then, is his place in the family, and his role in society? What nourishment, what fuel can he contribute? And so we come back to the pen: "The squat pen rests" (30, a repetition of the first half of line 2). "I'll dig with it" (31). The "squat pen" is the poet's spade and gun, to be used with the energy and precision with which his father and grandfather used their spades, and to be used, presumably, with the same life-sustaining effect.

Louise Erdrich "Indian Boarding School" (p. 468)

The runaways think of railroad tracks as "old lacerations" (4) and scars (6), and of their own "worn-down welts" as a highway—all of this, of course, a reflection of their experience of "ancient punishments" (16) at school. Even the names they inscribed in the wet cement of sidewalks and the outlines and veins of leaves they pressed into the cement are imagined as the scars of "old injuries" (24). In short, the violence done to the children is seen as reflected in violence done to the land.

Chapter 14

Figurative Language: Imagery
and Symbolism

For a discussion of the difference between *natural* symbols (items that are meaningful on the literal level but that mean much more too) and symbols that have no literal existence, such as a man who does not cast a shadow, see N. Friedman, "Symbol," in *Encyclopedia of Poetry and Poetics*, ed. Alex Preminger.

The references suggested for Chapter 13 are relevant here too. In addition, see Barbara Seward, *The Symbolic Rose*.

Among the highly relevant poems in Chapter 19, are Donne's "Valediction," Keats's "To Autumn," and Ginsberg's "A Supermarket in California." William Carlos Williams's "Spring and All" is an interesting example of a poem with almost no figurative language—until near the end.

William Blake "The Sick Rose" (p. 470)

"The Sick Rose" has been much interpreted, usually along the lines given in the text (See Reuben Brower, *The Fields of Light*, and Rosenthal and Smith, *Exploring Poetry*.) But E. D. Hirsch, Jr., in *Innocence and Experience*, argues that "The rose is being satirized by Blake as well as being infected by the worm. Part of the rose's sickness is her ignorance of her disease. Her ignorance *is* her spiritual disease because in accepting 'dark secret love' she has unknowingly repressed and perverted her instinctive life, her 'bed of crimson joy.'" Hirsch argues his point for a couple of pages.

We especially like Helen Vendler's comment on this poem in her introduction to *The Harvard Book of Contemporary American Poetry*:

> The world of the poem is analogous to the existential world, but not identical with it. In a famous created world of Blake's, for instance, there is a rose doomed to mortal illness by the love of a flying worm who is invisible. We do not experience such a poem by moving it piecemeal into our world deciding what the rose "symbolizes" and what the worm "stands for." On the contrary, we must move ourselves in to its amibience, into a world in which a dismayed man can converse with his beloved rose and thrust upon her, in his anguished jealousy, diagnosis and fatal prognosis in one sentence.... After living in Blake's world for the space of eight lines, we return to our own world, haunted and accused.

Allen Ginsberg has "tuned" the poem (MGM Records FTS-3083)

Thomas Hardy "Neutral Tones" (p. 47)

Brooks, Purser, and Warren, in *An Approach to Literature*, astutely point
out that the first stanza is conversational and somewhat slow, for the
speaker is trying to recollect all of the details. Notice especially the
dash at the start of the fouth line, making the line itself seem to be an
after-thought. In contrast, the last stanza is firm, emphasized by alliteration ("lessons . . . lover," "wrings with wrong"). The gray leaves of
the last line of the first stanza recur in the last line of the last stanza, but
now there is no sense of an afterthought; rather, each item (face, sun,
tree, leaves) seems firmly in place. Still, one does not want to minimize
the effect of lifelessness—the white sun, the "starving sod," the gray
leaves (doubtless there is a pun on "ash"), the numbed looks, and the
dull words exchanged. Hardy tells us almost nothing about the conversation, and nothing at all about why this love failed, but of course
that is part of the point. The point is the lifelessness of the encounter,
and (in the end) of subsequent encounters with others. No explanation for the decay is given, unless in "the God-curst sun" we hear a
suggestion that God is, for some unstated reason, hostile.

By the way, line 8 puzzles many readers. We paraphrase it thus:
"[We exchanged a few words] about which of the two of us lost the
more [i.e. suffered the more greatly from] our love affair."

Edgar Allan Poe "To Helen" (p. 472)

The best discussion that we have come across is an old one, by M. L.
Rosenthal and A. J. Smith, in *Exploring Poetry* (1955), pp. 603–04, in a
chapter on symbolism. Rosenthal and Smith begin by pointing out
that the speaker is telling a sort of story: "Helen's beauty, the speaker
says, has borne him 'homeward' gently and pleasurably—'o'er a per-
fumed sea.'" If the poem had ended with the second stanza, they add,
it might seem to argue that the beauty of the woman who is addressed
(if he is not addressing the original Helen) "has led him to appreciate
the kindred beauty of classical art." But in the third stanza "the emphasis on classical beauty is minimized." Helen has brought the
speaker, who has sailed on "desperate seas," to security, but she is
nevertheless still remote, strange, and statue-like in a window-niche.
By calling her Psyche he endows her "with a spiritual, unreachable
quality." Further, Rosenthal and Smith suggest, because the name
Psyche reminds us of the legend of Cupid and Psyche, in which the
beautiful Psyche inadvertently burned Cupid with a drop of oil from

her lamp and thus lost him as a husband, she is a "symbol both of beauty and of frustration. The poem therefore is not chiefly about the values of classical art. Rather, it may be about "the speaker's feelings for a particular woman," or it may even be "a confession of failure in love or in poetic achievement."

Thomas O. Mabbott, in his valuable edition, *Collected Works of Edgar Allan Poe* (1969) I,164 confidently offers a simpler, no-nonsense summary of the theme:

> It is spiritual love that leads us to beauty, a resting place from sorrow and the homeland of all that is sacred in our being. Beauty is the lasting legacy of Greece and Rome, and its supreme symbol is the most beautiful of women, Helen of Troy, daughter of Zeus, who brings the wanderer home and inspires the poet.

Who is the wanderer? Candidates include Odysseus, Dionysus, Menelaus, and Catullus. For instance, lines 2–5 may faintly recall Book XIII of the *Odyssey*, in which a Phaeacian bark carries the sleeping Odysseus to his native Ithaca. The various claims—none wholly convincing—are summarized in Mabbott's edition. Incidentally, the "desperate seas" of line 6 offer a nice example of a transferred epithet; the traveller is desperate, not the seas.

Poe revised the poem steadily, from 1831 to 1843. The most notable revisions are these:

Line 9: *from* beauty to fair *to* glory that was
Line 10: *from* And the grandeur of old *to* And the grandeur that was
Line 11: *from* that little *to* yon brilliant
Line 13: *from* folded scroll to agate book *to* agate lamp

Topics for Discussion and Writing

1. In the first stanza, to what is Helen's beauty compared? To whom does the speaker apparently compare himself? What does "way-worn" in line 4 suggest to you? To what in the speaker's experience might the "native shore" in line 5 correspond?
2. What do you take "desperate seas" to mean in line 6, and who has been traveling them? To what are they contrasted in line 8? How does "home" seem to be defined in this stanza (stanza 2)?
3. What further light is shed on the speaker's home or destination in stanza 3?

4. Do you think that "To Helen" can be a love poem and also a poem about spiritual beauty or about the love of art? Explain.

D. H. Lawrence "Snake" (p. 473)

Lawrence's "Snake," a sort of dialogue between, on the one hand, the "voice of my education" (which hates vitality and danger) and, on the other hand, what Lawrence elsewhere calls his "demon" (spontaneous self, which appreciates the snake's elemental nature), can cause little difficulty, though some students may miss the irony involved when the voice of education says, "If you were a man / You would take a stick and break him." The poem as a whole deflates this lifeless view of manhood. But the poem is richly ambiguous, metaphorically suggestive of evil and perhaps also of the phallus, and also (perhaps therefore) suggestive of power and vitality.

Additional Topics for Discussion and Writing

1. What do you think Lawrence's purpose was in writing "Snake"?
2. What does the speaker learn?
3. If you have read Emily Dickinson's "A narrow Fellow in the Grass" (text 531), write an essay of 500 to 750 words discussing the different purposes of Lawrence and Dickinson. How effectively does each poet fulfill these purposes? (The second question will probably require you to talk about tone, degree of amplification, and structure.)
4. Write an essay of 500 to 750 words reflecting on some early response to yours to part of the animal world. Note that the essay should describe your early response and also your mature reflection on it.

Samuel Taylor Coleridge "Kubla Khan" (p. 476)

Among the interesting discussions of "Kubla Kahn" are Brooks and Warren, *Understanding Poetry*, 4th ed.; Humphry House, *Coleridge* (House's material on "Kubla Khan" is reprinted in *Romanticism and Consciousness*, ed. Harold Bloom); Harold Bloom, *The Visionary Company*; Walter Jackson Bate, *Coleridge*; and Jerome J. McGann, *The Romantic Ideology*.

Most critics tend to see the fountain, river, and chasm as symbols of the poet's consciousness and "the pleasure dome" as a symbol of poetry. Charles Patterson (PMLA 89[October 1974]: 1033–1042) believes that the river (suggestive of poetic consciousness) is called "sacred" because it is "given over to and seemingly possessed by a god presenting through the poet's furor divinus a vision of beauty." The "deep delight" of line 44 is, Patterson suggests, "a daemonic inspiration, an unrestricted and amoral joy like that of the pre-Christian daemons." Patterson's judicious article deserves close study. These days, since drugs are in, the instructor also may wish to consult Elisabeth Schneider, *Coleridge, Opium, and Kubla Khan,* or Alethea Hayter, *Opium and the Romantic Imagination.* Apparently it is unsound to attribute the poem to opium. As someone has said, Coleridge didn't write "Kubla Khan" because he took opium; he took opium because he was the sort of person who writes poems like "Kubla Khan."

In Chapter 19, Blake's "Lamb" and "Tyger" are useful when talking about symbolism, as are Keats's "La Belle Dame sans Merci" and Yeats's "Sailing to Byzantium."

Additional Topic for Writing

"Kubla Khan" as a celebration of the energy of life. (It can be argued that even the references to ice and to the "sunless sea" and "lifeless ocean" in this context suggest mystery rather than lifelessness; certainly the Khan, the river, the fountain, the dome, the wailing woman, and the poet—among other things—combine to give a vision of a powerful and mysterious creativity.)

Adrienne Rich "Diving into the Wreck" (p. 479)

Most responses identify the wreck as either (1) the speaker's life (persons familiar with Rich's biography may identify it specifically as her unhappy marriage to a man who committed suicide in 1970, about three years before the poem was published) or (2) more broadly, our male-dominated society. Another way of putting it is to say that the poem is about sexual politics. The poem is discussed by Wendy Martin and by Erica Jong in *Adrienne Rich's Poetry,* ed. Barbara C. Gelpi and Albert Gelpi. Part of the following comment is indebted to their discussions.

Armed with a book of myths (an understanding of the lies society has created?) and a camera and a knife (an instrument of vision and an instrument of power?) she goes, alone, in contrast to Cousteau assisted by a team, to explore the wreck. (This sort of exploration can be

done only by the individual. One might add, by the way, that it is a
new sort of exploration, and exploration for which Rich had no maps.
Before the second half of the twentieth century, there was virtually no
poetry about what it was like to be a wife or a woman living in a male-
dominated society. The earlier poetry written by women was chiefly
about children, love, and God.) More exactly, she is there, exploring
the wreck ("I came to explore the wreck" implies that she is speaking
from the site itself). She has immersed herself in the primal, life-giving
element and has now arrived in order "to see the damage that was
done / and the treasures that prevail," that is to see not only what is
ruined but also what is salvageable. Her object is to find truth, not
myth (62–63).

Line 72–73, in which she is both mermaid and merman, and line
77, in which "I am she; I am he," suggest that she has achieved an
androgynous nature and thus has become the sort of new woman who
will tell the truth. According to lines 92–94, the names of such true
persons, or androgynes, persons who may rescue civilization, do not
appear in the book of myths.

Wallace Stevens "Anecdote of the Jar" (p. 482)

Steven's poem has evoked controversy, chiefly on whether the jar is a
symbol of man's superiority to nature or a symbol of man's corruption
of natural beauty. For a survey of various interpretations, see *College
English* 26(April 1965): 527–532. William York Tindall, in *Wallace Stevens*, p.24, argues that "the theme is interaction: The effect of the round
jar on its surroundings and of them on it. This artifact composes nature, but not entirely; for the slovenly place still sprawls. Wilderness
of bird and bush makes jar stand out, gray and bare." Frank Kermode,
in *The Romantic Image*, dismisses the controversy over whether "the
poet is *for* Nature or *for* Art." Kermode says:

> This is irrelevant, because the point of the jar's *difference*, and the manner
> of its difference, are what matters. It belongs to a different order of reality,
> already completely significant and orderly, fixed and immortal. In one
> sense it is more vital, in another sense less so, than the "slovenly wilder-
> ness" around it; the poem itself reconciles opposites by using the jar as a
> symbol . . . of what moves in stillness, is dead in life, whose meaning and
> being are the same.

See also Joseph N. Riddell, *The Clairvoyant Eye*, pp.43–44, and Harold Bloom, *Kabbalah and Criticism*.

A "Voices and Visions" video cassette of Wallace Stevens is available from HarperCollins. An audio cassette of Wallace Stevens reading is also available from HarperCollins.

Wallace Stevens "The Emperor of Ice-Cream" (p. 482)

On "The Emperor of Ice-Cream," first a comment by Stevens, in a letter (*Letters of Wallace Stevens*, Holly Stevens, ed.) of 16 May 1945. He says of "concupiscent curds" that the words "express the concupiscence of life, but, by contrast with the things in relation to them in the poem, they express or accentuate life's destitution, and it this that gives them something more than a cheap lustre" (p. 500).

If "emperor" suggests power and splendor, "ice cream" suggests pleasure, especially sensuous enjoyment, triviality, and transience. Put together, and in this context of a wake, the implication is that a human for a while shapes and enjoys the tawdry world, as the dead woman embroidered fantails on her sheets—which were too short. We can take pleasure in the world (there is certainly pleasure in the shifting diction and in the alliteration in line 3, "In kitchen cups concupiscent curds"), but if Stevens insists on the pleasure (cigars, ice cream, flirting girls), he also insists on looking at ("Let the lamp affix its beam") transience ("last month's newspapers," the dresser lacking knobs) and death (the corpse's horny feet). The two stanzas juxtapose a world of concupiscence and a world of death. The pleasures described, then, to return to Steven's letter, "accentuate life's destitution."

In another letter, published in the *Southern Review* (Autumn 1979): 773–774, Stevens freely paraphrases part of the poem: "let us have a respite from the imagination (men who are not cigar makers, blondes, costumes, theology), and, in short, suppose we have ice cream. Not that I wish to exalt ice cream as an absolute good, although my little girl might. It is a symbol, obviously and ironically, of the materialism or realism proper to a refugee from the imagination." Stevens goes on, however, to insist that "ambiguity [is] essential to poetry."

A "Voices and Visions" video cassette of Wallace Stevens is available from HarperCollins. An audio cassette of Wallace Stevens reading is also available from HarperCollins.

Chapter 15

Irony and Paradox

The chapter itself refers to I. A. Richard's essay on irony; reference may here be made to Cleanth Brook's *The Well-Wrought Urn*.

John Hall Wheelock "Earth" (p. 486)

The Martian astonomer who speaks confidently while "gazing off into the air" seems to be a pompous ass. Of course, it is the business of astonomers to gaze (sometimes) into air, but here the description seems to imply the astronomer's contempt for, or at least indifference to, his audience.

But it probably is more complicated. First, "drily" suggests that the astronomer may himself be speaking ironically. (The Elizabethans called irony "the dry mock.") Our students, by the way, seem to divide evenly between those who believe the astonomer is being satirized and those who believe the astonomer is speaking ironically. In any case, what he says makes sense; earth is inhabited by "intelligent beings" (4), and if the earth blows up, as here it is imagined to do, it will be because these people have blown it up. Yet the poem, ostensibly spoken by an astronomer who praises the intelligence of earthlings, of course condemns the misapplied intelligence.

For the report of another Martian, see Craig Raine, "A Martian Sends a Postcard Home" (text 622).

Percy Bysshe Shelley "Ozymandias" (p. 486)

James Reeves, in *The Critical Sense*, does a hatchet job on Shelley's "Ozymandias." (Ozymandias, incidentally, was the Greek version of the name User-ma-Ra, better known as Ramses II, the name the Greeks used for the thirteenth-century B. C. pharaoh who, like other pharaohs, built monuments to celebrate his own greatness. One such monument was a colossus sixty feet tall, carved in stone by Memnon. Diodorus, a Sicilian Greek historian of the first century, saw the statue and wrote that it was inscribed, "I am Osymandyas, king of kings; if any would know how great I am, and where I lie, let him excel me in any of my works." At some later date, the statue tumbled, leaving only fragments.) Reeve's objections include: "vast" (2) means "of great extent," but the legs would be tall rather than vast; "in the sand" (3) is hardly necessary after "in the desert"; if the visage is "shattered" (which Reeves takes to mean "broken to pieces"), it would be difficult to recognize the facial expression; the speaker says that the sculptor "well . . . read" the subject's passions, but we cannot know if this is true, since we have no other information about the subject; if it is argued that the inscription is evidence of cold-hearted tyranny, the sestet should begin "For," not "And"; to speak of "the decay" of a "wreck" is tautological; in lines 13–14 "boundless" makes unnecessary "stretch far away," and "bare" makes "lone" unnecessary. Some of Reeves's objections are telling, some are niggling; in any case, the power of the poem is chiefly in the essential irony and the almost surrealistic scene of legs arising in the desert, the face on the ground nearby, and no trunk anywhere.

A small point: Lines 4–8 are unclear, for it is not certain if "the hand . . . and the heart" belong to the sculptor, in which case the idea is that the sculptor "mocked" ("mimicked," "imitated in stone") the passions and "fed" them by creating them in stone, or if the hand and the heart belong to Ozymandia, whose hand mocked the passions of his foes and whose heart fed his own passions.

Shelley's friend, Horace Smith, a banker with a taste for literature, wrote a sonnet on Ozymandias at the same time that SHelley did. You may want to ask students to compare the two poems:

On a Stupendous Leg of Granite, Discovered Standing by Itself in the Desert of Egypt

In Egypt's sandy silence, all alone,
Stands a gigantic Leg, which far off throws
The only shadow that the desert knows.
"I am great Ozymandias," said the stone,
"The King of kings; this mighty city shows
The wonders of my hand." The city's gone!
Naught but the leg remaining to disclose
The sight of that forgotten Babylon.

We wonder, and some hunter may express
Wonder like ours, when through the wilderness
Where London stood, holding the wolf in chase,
He meets some fragment huge, and stops to guess
What wonderful, but unrecorded, race
Once dwelt in that annihilated place.

For additional background material on Shelley's poem, see H. M. Richmond, "Ozymandias and the Travellers," *Keats-Shelley Journal* 11(1962): 65–71. For a discussion of Shelley's poem and Smith's, see K. M. Bequette, "Shelley and Smith: Two Sonnets of Ozymandias," in *Keats-Shelley Journal* 26(1977): 29–31.

Linda Pastan "Ethics" (p. 487)

First, a word about the teacher and the ethical question posed. One may wonder what kind of teacher keeps asking the same question, year after year. (On the other hand, perhaps good teachers do ask the same questions year after year. They change the answers, not the quetions.) Why, by the way, does the stated ethical problem—an old chestnut—always involve a woman rather than a man? (We are reminded of Faulkner's comment that "If a writer has to rob his mother, he will not hesitate; the 'Ode on a Grecian Urn' is worth any number of old ladies.")

The poem begins by stating the ethical problem, but doesn't go on to answer it. Rather, it rejects the problem as arid, something perhaps fit for youngsters to debate (though in the poem the students don't care much about pictures or old people) but a concern that disappears when one is older and when one is "in a real museum" and is standing "before a real Rembrandt." We infer that the speaker, older and wiser, does care about both art and life, and knows that one doesn't have to choose between them. Art draws on life, and reveals life (lines 20–24), and both are "beyond saving by children" (25).

Although the speaker and her classmates were not much interested in the ethical problem that the teacher posed, other students may be. If so, you may want to set them loose on the first two lines of Yeat's "The Choice":

> The intellect of man is forced to choose
> Perfection of the life, or of the work.

Stevie Smith "Not Waving but Drowning" (p. 488)

All his life the dead man in Stevie Smith's "Not Waving but Drowning" sent messages that were misunderstood. His efforts to mask his loneliness and depression were more successful than he intended. His friends mistook him for a "chap" who "always loved larking," as they now mistake the cause of his death. But true friends would have seen through the clowning, the dead man seems to protest, in line 3 and 4 (when of course it is too late to protest or to explain). The second stanza confirms his view of the spectators. They are imperceptive and condescending; their understanding of the cause of his death is as superficial as their attention to him was while he was alive. But they didn't know him "all [his] life" (11). The dead man thus acknowledges, by leaving them out of the last stanza, that, never having risked honest behavior, he is at least as responsible as others for his failure to be loved and to love.

John Crowe Ransom "Bells for John Whiteside's Daughter" (p. 489)

Ransom's "Bells for John Whiteside's Daughter" has been discussed in Brooks, Purser, and Warren, *An Approach to Literature*. (Subsequently the same comment appears under Warren's name in *Kenyon Review* 5(Spring 1943): 238–240.)

Andrew Marvell "To His Coy Mistress" (p. 490)

Marvell's "To His Coy Mistress" is well discussed by J. V. Cunningham, *Modern Philosophy* 51(August 1953): 33–41; by Francis Berry, *Poets' Grammar*; by Joan Hartwig, *College English* 25(May 1964): 572–575; by Bruce King, *Southern Review* 5(1969): 689–703; and by Richard Crider, *College Literature* 12(Spring 1985):113–121. Incidently, "dew" in line 35 is an editor's emendation for "glew" in the first edition (1681). Grierson suggest "glew" means a shining gum found on some trees. Another editor, Margoulieth, conjectures "lew" that is, warmth.

Marvell's poem can be the subject of a paper involving a comparison with Herrick's "To the Virgins." Although both poems take as their theme the *carpe diem* motif, their tone and imagery differ greatly. For example, the sun in Herrick's poem ("the higher he's a-getting") does not race through the sky, but in Marvell's poem the lovers will force the sun to hurry. Or, again, in Herrick's poem the speaker is concerned not with satisfying his own desires but with the young women, whereas in Marvell's poem one strongly feels that the speaker is at least as concerned with himself as with the woman.

We have usually found it best to teach Herrick's poem before Marvell's partly because Herrick's is shorter, but chiefly because most students find it simpler.

John Donne "The Flea" (p. 492)

Donne's "The Flea" is discussed in a fine article by Patricia Spacks in *College English* 29(1968): 593–594. "The Flea," with the rest of Donne's *Songs and Sonnets*, has been edited by Theodore Redpath; the edition has much useful information, but this poem scarcely needs an editor's elucidation.

John Donne "Holy Sonnet XIV (Batter my heart three-personed God)" (p. 493)

"Batter my heart" has been discussed several times in *Explicator* (March 1953, Item 31: December 1953, Item 18; April 1954, Item 36; October 1956, Item 2). In *College English* 24(January 1963): 299–302, John Parrish summarized these discussions, rejecting the idea that in the first quatrain, especially in lines 2 and 4, God is compared to a tinker mending a damaged pewter vessel, and offering his own reading. All these are conveniently reprinted in the Norton critical edition of *John Donne's Poetry*, ed. A. L. Clements.

Our own winnowings from these essays follow. Although the first line introduces the "three-personed God," it is impossible to associate each quatrain with only one of the three persons. Still, the idea of the trinity is caried out in several ways: "knock, breathe, shine" becomes "break, blow, burn." And there are three chief conceits: God as a tinker repairing the speaker, damaged by sin; the speaker as a town usurped by satanic forces; God as a forceful lover who must ravish the sinful speaker; or (lest one get uneasy at the thought that Donne presents himself as a woman), God as a lover who must fully possess the speaker's soul (the soul is customarily regarded as female). "O'erthrow" in the first quatrian, in line 3, leads to the image of the besieged town in the second quatrain' "untrue" at the end of the second quatrain leads (because it can refer to marital infidelity) to the conceit of the lover in the third quatrain; and "ravish" in the final line can take us back to "heart" in the first line of the poem.

A useful, relatively long explication by M. T. Wanninger appeared in *Explicator* (December 1969), Item 37. M. H. Abrams, *Natural Supernaturalism*, pp. 50–51, points out that in "Batter my heart" Donne draws on revelation 21:5 ("Behold, I make all things new"), and that "the ultimate marriage with the Bridegroom, represented as the rape of the longingly reluctant soul" draws on "commonplaces of Christian devotion."

Topics for Discussion and Writing

How do you feel about an observation made in *Explicator* Spring 1980, to the effect that "no end" (1.6) is an anagram for "Donne"? What is the point? According to the author of the note," "This anagram is, I think, another of the many ingenious samples of Donne's playing upon his name for poetic effect." Is this reading helpful? Why? Why not?

Langston Hughes "Dream Boogie" (p. 494)

The *American Heritage Dictionary* defines boogie-woogie as "a style of jazz characterized by a repressed rhythmic and melodic pattern in the bass." "Repressed" has unconscious ironic echoes, since jazz grew in part from the white repression of blacks.

Many whites, noticing the musical accomplishments of some blacks, falsely assumed that these musicians were happy: If they weren't happy, why were they singing? But as Langston Hughes says in *The Big Sea*, blacks put their life into their music, singing "gay songs because you had to be gay or die; sad songs, because you couldn't help being sad sometimes. But gay or sad, you kept on living and you kept on going." In "Dream Boogie" Hughes says that if you "listen . . . closely," you can hear the injustice that in part gave birth to jazz and forced blacks to express their sorrow rhythmically and in a masked form. The enthusiasm of the opening line soon yields to a hint of a menace ("rumble," 3), and the point becomes almost explicit in the reference (4) to "a dream deferred." (Instructors who already have assigned "Harlem," text, 412, doubtless will make connections between the two poems.) In line 8–9 ("You think / It's a happy beat?") the speaker pretty clearly says it is an unhappy beat, but by putting the words in the form of a question, he stops short of making a flat assertion, and of course he doesn't—and lines 22–26 are explicit, for instance, in "We knows everybody / ain't free." The next passage (27–34), including the quotation from the Pledge of Allegiance, is hard-hitting, but the speaker then shifts to another manner, using the jive-talk that to unthinking whites suggests the happiness of blacks, but the message is clear to the reader.

In the preface to *Montage of a Dream Deferred* (1951) Hughes wrote:

> This poem on contemporary Harlem, like be-bop, is marked by conflicting changes, sudden nuances, sharp and impudent interjections, broken rhythms, and passages sometimes in the manner of the jam session, sometimes the popular song, punctuated by the riffs, runs, breaks, and disc-tortions of the music of a community in transition.

A "Voices and Visions" video cassette of Langston Hughes is available from HarperCollins. An audio cassette of Langston Hughes reading is also available from HarperCollins.

Langston Hughes "Theme for English B" (p. 495)

To our ear, lines 2–5, spoken by the instructor, immediately sound glib and unconvincing. We don't mean to say that we hear hypocrisy, only simple-mindedness, and we hear it for two reasons: (1) the short, rhyming lines sound jingly, like greeting-card verse, and (2) the stated idea' is pretty mindless; after all, to tell a student to let a page "come out of you— / Then, it will be true" is to talk foolishly about the truth and probably about writing. (Shades of Polonuis telling Hamlet to be true to himself. Of course, but what is the self? And what must one do in order to be true to oneself? Many of our students do not share our response on first reading the lines; rather, they take the instructor's lines to be serious thinking. But when they go on and read the next few lines of the poem, they then regard the instructor's lines in a different light.) In an case, as soon as a reader gets to line 6—the first line after the instructor's pep-talk—one hears a far more thoughtful voice: "I wonder if it's that simple." At least this student knows, as his instructor apparently does not know, that "It's not easy to know what is true for you or me / at twenty-two, my age" (16–17).

Lines 21–27 are relatively uncomplicated, as the speaker reveals that his likes and dislikes are pretty much those of any American male, white or black. (If it weren't for the reference to liking a pipe, we would say the likes could be those of women as well as of men.) But lines 28–40 are more complicated; they show the speaker facing the "American" idea (33) that we are all part of each other (Hughes embraced Whiman's vision). There are times when we don't want to be part of each other (34–35), but like it or not, we are connected (36). (Hughes thought it was possible to be a poet of the black experience and also a poet of America, or to be a universal poet.) In line 37 the student begins by saying (we think without conscious verbal irony) that he learns from his teacher. He then goes on (and from here on we cannot suppress the thought that the speaker engages in at least a little conscious irony) to "guess" that the teacher may learn from him, "although you're older—and white— / and somewhat more free." In the end, the student teaches the teacher.

A "Voices and Visions" video cassette of Langston Hughes is available from HarperCollins. An audio cassette of Langston Hughes reading is also available from HarperCollins.

Langston Hughes "Passing" (p. 497)

"To pass," in this context, is for a very light-skinned African-American to be taken as a white. A person who passes has "crossed the line" (11)—crossed the color line and also crossed the line that separates a black neighborhood (e.g. Harlem) from a white neighborhood ("downtown").

The gist of the irony in "Passing" is that by fulfilling their dream (15–16) of "passing," these African-Americans find that they are unhappy. They miss the world in which they grew up. The next poem in the text, Espada's "Tony Went to the Bodega," is also on this motif.

A "Voices and Visions" video cassette of Langston Hughes is available from HarperCollins. An audio cassette of Langston Hughes reading is also available from HarperCollins.

Martin Espada "Tony Went to the Bodega" (p. 497)

The basic irony of course is that Tony leaves the projects (i.e. his Hispanic background) for law school and Boston and (presumably) material success, but, finding that he is dissatisfied, he searches out the projects and a bodega. Why didn't he buy anything? Because it's enough for him to savor "la gente . . . hablando espanol." And now a smaller irony: earlier (15) we are told that as an incipient merchant he engaged in "practicing the grin on customers / he'd seen Makengo grin," but now, luxuriating in the "beautiful" atmosphere of the bodega, he "grinned / his bodega grin"—without any thought of trying to harm customers. Success, we are told at the end, is a return to one's roots.

Edna St. Vincent Millay "Love Is Not All" (p. 499)

Late in the poem a phrase in line 12 ("the memory of this night") identifies the speaker (a lover), the audience (the beloved), and the time (a night of love), but the poem begins drily, even rather pedantically. A somewhat professorial voice delivers a lecture on love, beginning authoritatively with four almost equally stressed monosyllables ("Love is not all"). Then, warming to the subject, the speaker becomes more expansive, with "It is not . . . nor . . . Nor . . . nor . . . And . . . and . . . and . . . and | . . . can not . . . Nor . . . nor," all in the octave. Of course in saying that love cannot do this and that we sense, paradoxically, a praise of love; if we have read a fair amount of love poetry, perhaps we expect the octave to yield to a sestet that will say what love *can* do. But this sestet too begins with apparent objectivity, as if making a concession ("It well may be"). Then, like the octave, the sestet introduces a romantic note while nominally proclaiming realism, although its images are somewhat less exotic (there is nothing like the "floating spar" of line 3, for instance) than the images of the octave. On the other hand, in so far as it introduces a more personal or a more intense note ("the memory of this night"), and reveals that the poem is addressed to the beloved, it is *more* romantic. In any case the sestet comes down to earth, and at the same times reaches a romantic height, in its last line, which consists of two sentences: "It may well be. I do not think I would." The brevity of these two sentences, and the lack of imagery, presumably convey a dry humor that the octave lacks, and at the same time they make an extemely romantic claim. (Surely "I do not think I would" is an understatement; in effect, it is a passionate declaration.) Put it this way: although the octave asserts, for expample, that love is not meat and drink and cannot heal the sick, and the first part of the sestet asserts that the speaker "might" give up the beloved's love in certain extreme circumstances, the understated passion of the conclusion serves to dismiss these assertions as unlikely-indeed, a reader feels, as untrue. Although to the rational mind "love is not all," to the lover it is "all," and a lover here is doing the talking.

Chapter 16

Rhythm and Some Principles of Versification

Paul Fussell, Jr.'s *Poetic Meter and Poetic Form*, rev. ed. (1979), is a readable discussion of metrics. Derek Attridge, *The Rhythms of English Poetry*, though more massive, is also readable and will be of special interest to teachers or students who themselves write poetry. John Hollander's *Rhyme's Reason: A Guide to English Verse* illustrates forms of verse with self-descriptive poems. Also of interest are Harvey Gross, *Sound and Form in Modern Poetry*, and *Mid-Century Poets*, John Ciardi, ed. (which includes useful comments by Wilbur, Roethke, Jarrell, and others). More difficult, and much more specialized, are W. K. Wimsatt, Jr.'s "One Relation of Rhyme to Reason," in his *The Verbal Icon*, and Charles O. Hartman, *Free Verse: An Essay on Prosody*.

We think it is a mistake to spend an hour discussing nothing but meter. It seems to us better to work some discussion of metrics into the daily meetings than to devote a meeting exclusively to this topic. The chapter is meant to provide a summary and a convenient dictionary, but instructors probably will already have made use of some the material. For example, the instructor, in teaching Keats's "On First Looking into Chapman's Homer," may have already mentioned (in commenting on the last line, "Silent upon a peak in Darien") that when a line in a predominatly iambic poem begins with a trochaic adverb or adjective, "we often get [Paul Fussell notes in *Poetic Meter*, p. 65] an effect of sudden quiet." Incidentally, a similar metrical effect occurs in Shakespeare's Sonnet 29 (printed in Chapter 19), where the ninth line (in effect the first line of the sestet begins with a trochee ("Yet in"), marking the start of an energetic rejection of the depressed condition set forth in the octave.

A. E. Housman "Eight O'Clock" (p. 504)

A. E. Housman's "Eight O'Clock" is discussed by Rosenthal and Smith, *Exploring Poetry*, and by Richard Wilbur, "Alfred Edward Housman," *Anniversary Lectures 1959* (Library of Congress), pp. 42–43. Wilbur points out that we learn almost nothing about the condemned man—not even what his crime was—we get only the last half-minute of his life. A clock strikes eight, the conventional hour for executions in England; to the victim, and to the reader, it is a machine that strikes down not merely hours but men. Note the ticking in "clock collected," and the effect of the enjambment in the seventh line, where the clock collects its strength and (after a heavy pause) strikes the hour and ends the man's life.

By the way, the Library of Congress owns a notebook draft of the poem, in which lines 3–4 run thus:

One, two, three, four, on jail and square and people
They dingled down.

Wilbur points out that the deletion of the reference to the jail is a great improvement. "Suspense," he says, "requires that the reason for the man's intent listening should not be divulged until we come to the second stanza. Contrast requires too that the 'morning town,' as it is called in the first stanza, be simply presented as a crowded market place down to which the steeple clock almost gaily 'tosses' its chiming quarters."

William Carlos Williams "The Dance" (p. 505)

Williams's "The Dance" is in free verse, but the abundance of dactyls (as in "Breughel's great picture," "dancers go round," "squeal and the blare") gives it a sort of stamping effect appropriate to sturdy dancers wearing wooden shoes.

A "Voices and Visions" video cassette of William Carlos Williams is available from HarperCollins. An audio cassette of William Carlos Williams reading is available from HarperCollins.

Theodore Roethke "My Papa's Waltz" (p. 506)

Writing of Roethke's "My Papa's Waltz" in *How Does a Poem Mean*, John Ciardi says that the poem seems to lack a "fulcrum" (Ciardi's word for a "point of balance" or point at which there is a twist in the thought, such as "Ah love" in line 29 of "Dover Beach"), but that the fulcrum "occurs after the last line." In his terminology, "The fulcrum exists outside the poem, between the enacted experience and the silence that follows it."

An audio cassette of Theodore Roethke reading is available from HarperCollins.

Gwendolyn Brooks "We Real Cool" (p. 507)

The unusual arrangement of the lines, putting what ordinarily would be the first syllable of the second line at the end of the first line, and so on, of course emphasizes the "we"—and therefore emphasizes the absence of "we" in the final line, which consists only of "Die soon," the "we" having been extinguished. The disappearance of the "we" is especially striking in a poem in which the "we" is so pleased with itself.

By emphasis we don't necessarily mean a heavy stress on the word. An emphasis can be gained by the slightest of pauses (even though the word is not followed by a comma or a shift in tone. In *Report from Part One* Brooks comments (p. 185) on this poem:

> The ending WEs in "We Real Cool" are tiny, wispy, weakly argumentative "Kilroy-is-here" announcements. The boys have no accented sense of themselves, yet they are aware of a semidefined personal importance. Say the "we" softly.

"We" presumably refers to a gang of seven confident pool players, but if seven is traditionally a lucky number, it brings these people no luck. The subtitle allows one to infer that at the Golden Shovel they are digging their own graves.

An audio cassette of Gwendolyn Brooks reading is available from HarperCollins.

Dylan Thomas "Do not go gentle into that good night" (p. 508)

One might at first think that a villanelle is an utterly inappropriate form in which to urge someone to "rage," but in Thomas's "Do not go gentle into that good night," addressed to a man on his deathbed, it proves appropriate because of its ritualistic, incantatory quality. In discussing the poem one can wonder why the night is "good." Probably because death is natural and inevitable (in 4 "dark is right"), but surely too there is a pun on "good night" as an equivalent to death. Further, "the last wave" (7) is probably both a final wave of water (suggesting the last flow of life) and a final gesture of the hand; "Grave men" (13) of course alludes both to serious men and to men near the grave.

Thomas's distinctions between "wise men," "good men," "wild men," and "grave men" have aroused various interpretations. W. Y. Tyndall, in *A Reader's Guide to Dylan Thomas*, suggests that wise men are philosophers, good men are moralists (perhaps Puritans), and wild men are "men of action and lovers of living." (He suggests that the grave men are poets.) M. W. Murphy, in *Explicator* 27, No. 6(February 1970), Item 55, suggests that the wise men who preach wisdom are contrasted with the good men who live a life of wisdom. Both rage against death because they have accomplished nothing, the words of the former and the deeds of the latter having gone unheeded. The wild men are hedonists—who at death discover they have not caught time—and, in contrast to those Dionysian figures, the grave men are ascetic Appollonians who have missed the joys of life but who now, near the grave, see what they have missed. In short, for all men life is incomplete and too brief, and no one should "go gentle into that good night."

We see the poem along these lines: Despite "good night," "at close of day," "the dying of the light"—terms that suggest death is to be welcomed—the speaker urges passionate resistance. The "wise men" (4–7) do not go gently, because they have come to realize that their wise words "had forked no lightning," that is had not given them, or anyone else, enough energetic illumination to accept death. The "Good men" of the third tercet, people who had presumably tried to do good deeds, see that their deeds are "frail." The "Wild men," the poets who "sang" of the vitality of nature, see that their celebrations were really elegies. The "Grave men" (there is, of course, a pun here) are highly serious people who, nearing death and seeing the joy they have lost, also rage. The speaker, then, tells his father, who is "on the sad height" of old age, to "curse" and to "bless" him, to curse presumably because the speaker will go on living in the world that the old man is losing, and to bless him because the speaker has instructed the father on how to die properly. "Curse, bless," then leads to "fierce tears."

If you are lucky, a pedantic student may ask you why "gentle" rather than "gently" is used. One answer is that "gentle" is an adjective referring to the understood subject "you," not an adverb modifying "go." In this view, Thomas is describing a condition he hopes his father will not be in, rather than describing the father's method of going. This point is clear if for "gentle" one substitutes, say, "ignorant." On the other hand, one can argue that "gentle" is not necessarily an adjective. Some authorities point out that verbs of motion and sensation take adverbs that do not end in *ly*: cf. "Go slow," "Think fast," "Sleep sound," and "Feel good."

An audio cassette of Dylan Thomas reading is available from HarperCollins.

Robert Francis "The Pitcher" (p. 509)

In presenting Robert Francis's "The Pitcher" to the class, ask if anyone knows the etymology of "eccentric" (cf. "eccentricity" in line 1). You may have to provide the answer yourself, but in any case you can explore with the students the ways in which a pitcher's art is "eccentricity."

Note that the first four stanzas do not rhyme, but they miss by only enough to "avoid the obvious" and to "vary the avoidance." "Aim" in line 1 comes as close as a word can to rhyming with "aim" in line 2, but the line drops off and misses by the merest fraction of a foot. And if obvious / avoidance and comphrehended / misunderstood aren't strictly consonant, they are eccentrically so. No question about consonance or slant rhyme in "wild / willed." But perfect rhyme is reserved for the last couplet, which everyone (except the by now paralyzed batter) can see is a perfect strike. The rhyme scheme, the econmical couplets, the tense but erratic repetition in sentence structure, the eccentric placement of caesuras (in 4 and 9), all of course contribute to the poem's wit in imitating the performance it describes.

We have found that students enjoy discussing the devices in the poem, one perception leading to another. But line 6 ("Throws to be misunderstood") and line 10 ("understood too late") can cause trouble. Is the poet saying that poets are wilfully obscure? Or that they like to challenge readers so that readers can have the pleasure of (after a little thought) enjoying complexity?

X. J. Kennedy "Nothing in Heaven Functions as It Ought" (p. 516)

The poem is a Petrarchan sonnet, with the traditional contrast between the octave and the sestet. Kennedy's contrast of heaven and hell is not surprising, then, but in the contrasting rhymes and versification he play an unexpected game. The off-rhymes and the hypermetric lines of the octave of course imitate the statement of the octave (things are askew), and the mechanical perfection of the sestet imitates the sestet's statement ("Hell hath no freewheeling part").

Kennedy has let us see an earlier version of the poem. You may want to invite students to compare the following version with the one in their text.

Nothing in Heaven Functions as It Ought (an early version)

Nothing in Heaven functions as it ought:
Peter snaps off a key stuck in the lock,
And his creaky gates keep crowing like a cock
(No hush of oily gold as Milton thought).

Gangs of the matryred innocents keep whoofing
The nimbus off the Venerable Bede
Like that of an old dandelion in seed.
The beatific choir take fits of coughing.

But Hell, sweet Hell, holds no unsteady part,
Nothing to rust nor rip nor lose its place.
Ask anyone: How did you come to be here?—
And he will slot a quarter into his face
And there will be a click and wheels will whir
And out will pop a neat brief of his case.

Walt Whitman "When I Heard the Learn'd Astronomer" (p. 518)

In our discussion of the poem, we emphasize the division of the one-sentence poem into two units of four lines each, but we concentrate our discussion on the length of the lines, and we say little about the thematic contrasts in the two parts; e.g., the speaker indoors versus the speaker out of doors, the speaker with other human beings versus alone in the presence of nature, the speaker amidst noise (the lecture, the applause) versus the speaker surrounded by silence, the speaker sitting and passive verses the speaker moving and active (though the activity seems almost effortless: "rising and gliding," "wander'd off," "Look'd up").

Notice too that we discuss the poem as an example of free verse—which it is— but we also mention that the final line of the poem is iambic pentameter. Moreover, though of course one does not want to read this line mechanically, stressing every second syllable, it is appropriate here (as rarely elsewhere in poetry) to stress the prepositions ("up" and "at") as well as the more obviously important words, "silence" and "stars."

A "Voices and Visions " video cassette of Walt Whitman is available from HarperCollins.

Carolyn Forche "The Colonel" (p. 519)

"The Colonel" comes from a book of poems. You may want to talk about the rather undefined genre of the prose-poem. A prose-poem looks like prose but is marked by a strong rhythm (often gained by repetition of grammatical contructions) and sometimes by adundant imagery. (The idea is that the chief characteristics of poetry are rhythm and imagery, and so a short piece of prose with these features can be called a prose-poem.) Having said this, we must add that we don't think there is much point in worrying much about whether "The Colonel" is poetry or prose.

Much of "The Colonel" probably is literally true. During one of her stays in El Salvador Forché may indeed have visited a colonel, and he may have said and done exactly what this colonel says and does. Until we are told that the ear "came alive" when dropped into the glass of water, there is nothing unbelievable in "The Colonel," partly, of course, because television has informed us that atrocities are committed daily.

Forché's first sentence ("What you have heard is true") suggests that the speaker is addressing someone who has just said, "I heard that you visited Colonel—. Did you really? What was it Like?" We get details about what seems to be a comfortable bourgeois existence ("Daily papers, pet dogs") and also some menacing details ("a pistol on the cushion beside him," "broken bottles were embedded in the walls"), all told in the same flat, matter-of-fact voice. The sixth sentence uses a metaphor, ("The moon swung bare on its black cord over the house"), but even journalists are allowed to use an occasional metaphonr , and a reader probably does not think twice about Forché's metaphor here, except perhaps to notice that it uses the same structure ("The moon swung bare . . . ") as the previous, factual sentences ("I was," "His wife carried," "His dauther filed," "There were"). Again, for the most part the language is flat; when the speaker next uses a metaphor (the ears are "like dried peach halves") she (or he) flatly apologizes for this flight of fancy: "There is no other way to say this." But the next to last sentece takes us into a metaphorical (or mysterious) world:"Some of the ears on the floor caught this scrap of his voice."

Much of the power of "The Colonel" comes from the contrast between the picture of the colonel's bourgeois private life (pets, television, lamb, wine, etc.) and his brutal public life, a contrast which Forche emphasizes by *not* commenting on (i.e. by allowing the reader to make the comment). The piece is masterful in what it doesn't say. The colonel asks how the visitor "enjoyed the country," but we don't hear the repsonse. We can, however, guess it by what follows: "There was some talk then of how difficult it had become to govern." Presumably the colonel becomes annoyed with the visitor's comments, though at first we aren't told this in so many words. Instead we are told what the colonel did (he got a sack of ears, dumped them on table, shook one in the faces of his guests, dropped it in a glass of water. Then we hear him: "I am tired of fooling around . . . . As for the rights of anyone, tell your people they can go fuck themselves." Irked but (as we see it) enormously confident, he says of the severed ears, "Something for your poetry, no?" Students might be invited to comment on the tone the colonel uses here. Is he complacent, wry, naive, or what?

Students might also be invited to comment on the last two sentences of "The Colonel." Does the next-to-last sentence indicate (let's say symbolically) that the oppressed people of the country know what is going on, and will ultimately triumph? Does the last sentence ("Some of the ears on the floor were pressed to the ground") mean that (1) some of the ears were pressed, presumably by being stood on, and (2) the dead were listening (and presumably waiting to be avenged)?

Chapter 18

Two Poets in Depth:
Emily Dickinson and Robert Frost

Emily Dickinson

Althought it is now somewhat dated, there is a useful guide to Dickinson criticism: *The Poems of Emily Dickinson: An Annotated Guide to Commentary Published in English, 1890–1977*, ed. Joseph Duchac (1979).

A "Voices and Visions" video cassette of Emily Dickinson is available from HarperCollins.

Emily Dickinson "These are the days when birds come back" (p. 525)

The time is Indian summer, that is, a day that seems summery but is late, hence it is a sort of sophistry of mistake or fraud. (By the way, it is not true that birds, deceived by Indian summer, return.) Lines 10–11 introduce religious imagery ("ranks of seed their witness bear," and the pun on alter-altar, which suggests a communion scene), anticipating the more overt religious images in the next two stanzas.

Some readers take the poem to suggest that just as the season can be deceptive, communion too can be deceptive or illusory. Other readers see the poem moving the other way: from the illusory season, which evokes nostalgic thoughts, to the real or firm joys of Christian immortatlity. Charles Anderson, in *Emily Dickinson's Poetry*, gives a substantive analysis. He suggests that the season's ambiguity provokes the question, "Does it symbolize death or immortality," and he answers that Dickinson does not give an answer but gives us "warning images poised in ironic tension."

Topics for Discussion and Writing

1. What season or weather is being talked about? Why does Dickinson use the words "mistake" (line 6) and "fraud" and "cheat" (line 7)?
2. Explain the pun on "altered" in line 11.
3. Take the first three stanzas as a group and summarize them in a sentence or two. Do the same for the last three. Then, in a sentence or two, state the relationship between these two halves of the poem.
4. Why "a child" in line 15?

Emily Dickinson "Wild Nights—Wild Nights!" (p. 526)

A reader tends to think of Emily Dickinson as the speaker of "Wild Nights" and therefore is perhaps shocked by the last stanza, in which a woman apparently takes on the phallic role of a ship mooring in a harbor. But perhaps the poem is spoken by a man. (In one of her poems the speaker says, "I am a rural man," in another the speaker refers to "my brown cigar," and in "A narrow fellow in the Grass"—included in our text—the speaker identifies himself as male in lines 11–12.)

Possibly we are superficial readers, but we don't attach to "Might I but moor–Tonight– / In Thee!" the strong sexual associations that several critics have commented on. Some but not all assume that the image suggests male penetration. Albert Gelpi, in *The Tenth Muse* (1975), pp. 242–43 says that "the sexual roles are blurred." He adds, "Something more subtle than an inversion of sexual roles is at work here, and the point is not that Emily Dickinson was homosexual, as Rebecca Patterson and John Cody have argued," but he doesn't clarify the point. (Patterson's disscussion is in *The Riddle of Emily Dickinson* [1951]; Cody's is in *After Great Pain* [1971].) Paula Bennett, in *My Life a Loaded Gun* (1986), drawing on a discussion by L. Faderman, seems to reject the idea of a male speaker. She says that "the imagery of the poem, with its emphasis on entering rather than being entered, is . . . far more appropriate for one woman's experience of another than for a woman's experience with a man" (p.61). Christine Miller too insists that the speaker is a woman. In *Feminist Critics Read Emily Dickinson*, ed. Suzanne Juhasz (1983), Miller says that the speaker is a woman but she adds that "The woman is the ship that seeks to 'moor—Tonight— / In Thee!'—an activity more representative of male than of female social behavior" (p.137). Our own simple view: a reader need not find an image of penetration in "moor"; rather, we think that in this poem the word suggests a longed-for security.

Is the poem sentimental? We don't think so, chiefly because it is brief, controlled, and (in "Tonight") it does not claim too much.

In *Explicator* 25 (January 1967), Item 44, James T. Connelly pointed out that in letter No. 332 (T. H. Johnson's edition, *Letters*, II, 463), Dickinson writes, "Dying is a wild Night and a new road." Looking at the poem in the light of this letter, Connelly concludes that "to die is to experience a wild night on a turbulent, surging sea. Only by plunging into this uncharted sea of Death can one at last reach the port of rest and calm. The poem, thus considered, is an apparent death wish: a personification and apostrophe to Death whose presence and company are paradoxically exhilerating luxury." We are unconvinced, partly because the poem speaks not of "a wild night" but of "Wild Nights," and we cannot see how the plural form lends itself to this reading.

Topics for Discussion and Writing

1. Probably "wild nights" refers chiefly to a storm outside of the lovers' room, but it can of course also describe their love. "Luxury" (from the Latin luxuria, which meant "excess" or "extravagance") in line 4 probably retains some of the meaning that it first had when it entered into English, "lust" or sensual enjoyment. What does the second stanza say about the nature of their love? How does the third stanza modify the idea?
2. What makes this lyric lyrical?
3. Do you think that the poem is sentimental? Explain.

Emily Dickinson "There's a certain Slant of light" (p. 526)

The poem seems difficult to us, and any questions about it therefore lead to difficulties, but perhaps our fifth question, below, on the rhyme scheme, is fairly straightforward. Some students may recognize that metrically the poem is close to the "common meter" or "common measure" (abbreviated C. M. in hymnals) of a hymn. (C. M. can be defined thus: stanzas of four lines, the first and third in iambic tetrameter, the second and fourth in iambic trimeter, rhyming *abcb* or *abab*.) In fact no two stanzas in the poem are metrically identical (if we count the syllables of the first line of each stanza, we find seven, six or seven, six, and eight), but despite such variations, the meter and especially the rhyme scheme (*abab*) seem regular. The second and fourth lines of each stanza have five syllables, and these lines end with exact rhymes, though the first and third lines of each stanza rely less on rhyme than on consonance. The regularity of the rhyme scheme, especially in such short lines, is something of a tour de force, and (because it suggests a highly ordered world) it might seem more suited to a neat little poem with a comforting theme than to the poem Dickinson has given us. Further, since the meter and some of the rhymes might occur in a hymn ("Despair," "Air"; "breath," "Death"), there is an ironic contrast between the form (a hymn, that is, a poem celebrating God's goodness) and the content of the poem.

But what, in fact, is the content? And what is the "certain Slant of Light" that, perceived on "Winter Afternoons," makes "Shadows— hold their breath"? No two readers seem to agree on the details, but perhaps we can offer a few inoffensive comments. Like Hopkins (cf. "God's Grandeur" [p.582]), Dickinson sees a divinity behind phenomena, but her nature-suffused-with-divinity differed greatly from his. "There's a certain slant of light" begins with "light," which might suggest life and eternal happiness (think of Newman's "Lead, kindly light"), but soon becomes darker, and ends with "the look of Death," The ending is not really a surprise, however, since the "certain Slant of light" is seen on "Winter Afternoons," that is a season when the year may be said to be dying and when light is relatively scarce, and a time of day when light will soon disappear.

This "Slant of light," we are told, "Oppresses, like the Heft / Of Cathedral Tunes." Surely "Oppresses" comes as a surprise. Probably most of us think that cathedral tunes (even funeral music) exalt the spirit rather than oppress it, and so most of us might have written something like, "That elevates, like the Lift / Of Cathedral Tunes." But of course most of us couldn't have written even this, since we would not have the imagination to think of light in aural terms ("Tunes") and in terms of weight ("Heft").

In any case, a certain appearance in nature induces in the poet a sensation that requires such words as "Oppresses," "Hurt," "Despair," "affliction," "Shadows," and "Death." These words might of course appear in a traditional hymn, but, if so, the hymn would move toward the idea that God helps us to triumph over these adversities. Dickinson, however, apparently is saying that on these wintry afternoons the slant of light shining in the air gives us a "Heavenly Hurt," that is it moves us to a painful consciousness of God and nature, and to a sense of isolation. In the final stanza presumably we are back to the "Winter Afternoons" of the first. Projecting herself into the surrounding world, the speaker personifies nature: "the Landscape listens"—but hears nothing further. (By the way, "listens" to or for what? A "Slant of light"? Again, as in the earlier comparison of light to "Cathedral Tunes," Dickinson uses synethesia.) If during the moment when one perceives the light or "listens" there is no further insight, and certainly no amerlioration of the "Heavenly Hurt," when "it goes" there is an intensification of despair, since one is left with "the look of Death." Is Dickinson evoking an image of the remote stare of a corpse? And is she suggesting that this stare corresponds to the paralyzed mental condition of those who have perceived the "Slant of light"?

Earlier in this brief discussion we contrasted Hopkins with Dickinson. But, as Charles R. Anderson points out in *Emily Dickinson's Poetry*, there is a connection between the two. The perception in this poem resembles Margaret's perception in "Spring and Fall" (p. 443), where the child senses "the blight man was born for."

Topics for Discussion and Writing

1. In the first stanza, what kind or kinds of music does "Cathedral Tunes" suggest? In what ways might they (and the light to which they are compared) be oppressive?

2. In the second stanza, the effect on us of the light is further described. Try to paraphrase Dickinson's lines, or interpret them. Compare your paraphrase or interpretation with that of a classmate or someone else who has read the poem. Are your interpretations similar? If not, can you account for some of the differences?

3. In the third stanza, how would you interpret "None may teach it"? Is the idea "No one can instruct (or tame) the light to be different"? Or "No one can teach us what we learn from the light"? Or do you have a different reading of this line?

4. "Death" is the last word of the poem. Rereading the poem, how early (and in what words or images) is "death" suggested or foreshadowed?

5. Try to describe the effect of the rhyme scheme. Then, a more difficult business, try to describe the effect of the rhyme scheme. Does it work with or against the theme, or meaning, of the poem?

6. What is the relationship in the poem between the light as one might experience it in New England on a winter afternoon and the experience of despair? To put it crudely, does the light itself cause despair, or does Dickinson see the light as an image or metaphor for human despair? And how is despair related to death?

7. Overall, how would you describe the tone of the poem? Anguished? Serene? Resigned?

Emily Dickinson "The Soul selects her own Society" (p. 528)

Richard Sewall, in *Voices and Visions*, ed. Helen Vendler, calls this poem Dickinson's "most famous 'choice' poem" (p.72), and indeed he leaves the choice of its subject to the reader; it may be read as concerned with the choice of a lover, or a friend, or a kind of spiritual life.

Even without being certain of the subject of this poem, one can sense how the form contributes to meaning. The even-numbered lines are shorter than the odd-numbered lines that precede them, and each even-numbered line ends emphatically with a monosyllable, thus contrasting with the previous lines with their feminine endings. And in the final stanza the short lines are even shorter (a mere two syllables each); the tight-lipped speaker leaves no doubt about the determination of the soul which has made a choice and now rejects all other suppliants, however noble. But details remain uncertain, and critics have not been so tight-lipped.

W. C. Jumper, in *Explicator* 29(September 1970), Item 5, suggests that the soul (feminine becuase Latin *anima* is feminine) has a "divine Majority" because Thoreau had said the *The Duty of Civil Disobedience* that "any man more right than his neighbors, consitstutes a majority of one." Jumper points out that the second stanza makes ironic use of two folktales, "The Querulous Princess" and "The King and the Beggar Maid." In the first of these tales, the wooers arrive in chariots, but the winner of her hand is he who will bow his head to enter through a low gate; in the second tale, the king kneels before a beggar maid and wins her. In "The Soul selects" the soul rejects two such humble wooers, having already made her choice.

The word "Valves" in the penultimate lines has especially disconcerted critics. *Explicator* 25(April 1967), Item 8, suggests that it is connected with "Door" in line 2 via two old meanings: (1)the leaves of a double or folding door and (2) the halves of the shell of a bivalve such as an oyster, which closes its valve when disturbed and thus remains "like Stone." Sewall takes "Valves" to refer to a double door and says that "the line simply dramatizes further the action of line two" (p.73).

Finally, we end with a remark by Anthony Hecht, printed in *Voices and Visions*, p.62:

"The Soul selects her own Society" has always been understood as a covert declaration of love. And it might be that. I suspect myself that it is not. It has to do, certainly, with the affinities one has with a very few people and how the soul, or anybody, makes exclusions and inclusions that are quite arbitrary; but I think this is meant to parallel the question of the Elect of God. So the soul in choosing its friends does very much what the deity does in discriminating between the saved and the damned. There is something very frightening about that; when we think of how ruthless we are about who our friends and enemies might be, at least inwardly, we are performing . . . the same act that God performs when he cuts us from all hope of salvation. The poem, I think, hovers on the brink of those curious mysteries which are interior and psychological, but are also exterior and theological.

Emily Dickinson "I heard a Fly buzz—when I died" (p. 528)

Dickinson's poem juxtaposes some conventional religious images ("that last Onset," "the King," "What portion of me be / Assignable") with the buzz of a fly, rather than with, say, choirs of angels, and so, as Charles R. Anderson suggests in *Emily Dickinson's Poetry*, "The King witnessed in his power is physical death, not God." Should one go further, and suggest that Death-as-fly equals putrefaction?

The last line of the poem ("I could not see to see") especially has attracted attention. Gerhard Friedrich (*Explicator* 13[April 1955], Item 35) paraphrases it thus: "Waylaid by irrelevant, tangible, finite objects of little importance, I was no longer capable of that deeper perception which would clearly reveal to me the infinite spiritual reality." The fall into skepticism, Friedrich says, demonstrates the inadequacy of the earlier pseudostoicism. John Ciardi took issue with this interpretation and suggested (*Explicator* 14[January 1956], Item 22) that the fly is "the last kiss of the world, the last buzz from life," reflecting "Emily's tremendous attachment to the physcial world"; the final line, in his view, simply means, "And then there was no more of me, and nothing to see with."

The Todd-Higginson editions gave "round my form" for "in the Room" (2), "The eyes beside" for "The Eyes around" (5), "sure" for "firm" (6), "witnessed in his power" for "witnessed—in the Room" (8), and "What portion of me I / Could make assignable—and then" for "What portion of me be / Assignable—and then it was" (10–11). It is worth discussing with students the differences these changes make.

Emily Dickinson "This World is not Conclusion" (p. 529)

First, a brief comment about Dickinson and religion. She clearly was not fond of the patriarchal deity of the Hebrew Bible. "Burglar! Banker—Father," she wrote of this deity, and in a note to Thomas Wentworth Higginson she says that the members of her family, except for herself, "address an Eclipse every morning—whom they call their Father." She seems to have been amused by preachers. She said, of one, that "the subject of perdition seemed to please him somehow."

Still, in the words of Charles R. Anderson, in *Emily Dickinson's Poetry* (1960), no reader can doubt that she "faced creation with a primal sense of awe" (p.17). And, as Anderson and everyone else points out, the Bible was "one of her chief sources of imagery" (p.18).

Now for "This World is not Conclusion." The first two lines sound like the beginning of a hymn ("Conclusion" presumably means "ending," not "inference drawn"). The poem is not divided into stanzas by white spaces, but clearly it moves in units of four lines. The first four lines assert that although a world beyond our own is (like music) invisible, we strongly sense it. "Positive" in line 4 perhaps refers both to our conviction that it exists and also to its goodness.

Line 5 introduces a complication: "It beckons, and it baffles." Although the rest of the stanza (i.e. line 6–8) seems to affirm the initial confident (positive) assertion, it also raises doubts in the reader, since it dismisses "Philosophy" and "Sagacity," and it characterizes life (or is it death?) as a "Riddle."

Lines 9–12 seem more positive. They remind us that although human experience "puzzles Scholars," martyrs have given their lives to affirm religious faith, to affirm (in the words of the first line) that "This World is not Conclusion."

Lines 13–16, however, present "Faith" in a somewhat less heroic light: "Faith slips—and laughs, and rallies—Blushes, if any see." Surely this is in a much lower key than "Men have borne / Contempt of Generations," a couple of lines earlier. The enduring power of faith is still affirmed (Faith "rallies"), but in "slips" and "Blushes, if any see" we seem to be presented with a rather adolescent world. Further, the last two lines of the stanza (15–16) similarly diminish Faith, showing it clutching after "a twig of Evidence," and inquiring of a "Vane" (a weathervane, a most unstable thing). Perhaps, too, "Vane" hints at emptiness, insubstantiality (Latin, *vanitas*).

The final four lines at first seem more affirmative. They begin with a strong assertion that calls up a picture of a vigorously gesticulating preacher, and they reintroduce imagery of music (now "Strong Hallelujahs roll"), but these lines at the same time are unconvincing, or, rather, almost comic. A reader may find in the preacher's abundant gestures a lack of genuine conviction. (One thinks of the marginal note in the politician's speech: "Argument weak; shout here.") The "Strong Hallelujahs" may strike a reader as less potent than the "Music" that was "positive" in lines 3–4. Are the gestures and the hallelujahs "Narcotics" that don't quite work, that is that don't quite convince us of the pious forthright assertion that "This World is not Conclusion"? Yet the poem ends with the word "soul"; if "Much Gesture, from the Pulpit" reveals a preacher who is not wholly convincing, we nevertheless cannot therefore lapse into the belief that this world is conclusion. Something "nibbles at the soul."

Topics for Discussion and Writing

1. Given the context of the first two lines, what do you think "Conclusion" means in the first line?
2. Although white spaces here are not used to divide the poem into stanzas, the poem seems to be constructed in units of four lines each. Summarize each four-line unit in a sentence or two.
3. Compare your summaries with those of a classmate. If you substantially disagree, reread the poem to see if, on reflection, one or the other of you seems in closer touch with the poem. Or does the poem (or some part of it) allow for two very different interpretation?
4. In the first four lines the speaker seems (to use a word from line 4) quite "positive." Do some or all of the following stanzas seem less positive? If so, which—and what makes you say so?
5. How do you understand "Much Gesture, from the Pulpit" (line 17)? Would you agree with a reader who said that the line suggests a *lack* of deep conviction? Explain.

Emily Dickinson "I like to see it lap the Miles" (p. 529)

Whoever first called a train an "iron horse" had the gift of the poet, but Dickinson goes much further in "I like to see it lap the Miles," catching the beast's energy and (in the last three lines) its docility. She is interested in the sound and sight of the train (these are playfully set forth with lots of alliteration, beginning with "like . . . lap . . . lick"), but she displays no interest in the train as a symbol of progress, no interest in people or goods getting anywhere. Indeed, her train ends up —for all its rushing and roaring— "At its own stable door."

Charles Dickens, in *American Notes* (1842), describes a train ride. You may want to ask your students to compare Dickens's account with Dickinson's.

On it whirls headlong, dives through the woods again, emerges in the light, clatters over frail arches, rumbles upon the heavy ground, shoots beneath a wooden bridge,which intercepts the light for a second like a wink, suddenly awakens all the slumbering echoes in the main street of a large town, and dashes on haphazard pellmell, neck-or-nothing, down the middle of the road. There—with mechanics working at their trades, and people leaning from their doors and windows, and boys flying kites and playing marbles, and men smoking, and women talking, and children crawling, and pigs burrowing, and unaccustomed horses plunging and rearing, close to the very rails—there—on, on, on—tears the mad dragon of an engine with its train of cars; scattering in all directions a shower of buring sparks from its wood fire; screeching, hissing, yelling, panting; until at last the thirsty monster stops beneath a covered way to drink, the people cluster around, and you have time to breathe again.

Emily Dickinson "Because I could not stop for Death" (p. 530)

In Dickinson's "Because I could not stop for Death," the fact that a grave is suggested in line 17–20 eludes many students; the reference to the grave contributes to toughening the poem. This stanza, by the way, is a good example of the closeness of some metaphors to riddles, a point worth discussing in class. Allen Tate, in a famous essay, praised the poem because "we are not told what to think." J. J. McGann, rightly taking issue with Tate, points out that "the message about the benevolence of Death is plain enough." McGann also takes issue with the widespread idea that in this poem death is a "gentlemanly suitor." He argues, on the contrary, that since the penultimate line speaks of "horses," Dickinson is talking not about a suitor—who would drive only one horse—but about an undertaker, who is driving a hearse. (McGann's essay originally appeared in *New Literary History*, 12 [1981], and is reprinted in *Literary Theories in Praxis*, [1987], ed. Shirley F. Staton.) Selections from a number of commentaries (including, among others, Allen Tate, *Reactionary Essays*; Yvor Winters, *In Defense of Reason*; and Richard Chase, *Emily Dickinson*) are collected in *Fourteen by Emily Dickinson*, ed. Thomas M. Davis. See also Clark Griffith, *The Long Shadow*, pp. 128–134, and Charles R. Anderson, *Emily Dickinson's Poetry*, pp. 241–246.

Topics for Discussion and Writing

1. Characterize death as it appears in line 1–8.
2. What is the significance of the details and their arrangement in the third stanza? Why "strove" rather than "played" (line 9)?

What meaning does "Ring" (line 10) have? Is "Gazing Grain" better than "Golden Grain"?

3. The "House" in the fifth stanza is a sort of riddle. What is the answer? Does this stanza introduce an aspect of death not present—or present only very faintly—in the rest of the poem? Explain.

4. Evaluate this statement about the poem (from Yvor Winters's *In Defense of Reason*): "In so far as it concentrates on the life that is being left behind, it is wholly successful; in so far as it attempts to experience the death to come, it is fraudulent, however exquisitely."

Emily Dickinson "A narrow Fellow in the Grass" (p. 531)

"Fellow" (and the pronouns "Him" and "His," rather than "it" and "its") and "rides" in the first stanza help to assimilate the snake to the human world, as does "comb" in the second stanza. In these two stanzas there is some emphasis on the unexpectedness of the snake. He is "sudden" but not menacing. And in the beginning of the third stanza he seems almost an eccentric neighbor: "He likes a Boggy Acre." In the fouth stanza the reference to a whiplash introduces a more threatening note; "Nature's People" in the next stanza seems to bring us back to the comfortable world of the first stanza, but with the last line of the poem ("Zero at the Bone") there is comminicated a terror that indicates a response to the snake as supremely hostile. (The snake is, after all, a traditional image of man's satanic enenmy.) The contrast between "a transport / Of cordiality" (which carries a sense of warmth, that is, warm-heartedness, via *cor*, heart) and the coldness of "Zero at the Bone" could hardly be greater.

Karl Keller, in a provocative book about Emily Dickinson, *The Only Kangaroo among the Beauty*, says (p. 268) that the poem "manages to make Freud trite." Keller says that Dickinson's "tighter breathing / And Zero at the Bone" indicate that "she finds her genitals alarmed," and that "she is shocked and attracted by the male erection ('His notice sudden is')." He patently misreads the poem when he says, "Her own sexual desires are, she says, very strongly aroused: she feels 'a transport / Of cordiality.'" But of course the poem says that for "Several of Nature's People" she feels that transport, "*but*" for this fellow she feels "Zero at the Bone."

Dickinson complained when the third line was printed with a

question mark at its end. Apparently "did you not" is less a question than a tagged-on conversational filler like "you know," and a question mark causes too long and too strong a pause. Yet another point about the punctuation: Lines 11–16, describing the boy (the speaker is a boy, not Emily Dickinson), stooping to pick up what he thinks is a whip-lash but what is in fact a snake that disappears, are unpunctuated (until the end of 16), and thus suggestive of the speed of the event.

Topics for Discussion and Writing

1. Many of Dickinson's peoms are rather like riddles. In this poem who or what is the "narrow Fellow in the Grass"?
2. How would you describe the speaker of this poem? What relationship does the speaker seem to establish with the reader?
3. In lines 17–20 Dickinson refers to "Several of Nature's People." Who or what might these be, in Amherst in the later nineteenth century? Check "transport" and "cordiality" in a dictionary, to see which meanings you think are especially relevant.
4. Why does Dickinson speak of the snake as "him" rather than "it," and of the animal world as "Nature's creatures"?
5. If you have read Lawrence's "Snake" (page 473), write an essay of 500 words indicating the *purposes* of Dickinson and Lawrence. Include a discussion of how effectively each poet fulfills these purposes.

Emily Dickinson "Further in Summer than the Birds" (p. 531)

We take the opening words, "Further in Summer," to mean that the crickets chirping in the grass are more advanced in their span of life (nearer to autumn and winter and death) than are birds. Moreover, their song is heard later in summer, and thus they remind us of the imminent end of the season. The song is pathetic, partly because the creatures are so small but probably chiefly because it reminds us of the passing of time and losses and of our consequent increasing loneliness. The final stanza provides another look. The first two lines of this stanza may mean that no disturbance as yet diminishes the beauty (no grace has been remitted, there is no "Furrow on the Glow" of summer), but we are somewhat inclined to take them as meaning: "Do not give back (reject) grace; the moment is undisturbed, that is, continue to experience the blessedness of the moment. If this reading is right,

"Yet" in the next line does not quite mean "but"; rather it means (we think) "still," "even so."

Charles Anderson discusses the poem at length in *Emily Dickinson's Poetry.*

Topics for Discussion and Writing

1. Paraphrase—put into your own words—the first line.
2. What is the "minor Nation," whose pathetic sounds (here said to be a celebration of the Mass) are heard in the grass?
3. In this context, what does "Grace" (line 6) mean?
4. Does "Enlarging Loneliness" (line 8) mean "making loneliness greater," or does it mean "setting loneliness free," that is, releasing us from loneliness?
5. Is Dickinson saying that nature teaches us that all of creation shares in God's grace? Or is she saying—especially in the last stanza—that we must give up our imagined idea that Christian grace is found in nature? Or is she perhaps saying something else?

Emily Dickinson "Tell All the Truth but tell it slant" (p. 532)

A student once brought up, by way of comparison, Polonius's

> And thus do we of wisdom and of reach,
> With windlasses and with assays of bias,
> By indirections find directions out. (*Hamlet* 2.1.64–66)

The last line especially seems to have affinities with Dickinson's first line, but the thrust of the two passages is fundamentally different. Polonius, worried about the behavior of his son Laertes, is sending Reynaldo to find out if Laertes has been misbehaving. He tells Reynaldo to slander Laertes, to see if Reynaldo's hearers deny the charges. Polonius thus is advocating deceit, whereas Dickinson is saying that because truth is too bright for our "infirm Delight," if we want to communicate, we must use indirection.

For Dickinson, the truth *is* splendid—it does "dazzle"—but we can perceive this splendor after we have become accustomed to it, and we arrive at this condition "gradually."

The word "slant" nicely plays against "Circuit," and on rereading it may be taken to anticipate the word "lightning," which is often represented by a diagonal line. In any case, one of the charms of the poem is the homely comparison in lines 5–6, where the need to tell the truth "slant" is compared to offering "explanation kind" to children who presumably have been frightened by lightning. Telling the truth "slant" or "in Circuit" is not an attempt to deceive, but to be "kind."

An extant draft of the poem shows that Dickinson comtemplated two possible changes, *bold* for bright in line 3, and *moderately* for gradually in line 7.

Emily Dickinson "A Route of Evanescence" (p. 532)

An old discussion, Grover Smith's in *Explicator* 8 (1949–50) item 54, seems to us to remain the most interesting. Snith points out that the phrase "A route of Evanescence" is "a metonymy equating the bird with its own path across the field of vision." Smith goes on:

> The visual effect is the converse of that obtained photgraphically by multiple rapid-exposures of a moving object on a single plate; here the poet describes not the simultaneous presence but the simultaneous vanishing of the bird at every point . . .

Speaking of the "revolving Wheel"—the wheel-like optical illusion produced by the rapid up and down motion of the wings—Smith points out that Dickinson's reference to the iridescent color on the bird's head and back uses synesthesia ("A Resonance of Emerald"). He also says that Dickinson uses onomatopoeia in this line and the next line ("A Rush of Cochineal"), though not every reader will agree that onomatopoeia occurs in "A Resonance of Emerald."

Equally challenging is his assertion that in the final two lines beside the image of the bird "is implicit that of a speeding railway train, the mail and express, and also that of the more common kind of mail— a letter . . . . A train travels upon a 'route', it is borne along by many a 'revolving wheel,' its sound is a 'resonance' and a 'rush,' and on it people 'ride.'" We confess that we don't see this image in the lines, and Smith himself is apparently a bit uneasy with the idea, since he himself points out that of course no train crosses the sea from Tunis, and no "easy Morning's Ride" will get us there.

Other points: the words Emerald, Cochineal (associated chiefly with North Africa), and Tunis bring the precious and the remote into the familiar garden. (By the way, we have been told that when humming birds leave New England they go to Mexico, not to North Africa.)

One of Dickinson's copies of the poem, according to Millicent Todd Bingham's *Ancestor's Brocades"* (1945), p. 37, included several alternatives for "revolving" in line 4: *delusive, dissembling, dissolving,* and *renewing.* (The present location of this manuscript is not known.)

Topics for Discussion and Writing

1. Dickinson in her letters refers to this poem as " A Humming Bird."
    What is she getting at in line 2?
2. Dickinson uses synesthesia (the description of a sensory impres-
    sion in terms of another sense) in "A Resonance of Emerald."
    What is the point of describing a color ("Emerald") in terms of
    sound ("Resonance")?
3. In line 7, why is "Tunis" preferable to, say "New York"?

Emily Dickinson "Those—dying, then" (p. 533)

The faith of her ancestors is, Dickinson apparently feels, no longer possible, but it serves to enrich behavior. An ignis fatuus (a phosphorescent light—caused by gases emitted by rotting organic matter—that hovers over a swamp) presumably resembles, how-ever weakly, the beautiful flames of heaven and the demonic flames of hell. It is only a will-o'-the-wisp, but at least it is *some*thing. The image of amputation is shocking, but it can be paralleled in the Bible, for example by "And if thy right eye offend thee, pluck it out, and cast it from thee . . . . and if thy right hand offend thee, cut it off, and cast it from thee" (Matthew 5:29–30)

Topics for Discussion and Writing

1. In a sentence or two, state the point of the poem.
2. Is the image in line 4 in poor taste? Explain.
3. What is an *ignis fatuus*? In what ways does it connect visually with
    traditional images of hell and heaven?

Emily Dickinson "Apparently with no surprise" (p. 533)

As in most nature poems, nature is humanized—but with a difference. If a flower is Wordsworthian in being at "play," the frost is not: It is a "blonde Assassin"; blond because it is white, and the fact that this color is usually associated with innocence makes the personification the more shocking. (See Frost's white spider in "Design," text 544). Note, too, that "at its play" can go with the frost as well as with the flower, in which case the frost is only playing, but happens to play too vigorously with a destructive (but unlamented) result. And still more shocking, at least on first reading, is the fact that God (like the sun) approves. God stands behind the world, approving of the accidental destruction of beauty and joy. One could, by agile philosophizing, justify the necessary destruction of beauty and joy—but the "accidental" destruction? The sun, as usual, measured off the days, but mysteriously withheld its warmth and allowed the frost to do its work. The flower, the sun, God, all seem indifferent; only human beings are shocked.

"Apparently," of course, has two almost opposed meanings: (1) evidently, clearly; (2) seemingly (but not really), as in "The magician apparently vanished into thin air." So the lack of surprise, and the impassivity of the sun and the approval of God *may* be unreal; maybe this is just the way things look or seem, not the way things really are. After all, it is only apparent (seemingly), not real, that flowers are "happy" and that they "play."

Topics for Discussion and Writing

1. What is the implication of the action described in lines 1–3?
2. Why is the frost's power called "accidental"?
3. Why is the assassin called "blonde"? What does this word contribute to the poem?
4. Is the last line shocking? Explain.

Robert Frost

Although in the text we give some of Frost's own comments on his poetry, here we want to quote two additional short comments. The first, from Frost's preface to his collection entitled *Aforesaid* (1954), is about the best way to read a poem:

A poem is best read in the light of all the other poems ever written. We read A the better to read B (we have to start somewhere; we may get very little out of A). We read B the better to read C, C the better to read D, D the better to go back and get something more out of A. Progress is not the aim, but circulation. The thing is to get among the poems where they hold each other apart in their places as the stars do.

The second passage we want to quote, from a letter to Louis Untermeyer, 1 January 1917, is a bit more cryptic. We read it to students when we begin studying his work, and we reread it occasionally during the course of the study.

> You get more credit for thinking if you restate formulae or cite the cases that fall in easily under formulae, but all the fun is outside saying things that suggest formulae that won't formulate—that almost but don't quite formulate. I should like to be so subtle at this game as to seem to the casual person altogether obvious. The casual person would assume that I meant nothing or else I came near enough meaning something he was familiar with to mean it for all practical purposes. Well well well.

A "Voices and Visions" video cassette of Robert Frost is available from HarperCollins. An audio cassette of Robert Frost reading is also available from HarperCollins.

Robert Frost "The Pasture" (p. 537)

"The Pasture" is a rare example of a poem that uses no figures of speech—no metaphors, no similes. Every word can be taken literally. But of course the entire poem is a sort of figure. By placing "The Pasture" at the opening of his *Collected Poems* Frost allows us to read it as a figure; the invitation to accompany the speaker on a trip to the pasture can be read as an invitation to accompany the poet on a trip to the poet's work—his poems.

Reuben Brower, in *The Poetry of Robert Frost*, rightly observes that in this poem "there is not a word or an order of words we might not use in talking," and that

> By using the commonest of leave-takings and a familiar phrase of artless begging, Frost balances perfectly the claims of both song and speech. Through the concealing art of this and other lines he aptly doubles his meanings, extending an invitation to seeing and doing country things while inviting his companion and the reader to a kind of poetry and to love. (p. 11)

In Daniel Smythe's *Robert Frost Speaks* Frost offers a comment on this poem:

> I have always had an interest in that word, "confusion." I don't think I really thought of it in this poem, but it could be thought of in connection with it. I wrote it a long time ago. I never had a greater pleasure than on coming on a neglected spring in a pasture in the woods. We clean out the leaves, then wait by to watch the uncloudiness displace the cloudiness. That is always a pleasure to me; it might be taken as a figure of speech. It is my place to see clarity come out of talk and confusion. You didn't need to know that was in the poem. But now you see that was the way it was used. (p. 56–57)

Robert Frost "Mending Wall" (p. 537)

Some critics applaud the neighbor in Frost's "Mending Wall," valuing his respect for barriers. For an extreme version, see Robert Hunting, "Who Needs Mending?" *Western Humanities Review* 17 (Winter 1963): 88–89. The gist of this faction is that the neighbor wisely realizes—as the speaker does not—that individual identity depends on respect for boundaries. Such a view sees the poem as a Browningesque dramatic monologue like "My Last Duchess," in which the self-satisfied speaker unknowingly gives himself away.

Richard Poirier, in *Robert Frost*, makes the interesting point that it is not the neighbor (who believes that "good fences make good neighbors") who initiates the ritual of mending the wall; rather it is the speaker: "I let my neighbor know beyond the hill." Poirier suggests that "if fences do not 'make good neighbors,' the *making* of fences can," for it makes for talk—even though the neighbor is hopelessly taciturn. For a long, judicious discussion of the poem, see John C. Kemp, *Robert Frost: The Poet as Regionalist* (1979), pp. 13".

Topics for Discussion and Writing

1. Compare and contrast the speaker and the neighbor.
2. Notice that the speaker, not the neighbor, initiates the business of repairing the wall (12). Why do you think he does this?
3. Write an essay of 500 words telling of an experience in which you came to conclude that "good fences make good neighbors." Or tell of an experience that led you to conclude that fences (they can be figurative fences, of course) are detrimental.

Robert Frost "The Wood-Pile" (p. 538)

The poem contrasts a human being, who "can forget his handiwork" because he lives for "turning to fresh tasks," with nature, a "frozen swamp" that is "Too much alike to mark or name a place by"; the swamp is not even a "here." but only something that tells the speaker he is "far from home." Nature is nothing in itself—or rather, nothing meaningful to man—until a human gives it meaning; in this poem, meaning is imposed on it by the person who built the woodpile. And even though the wood is not burning in the fireplace, it nevertheless has been made into something coherent, and it shows the mark of a human as its rots and "warm[s] the frozen swamp as best it could." Nature, then, needs man's collaboration, and, conversely, a human needs nature's collaboration, for nature completes what man has abandoned. On this last point, notice that "Clematis / Had wound strings round and round it like a bundle"—though the line also suggests that nature is reclaiming from humans what is hers. For an excellent discussion of the poem, see Richard Poirier, *Robert Frost.*

Topics for Discussion and Writing

1. What is the contrast that Frost makes between human beings and nature?
2. What does he say about the relationship between human beings and nature?

Robert Frost "The Road Not Taken" (p. 539)

The diverging roads are pretty similar; the speaker chose the one less worn, as "having perhaps the better claim," but three times we are told that the difference was negligible: "just as fair"; "Though as for that, the passing there / Had worn them really about the same"; "equally." It is important to notice that although a reason is given for the choice ("it was grassy and wanted wear"), we are led to doubt that there really was a clear basis for choosing. Certainly there is no moral basis. Moreover, we may feel that had the speaker chosen the other path, the ending of the poem would have been the same; that is, he would remember the alternative path and would fantasize that he might someday return to take it, and would at the same time know that he would not return. And so he would find that it too "has made all the difference." The sigh imagined in the last stanza is not to be taken as an expression of regret for a life wasted, but as a semi-comic picture of the speaker envisioning himself as an old man, wondering how things would have turned out if he had made a different choice—which is not at all to imply a rejection of the choice he did make.

Students are likely to take the poem too seriously, and to press it too hard for a moral, for example, that Frost says we should choose the "less traveled," the unconventional, path. We have tried to suggest that the first two lines of the last stanza are playful, a reading that is supported by a letter in which Frost spoke of the poem as "my rather private jest" (See *American Literature* 50 (November 1978): 478–479). As Lawrance Thompson says in his introduction to *Selected Letters of Robert Frost* (1964), p. xiv, Frost wrote the poem after returning to the United States from England. In England, his friend and fellow poet Edward Thomas liked to take Frost on wood-land walks, and then fretted that perhaps he should have chosen a different path, which would have revealed different flora. Of course, this bit of biography does not prove that the poem cannot refer to moral choice, but it may help students to ease up on the highly moral interpretations that many are prone to make.

Topics for Discussion and Writing

1. Frost called the poem "The Road Not Taken." Why didn't he call it "The Road Taken"? Which is the better title, and why?

2. Consider a choice that you made, perhaps almost unthinkingly, and offer your reflections on how your life might have been different if you had chosen otherwise. Are you now regretful, pleased, puzzled, indifferent, or what? (For instance, what seemed to be a big choice may, in retrospect, have been a decision of no consequence.)

3. Suppose that someone said to you that the poem is simply about walking in the woods and choosing one road rather than another. In an essay of 250 words, set forth your response. (You may, of course, agree with the view, in which case you will offer supporting evidence.)

4. In a paragraph discuss whether it would make any difference if instead of "yellow" in the first line the poet had written "Bright green" (or "dark green").

5. Why do you think that Frost says he (or, more strictly, the speaker of the poem) will later be telling this story "with a sigh"? Set forth your response in a paragraph.

Robert Frost "The Telephone" (p. 540)

A student of ours, Jane Takayanagi, wrote an entry in a journal that we think is worth reprinting. In our opinion she is right in seeing that a quarrel has precipitated the speaker's walk ("When I was just as far as I could walk / From here today"), but it is hard to convince someone who doesn't sense it. In an case, here is the entry from her journal.

> As the poem goes on, we learn that the man wants to be with the woman, but it starts by telling us that he walked as far away from her as he could. He doesn't say why, but I think from the way the woman speaks later in the poem, they had a fight and he walked out. Then, when he stopped to rest, he thought he heard her voice. He really means that he was thinking of her and he was hoping she was thinking of him. So he returns, and he tells her he heard her calling him, but he pretends he heard her call him through a flower on their window sill. He can't admit that *he* was thinking about her.
>
> This seems very realistic to me; when someone feels a bit ashamed, it's sometimes hard to admit that you were wrong, and you want the other person to tell you that things are OK anyhow. And judging from line 7, when he says "Don't say I didn't," it seems that she is going to interrupt him by denying it. She is still angry, or maybe she doesn't want to make up too quickly. But he wants to pretend that *she* called him back. So when he says, "Do you remember what it was you said?" she won't admit that she *was* thinking of him, and she says, "First tell me what it was you thought you heard." She's testing him a little. So he goes on, with the business about flowers as telephones, and he says "someone" called him. He understands that she doesn't want to be pushed into forgiving him, so he backs off. Then she is willing to admit that she did think about him, but still she doesn't quite admit it. She is too proud to say openly that she wants him back but does say, "I *may* have thought as much" And then, since they both have preserved their dignity and also have admitted that they care about the other, he can say, "Well, so I came."

Two other (small) points: (1) Why in line 11 does Frost speak of having "driven a bee away"? We think that maybe in a tiny way it shows the speaker's willingness to exert himself and to face danger. It's a miniature ordeal, a test of his mettle. (2) In line 17 the speaker says, "I heard it as I bowed." Of course "bowed" rhymes with "aloud," but putting aside the need for a rhyme, surely the phrase is better than, say, "I heard it as I stood," since it conveys a gesture of humility.

Robert Frost "The Oven Bird" (p. 540)

Whether or not one has ever heard an ovenbird, the idea that its song is exceptionally unmelodious is clearly suggested in lines 4, 6, and 10, where we get "he says" rather than "he sings." In case a reader missed the point while reading the first ten lines, Frost makes it explicit in line 12: "he knows in singing not to sing." Notice, too, other ways in which Frost deemphasizes the bird as a singer: The ovenbird "*makes* the solid tree trunks sound again," "he *knows*," and "he *frames*" a question.

Although Frost says in the opening line that everyone has heard the ovenbird, he carefully educates the reader who has not heard it, explaining that it is heard in the interval between "the early petal-fall / When pear and cherry bloom went down in showers" and "that other fall we name the fall." It is midsummer when leaves are abundant, but they are "old," and "the highway dust is over all." This time of stasis is no time for the usual sort of birdsong.

Ask your students how many of them have ever heard an ovenbird. (In some parts of the country few, if any, students will have heard it. By the way, the North American ovenbird is not a true ovenbird; i.e., it does not belong to the family Furnariidae, which contains birds who build elaborate domed nests of clay or who dig tunnels in the ground. The North American ovenbird is a wood warbler (Parulidae) which looks like a miniature thrush.) You might ask your students, too, after some discussion of "The Oven Bird" if they believe that in order to enjoy the poem one must have heard of an ovenbird. It's our guess that Frost adequately conveys the bird's song, partly in that stressed, unexpected "Loud" at the beginning of line 2 (it gains an even greater weight by being followed by a comma), and partly in the repetition of "mid" in this line ("mid-summer," "mid-wood") there is a suggestion of the repetition in a bird's song. Notice, too, that this line almost defies scansion; certainly it can't be called predominantly iambic. The poet, like the ovenbird, "knows in singing not to sing." Line 9 ("And comes that other fall we name the fall") sounds flat, and one isn't certain about how much stress to put on "we," "name," and "fall."

Robert Frost "Stopping by Woods on a Snowy Evening" (p. 541)

Our first question below calls attention to some of the manuscript readings. Others are line 9, "She gives her" (for "He gives his"); line 12, "Fall of flake" (for "downy flake"); line 15, "That bid me give the reins a shake," deleted and replaced by "That bid me on, and there are miles" (which was also deleted).

On "Stopping by Woods," see also John Lynen, *The Pastoral Art of Robert Frost,*and *Frost: Centennial Essays,* ed. Jac L. Tharpe. We number ourselves among the readers who see in the poem a longing for death ("frozen lake," "darkest evening of the year," "The woods are lovely, dark and deep" seem to support this view), but of course that is not what the poem is exclusively about. If there is a momentary longing for death in the poem, there is also the reassertion of the will to face the tasks of loving. As Frost put it, at the Bread Loaf Writers' Conference in 1960, "People are always trying to find a death wish in that poem. But there's a life wish there—he goes on, doesn't he?"

Frost reads the poem in *Robert Frost Reading His Own Poems* (Record No. 1, EL LCB, 1941), distributed by the National Council of Teachers of English.

Topics for Discussion and Writing

1. Line 5 originally read: "The steaming horses think it queer." Line 7 read: "Between a forest and a lake." Which version do you prefer? Why?

2. The rhyming words in the first stanza can be indicated by *aaba*; the second stanza picks up the *b* rhyme: *bbcb*. Indicate the rhymes for the third stanza. For the fourth. Why is it appropriate that the rhyme scheme differs in the fourth stanza?

3. Hearing that the poem had been interpreted as a "death poem," Frost said, "I never intended that, but I did have the feeling it was loaded with ulteriority." What "ulteriority" is implicit? How is the time of day and year significant? How does the horse's attitude make a contrast with the speaker's?

Robert Frost "The Need of Being Versed in Country Things" (p. 543)

Topics for Discussion and Writing

1. By the end of the second stanza the reader understands that the farmhouse has been destroyed by a fire. Why do you suppose (putting aside the matter of rhyme) in line 2 Frost wrote "a sunset glow" instead of (say) "a burst of flame"? And what is the effect

of the simile in line 4? That is, what do these comparisons contribute to the poem? (If you are unsure of the meaning of "pistil," check a dictionary.)

2. In the fifth stanza Frost uses personifications: "the lilac *renewed* its leaf," the "pump *flung up an awkward arm,* and "the fence post *carried* a strand of wire." What other personifications do do you find in the poem? What effect do these personifications have on you? And why do you suppose there are no personifications in the last two lines of the poem?

3. In a sentence or two or three, characterize the speaker. (Of course you can probably characterize him or her by means of an adjective or two or three; use the rest of the allotment to provide evidence, such as brief quotations.)

4. Much of the poem describes a scene, but the speaker also interprets the scene. How would you summarize the interpretation? How might you paraphrase the title? Does the speaker convince you of the "need" to be "versed in country things"?

5. Do you think the poem is sentimental? Or, on the other hand, cynical? Explain.

6. Suppose you were to write a parody of "The Need of Being Versed in Country Things." What scene might you use, or what objects might you personify? (A parody is an amusing imitation of the style of another work, often with an inappropriate subject. Thus, one might parody a sports writer by imitating his or her style, but the subject would not be an athletic event but, say, students engaged in peer review.) Suggestion: Consider the possibility of using your neighborhood or your workplace as a subject.

Our thoughts about the above questions may be of some interest.

1. Why "a sunset glow" in line 2, instead of say, "a burst of flame"? Frost's metaphor introduces, early in the poem, the motif that things are not what they seem. (Later, of course, his point will be that the birds seem to weep, but are not weeping.) The same might be said for the simile of the chimney as a pistil, in line 4, with the additional implication that the house is absorbed into nature.

2. The personifications in the fifth stanza suggest that the human perceiver of nature insists on finding human qualities in nature— a tendency that will be debunked (though that's too strong a word) by the end of the poem, where the speaker without figura-

tive language states the facts. Other personifications in the poem are: "the will of the wind" (7) and the "murmur" (15) of the birds.

3,4. Although at the end of the poem the speaker claims to be telling it as it is—that is insisting that nature is not lamenting the catastrophe—a reader probably feels that the speaker regrets that this is so. After all, much of the poem is devoted to evoking a highly sympathetic image of a busy farm that has been destroyed and turned almost into a part of nature itself. In our reading we hear some confidence in the assertion that the phoebes are not weeping, but this confidence is undercut by or at least suffused with deep regret. Put it this way: observers should understand that nature does not weep for humans losses, but (and this is not explicitly said but we think it is evident in the tone) this is a pity.

5. Our own feeling is that the poem is neither sentimental (maudlin, and influenced more by emotion than by reason) nor cynical (sneering). As we indicated in the preceding paragraph, we hear objectivity tinged with regret. Obviously other responses are possible.

6. This suggestion for writing calls for a parody. If you assign this topic, and receive some work of special interest, we hope that (after getting the student's permission) you will send it to us, with the student's name and address. If we think we can use it in the next edition of the book, we will get into touch with the student.

Robert Frost "Acquainted with the Night" (p. 543)

Some years ago a student of ours, Joseph Kang, wrote an explication of this poem. It seems excellent to us, and we reproduce it here with his permission.

The words in "Robert Frost's "Acquainted with the Night," except "luminary" in line 12, are all common ones, but if we look closely at these words we see some *unusual* implications. Take the title: "Acquainted with the Night." We are usually acquainted with a person or with a fact, not with the night. And so "night" must have some special suggestion that is not yet clear. And to be "acquainted" with someone or something usually implies familiarity (as in "I am acquainted with John Jones") but not thorough knowledge. "I have been one acquainted with the night," then, is an unusual and cautious statement.

The first stanza is matter-of-fact. It consists of three sentences, each beginning "I have," and each sentence fills exactly one line. It almost sounds flat, but is is not flat because as I have said, "acquainted with the night" is an unusual expression. Also, the repetition of words and grammatical structure makes for special emphasis. Furthermore, when "I have walked out" turns into "I have outwalked the furthest city light," we realize that we are being told about a special journey, not just a literal walk. We don't yet know what this journey was, but even if this walk beyond "the furthest city light" was a literal walk, Frost also means for us to take it as a walk beyond manmade illumination, civilization, order. It must have been meant as an experience with something dark in the way that grief, ignorance, loss of faith, or lonliness are dark.

The second stanza resembles the previous stanza but it is more expansive. It continues the use of "I have," but now only in the first two of its three lines, and only the first line is a complete sentence. And it introduces people other than the speaker, first in "the saddest city lane" (line 4), and next in the watchman (line 5). The lane cannot literally be sad; "saddest" implies that sad people live in the lane, or that the speaker feels sad when he thinks of the people who live in the lane. The watchman perhaps is one of these, and the speaker avoids his glance, explaining only that he is "unwilling to explain" (line 6). The speaker, then, not only is walking alone but also isolates himself from his fellows. That is, he feels isolated and therefore shuns contact.

The third stanza begins with "I have," as five of the previous six lines have begun, but it is even less closely patterned on the first stanza than the second was; that is, the poem becomes looser. In fact, the thought overflows the stanza; the first stanza of three lines was three sentences, and their tone was assertive, almost confident: "I have been one acquainted . . . I have walked out . . . and back" (there is a survivor's note of understated triumph in that "and back"), and I have "outwalked" again a note of triumph". But the quiet yet firm self-assertion then begins to dissolve. The second stanza was two sentences, and now the third stanza cannot contain even one complete sentence—the sentence flows into the next two stanzas, running almost to the end of the poem. To put it slightly differently, all but the last line of the octave (final eight lines) of this sonnet is a single sentence.

In the second stanza the speaker ignores human society, suggested by the watchman; in the third and fourth stanzas human society ignores the speaker, for the "cry" (line 8) is not directed to the speaker: it is "not to call me back or say good-bye" (line 10). In addition to this suggestion of mankind's indifference to the speaker, there is a suggestion that the speaker almost doesn't exist—even in his own perceptions: "I have stood still and stopped the sound of feet" (line 7). A paraphrase of the last six words might be, "and stopped producing the noise of footsteps." Thus, by standing still the speaker became inaudible not only to the city-dwellers but also to himself.

The "interrupted cry" on line 8 is sorrowful, for it is a "cry" and not a "call" or "shout" or "laugh." And the cry is mysterious because we do not know its cause, its source, its message, or why it is "interrupted." The fourth stanza continues to deepen the sense of mystery by referring to a clock "at an unearthly height." Maybe this is a real clock, perhaps with an illuminated face, high on a church or town hall, but it seems more likely that this "luminary" clock is something beyong "the furthest city light"; probably it is a metaphor describing the full moon, which is literally "unearthly." Its unearthliness is emphasized by the unusual use of the unusual word "luminary," for "luminary" is usually a noun meanigng " a source of illumination," but here it is used as an adjective. In any case, a real clock can be right or wrong, and it can tell us that the time is right or wrong for eating, sleeping, attending class, or whatever. But this "luminary clock," at an "unearthly height," offers no heavenly guidance and it cannot be either corrected or obeyed. The speaker can only look at the clock (whether a real clock or the moon) and increasingly sense that he has nothing to communicate with.

The last line of the poem, a complete sentence in itself, repeats the first line exactly, and it restores the tone of assurance. Now we have a sharper idea of what the speaker means when he says he has been "one acquainted with the night," but we still cannot say that the "night" equals or symbolizes this or that. "Loneliness," for example, is too simple a translation, because loneliness implies isolation from people, and in the poem we sense that the speaker's isolation may be not only from other people but also from himself (from a sense of any individual purpose) and also from a meaningless universe. Moreover, we must also say—and the poem is as much about this as it is about "the night"—that the speaker is not crushed by the experience. The poem is not a lament, and not a descent into self-pity. The speaker does not sadly say "I *am* one acquainted with the night"; rather, the experience is put at a distance by being set in the past: "I *have been* one acquainted with the night." And though the memory of the experience is still sharp, the speaker keeps his response under control. The closest he comes to telling us explicitly of his feelings is in the terse first and last lines. For the most part he shows us the situation rather than tells us his feelings, and thus he conveys a sense of control—a sense, we might say, of being able to deal with the experience, to survive it (since the last line repeats the first line we can say that he literally comes out where he went in), and even to get it down on paper.

Robert Frost "Desert Places" (p. 544)

Presumably the abundant alliteration and repetition of words, especially in the first stanza but, also in the third, help to suggest the thick snow falling fast, almost uniformly covering the land. The first three stanzas emphasize blankness, but of course a reader is as interested in the speaker's tone (elegiac and sonorous, but fused with some witty word-play); the fourth stanza emphasizes the speaker's response to heavenly emptiness (i.e., to the vast spaces and to lifelessness) by diminishing them with a reference to his inner "desert places." Reuben Brower, in *The Poetry of Robert Frost*, points out that in the fourth stanza "the scary place is thrust off 'there' by the emerging man of wit, by the mind that won't give way to 'absent-spiritedness.' But the gesture is a bit flamboyant and opens up a worse form of terror by bringing fear where the poet most lives alone. The taunting threat . . . is now replaced by a finer and more discreet irony" in the final lines.

The expression "desert places" appears in Chapter XVIII of *The Scarlett Letter*: Hester Prynne, outlawed from society, found that "Her intellect and heart had their home, as it were, in desert places, where she roamed as freely as the wild Indian in his woods." For two articles that seek to make much of the relation to Hawthorne, see A. J. von Frank and E. Stone in *Frost: Centennial Essays*, ed. Committee on the Frost Centennial of the University of Southern Mississippi. The poem (though not the alleged relation to Hawthorne) is also discussed by Brooks and Warren, *Understanding Poetry*.

Robert Frost "Design" (p. 544)

On Frost's "Design," see Randall Jarrell, *Poetry and the Age;* Richard Poirier, *Robert Frost*; Reuben A. Brower, *The Poetry of Robert Frost*; Richard Ohmann, *College English* 28 (February 1967): 359–367; *Frost: Centennial Essays*; and Reginald Cook, *Robert Frost: A Living Voice*, especially pp. 263–267. Brower is especially good on the shifting tones of voice, for example from what he calls "the cheerfully observant walker on back country roads" who reports "I found a dimpled . . ."—but then comes the surprising "spider, fat and white—to the "self-questioning and increasingly serious" sestet. Here, for Brower, "the first question (What had the flower to do . . . ') sounds like ordinary annoyance at a fact that doesn't fit in." The next question brings in a new note, and irony in "kindred." For Brower, with the last question ironic puzzlement turns into vision: "What but design of darkness to appall?" And then Brower syas that in the final line "the natural theologian pauses) he is only asking, not asserting—and takes a backward step. The title echoes the "Argument from Design," the argument that the universe is designed each creature fits perfectly into its environment: the whale is equipped for the sea; the camel for the desert), so there must be a designer, God. Notice that the word—"design"—has two meanings: (1) pattern and (2) intention, plan. Frost certainly means us to have both meanings in mind:

There seems to be a pattern and also an intention behind it, but this intention is quite different from the intention discerned by those who in the eighteenth and nineteenth centuries argued for the existence of a benevolent God from the "Argument from Design."

"Design" was published in 1922; below is an early 1912 version of the poem, entitled "In White":

> A dented spider like a now drop white
> On a white Heal-all, holding up a moth
> Like a white piece of lifeless satin cloth—
> Saw ever curious eye so strange a sight?—
> Portent in little, assorted death and blight
> Like the ingredients of a witches' broth?—
> The beady spider, the flower like a froth,
> And the moth carried like a paper kite.
>
> What had that flower to do with being white?
> The blue prunella every child's delight.
> What brought the kindred spider to that height?
> (Make we no thesis of the miller's plight.)
> What but design of darkness and of night?
> Design, design! Do I use the word aright?

The changes, obvious enough, are discussed by George Monteiro, in *Frost: Centennial Essays*, published by the Committee on the Frost Centennial of the University of Southern Mississippi, pp. 335–338.

By the way, an ingenious student mentioned that the first stanza has eight lines, corresponding to the eigth legs of a spider. And the second stanza has six, corresponding to the six legs of a moth. What to do? We tried to talk about the traditional structure of the sonnet, and about relevant and irrelevant conjectures, and about the broad overlapping area. About as good a criterion as any is, does the conjecture make the poem better?

Topics for Discussion and Writing

1. Do you find the spider, as described in line 1, cute or disgusting? Why?
2. What is the effect of "If" in the last line?
3. The word "design" can mean "pattern" (as in "a pretty design"), or it can mean "intention," especially an evil intention (as in "He had designs on her"). Does Frost use the word in one sense or in both? Explain.

Robert Frost "The Silken Tent" (p. 545)

The idea of comparing a woman to a silken tent in the summer breeze seems fresh enough to us (probably swaying silken tents have been compared to girls, but did anyone before Frost see it the other way around?), and given this idea, one would expect passages about gentle swaying. If one knew the piece were going to be an allegory worked out in some detail, one might expect the tent pole to be the soul. But who could have expected the brilliant connection between the cords and "ties of love and thought," and the brilliant suggestion that only rarely are we made aware—by "capriciousness"—of our "bondage"? The paradoxical idea that we are (so to speak) kept upright—are what we are—by things that would seem to pull us down is new to most students, who think that one "must be oneself." With a little discussion they come to see that what a person is depends largely on relationships. We are parents, or students, or teachers, or—something; our complex relationships give us our identity. Sometimes, in trying to make clear this idea that our relationships contribute to (rather than diminish) our identities, we mention the scene in Ibsen's *Peer Gynt* where, in an effort to get at his essential self, Peer peels an onion, each removed layer being a relationship that he has stripped himself of. He ends with nothing, of course.

In short, we think this poem embodies a profound idea, and we spend a fair amount of our class time talking about that idea. But we also try to look at the poem closely. Students might be invited to discuss what sort of woman "she" is. What, for instance, do "midday" and "summer" in line 2 contribute? Frost could, after all, have written "In morning when a sunny April breeze" but he probably wanted to suggest—we don't say a mature woman—someone who is no longer girlish, someone who is of sufficient age to have established responsibilities, and to have experienced, on occasion, a sense of slight bondage. Among the traits that we think can be reasonably inferred from the comparison are these: beauty, poise, delicacy (in lines 1–4), and sweetness and firmness of soul (5–7).

Topics for Discussion and Writing

1. The second line places the scene at "midday" in "summer." In addition to giving us the concreteness of a setting, do these words help to characterize the woman whom the speaker describes? If so, how?
2. The tent is supported by "guys" (not men, but the cords or "ties"

of line 10) and by its "central cedar pole." What does Frost tell us about these ties? What does he tell us about the pole?

3. What do you make of lines 12–14?

4. In a sentence, a paragraph, or a poem, construct a simile that explains a relationship.

Robert Frost "Come In" (p. 545)

This poem has fairly close associations with "The Need of Being Versed in Country Things" (the speaker at the end indicates his awareness that nature is *not* to be interpreted in the way that a less knowledgeable person might interpret it) and also with "Stopping by Woods on a Snowy Evening" (the temptation to enter into the darkness—to yield to some sort of impulse of self-surrender—is rejected, in favor of the assertion of the self in business as usual). The thrush's song is understood not as a "call to come in," but as "almost" (15) such a call (*cf.* the realism of the speaker of "The Need of Being Versed"), and the speaker is "out for stars," and therefore will "not come in" (*cf.* the end of "Stopping by Woods," where the speaker asserts the need to go for miles before he sleeps).

Rueben Brower in *The Poetry of Robert Frost*, speaks of "the doubling of tones in the poem" (p. 32). Among the examples that he gives are the title, which suggests a friendly welcome at the kitchen door, and also a more mysterious invitation, and (in line 2)the word "hark," which has an old-fashioned grandmotherly tone and also a poetic tone of religious wonder. Notice also the two sets of images, darkness (in most of the poem) and light ("But no, I was out for stars"). "Pillared dark," incidently, wonderfully connects the trees with columns, presumably those of a temple.

Robert Frost "The Most of It" (p. 546)

There are excellent discussions of the poem in Reuben Brower, *The Poetry of Robert Frost*, Randall Jarrell, *Poetry and the Age*, and Richard Poirier, *Robert Frost*. On the Yale recording of his poems, Frost suggests that the poem would be better titled, "Making the Most of It."

Robert Frost "The Gift Outright" (p. 547)

Since the somewhat paradoxical language may cause students difficulty, we find it useful to get the class to produce a paraphrase. There is usually some stumbling, but by the time the class gets to lines 12–13, with "Such as we were we gave ourselves outright / (The deed of gift was many deeds of war)"—one can pause, go back to the title, and in the light of what is now seen to be the gift (ourselves), effectively revise the paraphrase. Thus in the context of the entire poem the first line can be paraphrased. "We physically possessed the land before we had a national identity as Americans [lines 3–7 make it clear that we possessed—owned—the land], but because we ourselves were possessed by England [and presumably offered our allegiance to England, rather than being possessed by —obsessed by—the land of America], the land did not yet possess [enchant, serve as the object of our obsession] us." The paradox in 8–11 also requires comment: By not giving ourselves fully to our new land, we weakended rather than strengthened ourselves. Only when we surrendered to it —fully gave ourselves to it—did we find "salvation." The word "salvation" of course connects this action with a paradox central to Christianity; by dying to the old world, one gains life in the new world.

The paradoxes make for a kind of punning speech, notably in "possessed," and there are also multiple meanings in "deed" (deed of gift; deeds of war), "realizing" (becoming real; dawning on our consciousness), "artless" (without fine arts; without sophistication), and perhaps in "unstoried" (without a history; and perhaps without multi-level dwellings).

Topics for Discussion and Writing

1. Paraphrase the poem. (If you find lines 6–7 especially difficult, consider the possibility that "possess" may have multiple meanings: (1)to own; (2)to enchant. Thus, for instance, "possessed by" can mean "owned by" or "enchanted by, obsessed with.")
2. What is the gift referred to in the title? (In rereading the poem, pay special attention to lines 12–13.)
3. Consult the entry on "paradox" in the glossary. Then read the pages referred to in the entry, and write an essay of 500 words on paradox in "The Gift Outright."

Chapter 19

A Collection of Poems

We begin this chapter with some traditional (or popular) ballads, but later we print two literary ballads: Keat's "La Belle Dame sans Merci" (572) and Hardy's "Ah, Are You Digging on My Grave?" (579).

Albert B. Friedman, in *The Viking Book of Folk Ballads*, reissued as *The Penguin Book of Folk Ballads*, gives additional versions of "Sir Patrick Spence," a comic version of "The Three Ravens," and an American version of "Edward." An American version of "Edward" is recorded on an album, *Child Ballads Traditional in the United States*, 1, issued by the Library of Congress (AAFS L57). Some of these may be useful in class discussion.

Anonymous "Sir Patrick Spence" (p. 556)

Discussion of the questions (below) ought to fill a good part of the hour and ought to help students to see the virtues in this great ballad. One might also call attention to the fact that the poem does not begin with Sir Patrick—whose initial appearance is effectively held off and built up to—and to the fact that the first lines, with their reference to the king drinking, suggest a life of courtly ease that contrasts with Sir Patrick's life of seamanship. But notice too the dark or tragic implication in the second line: the wine is "blude-reid." And we should also call attention to the contrast between the nobles, who are "loath," to wet their shoes, and Sir Patrick, who is not eager for the trip and is much more than "loath," for he knows that the trip is virtually a death-mission. The nobles are associated with ladies with fans and combs. The courtiers will be mourned by the ladies, but we are not told of any mourners for Sir Patrick. However, we see Sir Patrick as master of the lords in death by virtue of having done his duty with full awareness.

Topics for Discussion and Writing

1. The shipwreck occurs between lines 29 and 32, but it is not described. Does the omission stimulate the reader to imagine the details of the wreck? Or does it suggest that the poem is not so much about a shipwreck as about kinds of behavior? (Our own response is that the poem is much more about loyalty than about a storm at sea.)

2. Do you think that lines 17–18 warrant the inference that the "eldern knicht" (5) is Sir Patrick Spence's enemy? (Maybe. There's no way of being sure, but, as we suggested a moment ago,

we think this poem is chiefly about Sir Patrick's loyalty. Whether the knight is malicious or not does not, finally, matter.)

3. What do you make of lines 13–16? (Students sometimes have trouble understanding the sharp transition. Apparently at first Sir Patrick thinks the order to sail is a joke, but then he sees it is serious, and he foresees the ironic consequences. The two states are sharply juxtaposed, without a transition.

4. In place of lines 37–40, another version of this ballad has the following stanza:

> The ladies crack't their fingers white,
>> The maidens tore their hair,
> A' for the sake o' their true loves,
>> For them they ne'er saw mair.

Which version do you prefer? (We prefer the first, since we find the second melodramatic.)

5. In the other version, the stanza that is here the final one (41–44) precedes the stanzas about the ladies (33–40). Which stanza do you think makes a better conclusion? Why? (We much prefer the version given in the text, since it ends quietly and with dignity.)

6. Understatement in "Sir Patrick Spence" (or, a slightly different way of putting it: Things unsaid in "Sir Patrick Spence").

Anonymous "The Three Ravens" (p. 558)

"The Three Ravens," like many other ballads, is filled with mystery: How did the knight die? Why does the doe bury him? Is the doe his lover? But against these uncertainties the poem gives us considerable detail: There are three ravens, the field is "green" (death and life coexist), hounds and hawks loyally guard the knight, and the doe cares for his corpse, protecting it from the birds who would make it their "breakfast." Having given us five stanzas in which death and life and bodily self-satisfaction and loyalty are juxtaposed, the poem goes on in its next four stanzas to show us only gentleness and self-sacrifice. The final stanza, with its reference to a "leman," pretty clearly indicates that the pregnant doe is the knight's beloved and, equally important, suggests that even though the knight is dead, his life was a sort of triumph since it earned such loyalty. The last stanza offers explicit moralizing, but the poem as a whole has *shown*, not preached.

Topics for Discussion and Writing

1. The hounds and the hawks are loyal followers of the knight, as is the doe. How do the references to the hounds and hawks in some degree prepare us for the doe? Do you think this preparation is necessary? Why, or why not?
2. Why does the poet include the ravens? Do they confuse a poem on loyalty, or do they provide an effective contrast? Do the ravens help to give a fuller, more realistic picture of life? Explain.
3. What is your response to the final two lines? Do they strike you as an intrusive comment? Explain.

Anonymous "The Twa Corbies" (p. 560)

"The Twa Corbies," unlike the "The Three Ravens," is a poem about *dis*loyalty—of hound, hawk, and lady—but we should not overlook the cozy, though macabre, domesticity of the fourth stanza, in which the corbies plan to dine and to patch their nest.

Topics for Discussion and Writing

1. The story in the poem is implied (in the second and third stanzas) rather than made explicit. In your opinion, what *is* the story? Is it the worse for being implicit? Explain.
2. Hair is usually "gowden" in ballads. What does this conventional detail tell us about the knight's age? Suppose instead of "gowden" (15) the poem said "graying." Would your response be different? How? Why?
3. What do you think the fourth stanza (especially 15–16) contributes to the poem?
4. Animals can't speak. Do you therefore find the poem absurd? Explain.

Anonymous "Edward" (p. 560)

Bertrand Bronson, in *The Ballad as Song*, suggests that "Edward" may not be a pure folk ballad. Perhaps the strongest evidence of a "literary" touch is the fact that the surprise ending in the last line—which forces us to reconstruct our understanding of the mother—is unusual for a ballad. In traditional ballads, Bronson points out, people ask questions in order to learn what they do not know (or, in the case of riddling ballads, in order to test someone), but in "Edward" the questions and answers serve a sophisticated technique of character revelation and of plot-telling. By the way, the motifs of questions and answers and last will and testament, found in "Edward" are also in "Lord Randal," which some undergraduates may know.

Topics for Discussion and Writing

1. The poem consists of two parts. How does the structure of the first part parallel that of the second?
2. What might have been the mother's motives? Do you think that the story would be improved if we knew the motives behind her "counseils"? Explain.
3. How can you explain Edward's statements about his wife and children?
4. Line 21 offers a surprise, but it is topped by the surprise in the final four lines. Can you reread the poem with pleasure once you know the surprises? Explain.

Anonymous "John Henry" (p. 562)

There is a wealth of information about the origin of "John Henry" in Guy B. Johnson, *John Henry*, and in Louis W. Chappell, *John Henry*. These books, and many other scholarly writings on John Henry, are summarized in Richard M. Dorson, "The Career of 'John Henry,'" *Western Folklore* 24(1965): 155–163, reprinted in *Mother Wit from the Laughing Barrel*, Alan Dundes, ed. Albert B. Friedman, *The Penguin Book of Folk Ballads*, prints six versions, and the song has often been recorded, e.g., by Huddie Leadbetter, *Leadbelly's Last Sessions*, Vol. I, Part Two (Folkways Records FA2941 C/D).

Although "John Henry" was composed by blacks, sung by blacks, sung to blacks, and is about a black hero, Eldridge Cleaver suggests (*Soul on Ice*, p. 164) that it suits the purposes of white racism: The black is all Body and no Brain. There is something to Cleaver's view, though ballads are scarcely likely to celebrate intellectual activity; when one thinks about the matter, one notices that ballads celebrating a white folk hero normally give him a touch of cunning and make him a fighter against injustice (e.g., Jesse James "had a hand and a heart and a brain," and he "stole from the rich, and he gave to the poor"). "John Henry" celebrates only physical strength (and sometimes sexual strength, in the reference to his women). But the vast majority of ballads celebrating white heroes are rather unimpressive sentimental pieces; "John Henry," however limited its view, has an aesthetic excellence that endures. And after all, no one expects any work of art to tell the *whole* truth.

Topics for Discussion and Writing

1. How does the first stanza contribute to John Henry's grandeur?
2. Some versions contain an additional stanza at the end:

> They took John Henry to the buryin' ground,
> And they buried him in the sand;
> And every locomotive come roarin' round
> Says "There lies a steel-drivin' man,"
> Says "There lies a steel-drivin' man."

Do you find the ending as given in the present text unsatisfactory? Do you have any doubt about John Henry's death?

Sir Thomas Wyatt "They Flee from Me" (p. 563)

Albert S. Guerard and J.D. Hainsworth, in *Essays in Criticism* 11(July 1961): 359–368, summarize most of the earlier criticism of this poem. A good deal of argument concerns "They" in line 1. Literally deer? Birds (falcons perhaps, or the doves of Venus)? Metaphorically, courtiers? Women? Possibly it is even a generalization and denotes only one woman, the poet's only mistress. And is "she" (12) the poet's mistress or not a real woman at all but the Goddess Fortune? This last view holds (not convincingly) that the motif of woman's inconstancy is metaphoric, a vehicle for the theme that Fortune is inconstant. In *An Introduction* we give the manuscript version of the poem. When it appeared in print in Tottel's *Songs and Sonnets* (1557), it was made more regular—and much less vigorous, although the last line of the revision has considerable merit. Here is Tottel's text; the points of chief difference are italicized.

The lover showeth how he is forsaken
of such as he sometime enjoyed

They flee from me, that sometime did me seek
    With naked foot stalking *within* my chamber.
Once have I seen them gentle, tame, and meek,
That now are wild, and do not *once* remember

That sometime they *have* put themselves in danger,
To take bread at my hand, and now they range,
Busily *seeking in* continual change.
        Thanked be fortune, it hath been otherwise
Twenty times better: but once *especial*,
In thin array, after a pleasant guise,
When her loose gown *did from her shoulders fall*,
And she me caught in her *armes* long and small,
And therwithal, *so* sweetly did me kiss,
And softly said: dear heart, how like you this?

        It was no dream: *for* I lay broad*a*waking.
But all is turned now through my gentleness
Into a *bitter* fashion of forsaking:
And I have leave to go of her goodness,
And she also to use newfangleness.
But, since that I *unkindly* so am served:
How like you this, what hath she now deserved?

Topics for Discussion and Writing

1. An analysis of the changes between the manuscript and the printed version.
2. Voice in "They Flee from Me."

William Shakespeare "Sonnet 29," "Sonnet 73," "Sonnet 116," and "Sonnet 146" (p. 564–66)

Shakespeare's 154 sonnets were published in 1609, although it is usually thought that most of them were composed in the middle 1590s, around the time *Romeo and Juliet* and *A Midsummer Night's Dream* were written. Francis Meres spoke of Shakespeare's "sugared sonnets" in 1598, and two were published in an anthology in 1599. The order of the sonnets is probably not Shakespeare's, but there are two large divisions (with some inconsistent interruptions). Sonnets 1–126 seem to be addressed to, or concerned with, a handsome, aristocratic young man who is urged to marry and thus to propagate his beauty and become immortal. Sonnets 127–152 are chiefly concerned with a promiscuous dark woman who seduces a friend, at least for a while.

Wordsworth thought the poems were autobiographical ("With this key Shakespeare unlocked his heart"), to which Browning replied, "If so, the less Shakespeare he." Scholars have not convincingly identified the friend or the lady, and of course the whole thing may be as fictional as *Hamlet*. Certainly it *sounds* like autobiography, but this is only to say that Shakespeare is a writer who sounds convincing. The chief argument that the poems really may be autobiographical is that the insistence that the friend marry is so odd a theme. As C. S. Lewis says in *English Literature in the Sixteenth Century*, what man (except a potential father-in-law) cares if another man gets married? One other point: Do the poems addressed to the beautiful friend suggest a homosexual interest? Certainly they suggest a *passionate* interest, but it doesn't seem to be erotic. "Sonnet 20," a bawdy and witty poem, expressly denies any interest in the friend's body. It seems reasonable to say that what the speaker of the sonnets wants from the friend is not sex but love.

"Sonnet 29" (When in disgrace with Fortune and men's eyes) (p. 564)

The rhyme scheme of "Sonnet 29" is that of the usual Shakespearean sonnet, but the thought is organized more or less into an octave and a sestet, the transition being emphasized by the trochee at the beginning of line 9. The sense of energy is also communicated by the trochee that begins line 10 and yet another introducing line 11, this last being especially important because by consonance and alliteration it communicates its own energy to the new image of joy ("Like to the lark"). As in most of Shakespeare's sonnets, the couplet is more or less a summary of what has preceded, but not in the same order: Line 13 summarizes the third quatrain: line 14 looks back to (but now rejects) the earlier quatrains.

The first line surely glances at Shakespeare's unimpressive social position, and line 8 presumably refers to his work. Possibly the idea is that he most enjoyed his work before it became the source of his present discomfort. Edward Hubler, in *The Sense of Shakespeare's Sonnets*, notes that "the release from depression is expressed through the image of the lark, a remembrance of earlier days when the cares of his London career were unknown."

To this it can be added that although the poem employs numerous figures of speech from the start (e.g., personification with "Fortune," synecdoche with "eyes" in line 1, metonymy with "heaven" in line 3), line 11, with the image of the lark, introduces the poem's first readily evident figure of speech, and it is also the most emphatic run-on line in the poem. Moreover, though heaven was "deaf" in line 3, in line 12 it presumably hears the lark singing "hymns at heaven's gate." "Sullen in line 12 perhaps deserves some special comment too: (1) The earth is still somber in color, though the sky is bright, and (2) applied to human beings, it suggests the moody people who inhabit earth.

Topic for Discussion and Writing

1. Disregarding for the moment the last two lines (or *couplet*), where does the sharpest turn or shift occur? In a sentence, summarize the speaker's state of mind before this turn and, in another sentence, the state of mind after it.

"Sonnet 73" (That time of year thou mayst in me behold) (p. 565)

Sonnet 73 is chiefly a meditation on growing old, though the couplet relates this topic to the theme of love that is the subject of many of Shakespeare's sonnets. All three quatrains, in varying degrees, glance at increasing coldness and darkness, and each successive quatrain is concerned with a briefer period. In the first, the human life is compared to a year; in the second, to a day; in the third, to a few hours. In the first quatrain, there is a further comparison; the boughs of the autumnal trees are compared (in "bare ruined choirs") to the churches that had fallen into decay after England broke with Rome. ("Sweet birds" refers primarily to the feathered creatures that recently sang in the boughs, but it also glances at choristers in the choirs.) Note, too, that it is reasonable to perceive, faintly, a resemblance between the shaking boughs and a trembling old person. The first quatrain, then, is rich in suggestions of ruined beauty and destroyed spirituality.

The second quatrain, by speaking of night as "Death's second self," explicitly introduces death into the poem. The third quatrain personifies the fire, speaking of its "youth" (i.e., the earlier minutes or hours of the blaze) and its "deathbed," and in its reference to ashes it introduces a common idea of the decayed body. (The idea, of course, is that the last embers lie on the ashes, which were the "youth" or earlier hours of the fire, and these ashes now help to extinguish the embers.) The year will renew itself, and the day will renew itself, but the firewood is utterly destroyed. In the final line the speaker is reduced to "that," not even "me."

"Sonnet 116" (Let me not to the marriage of true minds) (p. 565)

Although the poem is almost certainly addressed to a man, because it is a celebration of the permanence of love it can apply equally well to a woman or, in fact, to a parent or child.

The first words, "Let me not," are almost a vow, and "admit impediments" in the second line faintly hints at the marriage service in the Book of Common Prayer, which says, "If any of you know just cause or impediment . . . . " In line 2 "admit" can mean both "acknowledge, grant the existence of" and "allow to enter."

The first quatrain is a negative definition of love ("love is not . . . "), but the second quatrain is an affirmative definition ("O no, it is . . . "). The third begins as another negative definition, recognizing that "rosy lips and cheeks" will indeed decay, but denying that they are the essence to love; this quatrain then ends affirmatively, making a contrast to transience: "bears it out even to the edge of doom." Then, having clinched his case, the speaker adopts a genial and personal tone in the couplet, where for the first time he introduces the word "I."

Speaking of couplets, we can't resist quoting Robert Frost on the topic. Once, in conversation with Frost, the boxer Gene Tunney said something about the price of a poem. Frost replied: "One thousand dollars a line. Four thousand for a quatrain, but for a sonnet, $12,000. The last two lines of a sonnet don't mean anything anyway." Students might be invited to test the sonnets against this playful remark.

Topics for Discussion and Writing

1. Paraphrase (that is, put into your own words) "Let me not to the marriage of true minds / Admit impediments." Is there more than one appropriate meaning of "Admit"?
2. Notice that the poem celebrates "the marriage of true minds," not bodies. In a sentence or two, using only your own words, summarize Shakespeare's idea of the nature of such love, both what it is and what is is not.
3. Paraphrase lines 13–14. What is the speaker's tone here? Would you say that the tone is different from the tone in the rest of the poem?
4. Write a paragraph or a poem defining either love or hate. Or see if you can find such a definition in a popular song. Bring the lyrics to class.

William Shakespeare "Sonnet 146" (Poor soul, the center of my sinful earth) (p. 566)

Shakespeare's Sonnet 146 is well discussed in Edward Hubler, *The Sense of Shakespeare's Sonnets*, and more learnedly and elaborately discussed by Michael West in *Shakespeare Quarterly* 25(Winter 1974): 109–122. Also useful is *A Casework on Shakespeare's Sonnets*, Gerald Willen and Victor B. Reed, eds. See also an article by Charles A. Huttar, "The Christian Basis of Shakespeare's Sonnet 146," *Shakespeare Quarterly* 19(Autumn 1968): 355–365, which rejects a reading that the poem ironically argues that spiritual health is achieved by bodily subjugation. The rejected reading holds that the advice that the soul exploit the body must be ironic, since if it were not ironic, the soul would be guilty of simony, the sin of buying (or attempting to buy) salvation. According to this ironic reading, the poet really is pleading for the life of the body against a rigorous asceticism which glorifies the spirit at the expense of the body. But Huttar argues (by citing Biblical sources and Christian commentaries) that the poem argues in behalf of the traditional Christian doctrine that the soul should be the master of the body; the body (which must in any case die) should not be allowed to cause the soul to "pine." The poem, Huttar says, is close to Jesus's words in Matthew 6:20: "Lay up for yourself treasures in heaven, where neither moth nor rust doth corrupt, and where thieves do not break through and steal."

Topics for Discussion and Writing

1. In line 2, "My sinful earth" is doubtless a printer's error, an unintentional repetition of the last word of the first line. Among suggested emendations are "Thrall to," "Fooled by," "Rebuke these," "Leagued with," "Feeding." Which do you prefer? Why?
2. How would you characterize the tone of the first two lines? Where in the poem does the thought take its chief turn? What do you think is the tone of the couplet?
3. What does "array" (line 2) mean?
4. Explain the paradox in lines 13–14.
5. In a poem on the relation between body and soul, do you find battle imagery surprising? Commercial imagery (lines 5–12)? What other imagery is in the poem? Do you think the sonnet is a dull sermon?

John Donne "A Valediction
Forbidding Mourning" (p. 566)

Instructors may be so familiar with this poem that they may not recognize the difficulties it presents to students. The title itself leads
many students to think (quite plausibly) that it is about death, an idea
reinforced by the first simile. But this simile is introduced to make the
point that *just as* virtuous men can die quietly because they are confident of a happy future, *so* the two lovers can part quietly—that is, the
speaker can go on a journey—because they are confident of each other.

The hysterics that accompany the separation of less confident
lovers are ridiculed ("sigh-tempests," " tear-floods"); such agitation
would be a "profanation" of the relationship of the speaker and his
beloved and would betray them to the "laity."

Thus the speaker and the beloved are implicitly priests of spiritual
love.

The poem goes on to contrast the harmful movement of the earth (an
earthquake) with the harmless ("innocent") movement of heavenly bodies, thereby again associating the speaker and the beloved with heavenly
matters. (The cosmology, of course, is the geocentric Ptolemaic system.)
The fourth stanza continues the contrast: Other lovers are "sublunary,"
changeable, and subject to the changing moon. Such earthbound lovers
depend on the physical things that "elemented" their love ("eyes, lips, and
hands"), but the love of the speaker and his partner is "refined" and does
not depend on such stuff. Moreover, if their love is like something physical,
it is "like gold to airy thinness beat."

The three last stanzas introduce the image of a draftsman's (not an
explorer's) compass, and they also introduce the circle as a symbol of
perfection.

See Theodore Redpath's edition of *The Songs and Sonnets of John
Donne*, and see especially Clay Hunt, *Donne's Poetry*, and Patricia
Spacks, *College English* 29 (1968): 594–595. Louis Martz, *The Wit of Love*,
p. 48, says of line 20: "'Care less,' but is it so? The very rigor and intri-
cacy of the famous image of the compass at the end may be taken to
suggest rather desperate dialectical effort to control by logic and reason a situation almost beyond control."

Topics for Discussion and Writing

1. The first stanza describes the death of "virtuous men." To what is
   their death compared in the second stanza?

2. Who is the speaker of this poem? To whom does he speak and what is the occasion? Explain the title.

3. What is the meaning of "laity" in line 8? What does it imply about the speaker and his beloved?

4. In the fourth stanza the speaker contrasts the love of "dull sublunary lovers" (i.e., ordinary mortals) with the love he and his beloved share. What is the difference?

5. In the figure of the carpenter's or draftsperson's compass (lines 25–36) the speaker offers reasons-some stated clearly, some not so clearly-why he will end where he began. In 250 words explain these reasons.

6. In line 35 Donne speaks of his voyage as a "circle." Explain in a paragraph why the circle is traditionally a symbol of perfection.

7. Write a farewell note—or poem—to someone you love (or hate).

Robert Herrick "Upon Julia's Clothes" (p. 567)

A good deal has been published on this tiny poem. Much of what has been published seems odd to us, for instance, an argument that in the first stanza Julia is clothed but in the second is imagined as nude ("free" is alleged to describe her body, not her clothes), or that the first stanza describes her from the front, the second from the rear.

One of our students, Stan Wylie, seems to us to have written a far better discussion of the poem. He tells us that he began with this perception:

Two stanzas, each of three lines, with the same structure
Basic structure of first stanza: When X (one line), then Y (two lines)
Basic structure of second stanza: Next (one line), then Z (two lines)

Later, he noticed that the last line is much more personal than the earlier lines. Thinking further about this, he noticed that the whole poem is personal, in that it is not only about Julia's clothing, but about the effect of Julia, moving in silk, on the poet. The personal element appears as early as the first line, "*my* Julia." Here is his essay:

Herrick's Julia, Julia's Herrick

Robert Herrick's "Upon Julia's Clothes" begins as a description of Julia's clothing and ends as an expression of the poet's response not just to Julia's clothing but to Julia herself. Despite the apparently objective or detached tone of the first stanza and the first two lines of the second stanza, the poem finally conveys a strong sense of the speaker's excitement.

The first stanza seems to say, "Whenas" X (one line), "Then" Y (two lines). The second stanza repeats this basic structure of one line of assertion and two lines describing the consequence: "Next" (one line), "then" (two lines). But the coolness of "Whenas," "Then," and "Next," and of such rather scientific language as "liquefaction" (a more technical-sounding word than "melting") and "vibration," is undercut by the breathlessness or excitement of "Then, then" (that is very different from a simple "Then").

Finally, it is worth mentioning that although there is a personal rather than a fully detached note even in the first line, in "*my*" Julia," this expression scarcely reveals much feeling. In fact, it is a rather complacent touch of male chauvinism, with its suggestion that the woman is a mere possession of the speaker's. Not until the last line does the speaker reveal that, far from Julia being his possession, he is possessed by Julia: "O, how that glittering taketh me." If he begins coolly, objectively, and somewhat complacently, and uses a structure that suggests a somewhat detached mind, he nevertheless at last confesses (to our delight) that he is enraptured by Julia.

Other things, of course might be said about this poem. For instance, the writer says nothing about the changes in the meter and their contributions to the poem. Nor does he say anything about the sounds of any of the words (he might have commented on the long vowels in "sweetly flows" and shown how the effect would have been different if instead of "sweetly flows" Herrick had written "sweetly flits," and he might have commented on the spondees in "Then, then" and "O, how" and the almost-spondees in "Next, when," "each way free," and "that glittering"), but such topics might be material for another essay.

Robert Herrick "Delight in Disorder" (p. 568)

Almost every line except the last contains a word that, although describing clothing, suggests a bit of naughtiness or passion. The most obvious of these words are "disorder" (1), "wantonness" (2), "distraction" (4), "erring" (5), "Enthralls" (6), "neglectful" (7), "tempestuous" (10), "careless" (11), "wild" (12), "bewitch" (13), but even "kindles" (2), "thrown" (3), and "confusedly" (8) in this context hint of sexuality.

The metrical variations (e.g., line 2 begins with "Kindles," a trochee instead of an iamb, and line 10 contains dactyls) perhaps suggest, in a tiny, restrained way, this "sweet disorder" and the "wild civility." In any case, they prevent the poem from being "too precise in every part" (14).

John Milton "When I consider how my light is spent" (p. 568)

Milton's sonnets have been carefully edited by Ernst Honigmann (1966). Argument about the date Milton became blind need not concern us (Miltonists wonder how literally to take "Ere half my days"), but it should be noticed that one critic argues that the sonnet is not about blindness. (The common title "On His Blindness" has no authority; it was first used by a printer in 1752.) Lysander Kemp held (*Hopkins Review* 6 [1952]: 80–83) that the sonnet deals with the loss not of vision but of poetic inspiration, but Kemp's view has not been widely accepted. The most sensible view (to draw on Honigmann) is that the octave assumes that God requires ceaseless labor, and the sestet enlarges the concept of service to include those who, though inactive, are eagerly prepared for action.

Additional notes: In line 2, "this dark world and wide" suggests not only the dark world of the blind man, but also a religious stock expression for the sinful world; in line 7, "day-labor" suggests not only labor for daily wages, but also labor that requires daylight, i.e., the power of vision; in line 14, "wait" perhaps means not only "stay in expectation," but also "attend as a servant, to receive orders."

William Blake "The Lamb" (p.569); "The Tyger" (p. 569)

E. D. Hirsch, Jr., in *Innocence and Experience*, Harold Bloom, in *The Visionary Company*, and Hazard Adams, in *William Blake*, discuss these poems. "The Tyger" has engendered much comment. Of special interest are Martin K. Nurmi, "Blake's Revisions of 'The Tyger,'" *PMLA* 71 (September 1956): 669–685; Harold Bloom, *Blake's Apocalypse*; and two pieces by John Grant and Hazard Adams reprinted in *Discussions of Blake*, ed. John Grant. See also, for a collection of essays and extracts from books, *William Blake: The Tyger*, ed. Winston Weathers.

In the course of arguing on behalf of reader-response criticism, Stanley Fish, in *Is There a Text in This Class?*, has some fun calling attention to the diversity of opinions. He points out that in *Encounter* (June 1954), Kathleen Raine published an essay entitled "Who Made the Tyger?" She argued that because for Blake the tiger is "the beast that sustains its own life at the expense of its fellow-creatures," the answer to the big question ("Did he who made the Lamb make thee?") is, in Raine's words, "beyond all possible doubt, No." Fish points out that

Raine, as part of her argument, insists that Blake always uses the word "forest" with reference "to the natural, 'fallen' world." Fish then calls attention to E. D. Hirsch's reading, in *Innocence and Experience* (1964), in which Hirsch argues that "forest" suggests "tall straight forms, a world that for all its terror has the orderliness of the tiger's stripes or Blake's perfectly balanced verses." In short, for Hirsch "The Tyger" is "a poem that celebrates the holiness of tigerness." Hirsch also argues that Blake satirizes the single-mindedness of the Lamb.

We find all of this very baffling. We are not specialists in Blake, but it seems to us that both poems celebrate rather than satirize or in any way condemn their subjects. In "The Lamb" (such is our critical innocence), innocence is celebrated; in "The Tyger," energy is celebrated.

William Blake "London" (p. 570)

"London," from *Songs of Experience*, is a denunciation of the mind-forged manacles, that is, of manmade repressive situations, not a denunciation of cities with a glorification of rural life. The church assists in exploitation by promises of an eternal reward, the monarchy slaughters men for private gain, and marriage drives the unmarried (or the unsatisfactorily married) to harlots. "Chartered" (2), that is, not merely mapped but licensed, is perhaps almost acceptable for streets, but that the river, an image of freedom, should also be chartered is unnatural and intolerable. As the poem develops, it is evident that children are licensed (as chimney sweeps), soldiers are licensed (to kill and to be killed), and harlots are licensed (bought and sold). E. D. Hirsch, Jr., *Innocence and Experience*, suggests that there is a further meaning: Englishmen were proud of their "chartered liberties," rights guaranteed by Magna Carta, but "these chartered liberties are chartered slaveries." For "ban" in line 7 Hirsch offers four references: a summons to arms (king), a formal denunciation or curse (church), a proclamation of marriage, and a prohibition (king, church, marriage).

A few additional points: The church is "blackening" because (1) it is covered with the soot of an industrial (mechanistic) society; (2) it is spiritually corrupt; and (3) it corrupts people. The chimney-sweeper's cry appalls the church because the cry is a reproach, and "appalls" hints at "pall" (suggestive of the dead church) and at its literal meaning, "to make pale," that is, the hypocritical church is a whited sepulcher. In line 14, "the youthful Harlot's curse" may be a cry (thus linked with the infant's cry, the chimney sweeper's cry, and the soldier's sigh), or it may be the disease that afflicts her and is communicated to others. In *Poetry and Repression*, Harold Bloom offers the astounding suggestion that "the harlot's curse is not, as various interpreters have said, venereal disease, but is indeed what 'curse' came to mean in the vernacular after Blake and still means now: menstruation, the natural cycle in the human female . . . . [Blake knows that one] curse or ban or natural fact (menstruation) blasts or scatters another natural fact, the tearlessness of the new-born infant."

In an earlier version, "dirty" stood in lines 1 and 2 instead of "chartered," and "smites" instead of "blights" in line 16.

For an analysis of several reading of "London," see Susan R. Suleiman and Inge Crosman, *The Reader in the Text*. Also important is an essay by E. P. Thompson in *Interpreting Blake*, ed. Michael Phillips.

William Wordsworth "The World Is Too Much with Us" (p. 571)

The meaning of "the world" in line 1 is clarified in line 2: "Getting and spending." Our powers are bestowed on worldly (presumably commercial) things, rather than on perceiving Nature properly. We have given our hearts away, but this gift ("boon") is sordid, for our hearts are set on wrong things. Against the "world" Wordsworth sets nature. He defines nature through images of natural beauty (sea, flowers) and through mythological allusions (Proteus, Triton). That is, nature is both beautiful *and* wonderful, for those who perceive it. The sea and winds are "upgathered now like sleeping flowers," but they will reveal themselves in all their beauty and mystery when we turn to them. (Cf. Hopkins's "There lives the dearest freshness deep down things," in "God's Grandeur," text, 582.) Wordsworth does not say that paganism is preferable to Christianity; he says he would rather be a pagan than what "we" are, because the pagan still responded to the divinity in nature, whereas "we" have lost touch with it.

William Wordsworth "I Wandered Lonely as a Cloud (p. 571)

On 15 April 1802, Wordsworth and his sister, Dorothy, took a walk, during which they saw some daffodils near a lake. Dorothy recorded the experience in her journal, and this entry affords us something close to the raw material out of which Wordsworth's poem was made. The entry is not, of course, Wordsworth's own experience; Dorothy's experience was not William's, and Dorothy's words cannot exactly reproduce even her own experience. (It should be noted, incidentally, that Dorothy's description is not entirely "factual"; her daffodils rest their heads, glance, dance, etc.) Still, the entry gives us something of the phenomena that stirred an "emotion in Wordsworth, and for Wordsworth, poetry was made out of emotion recollected in tranquillity." Below is the entry from Dorothy's journal. (We sometimes photocopy the entry and ask the students to discuss the poem in light of the entry.)

It was a threatening, misty morning, but mild. We set off after dinner, from Eusemere. Mrs. Clarkson went a short way with us, but turned back. The wind was furious, and we thought we must have returned. We first rested in the large boat-house, then under a furze bush opposite Mr. Clarkson's. Saw the plough going in the field. The wind seized our breath. The lake was rough . . . . When we were in the woods beyond Gowbarrow Park we saw a few daffodils close to the water-side. We fancied that the lake had floated the seeds ashore, and that the little colony had so sprung up. But as we went along there were more and yet more; and at last, under the boughs of the trees, we saw that there was a long belt of them along the shore, about the breadth of a country turnpike road. I never saw daffodils so beautiful. They grew among the mossy stones above and about them; some rested their heads upon these stones as on a pillow for weariness; and the rest tossed and reeled and danced, and seemed as if they verily laughed with the wind, that blew upon them over the lake; they looked so gay, ever glancing, ever changing. This wind blew directly over the lake to them. There was here and there a little knot and a few stragglers a few yards higher up; but they were so few as not to disturb the simplicity, unity, and life of that one busy highway. We rested again and again. The bays were stormy, and we heard the waves at different distances, and in the middle of the water, like the sea. Rain came on— we were wet when we reached Luff's, but we called in.

Two years after the walk, William presumably recollected and contemplated the emotion, and wrote "I Wandered Lonely as a Cloud," leaving out the threatening weather, the plough, the boathouse, the miscellaneous flowers and even the first group of daffodils, and the people (including Dorothy). Notice, too, that the sense of effort which Dorothy records ("we thought we must have returned," "we first rested," etc.) is not in the poem: The speaker "wandered," and he lies on his couch in "vacant or in pensive mood"; if he acts, it is with spontaneous joy, but chiefly it is the daffodils that act ("Fluttering and dancing in the breeze," "tossing their sprightly heads," etc.).

On Dorothy Wordsworth's *Journals* and William Wordsworth's "I

Wandered Lonely as a Cloud," see Carl Woodring, *Wordsworth*: Edward Rosenheim, *What Happens in Literature*; David Perkins, *Wordsworth*; and especially Frederick Pottle's essay in *Yale Review* 40(Autumn 1950): 27–42, reprinted in *Wordsworth*, Gilbert T. Dunklin, ed.

Topic for Writing

Wordsworth first published the poem in 1807, but the version printed here (which is the one everyone knows) is that of 1815. The differences between the first and second versions are these: In the first version lines 7–12 are lacking; line 4 has "dancing" instead of "golden"; line 5 has "Along" instead of "Beside"; line 6 has "Ten thousand" instead of "Fluttering and"; line 16 has "laughing" instead of "jocund." Evaluate the revisions. In particular what does the added stanza contribute?

John Keats "La Belle Dame sans Merci" (p. 572)

"La Belle Dame" is elaborately discussed in Earl Wasserman, *The Finer Tone*, and more reasonably discussed in books on Keats by Walter Jackson Bate, Douglas Bush, and Charles Patterson, and in Harold Bloom *The Visionary Company*. Here are a few points: In the first stanza, nature ("withered") reflects the condition of the knight ("*palely* loitering"). The second stanza further establishes the time as autumn, and though nature is abundant ("The squirrel's granary is full"), the knight seems starved, and the implication is that he is approaching winter, that is, death. Line 22 ("And nothing else saw all day long") indicates his total absorption in the lady's song, which (along with "roots of relish sweet, / And honey wild, and manna dew") nourished him for a while, and brought him to a vision of people who resemble him in his present condition ("pale"). This vision is presumably a vision of mortality, and he awakes to find himself "On the cold hill's side"—in the physical world unredeemed by the imagination.

Topics for Discussion and Writing

1. In the first three stanzas the speaker describes the knight as pale, haggard, and so forth. In the rest of the poem the knight recounts his experience. In a few sentences summarize the knight's experience, and indicate why it has caused him to appear as he now does.

2. The *femme fatale*—the dangerously seductive woman—appears in

much literature. If you are familiar with one such work, compare it with Keat's poem.

3. What characteristics of the popular ballad (see the note on p. 555 of text) do you find in this poem? What characteristic does it *not* share with popular ballads? Set forth your response in an essay of 500 words.

John Keats "To Autumn" (p. 579)

The poem is discussed in books on Keats by Walter Jackson Bate, Douglas Bush, and Helen Vendler, and also in Reuben Brower, *The Fields of Light*, and in Geoffrey Hartman, *The Fate of Reading, and Other Essays*. Some gleanings: One can see, in the three stanzas, the progress of autumn from the energetic first stanza (note "load," "bless," "bend," "fill," "swell," "set budding") with its "apples" and "mellow fruitfulness" before the harvest to the more languid second stanza with its "half-reaped furrow" and its cider press with "last oozings," and then the "stubble plains" in the third. We move from richness and fruition in the first stanza, to a sense of loss and also of drowsiness in the second, and finally to a full awareness of death in the third ("soft dying," "mourn," "wailful"), though death is seen in the context of fulfillment. Thus the images of death are in various ways modified. If the day is dying, it is "soft-dying," and if we get stubble rather than swaying grain, the stubble is "rosy."

One can also see the progress of a single day: The "maturing sun" of the first stanza may suggest noon, the resting figure of second suggests midafternoon, and then "the last oozings hours by hours" suggest late afternoon; and of course the third stanza explicitly indicates the end of the day, by "soft-dying day" and "gathering swallows." There is also a movement from the cottage garden with its fruit trees and flowers in the first stanza, to the granary, cider press, and fields of a farm in the second, and then to the hills and skies (though including the "garden-croft") of the third.

Alfred, Lord Tennyson "Ulysses" (p. 575)

Robert Langbaum, in *The Poetry of Experience*, and Christopher Ricks, in *Tennyson*, offer some good remarks; Paul Baum, in *Tennyson Sixty Years After*, assaults the poem. Henry Kozicki, in *Tennyson and Clio* (a book on Tennyson's philosophy of history), argues that "Ulysses" reveals Tennyson's optimism about historical progress and his despair about the role of a hero. For a review of much that should not have been written, see L. K. Hughes in *Victorian Poetry* 17(Autumn 1979): 192–203. By the way, it is worth mentioning to students that Homer's hero wanted to get home, Sophocle's (in *Philoctetes*) is a shifty politician (as is Shakespeare's) and Dante's Ulysses (*Inferno* XXVI) is an inspiring but deceitful talker whose ardent search is for *forbidden* things.

The first five lines emphasize, mostly with monosyllables, the dull world Ulysses is leaving. With line 6 ("I cannot rest from travel") we see a rather romantic hero, questing for experience, and indeed "experience" is mentioned in line 19, but it must be added that something is done in the poem to give "experience" a social context: Ulysses has fought for Troy (17), he wishes to be of "use" (23), and he wishes to do "some work of noble note" (52). Lines 22–23 apparently say the same thing four times over, but readers are not likely to wish that Tennyson had deleted the superbly appropriate metaphor of the rusting sword. "Gray spirit" (30) and "sinking star" (31) help (along with the heavy pauses and monosyllables in 55–56) to define the poem as a piece about dying, though students on first reading are likely to see only the affirmations. Even the strong affirmations in 57 ff. are undercut by "sunset" (60), "western" (61), etc. But the last line, with its regular accents on the meaningful words, affords a strong ending; perhaps the line is so strong and regular that it is a bit too easy. In line 45 Ulysses directly addresses the mariners, yet we hardly sense an audience as we do in Browning's dramatic monologues. If he is addressing the mariners, who are aboard, where is he when he refers to "this still hearth" (2) and when he says, "This is my son" (33)? (Some critics claim that lines 1–32 are a solioquy: Ulysses supposedly would not speak publicly of Ithaca as stagnant and savage, or of his wife as "aged." Lines 33–43 are his farewell to the Ithacans, and the remainder is an address to his mariners.)

Probably the reader ought to see the poem not as a muddled attempt at a Browingesque dramatic monologue, but as a somewhat different type of poem–a poem in which the poet uses a fairly transparent mask in order to express his state of mind and to persuade his readers to share that state of mind. The poem thus is closer to, say, "Prufrock," than it is to "My Last Duchess."

Topics for Discussion and Writing

1. Ulysses's voice.
2. Ulysses: hero or suicidal egotist?
3. Ulysses as he sees himself, compared with Ulysses as we see him.

Robert Browning "Porphyria's Lover" (p. 576)

Compared with "My Last Duchess," this poem has more story and less of the diction of a particular speaker, but students can fairly soon see that the interest in "Porphyria's Lover" is not only in what happened but also in the speaker's mind. His insane egotism led him to attempt to preserve forever Porphyria's love for him. He believes that although she struggles to offer her love, her weakness (21–25) made her require his assistance. (Interestingly, in 6–15 she seemed energetic and efficient; perhaps there is even something a bit too efficient in making the fire before speaking to her lover.) But his egotism is tempered with solicitude (41–42, 50–54), making him less monstrous but certainly mad. Inevitably, discussion in class centers on the lover's motives (do we believe them?), but it is useful to spend some time on the question of why readers enjoy the story of a mad strangler.

As for question 2 below, which asks the students to serve as the murderer's lawyer: Probably the best defense is a plea of insanity, which in some twenty-five states in the United States means that a defendant who did not know what he or she was doing or that the acts were morally wrong is not criminally liable. Evidence that the speaker is insane: (1) He sees nature as hostile (the wind is "sullen," vexing the lake and tearing down the trees "for spite"); (2) he thinks Porphyria "worships" him—though perhaps she does, we can't tell; (3) he thinks that Porphyria, now dead, has her "utmost will"; and (4) he has sat "all night long" with her head on his shoulder.

By the way, a plea of insanity is usually accepted to mean that the defendant not only was mentally ill but was so ill that he did not have the capacity to control his actions or (and this is rather different) to appreciate the wrongfulness of the action. Thus a killing may be carefully planned and executed exactly according to plan, but the defendant may be judged not guilty by virtue of insanity. John Hinckley, Jr., who shot President Reagan, was so judged, although the prosecution argued that Hinckley planned carefully and was aware that he would get attention by attacking the president. In reaction to the Hinckley decision, some states have recently changed the laws governing the use of the insanity plea. That is, some states that used to allow juries to acquit a defendant if the prosecutor failed to prove beyond a reasonable doubt that the defendant was sane at the time the crime was committed now shift the burden to the defense: The defense must prove that the defendant was insane. The change is a big one, for the traditional constitutional concept of a criminal trial was that the defendant need do nothing to prove his or her innocence; the burden of proof was on the prosecutor. Students wishing to do some research on the insanity plea might look at two books: William J. Winslade and Judith Wilson Ross, *The Insanity Plea*, and Norval Morris, *Madness and the Criminal Law*.

Topics for Discussion and Writing

1. Exactly why did the speaker murder Porphyria?
2. You are a lawyer assigned to defend the speaker against the charge of murder. In 500 to 750 words, write your defense.

Matthew Arnold "Dover Beach" (p. 578)

"Dover Beach" begins with the literal—the scene that hits the eye and ear—and then moves in the second stanza to Sophocles' figurative tragic interpretation, in the third to Arnold's figurative religious interpretation, and finally—the image of the sea now being adandoned—to the simile of the world as a "darkling plain" whose only reality is the speaker and the person addressed. The end thus completes the idea of illusion versus reality that began in the first stanza, where the scene that was "calm" (1), "fair" (2), and "tranquil" (3) actually contained the discords implicit in "grating roar," "fling," and so on. In fact, even the "tonight" of the first line implies some conflict, for the word suggests that on other nights the sea is *not* calm.

For a thought-provoking reading of "Dover Beach", consult A. Dwight Culler, *Imaginative Reason: The Poetry of Matthew Arnold*. Culler argues (perhaps too ingeniously) that although some critics complain about a lack of unity in the imagery (no sea in the last section, and no darkling plain in the first), "the naked shingles *are* the darkling plain, and that we have no sea in the last section is the very point of the poem. The sea has retreated from the world . . . . " To this point of Culler's we add that the "pebbles" flung about by the waves (10) are an anticipation of "ignorant armies" that are "swept with confused alarms of struggle and flight" (36). For parodies of critical methods, see Theodore Morrison in *Harper's Magazine* 180(February 1940): 235–244, where "Dover Beach" serves as grist for critics' mills.

Topics for Discussion and Writing

1. What are the stated and implied reasons behind Arnold's implication that only love offers comfort?

2. The sea, described in the first stanza puts the speaker in mind of two metaphors, one in the second stanza and one in the third. Explain each of these metaphors in your own words. In commenting on the first, be sure to include a remark about "turbid" in line 17.
3. Is there a connection between the imagery of the sea in the first three stanzas and the imagery of darkness in the last stanza?

Thomas Hardy "Ah, Are You Digging on My Grave?" (p. 579)

The narrative structure, as well as the motif of the unquiet grave (see the ballad of that title in Albert B. Friedman's *The Penguin Book of Ballads*), of course derives from traditional ballads.

Also ballad-like is the use of the cliches or stock epithets (e.g., "My loved one," "My nearest, dearest kin"), but note that the chief cliche of thought (in the next-to-last stanza, with its stock idea of animal fidelity) is offered only so that it may be debunked in the final stanza.

It is worth asking students whether, if the author of this poem were not named, they would take it to be a genuine traditional ballad rather than a literary derivative. It is also worth discussing Samuel Hynes's contention (*The Pattern of Hardy's Poetry*, p. 53) that the poem—based on the idea that no affection survives death—is neither true (as Hardy's own poems to his dead wife demonstrate) nor effective (Hynes finds the poem's irony "gross and automatic," "clumsy and cynical").

Thomas Hardy "The Convergence of the Twain" (p. 580)

The biggest and perhaps the most luxurious ship ever built up to that time, the supposedly insinkable *Titanic* (it had sixteen watertight compartments), collided with an iceberg and sank in the Atlantic on 15 April 1912, during her maiden voyage from Southampton to New York, with a loss of 1513 lives. Many of those who were drowned were rich and famous.

Hardy completed the poem on 24 April 1912. He lost two acquaintances in the wreck, but the poem is not an elegy; rather it is a sort of narrative and philosophical lyric which tells of the destruction (fashioned by "the Immanent Will") that awaits "the Pride of Life." The poem contains eleven stanzas, the first five of which descirbe the "vaingloriousness" that rests at the bottom of the sea, "Deep from human vanity." The sixth stanza, beginning, "Well:" makes an emphatic transition, and the remaining five introduce the "Shape of Ice" and tell of "the intimate welding" of ship and iceberg. (Note that "welding—which almost sounds like "wedding—leads in the last line to "consummation"; the ship [female] at last meets her "mate.") The first two lines— notably brief—of stanzas 2, 3, 4, and 5 call attention to pride ("mirrors meant / To glass the opulent," etc.) and the last line— notably long and sonorous—of each of these stanzas calls attention to the humbling of pride ("The sea-worm crawls," etc.).

The poem is not merely about the contrast between vain ambition and death; it is, of course, also about the government of the universe. The "moon-eyed fishes" formulate a question in line 13, but they cannot answer it. Hardy can. For Hardy, "the Spinner of the Years" stands behind these ambitions, preparing their "mate."

Gerard Manley Hopkins "God's Grandeur" (p. 582)

The world (including the human world) has divinely created beauty in its charge (care), but "charged" in line 1 is also a scientific term (referring to electricity), leading to "flame out" in the next line; "foil" in line 2, Hopkins explained in a letter, refers to "foil in its sense of leaf or tinsel." Most of the first quatrain asserts the grandeur of God, whose divine energy may be manifested either suddenly ("flame out") or slowly ("ooze of oil / Crushed"). "Crushed," at the beginning of line 4, is part of this celebration (probably alluding to olives or seeds), but this word itself of course also suggests destruction, and the rest of the octave is about human corruption of the self and of nature. "Man's smudge" in line 7 probably alludes to original sin as well as to the destruction wreaked on the countryside by factories. The octave thus moves from an excited or urgent proclamation of God's grandeur to a melancholy reflection on our insensitivity to this grandeur. The sestet reintroduces a joyous affirmation of God's grandeur. Lines 13 and 14 allude to the traditional representation of the Holy Ghost as a dove, but of course Christ is here seen also as the dawning sun, giving warmth and light, and thus we go back to the reference to light in line 2; "bent world" probably evokes the curature of the horizon, the world distorted by sin, and perhaps backbreaking labor.

Paul L. Mariani, in his excellent *Commentary on the Complete Poems of Gerard Manley Hopkins*, suggests that the last lines are connected with the first quatrain: "If we can picture the dawning sun before it breaks over the horizon, we may recall how the rich light seems precisely to

'gather to a greatness' in density and brightness . . . until the orb of the
sun itself seems to spring forth, and then the sun flames out in strong
rays like wings from its center." W. H. Gardner, in *Gerard Manley Hopkins*, II, 230, suggests that the obvious meaning of the poem is that the
world is a reservoir of divine power, love, and beauty, and that the
deeper meaning is that life must be jarred before the presence of God
can be felt. On "verbal resonance" and other sound effects in the poem,
see Brooks and Warren, *Understanding Poetry*, 4th ed., pp.538–540. See
also Terry Eagleton in *Essays in Criticism* 23(1973): 68–75. Students might
be invited to compare the poem with this entry (8 Dec. 1881) from one of
Hopkins's notebooks, reprinted in *The Sermons . . . of Gerard Manley Hopkins*, ed. Christopher Devlin, p. 95: "All things therefore are charged with
love; are charged with God and if we know how to touch them give off
sparks and take fire, yield drops and flow, ring and tell of him."

Topics for Discussion and Writing

1. Hopkins, a Roman Catholic priest, lived in England during the last
   decades of the nineteenth century—that is, in an industrialized society. Where in the poem do you find him commenting on his setting? Circle the words in the poem that can refer both to England's
   physical appearance and to the sinful condition of human beings.

2. What is the speaker's tone in the first three and a half lines
   (through "Crushed")? In the rest of line 4? In lines 5–8? Is the second part of the sonnet (the next six lines) more unified in *tone* or
   less? In an essay of 500 words, describe the shifting tones of the
   speaker's voice. Probably after writing a first draft you will be
   able to form a thesis that describes an overall pattern. As you revise your drafts, make sure (a) that the thesis is clear to the reader,
   and (b) that it is adequately supported by brief quotation.

Ezra Pound "In a Station of the Metro" (p. 582)

While these two lines have not generated quite as much commentary
as the "two-handed engine" in "Lycidas," they have generated a good
deal—beginning with Ezra Pound. In *T.P.'s Weekly* (6 June 1913)
Pound talked about the poem, and then elaborated his comment, as
follows, in *Fortnightly Review* (1 September 1914):

> Three years ago in Paris I got out of a "metro" train at La Concorde, and
> saw suddenly a beautiful face, and then another and another, and then a

beautiful child's face, and then another beautiful woman, and I tried all that day to find words for what this had meant to me, and I could not find any words that seemed to me worthy, or as lovely as that sudden emotion. And that evening, as I went home along the Rue Raynouard, I was still trying, and I found, suddenly, the expression. I do not mean that I found words, but there came an equation . . . not in speech, but in little splotches of color.

. . . The "one image poem" is a form of super-position, that is to say, it is one idea set on top of another. I found it useful in getting out of the impasse in which I had been left by my metro emotion. I wrote a thiry-line poem, and destroyed it because it was what we called work "of second intensity." Six months later I made the following hokku-like sentence ["In a Station of the Metro"]. I dare say it is meaningless unless one has drifted into a certain vein of thought. In a poem of this sort one is trying to record the precise instant when a thing outward and objective transforms itself, or darts into a thing inward and subjective.

What is left for commentators to say about the poem? A great deal, since Pound says nothing about any of the specific words in the poem. Thomas Hanzo in *Explicator*, February 1953, made the following points:

1. "In the first line the word 'apparition' suggests the supernatural or the immaterial and a sudden and unexpected appearance."
2. "Since only faces are mentioned," we have a sense of "bodiless" substances.
3. "The faces are likened to 'petals on a wet, black bough.' We know therefore that they are the faces in the windows of a train which has drawn up at the station, for the likeness can only be between the faces framed in the windows of the long, dark train and petals which have fallen on a bough after a rain."
4. "The important point of similarity is that the train has made one of its momentary stops, just as the bough is only momentarily black because it is wet from the rain which has just broken the petals from their stem."
5. What interest Pound is *not* that beauty can be found in a subway (a point made by Brooks and Warren), "but that the vision of beauty has occured in the one instant before it vanishes, when it has been released from the accidents and particularly of its material embodiment."

John Espey, writing in the June 1953 issue of *Explicator*, took issue with some of Hanzo's points. Espey argued that Pound's comment (unlike

Espey's) keeps the faces "precisely where the poem places them, 'in the crowd,'" rather than in the windows of subway cars drawn up for a moment at the station. Further, Espey points out, the Parisian subway cars were not dark either inside or out, since they were illuminated and they had colorful exteriors.

What to do? Hanzo's comment that the detached petals can be taken to refer to faces in the windows strikes us as reasonable and perceptive, especially since "apparition" allows for a sort of disembodiment corresponding to faces viewed without bodies, but against this is Pound's own statement that the faces were in the crowd—presumably the crowd he saw on the platform as he got out of the car. Well, we all know that we don't have to take the author's word (Wimsatt and Beardsley taught us this truth in "The Intentional Fallacy"); still, one wants to think as carefully about an author's comments as one does about a critic's.

Let's start over. We can probably all agree that although the most memorable (because the most visual?) thing in the poem is the image of "Petals, on a wet, black, bough," the word "apparition" is extremely important, since it (paradoxically) makes somewhat ghostly or unreal the vivid image of the faces as petals. Yoshiyuki Iwamoto, in *Explicator* February, 1961, presses this point. He begins by arguing that the second line adds up to something like this: life is violent (the rain-storm), and such violence is essential to the continuity of life. But, he says, the word "apparition" calls all of this into doubt, and thus the poem as a whole is linked to Buddhist thought about the unreality of the tumultuous life that we think is real. There is surely plenty here that can provoke lively debate in class.

Other points:

1. "The transition from the Metro station to the wet boughs somewhere outside liberates us from 'space limits,' and the transition from the present faces to the remembered petals breaks down 'time limits,'" (Hugh Witemeyer, *The Poetry of Ezra Pound* [1969], p. 34.)
2. Perhaps we can more humbly reword Witemeyer's point along these lines: the second line perceives beauty in the subway (underground, enclosed) and also takes us out of the subway, above ground and in the open air, and in connection with "apparition" suggests the mystery of existence. (If we seem to be making a fuss about "apparition," consider how different the poem would be if the word were "appearance."
3. Can one go further and say that this poem, often thought of as

simply a vivid image, not only suggests (a) the fragility or transience of life, and (b) the mystery of life, but it also suggests (c) the pathos of urban, mechanized life?

A "Voices and Visions" video cassette of Ezra Pound is available from HarperCollins. An audio cassette of Ezra Pound reading is also available from HarperCollins.

A. E. Housman "Shropshire Lad #19 (To an Athlete Dying Young)" (p. 583)

Brooks and Warren, *Understanding Poetry* 4th ed., print two manuscript versions of the poem—the first a very incomplete sketch, the second a rather full one.

William Butler Yeats "Leda and the Swan" (p. 584)

On Yeats's "Leda," see Richard Ellmann, *The Identity of Yeats*, which includes three earlier manuscript versions. Also useful for discussion of "Leda" are Leo Spitzer's essay in *Modern Philology* 51(May 1954): 271–276; the comment in M. L. Rosenthal and A. J. Smith, *Exploring Poetry*; and Helen Vendler's fifth chapter in her *Yeat's Vision and the Later Plays*.

Among Vendler's points are these: (1) the question at the end—no mere rhetorical question—represents a remarkable departure from the sestet of the traditional sonnet, which customarily has a neat unity; (2) although in the octave Leda is assaulted or caught, she is "caught up," enraptured, in the sestet (her thighs are "loosening," not "loosened," and she feels the "heartbeat" and she sense the "glory" of her attacker); and (3) Leda presumably does not acquire all of Jove's knowledge, but she does have a glimpse of divinity that is ordinarily unavailable.

Yeats saw political significance in the myth of beauty and war engendered by a god, but, as he tell us, when he was composing "Leda and the Swan" the political significance evaporated:

> After the individualistic, demogogic movements, founded by Hobbes and popularized by the Encyclopaedists and the French Revolution, we have a soil so exhausted that it cannot grow that crop again for centuries. Then I thought "Nothing is now possible but some movement, or birth from above, preceded by some violent annunciation." My fancy began to play

with Leda and the Swan for metaphor, and I began this peom, but as I
wrote, bird and lady took such possession of the scene that all politics went
out of it.

Note: one might invite students to contrast this poem with Adrienne Rich's "Rape" (p. 614)

An audio cassette of W. B. Yeats reading is available from
HarperCollins.

William Butler Yeats "The Second Coming" (p. 584)

The words "Second Coming" normally refer to Christ's return to earth
on the last day, predicted in Matthew 24, but in his poem with this title
Yeats draws also on St. John's vision in Revelations of the coming of
the beast of the Apocalypse, Antichrist, a great antagonist who was
expected to set himself against Christ in the days just before the Second Coming. Yeats wrote the poem in 1919, probably stimulated by
the Russian Revolution of 1917, but he later spoke of the poem as
prophesying the rise of fascism. In a complex prose work, *A Vision*
(1925), Yeats sets forth his cyclical theory of history. According to this
theory of cycles or "gyres" (1) "each age unwinds the threads another
age had wound." Thus Persia (the east) fell and Greece (the west)
arose; Rome (the west) fell and Byzantium, later called Constantino-
ple and now called Istanbul (the east), rose; Byzantium fell and the
west rose in the renaissance, "all things dying each other's life, living
each other's death." The Age of Christianity, an age that is "levelling,
unifying, feminine, humane, [with] peace its means and end," will be
followed by an age which is "hierarchical, multiple, masculine, harsh,
surgical." Having offered this capsule comment of Yeats's view of history, we want to add that the poem of course has an independent life.
In Yeats's poem, "the Second Coming" is not a Christ but of an An-
itchrist in the form of a sphinx ("lion body and the head of a man").

Although *A Vision* is a great help, it also is an impediment, a
dragon at the gate, inhibiting some readers from daring to enjoy "The
Second Coming" until they have mastered Yeat's theory of history as
set forth in *A Vision*. But even without *A Vision*, a reader can enjoy the
poem and can comment on it.

The poem begins with "Turning," thus introducing the idea of
continuous motion that is at the heart of the poem. The image of the
falcon going beyond the falconer's control, and specifically of the wid-

ening gyre, leads to the third line: "Things fall apart; the centre cannot hold." And from the sky we move to "the world" (4) and then to the sea (the "blood-dimmed tide" of 5). "The ceremony of innocence" (6) probably refers to baptism, but it also may suggest that ceremoniousness and innocence—the only possible protection in a bloody age—no longer afford protection.

The second stanza begins by offering the only explanation adequate to the experience, and the speaker finds some confirmation in the fact that the Universal Spirit, in which the individual soul participates, sends forth a sign, "a vast image." This image, though part human, is bestial, embodying a quality overlooked by both Greek reason and Christian faith. The "twenty centuries" (19) of Christianity have stimulated their antithesis; the "rocking cradle" (20) of Christ has awakened the "rough beast" whose time has come round, and who will now manifest itself at Bethlehem, birthplace of Christ.

An audio cassette of W. B. Yeats reading is available from HarperCollins.

Topics for Discussion and Writing

1. What is the connection between the first two lines, about the falcon and falconer, and line 3, "Mere anarchy is loosed upon the world"?

2. Do you imagine that an educated pagan of, say, the seond or third century A.D. might have said of the new creed and its adherents that "things fall apart" (3) and that "the best [of our age] lack all conviction, while the worst / Are full of passionate intensity"?

3. Why is the best slouching "toward Bethlehem" (22)? What line earlier in the poem connects with Bethlehem?

William Butler Yeats "Sailing to Byzantium" (p. 585)

The literature on this poem is enormous. Among the readable pieces are M. L. Rosenthal and A. J. Smith, *Exploring Poetry*; and Elder Olson in *University Review* 8(Spring 1942): 209–219, reprinted in *The Permanence of Yeats*, James Hall and Martin Steinmann, eds. Less readable, but highly impressive, are Curtis Bradford's study of Yeat's interest in Byzantium and of the manuscripts, in *PMLA* 75(March 1960): 110–125, reprinted in *Yeats*, John Unterecker, ed., and Jon Stallworthy's discussion of the manuscripts in *Between the Lines*. For a hostile discussion of the poem, see Yvor Winters, *Forms of Discovery*. The capital of the

Eastern Roman Empire (330 to 1453 A.D.) and the "holy city" of the Greek Orthodox Church, Byzantium's culture is noted for mysticism, the preservation of ancient learning, and exquisitely refined symbolic art. In short, its culture (as Yeats saw it) was wise and passionless. In *A Vision*, his prose treatment of his complex mystical system, Yeats says:

> I think that in early Byzantium, maybe never before or since in recorded history, religious, aesthetic and practical life were one, that architect and artificers—though not, it may be, poets, for language has been the instrument of controversy and must have grown abstract—spoke to the multitude and the few alike. The painter, the mosaic worker, the worker in gold and silver, the illuminator of sacred books, were almost impersonal, almost perhaps without the consciousness of individual design, absorbed in their subject matter and that the vision of the whole people. They could copy out of old Gospel books those pictures that seemed as sacred as the text, and yet weave all into a vast design, the work of many that seemed the work of one, that made building, picture, pattern, metal-work or rail and lamp, seem but a single image.

An audio cassette of W. B. Yeats reading is available from Harper-Collins.

Topics for Discussion and Writing

1. The patterns of organization in "Sailing to Byzantium."
2. The poem can be said to record a debate between opposing desires. What are those desires?
3. Summarize the poem, perhaps in three or four sentences, and then explain Yeat's view of the happiness of old age, comparing it to more customary views of old age.

William Butler Yeats "For Anne Gregory" (p. 586)

One can imagine Yeats, at 65, writing about a woman of 19, in response to her somewhat petulant and innocent assertion that she wants to be loved "for herself alone." Presumably she means by this her intellectual and psychological characteristics, her mind and her personality. Yeats, more or less in the role of The Wise Old Man, asserts in the first stanza that it is simply a fact that youthful lovers will be taken by her physical beauty—a beauty, by the way, that seems formidable (note "ramparts")—and thrown into despair. The old Yeats presumably remembers his own youthful feelings, but note his reference to "an old religious man" who "found a text" to prove that only God could overlook her hair and love her for herself alone. If the old man "found" the text, presumably he was looking for it. The implication seems to be that beauty captivates not only "a young man, / Thrown into despair" (1 and 2), but also "an old religious man"—to say nothing of an old irreligious man, or of Yeats—and that such a man, feeling ashamed, might well search for a text that would explain or justify his apparently indecorous feelings.

Of course Yeats is speaking somewhat playfully, even teasingly, but the overall intention is to help this young female friend ("my dear,"16) accept her exceptional beauty. She may think of her hair as yellow, and she may imagine dying it "Brown, or black, or carrot," but for Yeats, and for " young men in despair," it is "great honey-colored / Ramparts," sweet, yet magnificent and beyond reach.

If one wants to move away from the poem a bit and turn to a larger issue, one might ask whether the poem is sexist. Can we imagine a poem consisting of a dialogue between an older woman and a young man, in which the woman assures the man that young women can never love him for himself alone, but only for his blond (or raven-black) hair (or profile, or body)? If one can't imagine such a poem, *Why* can't one? Is it because a sexist view prevents us from imagining an old woman giving good advice to a young man? Or is it perhaps because Yeat's poem touches on a truth, that is, young men are captivated by youthful female beauty, whereas the hypothetical poem is false; that is, young women are not taken chiefly by youthful male beauty? Or is it sexist to assume that, confronted with the opposite sex, the primary interests of young men and young women differ?

Topics for Discussion and Writing

1. What can you imagine Anne saying that provoked the poem?
2. In the first stanza Anne's hair is described both as "great honey-colored ramparts" and as "yellow." Why does the speaker use these two rather different characterizations? Judging from the second stanza, how would Anne describe her hair?
3. If you did not know that Yeats was 65 when he wrote the poem, would you be able to deduce from the poem itself that the speaker of the first and third stanzas is considerably older than Anne?
4. Anne says that she wants to be loved "for myself alone." Exactly what do you think this expression means?

5. Why would "an old religious man" search until he found a text that would prove that only God could love her for herself alone? Do you think Yeats shares this view?
6. In a sentence or two characterize Yeats as he reveals himself in this poem, and then characterize Anne.

An audio cassette of W. B. Yeats reading is available from Harper-Collins.

Edwin Arlington Robinson "Mr. Flood's Party" (p. 587)

Cleanth Brooks, R. W. B. Lewis, and R. P. Warren, in *American Literature* II, 1844, point out that among Robinson's poems, "Mr. Flood's Party" is fairly unusual in its shifts of tone. There is the language of the poet, making, for example, a reference to the medieval epic, *The Song of Roland* (or possibly to Browning's "Childe Roland"), and there is the contrasting language of Mr. Flood speaking to himself: "Well, Mr. Flood, / Since you propose it, I believe I will." But of course the effect of the reference to Roland is both to diminish Mr. Flood, by almost comically comparing this tippling old man to a heroic warrior, and also to elevate him by reminding us of the heroism of the lonely man. Notice too that Mr. Flood himself uses the "poetic diction" of "the bird is on the wind" (quoting from *The Rubayat*, and "auld lang syne." Another point: The poem is saved from sentimentality (the old man now friendless) largely by Flood's slightly comic (as well as pathetic) politeness.

William Carlos Williams "Spring and All" (p. 588)

This, the first poem in his book (1922) of the same title, is preceded by eleven pages of prose, the gist of which is the defense of a "new" American experimental writing. This introduction concludes with the words "THE WORLD IS NEW," and then the poem bursts upon us. It begins with the reference to the hospital (stock responses—which Williams dedicated his life to opposing—conjure up ideas of sickness and death, reinforced in "cold" and "dried," but it turns out that the poem moves on to the recovery of health, which after all is what hospitals are for); it moves on to a vivid and concrete description of bushes and trees that appear "Lifeless," then to a spring that "quickens," and finally back to the bushes and trees that "begin to awaken." What is "contagious" turns out to be not sickness, death, winter (all stock responses), but spring, and probably this contagious quality of spring is what the "All" of the title implies.

Characteristically, Williams seems "unpoetic": Although in line 2 "the surge of clouds" is metephoric (clouds as waves), and in line 7 "standing water" is a metaphor (though only a dead metaphor), one can say that in the first part of the poem figurative language is conspicuously absent. Not until line 15 ("dazed spring approaches") does figurative language emerge; the following stanza (16–20)continues the image of nature as human ("They enter the new world naked"), making it clear that the hospital is as much a place of birth as of death, and essentially a place where life is preserved, but the poem also continues to record sharp literal perceptions ("the stiff curl of wildcarrot leaf"), enhancing the last, metaphoric words: "rooted they / grip down and begin to awaken." The slight increase in the number of verbs (they are sparse in the beginning) helps to suggest the life that is pushing through the deadness. Whether literal or metaphoric, the lines seek (to borrow words which Williams used of his *Kora in Hell*)"to refine, to clarify, to intensify that eternal moment in which we alone live." See also, for a long discussion, Bram Dijkstra, *Cubism, Stieglitz, and the Earlier Poetry of William Carlos Williams*.

A "Voices and Visions" video cassette of William Carlos Williams is available from HarperCollins. An audio cassette of Williams reading is also available from HarperCollins.

Marianne Moore "Poetry" (p. 589)

See Lloyd Frankenberg, *Pleasure Dome*, pp. 137–141, and R. P. Blackmur, *Languages as Gesture*, pp. 266–268. In an interview in *Paris Review*, reprinted in *Writers at Work, Second Series*, Moore comments on her extensive use of quotations:

> I was just trying to be honorable and not to steal things. I've always felt that if a thing has been said in the *best* way, how can you say it better? If I wanted to say something and somebody has said it ideally, then I'd take it but give the person credit for it. That's all there is to it. If you are charmed by an author, I think it's very strange and invalid imagination that doesn't long to share it. Somebody else should read it, don't you think?

And perhaps the following comment, also in the interview, is relevant:

Do the poet and scientist not work analogously? Both are willing to waste effort. To be hard on himself is one of the main strengths of each. Each is attentive to clues, each must narrow the choice, must strive for precision . . . . The objective is fertile procedure. Is it not?

An audio cassette of Marianne Moore reading is available from HarperCollins. A "Voices and Visions" video cassette of Marianne Moore is also available from HarperCollins.

T. S. Eliot "The Love Song of J. Alfred Prufrock" (p. 591)

Among the useful introductory books are Elizabeth Drew, *T. S. Eliot*; Northrop Frye,*T. S. Eliot*; and Grover Smith, *T. S. Eliot's Poetry and Plays*. On "Prufrock," see also Rosenthal and Smith, *Exploring Poetry*; High Kenner,*The Invisible Poet: T. S. Eliot*, pp. 3–12; and Lyndall Gordon, *Eliot's Early Years*. It is well to alert students to the fact the "Prufrock" is not a Browningesque dramatic monologue with a speaker and a listener, but rather an internal monologue in which "I" (the timid self) addresses his own amorous self as "you." (Not every "you" in this poem, however, refers to Prufrock's amorous self. Sometimes "you" is equivalent to "one.") Possibly, too, the "you" is the reader, or even other people who, like Prufrock, are afraid of action.

Among the chief points usually made are these: The title proves to be ironic, for we scarcely get a love song: "J. Alfred Prufrock" is a name that, like the speaker, seems to be hiding something ("J.") and also seems to be somewhat old-maidish ("Prufrock" suggests "prude" and "frock"); the initial description (especially the "patient etherised") is really less a description of the evening than of Prufrock's state of mind; mock heroic devices abound (people at a cocktail party talking of Michelangelo, Prufrock gaining strength from his collar and stickpin); the sensuous imagery of women's arms leads to the men in shirtsleeves and to Prufrock's wish to be a pair of ragged claws.

Topics for Discussion and Writing

1. How does the speaker's name help to characterize him? What suggestions—of class, race, personality—do you find in the name? Does the poem's title strike you as ironic? If so how or why?
2. What qualities of big-city life are suggested in the poem? How are these qualities linked to the speaker's mood? What other details

of the setting—the weather, the time of day—express or reflect his mood? What images do you find especially striking?

3. The speaker's thoughts are represented in a stream-of-consciousness monologue, that is, in what appears to be an unedited flow of thought. Nevertheless, they reveal a story. What is the story?

An audio cassette of T. S. Eliot reading "The Love Song of J. Alfred Prufrock" is available from HarperCollins. A "Voices and Visions" video cassette of T. S. Eliot is also available from HarperCollins.

John Crowe Ransom Piazza Piece" (p. 595.)

"Piazza Piece" is a sonnet, and sonnets often treat the theme of love, but few if any others treat the old theme of "Death and the Maiden." It should be read aloud, and when it is read aloud, the apparently odd placement of "listen to an old man not at all" seems perfectly right, catching the old-fashioned tone of the suitor.

Not all students will know that "piazza" (Italian for square) in parts of the United States denotes a porch, verandah, or balcony; nor will they know that in the earliest days of automobiling the roads were not paved or covered with asphalt, so riders— in open cars, of course—wore dustcoats, coats that were ankle-length. Ransom, a Southerner who was born in 1880, catches the politeness and nostalgia that characterized (and still characterize) much of the South when a respectable woman was still "a lady," and a man was "a gentleman," and "Sir" was in common use.

Topics for Discussion and Writing

1. Who speaks the first eight lines? What words especially characterize him? He is "gentleman in a dustcoat," but who else is he? What is a "dustcoat" or a "duster"? Why is this garment especially appropriate here? Characterize the speaker of the six remaining lines.

2. In lines 9–10, she is waiting for her "truelove." In line 14 she is still "waiting." For whom does she think she is waiting? For whom does the reader know she is waiting? How do you know?

Archibald MacLeish "Ars Poetica" (p. 595)

See Donald Stauffer, *The Nature of Poetry*, pp. 121–125, and W. P. Standt in *College English* 19(October 1957): 28–29. Standt points out that in the first and second sections there are similes, but in the third section we move from similarity to identity; i.e., metaphors replace similes. Moreover, identity is stressed in the quasi-mathematical formula at the beginning of the third section.

This poem, like Moore's "Poetry," easily gets the class into a discussion of the nature of art. (Moore's poem is not concerned explicitly with "modern" poetry, but with new poetry of any period.) And a discussion of MacLeish's poem inevitably gets into whether MacLeish practices his precepts; the abundant detail gives us a sense of felt reality ("be"), but doesn't MacLeish also "mean"? Certainly "a poem should not mean but be" has meaning; and note, too, that MacLeish is not content to give us "An empty doorway and a maple leaf," for he prefaces this with an explanation, telling us that it stands "for all the history of grief."

It is useful to ask students to comment in detail on the figures. The figure of an empty doorway and an autumn leaf standing for grief is clear enough, but how is "a poem ... motionless in time / As the moon climbs"? Perhaps the idea is that a poem, because it stirs the emotions, seems to move, yet it is itself unchanging.

An audio cassette of Archibald MacLeish reading is available from HarperCollins.

Wilfred Owen "Dulce et Decorum Est" (p. 596)

There are plenty of comments about the horrors of war—for instance Tacitus's "they make a desert and call it peace," and Sherman's "War is Hell"—but even Tacitus and Sherman probably believed that war is necessary and can be heroic. It's our guess that they would even have agreed with Horace: "*Dulce et decorum est / Pro patria mori.*"

Owen is asserting that modern war is so dehumanizing that Horace's line—if it were ever true—is now certainly false. We say "dehumanizing" because even from the start Owen gives us images of ruined creatures: "Bent double," "old beggars," "hags." There is nothing here of Tennyson's Light Brigade charging manfully into the Valley of Death.

Death comes to a battered, knock-kneed, limping soldier who is seen as "flound'ring" rather than falling in some heroic pose. The speaker relives the sight of witnessing (through the eye-piece of his gas mask) his companion destroyed by what seemed to be a sea of poison gas, but equally horrible is the memory of the appearance of the dead body when it was carted away.

It's probably true to say that as long as war was (for the most part) something executed by professionals in remote places, politicians and poets and even the mass of citizens comfortable at home could find it easy to praise war. Speaking of war as it was in the eighteenth century, the Swiss philosopher Emerich de Vattell (1714–1767) said, "The troops alone carry on war, while the rest of the nation is at peace." But modern war—it is sometimes said that the Civil War was the first modern war—is quite another thing. First, an army can get its supplies from remote sources, which means from the civilians back home, who therefore become fair game for the enemy. Second, newspaper photography and television have brought the horrors of the battlefield into the home—and this, in effect, is what Owen does in the poem.

What of the structure of the poem? The first stanza (8 lines) consists of two quatrains (*ababcdcd*). Line 4 ends with a period, so why did Owen not begin a new stanza with line 5? Apparently he thought of the first two quatrains as an octave— possibly he even began by thinking he would write a sonnet. The next stanza is a sestet, rhyming *efefgh*. The fifth and sixth lines of this sestet will rhyme with the next two lines, so from the point of view of the rhyme scheme Owen has again written two quatrains, but he interrupted the second of these two, separating it from its last two lines by putting a space between lines 14 and 15. Surely this arrangement of lines has a meaning, and probably has an effect. Although the speaker uses "we" in line 2 and "our" in line 4, and thus identifies himself with the scene, until the last line of the sestet (i.e., until the second half of line 14) the impression is chiefly of a description of something out there, rather than a revalation of the self. But if for fifteen and a half lines the speaker seems chiefly to be an observer, the second half of the sixteenth line emphatically introduces the speaker's response: "I saw him drowning." In the next stanza, which consists of only two lines (15–16), considerable emphasis is given to the dead man, but an even greater emphasis is given to the speaker's response to the sight:

> In all my dreams, before my helpless sight,
> He plunges at me, guttering, choking, drowning.

The final stanza (twelve lines—three quatrains, the third of which grimly rhymes "glory" with "*mori*") begins by drawing the reader ("you") into the nightmare world of the narrator and the dead soldier. The speaker insistently holds onto this "you," addressing him (or her?) not only in line 17, but also in 21 and ironically (as "My friend") in line 25. The poem ends with a noble Latin sentiment, but this ending is scarcely designed to provide a quiet or upbeat ending; rather, it is designed to keep the squirming reader squirming.

E. E. Cummings "in Just-" (p. 597)

Like Gerard Manley Hopkins, Cummings sought to invigorate language, partly by means of unusual words. Unlike Hopkins's coinages, Cummings's are, for the most part, immediately accessible to students. Readers don't have difficulty with the language in this poem (e.g., they recognize a child's voice in "eddieand bill" and "bettandisbel"), but the allusion to Pan (in the "goat-footed / balloon Man") escapes most of them. If no one in the class knows who Pan is, our old-fashioned practice is to tell the students to look up Pan in an encyclopedia or dictionary of mythology and to report their findings at the next meeting, at which time most of them will see the appropriateness of Pan, a pastoral figure and a piper. Oddly (to our mind) one interpreter of the goat-footed balloon man sees (*College English* 23[January 1962] a symbol of "shady adult knowledge."

One other point: Most students, in the course of class discussion, will see that the repeated "wee" (5, 13, 24) works several ways: The balloon man is "little" (3); his whistle makes the sound of "wee"; "wee" is a child's exclamation of delight; and "we" children go running to buy balloons.

E.E. Cummings reads on two audio cassettes that are available from HarperCollins.

Topics for Discussion and Writing

1. In the first ten lines, what words are especially surprising in a love poem addressed to the beloved?
2. Paraphrase the second stanza, putting it into your own words in such a way that the gist of the idea is immediately clear to your reader.
3. Make a list of the ideas or topics that, almost without thinking, you might ordinarily expect in a conventional love poem—for instance, the beauty of the beloved. Then, in a paragraph or two,

indicate which of these ideas Auden includes, and what other ideas he surprisingly introduces.

4. How would you characterize the speaker of the poem? Bitter? Resigned? Ecstatic? Or what? You need not limit your answer to a single word; you will probably need a paragraph.

An audio cassette of W. H. Auden reading is available from HarperCollins.

W. H. Auden "Musèe des Beaux Arts" (p. 598)

Useful pieces on "Musee" are in *College English* 24(April 1963): 529–531; *Modern Language Notes* 76(April 1961): 331–336; *Textual Analysis*, ed. Mary Ann Caws (a relatively difficult essay by Michael Riffaterre); and *Art Journal* 32(Winter 1972–1973): 157–162—the last useful primarily because it includes reproductions of Brueghel's work and reprints other poems relating to his pictures. We reproduce Brueghel's picture of Icarus (in the Brussels Museum of Fine Arts, hence Auden's title); for a color reproduction see Timothy Foote, *The World of Brueghel*. Auden glances at some of Brueghel's other paintings (the children skating, in *The Numbering of Bethlehem*, are indifferent to Joseph and Mary, who are almost lost in a crowd; the dogs and the horses in *The Massacre of the Innocents*), and his poem accurately catches Brueghel's sense of nature undisturbed by what rarely happens to the individual.

As Otto Benesch points out (*The Art of the Renaissance in Northern Europe*, p. 99), in *Icarus* Brueghel gives us a sense of cosmic landscape. Plowman, shepherd, and fisherman go about their business, unaware of Icarus, who is represented in the lower right hand corner simply by his lower legs and feet, the rest of him being submerged in the sea. Daedalus is nowhere represented; the yellow sun sets in the west, and the sea, coasts, and islands are transfigured with a silvery light. It should be noted that in Ovid's account in *Metamorphoses*, VIII, pp. 183–235, the plowman, shepherd, and fisherman beheld Icarus and Daedalus with amazement, taking the two for gods. Given Brueghel's diminution of Icarus—legs and feet, unnoticed by the other figures in the picture—it is fair to say that Brueghel is offering a comment on the pride of scientists. James Snyder, who makes this point in *Northern Renaissance Art*, p. 510, also calls attention to the shiny pate of a recumbent man, a dead man, at the left margin, halfway up and all but invisible even in the original painting. This image, Snyder says, "assuredly is meant to express the old Netherlandish saying, 'No plow stops over the death of any man,' or over Brueghel's Everyman, a clever footnote that reveals, after all, that peasant wisdom can be as profound as that of the ancients."

Students are first inclined to see Auden's poem as an indictment, of indifference; our own view is that Auden gives the daily world its due, especially in such phrases as "doggy life" and "innocent behind"; that is, he helps us see that all of creation cannot and need not suffer along with heroes. Auden's poem evoked a pleasant reply by Randall Jarrell, "The Old and the New Masters," *Collected Poems* (1969), pp. 332–333. It begins, "About suffering, about adoration, the old masters / Disagree . . . . "

An audio cassette of W. H. Auden reading is available from HarperCollins.

Topics for Discussion and Writing

1. Reread the poem (preferably over the course of several days) a number of times, jotting down your chief responses after each reading. Then, in connection with a final reading, study your notes, and write an essay of 500 words setting forth the history of your final response to the poem. For example, you may want to report that certain difficulties soon were clarified, and that your enjoyment increased. Or, conversely, you may want to report that the poem became less interesting (for reasons you will set forth) the more you studied it. Probably your history will be somewhat more complicated than these simple examples. Try to find a chief pattern in your experience, and shape it into a thesis.

2. Consider a picture, either in a local museum or reproduced in a book, and write a 500–word reflection on it. If the picture is not well known, include a reproduction (a postcard from the museum, or a photocopy of a page of the book) with your essay.

W. H. Auden "The Unknown Citizen" (p. 599)

In "The Unknown Citizen" the speaker's voice is obviously not the poet's. The speaker—appropriately unidentified in a poem about a society without individuals—is apparently a bureaucrat. For such a person, a "saint" is not one who is committed to spiritual values, but one who causes no trouble.

An audio cassette of W. H. Auden reading is available from HarperCollins.

Topics for Discussion and Writing

1. What is Auden satirizing in "The Unknown Citizen"? (Students might be cautioned to spend some time thinking about whether Auden is satirizing the speaker, the citizen, conformism, totalitarianism, technology, or what.)
2. Write a prose eulogy of 250 words satirizing contemporary conformity, or, if you prefer, contemporary individualism.
3. Was he free? Was he happy? Explain.
4. In a paragraph or two, sketch the values of the speaker of the poem, and then sum them up in a sentence or two. Finally, in as much space as you feel you need, judge these values.

Elizabeth Bishop "The Fish" (p. 600)

Bishop's poem gives a highly detailed picture of a "venerable" heroic fish that, with its "medals" and its "beard of wisdom," becomes a symbol of courageous endurance. From the colors of the fish, seen and imagined ("brown skin," "darker brown," "rosettes of lime," "tiny white sea-lice," "white flesh," "dramatic reds and blacks," "pink swim-bladder," "tinfoil"), and from the colors of the old fish-lines, the poem moves to the rainbow in the oil in the bilge (the lowest part of the hull). The rainbow—the sign of hope and of God's promise to Noah to spare humanity—grows in the imagination until it fills "the little rented boat," illuminating (we might say) the speaker, who, perceiving the heroic history of the captive, forbears to conquer and returns the fish to the water.

Topics for Discussion and Writing

1. Underline the similes and metaphors, and think about their implications. Of course they help to describe the fish, but do they also help to convey the speaker's attitude toward the fish?
2. Why does the speaker release the fish at the end of the poem?

For a discussion of the poem, see Bonnie Costello, *Elizabeth Bishop.*

Elizabeth Bishop "Poem" (p. 602)

First, the title. We tell students in our composition classes that a piece of writing—whether by a student or by a professional—begins with the title; this poem provides a sort of test case. Bishop's titles are usually less laconic than this one, so we assume that this title too is significant. The poem is partly about a painting, and therefore about the effects of works of art; this title, then, reminds us at the start that we are confronting a work of art, or, to put it a little differently, Bishop's poem is itself, as an artifact, analogous to Uncle George's picture, a work of art, a concrete embodiment of a perception, and an object that will stimulate the mind of the perceiver.

We find touches of wry humor in "that awful shade of brown" ("awful" is also deeply disturbing), in the reference to "the artist's specialty," and in the bird that looks like a flyspeck—or the flyspeck that looks like a bird (12, 25, 26–27); there is a sort of humor, too, in the remembered monologue of the giver of the picture, presumably the speaker's mother or father (39–44). But any wryness that occurs after this last passage lacks humor; the remaining lines are not quite bitter, but they convey a strong sense of diminution or loss, as in "Which is which? / Life and the memory of it cramped, / dim, on a piece of Bristol board . . . ," and especially in "the little of our earthly trust. Not much / About the size of our abidance / along with theirs; the munching cows . . . . "

"Earthly trust" and "abidance" in the lines just quoted have a puritanical ring—though there is probably also a pun in "earthly trust," given the earlier financial references ("dollar bill," "never earned any money in its life," and "handed along collaterally"—another pun here). At the start the diminutive is engaging (the "tiny" cows, the "wisp" of the steeple), but soon the references to the small and the transient or the brief become disquieting. The picture is "done in an hour, 'in one breath'"; Uncle George abandoned Canada; "Life and the memory of it cramped, / dim, on a piece of Bristol board"; the speaker of the remembered conversation, who will "probably never / have room to hang these things again," is quite likely moving to smaller quarters. (Such a move is usually provoked by the loss of part of one's family.) We get "little . . . for free" (58), and though what we get on earth we treasure in memory, it cannot last. Right now, at least in memory, there are "spring freshets," but autumn and winter will come: the elms will be "dismantled" (64); that is, their covering or mantle of leaves will fall, or perhaps the branches will be lopped and the trees themselves will be chopped down. Although the reference to dismantling is powerful, it is not the last word; the poem ends with "the geese," and, after all, the little picture itself continues to survive. Art—including Bishop's poem (again we emphasize the importance of the title—is one of the things we "get for free." (One might, in class, compare this poem with Keat;s "Ode on a Grecian Urn," another poem about transience and art.) Helen Vendler, in *Part of Nature, Part of Us*, at the end of her discussion of Bishop's poem offers a somewhat different interpretation:

> As lightly as possible, the word "dismantled" . . . refutes the whole illusion of entire absorption in the memorial scene; the world of the poet who was once the child now seems the scenery arranged for a drama with only too brief a tenure on the stage—the play once over, the set is dismantled, the illusion gone. The poem, having taken the reader through the process that we name domestication and by which a strange terrain becomes first recognizable, then familiar, and then beloved, releases the reader at last from the intimacy it has induced. Domestication is followed, almost inevitably, by that dismantling which is, in its acute form, disaster . . . .

Earlier in the essay Vendler points out that "the place" depicted in the painting is described three times: first, visually; then, after "Heavens, I recognize this place," as a remembered landscape (but the painting remains a painting, consisting of "titanium white," etc.); and finally as something not merely seen by the eye or contemplated by the mind but perceived (Vendler says) "by the heart, touched into participation." See, in addition to Vendler, Bonnie Costello, *Elizabeth Bishop*.

Robert Hayden "Frederick Douglass" (p. 604)

The second question, below, asks why the subject of the sentence delayed so long. We take it that Hayden is seeking to instill in the reader a sensation corresponding (in an infinitely tiny way, of course) to the agonized sense of waiting that blacks for more than a century have experienced.

Another point: The words "mumbo jumbo" in line 6 perhaps deserve a comment. Among certain West African tribes, Mumbo Jumbo is or was revered as a god who protects the people from evil. In white America, where African religion was scarcely regarded with sympathy or even with tolerance, the words came to mean gibberish. Hayden neatly turns the tables, applying the term not to the language of Africans or African-Americans but to the language of white politicians.

Topics for Discussion and Writing

1. When, according to Hayden, will Douglass "be remembered"? And *how* will he be remembered?
2. "Frederick Douglass" consists of two sentences (or one sentence and a fragment). In what line do you find the subject of the first sentence? What is the main verb (the predicate) and where do you find it? How would you describe the effect of the long delaying of the subject? And of the predicate?
3. Does Hayden assume or seem to predict that there *will* come a time when freedom "is finally ours" (line 1), and "belongs at last to all" (line 3)?
4. Hayden wrote "Frederick Douglass" in 1947. In your opinion are we closer now to Hayden's vision or farther away? (You may find that we are closer in some ways and farther in others.) In your answer—perhaps an essay of 500 words—try to be as specific as possible.
5. "Frederick Douglass" consists of fourteen lines. Is it a sonnet? (For a discussion of the sonnet form, see pages 229–230.)

Robert Hayden "Those Winter Sundays" (p. 604)

Students can learn something about writing by thinking about the length of the four sentences that constitute this poem. The first stanza consists of a fairly long sentence (four and a half lines) and a short one (half a line, completing the fifth line of the poem). The brevity of that second sentence reinforces the content—that no one thought about the father—and the brevity also, of course, adds emphasis by virtue of its contrast with the leisurely material that precedes it. Similarly, the fourth sentence, much shorter than the third, adds emphasis, an emphasis made the more emphatic by the repetition of "What did I know?"

Next a confession: We thought about glossing "offices" in the last line, for students will almost surely misinterpret the word, thinking that it refers to places where white-collar workers do their tasks. But we couldn't come up with a concise gloss that would convey the sense of ceremonious and loving performance of benefits. And it may be just as well to spend some class time on this important word, because the thing as well as the word may be unfamiliar to many students. After the word has been discussed, the poem may be read as a splendid illustration of an "office." Like the father in the poem, who drives out the cold and brings warmth (by means of love, of course, as well as coal) to an unknowing child, an "austere and lonely" writer performs an office, shaping experience for another person's use.

One may want to raise the question in class of whether the knowledge that the author was black affects the poem's meaning.

Topics for Discussion and Writing

1. In line 1, what does the word "too" tell us about the father? What does it suggest about the speaker (and the implied hearer) of the poem?
2. What do you take to be the speaker's present attitude toward his father? What circumstances, do you imagine, prompted his memory of "Those Winter Sundays"? What line or lines suggest those circumstances to you?
3. What is the meaning of "offices" in the last line? What does this word suggest that other words Hayden might have chosen do not?

Henry Reed "Naming of Parts" (p. 605)

Most students will immediately hear—if the poem is read aloud in class—two voices. One voice is that of a riflery instructor, who maddeningly uses—four times in the first four lines—what has been called the "Kindergarten We"; and he uses it again in lines 6, 12, 20, 21, and 30. But from the middle of the fourth line of each stanza to the end of the stanza there is a countervoice, or, rather, we hear the thoughts of the recruit, whose mind turns from the numbing lecture to thoughts of "the neighboring gardens" (5) and of spring. Some of the instructor's phrases (e.g., in 10, where he speaks about slings, "Which in your case you have not got") are echoed but given a different context by the student ("in our case we have not got," in 12, the silence of the trees in spring).

The poem is delightfully comic, not least because of the boring talk of the instructor, because of the contrast between his talk and the recruit's thoughts, with puns on "easing the spring" (22, 24, and 25) and "point of balance" (27–28), and with mildly dirty allusions, but we don't think we are being hypersubtle when we say that these sexual puns arise from a not-at-all-comic desperation in the recruit's mind. Forced to listen to the droning instructor, who is talking about how to kill, the recruit mentally escapes to the abundant life going on around him. There is an assault in nature, too ("The early bees are assaulting and fumbling the flowers," 22), but that assault (in contrast to the instructor's lesson) is life-producing.

Dylan Thomas "Fern Hill" (p. 605)

"Fern Hill" is discussed in William York Tindall, *A Reader's Guide to Dylan Thomas; Explicator* 14(October 1955), Item 1; C. B. Cox in *Critical Quarterly* 1(Summer 1959): 134–138; and Elizabeth Drew and George Conner, *Discovering Modern Poetry*. Thomas recites the poem on Caedmon Records 1002. James G. Kennedy in *College English* 31(March 1970): 585–586, dwelling on the last two lines ("Time held me green and dying / Though I sang in my chains like the sea"), argues that the child "may have been stunted by his being let alone, as if he were a unique being, and by his being furnished with unrealistic ideas about the world . . . . The last line of 'Fern Hill' is powerful in its evocation of how the mind of bourgeois man may be fettered for life by a *laissez-faire* boyhood." This quotation should provoke lively response.

The poem is a sort of ode, celebrating the landscape of the poet's childhood and his innocence. But this innocence or joy is seen as transient, for time conquers everything. As early as the fourth line an *adult* perception is given: "Time let me hail . . . ," though in line 7 the expression "once below a time" suggests that the boy himself had no awareness of time. In the final stanza the childhood farm has "forever fled," since the speaker is fully aware of the changes wrought by time, but surely we feel that the loss is not total, for the poet is a singer and thus he is engaging in the same activity that the child engaged in. The last line ("Though I sang in my chains like the sea") does not merely comment on the ignorance of the child; after all, the mature poet sings "in . . . chains" of meter.

Two audio cassettes of Dylan Thomas reading are available from HarperCollins.

Topic for Writing

Evaluate the thesis that Thomas's poem is about nature deceiving the speaker by furnishing him with an unrealistic attitude toward reality.

Randall Jarell "The Woman at the Washington Zoo" (p. 607)

Jarrell discusses the poem, especially its progress through several drafts, in Brooks and Warren, *Understanding Poetry*, 4th ed., reprinted in *The Poet's Work*, Reginald Gibbons, ed. We extract a few comments, but the entire discussion is recommended. The speaker, a woman employed by the government, despairingly feels that her faded navy blue print dress is a sort of uniform. She knows that she attracts no attention, and that her days (like her work and her clothes) are humdrum. She looks into the eyes of the caged animals and sees a reflection, that is, sees herself as caged. The animals, however, are *not* like her.

As Jarrell says in his commentary, the poem begins with "colored women and colored animals and colored cloth—all that the woman sees as her opposite"; the saris of Indian and Pakistani women in Washington, he explains in the commentary, seem to be "cloth from another planet." "Inside the mechanical official cage of her life, her body," Jarrell explains, "she lives invisibly; no one feeds the animal— . . . the cage is empty," whereas the caged wild animals retain their identity as wild animals. The natural, wild world ("sparrows," "pigeons," and then, more loathsome, "buzzards") visits the caged wild beasts, but no one of her tribe comes to her. She herself has become dead flesh, like the buzzards' food. "Her own life is so terrible to her that to change, she is willing to accept even this, changing it as best she can." She hopes that under the ugly bird's red head and black wings is a human being (not a lifeless creature like herself) who will change her body by love.

William Stafford "Traveling Through the Dark" (p. 608)

The speaker is matter-of-fact, but by the end of the poem we realize that he is not only thoughtful in the sense of considerate of others (unlike the motorist who killed the deer, he pushes the deer off the road so that others won't have an accident) but also thoughtful in the sense of meditative. Although he realizes that he cannot possibly save the unborn fawn, he cannot dispose of the doe casually, knowing that he will also be killing its fawn.

We take it, then, that when he says "I thought hard for us all" (line 17) he means not only "our group" (line 10), but everything including the fawn. He briefly hesitates—his "only swerving"—but he does what he has to do, lest a motorist "swerve [and] . . . make more dead" (line 4).

In teaching this poem we usually try to reserve comment on the title until late in the discussion. If the poem has been talked about for a while, students can usually see that the title implies something about the human condition. All of us are "traveling through the dark," moving through a difficult, demanding world, sometimes swerving a bit, but by and large guided by principles. The resonance of Stafford's title will become especially clear if you ask students how it compares with some invented title, such as "The Dead Deer," or "On the Edge of the Wilson River."

A postscript. Is it absurd to compare the poem to Frost's "Stopping by Woods on a Snowy Evening"? We have in mind especially Frost's contrast between the speaker and the little horse that, being only a horse, can't share the speaker's values. In Stafford's poem, the automobile serves somewhat as the horse; its parking lights are on, and its engine purrs steadily. No swerving here, no decisions to make. But unlike machines, human beings have to make hard decisions in a world of danger (the tail-light turns the exhaust red).

Topics for Discussion and Writing:

1. What do we know (or believe we know) about the speaker of these lines?
2. Rereading the second stanza, note the pauses in line 6. What do they seem to tell you about the speaker's frame of mind?
3. Line 11 also has three pauses. In reading the line what do you sense about the speaker's feelings?
4. Line twelve tells us that the speaker hesitated—and then the poem hesitates. Instead of moving forward to the conclusion of the story, the fourth stanza offers some description. What is described and how is it described? Try to imagine the poem without stanza 4. Do you find the stanza necessary? If so, why?
5. In the final stanza who does "us all" refer to? Does it include the same members as "our group" (in line 15) or not? Why does the speaker characterize his thinking (in line 17) as "swerving"?
6. In light of your reading of the poem, what meanings does the title have?
7. What choices does the speaker of "Traveling" have? Do you think he makes the right choice? Explain.

Lawrence Ferlinghetti "Constantly risking absurdity" (p. 609)

Ferlinghetti has insisted that poetry be read aloud, and as a consequence, he writes poetry that is easily intelligible to auditors. (Not surprisingly, the one allusion in Ferlinghetti's poem is not to mythology or literature, but to the liveliest and most popular art, film.) Easy intelligibility, however, means that the poet is "constantly risking absurdity." Of course the point is not to be absurd; absurdity is a risk one runs in trying to "perceive / taut truth" as one approaches "Beauty" and hopes to catch her. The shape of the poem on the page more or less imitates the progress and the pauses of a performer on a tightrope, and perhaps it also imitates his balancing pole extending far out on each side. The poem is obviously related to many of William Carlos Williams's poems, especially to "The Artist." And it is worthwhile to remind students of Frost's comment that a poem is a "performance in words." In addition to Ferlinghetti's typographical performance on paper, the word-play is part of the act ("climbs on rime," of "balancing on eyebeams," "sleight-of-foot tricks," " with gravity").

Richard Wilbur "Love Calls Us to the Things of This World" (p. 610)

Wilbur's poem is a sort of reply to the First Epistle to John 2:15: "Love not the world, neither the things that are in the world."

The title of Wilbur's poem speaks of "things of this world," but the poem begins with other-worldly words: "spirited," "soul," "bodiless," followed by such related words as "air," "rising," and "flying." The vision, of course, is not really of heaven but of laundry (bedsheets, blouses, smocks) hung out to dry on a clothesline extended between pulleys—a sight unfamiliar to many of today's students, who may know only of the laundromat with its driers. (The pun in "awash," in line 5, usually escapes their notice.)

The delightful vision of bodiless garments fluttering in the breeze seems at first (16–20) a rebuke to the workaday world. But line 21 marks a shift, and the second half of the poem moves to the world's "hunks and colors" (a contrast with the earlier diction of weightlessness and whiteness) which, when warmed by the sun, become acceptable to the soul (21–24). The waking body, with its soul, celebrates the things of this world: thieves in clean linen (such as is described in the airy opening lines); lovers, "fresh and sweet," who clothe themselves, but will undo their clothing when they make love; and "the heaviest nuns . . . [in] dark habits," whose dark clothing contrasts with the white laundry at the beginning, but is no less spiritual. The nuns, dedicated to the spiritual world (but surely there is a pun in "dark habits"), keep an especially "difficult balance" as they move through the things of this world.

Anthony Hecht "The Dover Bitch" (p. 611)

Andrews Wanning, to whom the poem is dedicated, is a teacher of literature. Like the title, the subtitle ("A Criticism of Life") is derived from Matthew Arnold, who in "The Study of Poetry," *Essays in Criticism, Second Series,* speaks of poetry as "a criticism of life." Hecht's poem, which at first glance is a parody of Arnold, therefore is also a criticism of poetry (though Arnold's "Dover Beach"—text, 578—survives it), and, as we will argue in a minute, also a criticism of life. Inevitably Hecht's poem must be discussed in connection with Arnold's, but sooner or later the discussion probably ought to get to matters of tone in "The Dover Bitch."

Much of Hecht's poem purports to give the girl's point of view, though we should remember that the speaker is not the girl, but a rather coarse fellow who knows her. This speaker sympathizes with her (to "be addressed / As a sort of mournful cosmic last resort / Is really tough on a girl"), but his sensibilities are not of the finest (he tells us that although she is "Running to fat," he gives her "a good time"). If he introduces a note of sexuality that is conspicuously absent from Arnold's poem and that affords some comedy, one's final impression may be that the poem shows us the bleak, meaningless, loveless world that Arnold feared. As Christopher Ricks puts it in *Victorian Studies* 6(1968), Hecht's brilliant and poignant poem is by no means flippant . . . . Having subjected Arnold to an unprecedented skepticism, [the poem suddenly reveals] the superiority of Arnold—and of all he epitomized—to that knowing speaker whose worldliness was at first refreshing. The poem, we realize, is in important ways a tribute to Arnold, though hardy a reverential one . . . " (pp. 539–540).

Allen Ginsberg "A Supermarket in California" (p. 612)

The poem evokes Walt Whitman by name and evokes his poetry in the long, unrhymed lines and in the catalogs of commonplace objects of American life. But Ginsberg's America is not Whitman's, for Ginsberg makes the point that Whitman too was lonely while he lived and finally encountered the loneliness of death. The allusion to the Spanish poet Garcia Lorca is to his poem on Walt Whitman, and also calls to mind yet another homosexual poet whose love was unreciprocated. As we see it, the "self-conscious" poet, his head aching (1), draws inspiration from Whitman, who lived in an earlier and more innocent age, an age when a man could unselfconsciously celebrate male beauty and comradeliness. But that age is "the lost America of love" (11), and in any case the Whitman who celebrates it and who is the poet's "courage-teacher" (13) was himself "lonely" (again 13) and, like all mortals, at last lost all. By the way, in the first sentence, Ginsberg seems to confuse the Lethe (the river of forgetfulness) with the Styx (the river across which Charon poled his ferry).

Adrienne Rich "Living in Sin" (p. 613)

If some of the woman's perceptions seem to indicate hyperesthesia (she hears "each separate stair . . . writhe"), for the most part her perceptions are fairly ordinary: "last night's cheese," bugs among the saucers, and so on. The man, however, does not perceive even these, and for the moment—since we see him through her eyes—he seems utterly oafish. Notice the description of the apartment, imagined as an attractive still-life ("A plate of pears, / a piano with a Persian shawl, a cat / stalking the picturesque amusing mouse," in contrast to the apartment with "dust upon the furniture of love," scraps of food, a piano that is "out of tune," and a lover (temporarily absent) who needs a shave. Later she is back in love—more concerned with the man than with the things around them—but this is not a love poem, and the real interest is in the woman's diminished (more reasonable) view of love, even though she is now back in love. The "sin" of the title is not a matter of cohabiting without the blessing of the church; rather, the "sin" is that she has seen through the myth of romantic happiness in difficult circumstances. If the stairs no longer "writhe," she is nevertheless conscious of them and of the "relentless day." Presumably never again will she think the studio will "keep itself"; now she knows that love in not the whole of life.

Adrienne Rich "Rape" (p. 614)

We can think of a number of earlier poems about rape—one of them, Yeats's "Leda and the Swan," is in our text—and it occurs to us that in virtually all of them the suffering of the woman is transformed by a mythic vision. (So far as we know, all poems on Philomela turn the violated woman not only into a bird, as Ovid did, but also into a symbol that presumably should be contemplated with sweet melancholy.)

Rich's poem is different. The violated woman is not metamorphosed and mythologized. She is, at the end of the poem as at its beginning, an ordinary woman, a "you" who lives in a violent male world, a world in which everyone else is rapist, cop, father, stallion, unsympathetic confessor. The victim of the rape is victimized a second time when, "the maniac's sperm still greasing your thighs, / . . .

You have to confess / to him, you are guilty of the crime / of having been forced." In Ovid, the authorities (the gods) take pity on the victim and metamorphose her, but in Rich's poem the police officer takes pleasure in the victim's distress: "the hysteria in your voice pleases him best." The first rapist is a "maniac," but the second, the police officer-confessor, is empowered by society, and so at the end the victim is diminished rather than elevated into the world of myth.

Linda Pastan "Marks" (p. 615)

The graders (husband, son, daughter) give steadily lower marks to the speaker, moving from A to B plus to "average," and then to "pass" (which everyone knows can mean just barely passing); but the speaker, in a surprise ending, then awards a sort of mark or academic label to herself, a label which might seem to suggest a still further diminution but which here suggests a course of vigorous action that will greatly affect those who so casually have been grading her: "I'm dropping out."

But how seriously, we ask our students, does a reader take the poem? To our ear, the speaker is good-natured and at least semi-playful. She mocks the treatment she receives from those who take her for granted, but the mockery (if that is not too strong a word) seems genial enough—though perhaps that is what many a complacent man thought until his wife explained that, no, she wasn't kidding and, yes, she really was walking out on him (shades of Ibsen's Nora). Perhaps it comes down to this: Does your ear hear a voice that conveys affection even while it complains and threatens—or does it hear a voice speaking in deadly earnest?

Sylvia Plath "Daddy" (p. 615)

C. B. Cox and A. R. Jones point out, in *Critical Quarterly* 6 (Summer 1964): 107–122, that literature has always been interested in perverse states of mind (Greek and Roman interest in the irrational; Elizabethan interest in melancholy, jealousy, madness, etc.; and Browning's dramatic monologues). The "fine frenzy" of the poet himself (in the words of Shakespeare's Theseus), once associated with inspiration and even divinity, in the twentieth century links the poet with the psychotic personality. And apparently a sensitive (poetic) mind can make only a deranged response in a deranged world. Plath's "Daddy" begins with simple repetitions that evoke the world of the nursey rhyme (and yet also of the witches in Macbeth, who say, "I'll do, I'll do, and I'll do"). The opening line also connects with the suggestion of the marriage service ("And I said I do") in line 67. The speaker sees herself as tormented yet also as desiring the pain inflicted by her father/love ("Every woman adores a Fascist"). She recognizes that by accepting the need for love she exposes herself to violence. The speaker's identification of herself with Jews and the evocation of "Dachau, Auschwitz, Belsen" suggest some identity between the heroine's tortured mind and the age's. Death, Cox and Jones go on to say, is the only release from a world that denies love and life. The "Daddy" of the poem is father, Germany, fatherland, and—life itself, which surrounds the speaker and which the speaker rejects.

In *Commentary* (July 1974 and October 1974), there is an exchange of letters on the appropriateness of Plath's use of Nazi imagery in a poem about her father. Roger Hoffman, in the July issue, argues that the imagery is valid because in a child's mind an authoritarian father is fearsome. Irving Howe, in October (9–12), replies that this argument is inadequate ground "for invoking the father as a Nazi." The speaker of the poem is not a child, Howe says, "the grown-up writer, Sylvia Plath." He goes on: the " unwarranted fusion of child's response and grown-ups' references makes for either melodrama or self-pity." Howe also rejects Carole Stone's argument (July) that the images are acceptable because "one individual's psyche [can] approximate the suffering of a people." Howe replies that the victims of the concentration camps didn't merely "suffer"; they were methodically destroyed. He questions the appropriateness of using images of the camps to evoke personal traumas. There is, he says, a lack of "congruence" between the object and the image, "a failure in judgement." Some useful criticism can also be found in *The Art of Sylvia Plath*, ed. Charles Newman.

A "Voices and Visions" video cassette of Sylvia Plath is available from HarperCollins. An audio cassette of Sylvia Plath reading is also available from HarperCollins.

Topic for Discussion

The speaker expresses her hatred for her father by identifying him with the Nazis, herself with the Jews. Is it irresponsible for a poet to compare her sense of torment with that of Jews who were gassed in Dachau, Auschwitz, and Belsen?

N. Scott Momdady "The Eagle-Feather Fan" (p. 618)

One way to begin a discussion of the poem is to invite students to comment on who the speaker is, and what he (or she?) is doing. We take it that the Native American speaker is holding a fan while dancing an eagle-dance, which imitates the scudding, circling flight of an eagle (lines 12–13). The speaker is accompanied by drum music and by singing (14). Perhaps the speaker too is singing these words; if not, he (we assume the speaker is a male, but we are not familiar with the dance) thinks them.

Although the first line, "The eagle is my power," seems to suggest that the speaker dominates the eagle, as the poem proceeds—as the dance proceeds—the speaker is swept up or possessed by the eagle (represented by the eagle-feather fan), or, better, the speaker and the eagle become one. Notice that early in the poem the speaker emphasizes that his hand holds the fan, but later he says that the fan bears his fingers (9), and that his bones are "hollow," that is like a bird's. The unity of the human world with the surrounding natural world can hardly go further.

Topics for Discussion and Writing

1. In the first two lines the speaker seems to assert his possession of both the power of the eagle and the fan. At what point does he begin to relinquish possession and control?
2. What effect do the singing and drums have? As the eagle "scuds" and "circles" (in lines 12 and 13) what do we imagine the speaker to be doing?
3. Imagine or write a prose paragraph describing the scene depicted in "The Eagle-Feather Fan." What advantage does the poem have over a prose "translation"?
4. Compare "The Eagle-Feather Fan" to any one or two of the poems about nature in this book, focusing on the relationship between consciousness and the natural enviornment.

Lucille Clifton "in the inner city" (p. 618)

This poem—from a book called *Good Times*—catches a distinctive voice, meditative and colloquial, the colloquialisms never slipping into merely cute dialect or local color.

Pat Mora "Sonrisas" (p. 619)

First, a reminder that another poem by Mora, "Immigrants," appears in Chapter 1.

Most students will quickly see that the two stanzas stand for the "two rooms" (worlds, we might ordinarily say) in which the Chicano speaker lives. (Interestingly, the word "stanza" comes from an Italian word meaning "room," "stopping place"; a stanza is a room in a poem.) The first room in "Sonrisas" is a room of Anglo culture, "careful," usually unsmiling and when there are smiles the smiles are "beige" (cautious, neutral, certainly not enthusiastic). This is a world of "budgets, tenure, curriculum," that is the orderly world of the establishment. The second room is a room of Chicano culture, a world of coffee-breaks, "laughter," "noise," scolding (presumably affectionate) and "dark, Mexican eyes" that contrast with the beige smiles and eyes of unspecified color in the first stanza. If the first stanza hints at the world of power and therefore of money (in "budgets, tenure, curriculum"), this stanza hints very gently at a world a relative poverty in "faded dresses," but it seems evident that for the speaker this world is more attractive, more (we might say) human.

Don L. Lee "But He Was Cool or: he even stopped for green lights (p. 619)

Lee's poetry, like some of the poetry of Imamu Amiri Baraka (LeRoi Jones), owes something to William Carlos Williams and to Williams's descendants, the Beat poets, though of course the Beats were indebted to the rhythms of jazz, and so ultimately the chief sources are black speech and black music. The influence of black speech is apparent in a quality that Stephen Henderson (*Understanding the New Black Poetry*, pp. 33–34) calls "virtuoso naming and enumerating," a technique [that] overwhelms the listener," which may be derived from "the folk practice of fiddling and similar kinds of wordplay." There is also a fondness for hyperbole, combined with witty, elegant coolness.

Sharon Olds "I Go Back to May 1937" (p. 620)

One way of getting a lively discussion going is to mention that although poets often adopt a persona, Olds's "I Go Back" strikes most readers as autobiographical. What do the students think about Olds disclosing such intimate (and potentially embarrassing) family history?

Topics for Discussion and Writing

1. Summarize the poem in a sentence or two. (In summarizing, try to convey a sense of the speaker's changes of attitude, a sense of development. You may want to use a structure something like this: "The speaker begins by envisioning her parents at college and thinks . . . but . . . because . . . and then . . . . " That is, if you find in the poem *a sequence* of thought, rather than a collection of unconnected thoughts, try to give your reader a sense of that sequence.)

2. What do you take to be the speaker's attitude toward her parents? Does the poem give us enough information to let us comment on the speaker's attitude toward herself? If so, what is this attitude?

3. Discuss the poem with a friend or two, then read it aloud, and compare your oral interpretations. How do they differ (for example, in the tone in which you read a certain line), and why?

4. A collaborative exercise: Divide the class into groups of five, and ask each group to discuss the poem and to come up with one paragraph interpreting the poem. Then have a member of each group read the paragraphs aloud in class, and have the class discuss the differences.

5. "I go back to May 1937" doesn't rhyme, and its lines vary in length. Do you agree that it is a poem, or is it really prose printed in a strange way? Explain.

Nikki Giovanni "Master Charge Blues" (p. 621)

For some comments on blues, see the note on Langston Hughes's "Evenin' Air Blues," in this manual, p. 128.

Craig Raine "A Martian Sends a Postcard Home" (p. 622)

We like to begin most discussions by talking about the title—about what expectations are set up by the title—and we especially recommend the procedure for this poem. Most students will find the combination of "Martian" and "postcard" at least a bit incongruous (Martians have spaceguns and "thoughtgrams"); some students (even without having read the poem) will guess that the poem will be the report of a traveler impressed by the strange things he sees on earth. And, of course, an outsider's report of something strange (here, a Martian's report of things on earth) may itself seem to be strange when read by those who are familiar with the thing described (here, we earthlings). A large part of the point of such writing is to help us to see freshly things we have taken for granted.

The Martian, in his report, of course gets a few things slightly wrong. He thinks that all books are called "Caxtons" and that all cars are called "Model T." Probably the hardest part of the poem is the opening, the first four lines, describing books ("mechanical birds with many wings") which can make one cry ("cause the eyes to melt") and can make one laugh ("cause . . . the body to shriek without pain"). The car (13), the rear-view mirror (15–16), and the watch and clock (17–18) cause little difficulty; the telephone (19–24) is fairly easily guessed, even though American phones, unlike English phones (at the time when the poem was written) do not make a snoring noise when lifted from the cradle. The bathroom (25–30) is only a little more riddling. Raine (at a poetry reading) mentioned that the Martian, who during his short visit presumably saw only children cry, assumes that when adults suffer and cry, they do so privately, in the "punishment room" (26) where there is water but no food. (Martians apparently do not excrete.) In the final two lines, the Martian, speaking of couples dreaming, thinks they are reading "with their eyelids shut." The poem thus ends, as it begins, with reading.

But what does one make of what the Martian makes of us? He (or she?) seems to be very decent, sensitive to earthly phenomena, and endowed with the gift of metaphor, the sign of the poet. (In fact, when Raine reads the poem to audiences, he usually says that the Martian is not only a Martian, but also a metaphor for the poet.) The passage on mist is a good example: "the world is dim and bookish / like engravings under tissue paper" (9–10) (In our discussion of metaphor in the text we make the point that metaphors are closely related to riddles. In Richard Wilbur's "Love Calls Us to the Things of This World" (text 610), the description of laundry drying in the breeze is a fresh, metaphoric view of what used to be a familiar sight. Many passages in Raine's poem are similarly close to riddles.)

The Martian reports phenomena, but (luckily for us?) does not judge our actions. Earthlings thus come off pretty well, especially if we contrast this poem with another Martian report, John Hall Wheelock's "Earth" (text p. 486).

One other point: We have been able to explain a few puzzling de-

tails (especially the mistaken account of why adults go to the bathroom) because the poet has told us what's going on. But is the poet's
intention binding? Suppose a reader says that the last two lines describe not people dreaming, but people falling asleep while watching
television. Are they wrong?

Joy Harjo "Vision" (p. 623)

The view that the earth is sacred is found in many societies but it is
apparently especially strong in the thought of Native Americans.

Some students—not necessarily only those who are Native
Americans—may know something about Native American beliefs,
and they may provide a way of entry to the poem. It may also happen
that some students may know that according to Genesis 9.12–17 God
established the rainbow as a token of a covenant with Noah and his
descendants. If this concept come us, you may want to contrast it with
Harjo's poem and to compare Harjo's poem with Wordsworth's "My
Heart Leaps Up":

> My heart leaps up when I behold
> A rainbow in the sky:
> So was it when my life began;
> So is it now I am a man;
> So be it when I shall grow old,
>   Or let me die!
> The Child is father to the Man;
> And I could wish my days to be
> Bound each to each by natural piety.

For Wordsworth, "piety" is "natural piety," something rooted in the
human being's perception of (responsiveness to) nature, rather than
something based on Scripture. We take it that Harjo's vision is close to
Wordsworth's.

We are not saying, of course, that the visions are the same, but we
do find a close resemblance in the emphasis on the perception of nature as animating the human. For Harjo, the rainbow animates the
earth, giving "horses / of color" to humans, "horses that were within
us all of this time / but we didn't see them . . . . "

Rita Dove "The Fish in the Stone" (p. 624)

This poem touches on the sensuous and even magical experience of
scientific thought. The fossilized fish in the stone is here imagined as
having thoughts and desires: "The fish in the stone / would like to fall

/ back into the sea." Why? "He is weary / of analysis, the small / predictable truths." Invite students to offer their opinions as to what these "small / predictable truths" may be. Are they the truths that the paleontologist utters, concerning the dating of the fossil? And what of the fifth stanza, "the fish in the stone / knows to fail is / to do the living a favor"? Has the fish "failed" by dying, and done the living a favor by becoming a fossil that offers information and that also reminds the beholder of the unfathomable mysteries of life?

This presumably sober-colored fossil looks with some disdain at the ant which, pressed in amber, has the garish coffin of a gangster. The fish, in fact, has an understated appearance, its anatomy resembling the leaves of a fern that offers "secret delight" to the scientist, who, touching the fine ridges of the fossil, "strokes the fern's / voluptuous braille."

Students might be invited to discuss the effect of the short lines. How would the poem sound—how would its effect on us be changed—if, for instance, the first stanza were printed as one long Whitmanesque line, and if the first three lines of the second stanza were another such line, and the next four yet another?

In a letter to us, Ms Dove says:

> There is a suggestion in the poem that the fish fossil is merely the imprint of a creature that the scientist can never fully comprehend; he / she may finger its impression, seeking to possess it like a lover, but there is an essence of "fish-being" that is lost to us forever—silence that is constantly moving, and that intangible, great truth is invisible under the harsh white light of the laboratory. In this sense the poem, although inviting the reader to explore the mysteries of science, warns that there is more to understanding existence than empirical thought or deductive reasoning.

Rita Dove "Daystar" (p. 625)

The poem comes from Dove's Pulitzer-prize book, *Thomas and Beulah* (1986), which contains sequences of poems about blacks who migrated from the South to the North.

In thinking about a poem, one can hardly go wrong in paying attention to the title. Here, why "Daystar"? "Daystar" can refer either to a planet—especially Venus—visible in the eastern sky before sunrise, or to the sun. Both meanings are probably relevant here. The speaker's brief period of escape from (at one extreme) the children's diapers and dolls and (at the other) Thomas's sexual demands is perhaps like the brief (and marvelous) appearance of a planet at a time that one scarcely expects to see a heavenly body; and this moment of escape—a moment of wonderful independence—is perhpas also like the sun, which stands in splendid isolation, self-illuminating. Sometimes, as she sits "behind the garage," she is closely connected to the visible world around her (the cricket, the maple leaf), but sometimes, with her eyes closed, she perceives only her self. (The mention, in the last line of the poem, of "the middle of the day" perhaps indicates that the chief meaning of "daystar" here is the sun, but we see no reason to rule out the suggestion of the other meaning.)

Judith Ortiz Cofer "My Father in the Navy: A Childhood Memory (p. 626)

Most students will quickly see the imagery of death ("stiff and immaculate / in the white cloth, / an apparition") and the Christian imagery ("halo," "When he rose," "kept vigil." "like an angel / heralding a new day"). The sailor-father comes back to the living world from "below," and thus would seem to resemble the risen Jesus. But, at least as we understand the poem, it is the living (the speaker and her siblings) who, so to speak, bring life to the "apparition," whereas of course in Christian thinking it is Jesus who animates human beings, that is gives them the possibility of eternal heavenly life.

David Mura "An Argument: On 1942" (p. 626)

Mura is a *sansei*, a third-generation Japanese-American. Born in 1952, he of course did not experience internment in the relocation camps of 1942. The poem is rooted in the fairly widespread difference today between the attitude of, on the one hand, most of those who experienced the camps (chiefly *issei* [first-generation] and their American-born children, *nissei* [second-generation], and on the other hand, many *sansei*, who were born after World War II, and who cannot understand how their parents and grandparents allowed themselves to be so subjugated.

Mura's poem—in effect an argument between the poet and his mother—begins in the son's voice. Between the fourth and the fifth lines, however, the mother interrupts (or at least she does so in the son's imagination), and the poet reports her words:"—No, no, she tells me. Why bring it back? The camps are over." The mother wishes to forget the experience, or at least not to dwell on it, but her son, she says, is "like a terrier . . . gnawing a bone." For her, the experience was chiefly boring (line 9). (Of course one can say that she has repressed her memories of humiliation—but one can also entertain the possibility that for a child the experience was indeed chiefly boring.) For the son, who did not experience it but who now looks at it through the eyes of a mature Japanese-American writing in the late 1980's, the thought of the indignity it galling.

What does a reader make of the conflict? Presumably the reader can hold both views, sharing the youth's sense of outrage but also understanding the mother's view—which, incidentally, is given the climactic final position: "David, it was so long ago . . . how useless it seems . . . " In fact, it seems entirely possible that the poet himself holds both views. At least to our ear he voices them with equal effectiveness.

After we had written the preceding remarks, we received the following comment from David Mura:

> The poem starts with an imaginary poem in my voice, a lament for the world that was destroyed by the internment order. I'm both attracted to and wary of the romantic cast to such a voice, and in the poem, my mother gives another version of the past, one which downplays the effect of the camps and argues against over-romanticizing both the past and past sufferings. In the end, I think there's a great deal of denial in my mother's version of the past, and yet, her version is a reality with which I must contend; after all, she was there, and I wasn't (of course, her presence at these events doesn't necessarily mean her interpretation of them can't be wrong). Both her version and my version exist in the poem as realities which the reader must confront. As with much of my work, I think of this poem as a political poem.

For another poem about the internment of Japanese-Americans in 1942, see Mitsuye Yamada, "To the Lady" (p. 450).

Chapter 20

Some Elements of Drama

Among useful basic studies are S. Barnet et al., eds. *Types of Drama* (an anthology with introductions and critical essays); Cleanth Brooks and Robert Heilman, eds., *Understanding Drama* (an anthology with a good deal of critical commentary); J. L. Styan, *The Elements of Drama*; and Eric Bentley, *The Life of the Drama*.

Susan Glaspell "Trifles" (p. 637)

Some students may know Glaspell's other version of this work, a short story entitled "A Jury of Her Peers." Some good class discussion can focus on the interchangeability of the titles. "Trifles" could have been called "A Jury of Her Peers," and vice versa. A peer, of course, is an equal, and the suggestion of the story's title is that Mrs. Wright is judged by a jury of her equals—Mrs. Hale and Mrs. Peters. A male jury would not consist of her equals because—at least in the context of the story and the play—males simply don't have the experiences of women and therefore can't judge them fairly.

Murder is the stuff of TV dramas, and this play concerns a murder, of course, but it's worth asking students how the play differs from a whodunnit. Discussion will soon establish that we learn, early in "Trifles," who performed the murder, and we even know, fairly early, *why* Minnie killed her husband. (The women know what is what because they correctly interpret "trifles," but the men are baffled, since they are looking for obvious signs of anger.) Once we know who performed the murder, the interest shifts to the question of whether the women will cover up for Minnie.

The distinction between what the men and the women look for is paralleled in the distinction between the morality of the men and the women. The men stand for law and order, for dominance (they condescend to the women, and the murdered Wright can almost be taken as a symbol of male dominance), whereas the women stand for mutual support or nurturing. Students might be invited to discuss *why* the women protect Minnie. Is it because women are nurturing? Or because they feel guilt for their earlier neglect of Minnie? Or because, being women, they know what her sufferings must have been like, and feel that she acted justly? All of the above?

The symbols will cause very little difficulty. (1) The "gloomy" kitchen suggests Minnie's life with her husband; (2) the bird suggests Minnie (she sang "like a bird," was lively, then became caged and was broken in spirit).

The title is a sort of symbol too, an ironic one, for the men think (in

Mr. Hale's words) that "Women are used to worrying over trifles." The men in the play never come to know better, but the reader-viewer comes to understand that the trifles are significant and that the seemingly trivial women have outwitted the self-important men. The irony of the title, is established by the ironic action of the play.

Does the play have a *theme*? In our experience, the first theme that students may propose is that "it's a man's world." There is something to this view, but (1) a woman kills her husband, and (2) other women help her to escape from the (male) legal establishment. Do we want to reverse the first suggestion, then, and say that (in this play) it is really a woman's world, that women run things? No, given the abuse that all of the women in the play take. Still, perhaps it is fair to suggest that one of the things the play implies is that overbearing male behavior gets what it deserves—at least sometimes. Of course, when put this way, the theme is ancient; it is at the root of the idea of *hubris*, which is said to govern much Greek tragedy. Glaspell gives it a very special twist by emphasizing the women's role in restoring justice to society.

Chapter 21

Tragedy

On tragedy, consult T. R. Henn, *The Harvest of Tragedy*; F. L. Lucas, *Tragedy* (especially good on "recognition" and "reversal"); Oscar Mandel, *A Definition of Tragedy*; Herbert J. Muller, *The Spirit of Tragedy*; Richard B. Sewall, *The Vision of Tragedy*; *Tragedy: Modern Essays in Criticism,*, Richard B. Sewall and Laurence Michel, eds.; and George Steiner, *The Death of Tragedy*.

William Shakespeare *Othello* (p. 657)

A video cassette of Shakespeare's *Othello* is available from HarperCollins.

The following scene-by-scene commentary seeks to digest a fair amount of reading, done over many years. It makes no claim to originality; the chief sources are given at the end of this discussion.

Inevitably much classroon discussion will focus on the matter of Othello's blackness. (At the end of this commentary we cite some bibliographic references on the topic, but here we will simply say that nineteenth-century efforts to lighten Othello's color—to turn him into a "tawny Moor" rather than a black—now seem absurd. The gist of the idea was that Desdemona *couldn't* have fallen in love with a black. But of course Shakespeare's point is that this is exactly what she has done—to the horror of her father. Notice, by the way, that no one in the play expresses surprise or annoyance that a person of color commands the Ventian forces. Othello had been an honored guest at Brabantio's household, and he is esteemed by the other Venetians. Even Iago expresses no prejudice against a black commander. Race becomes an issue only when he becomes Desdemona's husband.

Was Shakespeare a racist? Perhaps the best answer to the question is to point to the fact that he made Othello a tragic hero, that is he presented a black in a role that possessed enormous prestige. Othello is said to be a Moor, but he has Negroid features. Notice, for instance, Brabantio's characterization of Othello as "sooty" and notice Roderigo's use of the term "thick-lips." Like the other Elizabethans, Shakespeare seems not to have made much of a distinction between Moors and blacks.

Putting aside the disputed case of Othello, in Elizabethan drama Moors are either villainous (lustful, cruel) or foolish. Our own view, put bluntly, is this: Othello resembles the stock Moor in being passionate, savagely ferocious, and gullible, but—and this is the important thing— he is a tragic *hero*, and the final view of him, when he speaks calmly, judges himself as a murderer, and then executes justice on himself, is that he is (as he is called in the play) "the noble Moor." (We'll comment on some of these points in our scene-by-scene discussion.)

1.1. Othello will not be mentioned until line 30, and not named until 1.3.47. The play begins with the splutterings of Roderigo and the blasphemy of Iago ("'Sblood"), with talk of "this," "such a matter," "him," and so on. All of this negative comment will ultimately serve to set off the poised, magnificent behavior of Othello when he finally makes his first appearance. We had heard of someone engaged in "loving his own pride and purposes" (11), of someone given to "bombast circumstance" (12), and instead we see a man of poise and authority. (Many students are familiar with *Macbeth*, where the hero is elaborately praised before we meet him. You may, then, want to contrast the introduction to Othello with the introduction to Macbeth.)

Iago's speech misleads us about Othello, but it reveals Iago as a man filled with contempt and envy. Line 18 ("A fellow almost damned in a fair wife") is especially interesting, since it indicates Iago's low view of human nature; for Iago, a man with an attractive wife is bound to be cuckolded. In line 39 ("I follow him to serve my turn upon him") Iago clearly reveals that he is the Machiavel, the unscrupulous villain. But he is doubtless sincere in his contempt for honest, dutiful persons. For Iago, a dutiful person is an "ass" (44). The people who have some "soul" are those who "do themselves homage" (51)! By line 62 ("I am not what I am"), with its inversion of God's "I am what I am (Exodus 3.14), we have seen the complete self-serving villain.

We have already noticed Iago's comparison of an honest man to an ass; in line 68 he uses another animal image when he urges Roderigo to "plague" Othello " with flies." Notice, too, "poison his delight" (65), a remark characteristic of the poisoner Iago. Animal images abound in Iago's speech to Brabantio: "An old black ram / Is tupping your white ewe" (85–86), in the speech beginning with line 105 we get "Barbery horse," "neigh," "coursers," "gennets," and a moment later "the beast with two backs." Later in the play, when Othello has been infected by Iago's poison, Othello will use animal imagery. In 4.2.60 Othello's mind turns to a "cistern for foul toads / To knot and gender in."

In line 105 Iago uses prose, and it is fair to say that he is the chief speaker of prose. One can almost say that he adopts prose—the language of "honest Iago"—as a disguise, though in 2.1.165 he uses prose in an aside, that is when he is not attempting to present himself as an honest, plain-speaking man.

That Roderigo and Brabantio are racists is evident, for instance from Roderigo's reference to "the gross clasps of a lascivious Moor" and from Brabantio's remark, addressed to Roderigo, "O, would you had had her," a comment that indicates Brabantio would rather see his daughter married to a fool than to a black man. In fact, by the last line of the scene Brabantio, so distressed by the thought that his daughter is with Othello, now sees merit in Roderigo, and calls him "good Roderigo."

1.2. Iago unsuccessfully tries to stir Othello against Brabantio, and unsuccessfully tries to persuade Othello to hide (an action which would make Othello seem guilty). Read aloud, or ask two students to read aloud, the first 27 lines of the scene. The difference between Iago's energetic first speech (1.2.1–5), and Othello's dignified and restrained first speech (only half a line" "'Tis better as it is") is evident. (By the way, when Iago says, in lines 4–5, "Nine or ten times / I had thought to have yerked him here, under the ribs," many actors who play Iago, daringly poke Othello's ribs. The business is extremely effective.)

In the previous scene, in lines 11–12, Iago had spoken of Othello's "bombast circumstance" (stuffed roundabout talk). Othello's first big speech (17–27) does indeed have unusual words ("out-tongue," "promulgate," "unhoused," "circumstance") but surely the Othello whom we now see is not the Othello that Iago had led us to expect. Rather, in Othello's hyperbole we hear the diction of the great hero, especially in "I would not my unhoused free condition / Put into circumscription and confine / *For the sea's worth*." Othello is a prince ("I fetch my life and being / From men of royal siege"), and he speaks like one. In fact, one sign of his greatness is that he is *not* moved to action by Iago's words. Nor is he moved by Iago's attempt to make him act suspiciously ("You were best go in"): "My parts, my title, and my perfect soul / Shall manifest me rightly." It soon turns out that the officers with torches are indeed seeking Othello, but not for any shameful action. Rather, they need the great general. Soon, however, we get Brabantio, Roderigo, and others, and what might become a street brawl is quickly extinguished by Othello's majestic words: "Keep up your bright swords, for the dew will rust them." In Othello's remark that the dew will rust the "bright swords," there is perhaps a suggestion that these swords are the pretty ornamental toys of civilians, not the swords of real warriors.

Brabantio, horrified at the thought of Desdemona loving a black man (cf. "sooty bosom"), can attribute her interest in Othello only to magic ("thou hast enchanted her," "chains of magic"). The very fact, however, that she has shunned "The wealthy, curled darlings of our nation" is a sign that she was looking for a man of unusual qualities. Othello's response is again to refuse to get drawn into a brawl, and the scene ends with Brabantio sounding rather like Egeus in *A Midsummer Night's Dream* (another father enraged by the behavior of his daughter), as he talks of bringing his case to the Duke.

1.3. In Shakespeare's source (Cinthio's prose story), by the way, Othello is ordered to Cyprus on a routine change of command. Shakespeare invents the Turkish threat in order (1) to emphasize Othello's importance, (2) to show Desdemona's devotion (she will accompany him even in danger), and (3) to add an ominous note to the play. (Cyprus, incidentally, became part of the Venetian Empire in 1473, but was conquered by the Turks in 1571, that is only some 30 years before *Othello* was written, and was annexed by Great Britain in 1914. It is now divided between Turkey and Greece. So much for history; now to return to the play.) As Maynard Mack points out in "The Jacobean Shakespeare," the tragic hero often goes on a journey: Romeo to Mantua, Hamlet to England, Lear to the heath, Macbeth to the witches, Othello to Cypress. The journey is something of a symbol of the psychological changes taking place, or of the new responses.

In 1.3.48 there is a nice touch: The Duke greets Othello ("Valiant Othello") first, and then a moment later notices Brabantio. Clearly Othello is more important to the welfare of Venice than is Brabantio, though the Duke does what he can to praise Brabantio ("We lacked your counsel and your help tonight").

Othello's address to the court (1.3.76ff) deserves to be read aloud in its entirety. When Othello says of the charge that he has taken Brabantio's daughter, "It is most true" (78), presumably there is a gasp in the court. He then gives his history, in appropriately heroic language ("nine moons wasted," for "nine months") and he tells how he won Desdemona. (Brabantio's assertion that she was "A maiden never bold, / Of spirit so still and quiet that her motion / Blushed at herself" is probably true—until she met Othello.) Othello then sketches his rise, from slave (though of princely origin) to hero, more or less paralleling what we have seen in the play, that is the rise from the low thing depicted by Iago to the poised, commanding figure who now speaks. Later the play will show us Othello descending into savagery when he murders Desdemona, then rising again at the end.

In 1.3.159–60 ("She swore in faith 'twas strange, 'twas passing strange; / 'I was pitiful, 'twas wondrous pitiful") we almost hear Desdemona's voice, and a moment later she enters, as the Duke testifies to Othello's integrity by saying, "I think this tale would win my

daughter too." Desdemona greets her father courteously ("My noble
father"), and explains that she has a divided duty—to her father but
another to her husband. He apparently has learned nothing, however,
since he says that if he had other children he would "hang clogs on
them." Brabantio is unattractive, but perhaps we can share his contempt for the Duke's rhymed (and glib-sounding) efforts to comfort
him. That is, after hearing the Duke's moralizing, we perhaps can feel
the truth of Brabantio's mocking response: "So let the Turk of Cyprus
us beguile: / We lose it not so long as we can smile."

Why does the Duke shift to prose after Brabantio's response? Perhaps to indicate a shift from passion to practical business.

Desdemona's response, in which she says that she "saw Othello's
visage in his mind," and that she had consecrated—an important
word—her "soul and fortunes" to Othello's "honors and his valiant
parts," makes it clear why she shunned "the wealthy, curled darlings"
of Venice. Still, if Desdemona's love for Othello includes an appreciation of his virtue, she is also fully aware of the sexual aspects of marriage ("The rites for why I love him are bereft me"). In his reply, when
he urges the Venetians to let Desdemona go to Cyprus with him,
Othello insists that he is not speaking in order to satisfy his own physical longings ("the young affects / In me defunct"); perhaps, as he
goes on to insist that Cupid cannot move him, we hear a touch of hy-
bris—at least in retrospect, when we know of his response to Desdemona's apparent infidelity.

As almost all commentators have pointed out, the first person to
suggest that Desdemona may be unfaithful is *not* Iago but Brabantio:

> Look to her, Moor, if thou hast eyes to see:
> She has deceived her father, and may thee.

Iago will later remind Othello of this. But for now Othello's response is characteristic and significant:

> My life upon her faith.

Her fidelity, her virtue, is something that Othello is fully confident of,
and he would stake his life on it. Later, when he thinks she is false, he
will take her life, and at the end, when he learns that she is indeed
innocent, he will give up his own life. For Othello, Desdemona's virtue and Othello's love for her are matters of life and death.

It's important for students to understand that when Roderigo says,
"It is not in my virtue" to stop loving Desdemona, "virtue" means

"power," not "moral quality." Iago, in his response, uses some of the animal imagery that often salts his speech (guinea hen, baboon). Iago's speech is complicated but the gist is that we can control ourselves because "our wills are gardeners," and they can uproot unwanted things. Further, "We have reason to cool our raging motions." Of course all of this is said in order to work on Roderigo, and it may not reflect Iago's true beliefs, but in any case a reader of the play will see, in Othello's later behavior, how little reason can do to calm "our raging motions."

One thing Iago says to Roderigo that surely is true is this, "I hate the Moor," a statement he repeats a moment later, when alone, having dismissed the "snipe" Roderigo (another animal image). Iago gives a reason for his hatred of Othello: "It is thought abroad that 'twixt my sheets / H'as done my office." Iago admits that he does not know if the rumor is true but nevertheless he will assume the truth of it. (In 2.1 he repeats his suspicion that "the lusty Moor / Hath leaped into my seat," and later in the scene he says that he also suspects Cassio: "For I fear Cassio with my nightcap too.")

One of the most important passages in Iago's speech is his comment on Othello:

> The Moor is of a free and open nature
> That thinks men honest that but seem to be so.

That is, Iago will undo Othello by preying on Othello's *virtue*. (We assume that Othello's faith in apparent honesty is an admirable trait, not a tragic flaw.)

In this speech Iago has been trying to think of a plan ("How? How? Let's see") and at the end in effect says he is in league with the devil: "Hell and night / Must bring this monstrous birth to the world's light." A word about the diabolic imagery in the play, then, may be useful. In *Shakespeare Survey 5* S. L. Bethell points out that in the first act Iago has eight diabolic images, and Othello has none (though in one Iago says he hates "hell-pains"). In the second act Iago has six diabolic images, and Othello again has none. Then comes the change, as Iago works on Othello: in the third act, Iago has only three, but Othello has nine. In the fourth act, Iago has one, Othello has ten. In the fifth, Iago has none, and Othello has six. (For Iago's relation to the Vice of medieval drama, and thus for his connections with the devil, see Bernard Spivack, *Shakespeare and the Allegory of Evil*.)

2.1. The storm in this scene—Shakespeare's addition to the source—adds a note of danger, and, equally important, it emphasizes the power of love. The news that "Our wars are done" (20) comes as a surprise. Probably the audience expected to see a heroic play, but the play turns out to be almost a bourgeois drama, a play not about a great general's success or failure in war, but about a man's failure in a domestic relationship. This is not to say, however, that Othello does not exhibit greatness; on the contrary, he exhibits it in his exalted love for Desdemona, and especially in his final understanding of how he has betrayed his love.

Cassio testifies to Desdemona's greatness, especially in his speech to the effect that the tempests themselves yield to "the divine Desdemona" (73). The whole speech (67–86) is worth reading in class, especially its last three lines, where Desdemona is almost imagined as surrounded by divinity:

> Hail to thee, lady! and the grace of heaven,
> Before, behind thee, and on every hand
> Enwheel thee round.

Othello, then, is flanked by the devilish Iago and the heavenly Desdemona. Next comes a passage of 90 lines in which Desdemona says very little—presumably she is silently anxious about Othello—while Iago jokes at the expense of women. But for all his joking, Iago is also carefully observing, and he notices that Cassio takes Desdemona by the hand:

> Ay, well said, whisper! With as little a web [net] as this will I ensnare so great a fly as Cassio.

It is characteristic that Iago, who from the start of the play has used a variety of animal images, here sees Cassio as an insect.

Othello's first speech in the scene includes some especially significant words: "O my soul's joy" (Desdemona is an almost spiritual force to him), and "If it were now to die, / 'Twere now to be most happy" (a passage that is true; he will live and will become unbearably unhappy). A moment later he says,

> I cannot speak enough of this content;
> It stops me here [*touches his heart*]; it is too much of joy."

In passages like this we see the depth of Othello's love. When he kills Desdemona, then, it is *not* simply because he is at bottom a barbarian with a veneer of civilization; he kills her partly (chiefly?) because she is of overwhelming importance to him, and he cannot tolerate the thought that this heaven-seeming creature is untrue.

They kiss, and Othello playfully expresses the hope that their kisses will be "the greatest discords," but Iago picks up the musical metaphor. Music suggests harmony, but Iago thrives on discord, so against Othello's view of love we hear Iago's cynical comment: "O, you are well tuned now! / But I'll set down the pegs that make this music."

In his long prose speech to Roderigo Iago says that Othello told Desdemona "fantastical lies," but surely this is *not* what the audience thinks. Possibly Iago is simply trying to decieve Roderigo, but possibly he believes what he says. That is, perhaps Iago really cannot conceive of such things as love and greatness of spirit. When Roderigo says that Desdemona is "full of most blessed condition," Iago replies,

> Blessed fig's end! The wine she drinks is made of grapes. If she had been blessed, she would never have loved the Moor. Blessed pudding! Didst thou not see her paddle with the palm of his hand?

Again, probably he is concerned chiefly with deceiving Roderigo, but we can reasonably also think that he believes what he says. In fact, he says something to this effect a moment later, when, returning to blank verse in a soliloquy, he says,

> That Cassio loves her, I do well believe't;
> That she loves him, 'tis apt and of great credit.

The entire speech is of great importance, but a few lines are of special significance. Iago characterized Othello as "of a constant, loving, noble nature"; this is important, for it helps us to see that Othello will be destroyed partly by his *virtue*, not simply by what is conventionally called the "tragic flaw." (Somewhat similarly, Claudius and Laertes know that because Hamlet is "noble" he will not examine the foils closely enough to see that one was sharp and poisoned.) Next, Iago gives us the astounding information that he too loves Desdemona, but he immediately describes this love in such a way that we understand it is nothing at all like Othello's love for her, or, indeed, like anything that we can reasonably call love. In a moment he will say that he thinks Cassio too may have slept with Emilia, and now we see clearly that he is crazily looking for reasons to justify his hatred of Othello. Finally, notice in this speech that he talks of Roderigo as a dog (used in hunting) and of Othello as an "ass."

Why does Iago deliver this speech in verse, since he has been speaking prose a moment ago? Probably the best answer is this: Although he is a villain, his "natural" language is verse, and when he speaks in prose he is in effect speaking in disguise, that is he is affecting a simple honesty that he does not possess.

2.2. Prose, since it is a proclamation. That is, since the "normal" language of the play is verse, a passage that is in some special language, such as a proclamation, is customarily given in a different language—prose. (Virtually all letters in Shakespeare are in prose.) The chief function of the scene presumably is to prepare us (via "sport and revels") for Cassio's drinking.

2.3. If you ask students to perform (text in hand) brief passages in class, you may want them to do the first part of the scene between Iago and Cassio, when Iago utters lewd implications about Desdemona (e.g. "sport for Jove," "full of game," "a parley to provocation," "happiness to their sheets"), and Cassio politely fends them off.

When Iago succeeds in getting Cassio drunk and combative, we again see Iago as the devilish introducer of discord. Notice in Othello's speech the reference to the Turks ("Are we turned Turks?"), where the Turks are contrasted with the Christians. Later Othello—a Christian—will, so to speak, turn Turk, that is behave lawlessly, barbarously. (Although in fact during the Renaissance Christian nations sometimes had peaceful dealings with Moslems, Moslems nevertheless were conventional symbols for barbarians. As we will see, at the very end of the play Othello, speaking of the terrible injustice he inflicted on Desdemona, will in effect speak of himself as a "circumcised dog," that is as a Moslem. Shakespeare's use of Moslems as symbols of barbarism can make the play difficult to teach—he *does* sometimes use racial stereotypes—but one can hope that students, and even Moslem students who may well feel uncomfortable, will be able to take the passages as symbolic rather than as an accurate statement about what Turks in fact are or were.

Othello's anger in this scene has two causes: he sees his soldiers behaving unprofessionally, and, second, he cannot understand the cause of their behavior. The result is that he acts decisively but unjustly. In his statement that he will punish the offender even if the offender is his twin, we get some preparation for the stern judgement he will, in a later crisis, inflict upon Desdemona. "Cassio, I love thee; / But never more be officer of mine." Later, when Desdemona seems to him to behave in unworthy fashion, he will cut her off.

After Othello and then Cassio leave, Iago soliloquizes, associating himself with "devils." Equally important is the end of the soliloquy, in which he says he will use Desdemona's *virtue*—certainly not a weakness—to undo Desdemona, Othello, and Cassio.

> I'll pour this pestilence into his ear;
> That she repeals him for her body's lust;
> And by how much she strives to do him good,
> She shall undo her credit with the Moor.
> So will I turn her virtue into pitch,
> And out of her own goodness make the net
> That shall enmesh them all.

3.1. Although the old idea that comic scenes in tragedy served to provide "comic relief" is no longer widely held—it is now usually said that they deepen the tragedy by providing some sort of ironic counterpoint—this scene perhaps does serve chiefly to get some laughs. Or, more precisely, it got some laughs in its day. Today the jokes are obscure—for instance, "put your pipes into your bag" probably refers not only to putting away bagpipes but also to "pipes" as genitals. Truth to tell, we skip this scene when we teach the play.

3.2. Probably this tiny scene exists chiefly to explain why Othello is not present during Cassio's interview with Desdemona.

3.3. This long scene, at the center of the play, is of enormous importance. As the central scene, it thus corresponds to, say, the scene in *Julius Caesar* where Brutus kills Caesar, or the scene in *Hamlet* where Hamlet does not kill the king at prayer, or the scene in *Macbeth* where Banquo and Fleance leave the court. That is, it contains a turning point: Iago manipulates and transforms Othello. Iago begins with such bits as "Ha! I like not that" and "No, sure, I cannot think it / That he would steal away so guilty-like." At first he seems to make little progress, since Desdemona reassures Othello that Cassio admires him. Othello says to Desdemona, "Let him come when he will," and "I will deny thee nothing—a phrase that he repeats a moment later. Especially significant are his words,

> Perdition catch my soul
> But I do love thee! And when I love thee not,
> Chaos is come again.

Here we get both a glimpse of Othello's love for her, and an anticipation of the terror that is to come. (At the end of the play he will say that the devilish Iago has ensnared his soul.)

If you ask students to perform part of this scene, you may want to coach them especially about the powerful repetitions ("thought," "think," "indeed," "indeed," "honest," "honest,") that so exasperate Othello and drive him to say to Iago, "By heaven, thou echoest me." Consider these lines from the end of one of Othello's speeches:

> If thou dost love me,
> Show me thy thought.

To which Iago replies:

> My lord, you know I love you,

a response that is calculated to heighten Othello's uncertainty:

> I think thou dost.

What Iago is doing is making Othello so uncertain that Othello will ultimately out of desperation fasten on almost anything and take it for a certainty. So clever is Iago at seeming to hide his purpose that Othello bursts out, "By heaven, I'll know they thoughts." Iago can, then, in a moment, say to Othello,

> She did deceive her father, marrying you.

He is right, but what he is doing is using Desdemona's act of love as an example of her willingness to deceive. And Othello is now so at a loss that in a moment he will say to Iago, "I am bound to thee forever"—words that a lover might say to his beloved, but now, in a sense, Iago rather than Desdemona has become Othello's beloved. Notice, too, the language of love in the last line in this scene, Iago's "I am your own forever." (We are not suggesting a homosexual interpretation of the relationship between Iago and Othello, though in fact such an interpretation has often been given.)

Iago plays on Othello's condition as an outsider in Venice ("In Venice they [i.e. wives] do let heaven see the pranks / They dare not show their husbands"), and also on Othello's racial fears, reminding Othello that Desdemona had rejected proposed matches "Of her own clime, complexion, and degree." What in fact had been a bold, loving act of Desdemona is now used as proof of some sort of vice, something "rank," something showing "Foul disproportions, thoughts unnatural." Othello, alone, mentions that he is black, and that he is getting on in years, and he concludes (despite all that Desdemona has said earlier in the play, for example that she saw Othello's visage in his mind) that she cannot love him. Yet when she appears, the very sight of her causes him to say,

> If she be false, heaven mocks itself!
> I'll not believe it.

And a moment later he says, "I am to blame," that is the very sight of Desdemona banishes his doubts—for a while.

When Othello pushes away Desdemona's handkerchief, and the handkerchief falls, Othello says "Let it alone." The antecedent of "it" may be the handkerchief—perhaps she tries to retrieve it, or it may be Othello's forehead. In both cases, however, Othello is responsible for Desdemona's loss of her handkerchief—either because he prevents her from picking it up, or because she is concentrating on his head. It is wrong, then, to say that the whole tragedy depends on the accidental loss of a handkerchief. One feels that Iago is so masterful a villain that even without the handkerchief he would be able to destroy the noble Moor. Iago rightly says that "Trifles light as air / Are to the jealous confirmations strong / As proofs of Holy Writ." That is, the loss of the handkerchief does not by itself bring about the catastrophe; it merely *helps*. (By way of contrast, in *Romeo and Juliet*, the delay of Friar John—an accident—is entirely responsible for the deaths that follow.) One can almost say that the real function of the handkerchief is not to destroy Othello but to establish Iago's guilt at the end of the play.

Othello leaves the stage, and Iago soon enters. After Emilia's exit, Iago soliloquizes, finishing the soliloquy in what has been called "the Othello voice," that is the grand, exotic language that Othello uses, for instance in his address to the senators. The following grand lines are presumably a sign that Iago now possesses Othello's mind:

> Look where he comes! Not poppy nor mandragora,
> Nor all the drowsy syrups of the world,
> Shall ever medicine thee to that sweet sleep
> Which thou owedst yesterday.

And as proof of Iago's words that Othello will never again be tranquil, we immediately hear Othello's tormented mind, expressing itself in language that lacks any touch of grandeur: "Ha! ha! False to me?" and "Avaunt! be gone! Thou hast set me on the rack."

A moment later, however, when Othello bids farewell to his past, he does so in language that is worthy of him: "Farewell content! / Farewell the plumed troops, and the big wars / That makes ambition virtue! O, farewell . . . . / Farewell! Othello's occupation's gone." (The entire speech of course should be read aloud in class.)

Othello, his mind poisoned, is now crazily insistent on proof. We can almost say the he *wants* proof of Desdemona's infidelity: "Villain, be sure thou prove my love a whore!" And again, "I'll have some proof." He is saying that he won't believe Iago until Iago can offer further proof, but we feel that he will welcome the proof. Iago talks of the difficulty, using base images ("topped," "as prime as goats, as hot as monkeys, / As salt as wolves"), and soon the noble Moor (3.3.446) is reduced to a barbarian: "I'll tear her all to pieces!" (It is significant that he utters this horrible line even *before* the evidence of the handkerchief is introduced. As we have already suggested, some critics have made too much of the idea that the tragic outcome hinges on the accidental loss of Desdemona's handkerchief.)

In another moment Othello announces that he has given up his love for Desdemona:

> Look here, Iago:
> All my fond love thus do I blow to heaven.
> 'Tis gone.

Then we get another speech (about "the Pontic Sea") in the Othello voice, in which Othello is joined by a kneeling Iago ("Witness, you ever-burning lights above . . . "). Othello says to Iago, " I greet thy love, / Not with vain thanks but with acceptance bounteous, " and Iago replies, in the last words of the scene "I am your own forever." It is as though Iago and Othello now are lovers, not Desdemona and Othello.

This quick tour of an immensely important scene has skipped a good deal. Even as we write these lines we notice, for instance, the two speeches immediately preceding Iago's closing speech. In the first of these, Iago cunningly suggest—by seeming *not* to suggest it—that Othello kill Desdemona. "My friend [i.e. Cassio] is dead. 'Tis done at your request. / But let her live." To which Othello replies, in language that shows he is all but crazy, "Damn her, lewd minx! O, damn her! Damn her!" Most students are not likely to *hear* the changes in

Othello's voice (which of course reveal changes in his state of mind) if they simply read the play silently. On the other hand, if they read some scenes aloud, they will indeed perceive the changes.

3.4. The scene begins with an exchange with a clown, often deleted in modern productions. Notice, after the clown's departure, that Desdemona refers to Othello as "the noble Moor," and says that he is *not* jealous. Surely we are to assume that Otheelo indeed is noble, and indeed is not normally jealous. Iago's genius is that he can somehow undermine Othello's nobility by arousing in him a fit of jealousy.

In asking for the handkerchief, Othello again speaks in the Othello voice. For instance, he does not say that the sibyl was two hundred years old; rather he says that she "had numbered in the world / The sun to course two hundred compasses." A moment later, however, his language degenerated to lines such as "Ha! Wherefore?" and "Say you?" and "Fetech't, let me see't!"

4.1. The scene begins in blank verse, the normal medium, we might say, for the tragedy, but at line 35 Othello shifts to prose, in a speech in which he sputters hysterically ("Lie with her? Lie on her— We say lie on her when they belie her.—Lie with her! Zounds"). The prose here is a sign of Othello's mental deterioration. After Othello falls into a trance, Iago speaks in verse, a sign of his self-mastery: "My medicine works! Thus credulous fools are caught . . . . "

We already called attention to the savegery of one of Othello's lines, "I'll tear her all to pieces," and now we encounter others. Spying on Cassio, Othello says, in an aside, "O, I see that nose of yours, but not that dog I shall throw it to." Later in the scene he will say of Cassio, "I will chop him into messes. Cuckold me!" And, no less horrifying, he will strike Desdemona. Some commentators have taken this language and this behavior to indicate that Othello is fundamentally a savage, a primitive man who has acquired the veneer of Western civilization but who relapses into his natural barbarism when pressed. But this view is too simple. For one thing, the pressure on Othello has been enormous. He has seen (or thought he has seen) the thing he most valued (remember, "My life upon her faith") prove to be foul. His world has fallen apart, just as (say) Hamlet's has fallen apart with the remarriage of his mother and with his perception that Ophelia is spying on him. Further, interspersed with passages of savagery are passages that indicate his continuing perception of Desdemona's worth (e.g. "O, she will sing the savageness out of a bear"), and passages that indicate he believes he is acting justly. For instance, he says that he does what he does in order to prevent Desdemona from contaminating others. Our point is this: Othello *does* indeed act barbarously, but Shakespeare also reminds us that Othello is much more than a barbarian. If, for instance, we hear the voice of savage egotism in "Cuckold me!" we hear something other than sheer egotism and savagery when Othello speaks of the "justice" of strangling her in the very bed that (he thinks) she has contaminated. Notice too, a line he speaks to Iago: "But yet the pity of it, Iago. O Iago, the pity of it, Iago."

Nothing that we have just said should be taken as suggesting that when he strikes Desdemona, and then a moment later when he humiliates her by causing her to "turn, and turn," he is less than terrifying. Still, after his explosive "Goats and monkeys!"—Othello now uses the bestial language of Iago—an audience probably shares Lodovico's astonishment:

> Is this the noble Moor whom our full Senate
> Call all in all sufficient? Is this the nature
> Whom passion could not shake? whose solid virtue
> The shot of accident nor dart of chance
> Could neither graze nor pierce?

Here we get a reminder of the heroic Othello, the Othello that we saw earlier in the play.

4.2. At the beginning of the scene Othello is relatively calm. Probably an audience thinks that Emilia may persuade him to put aside his suspicions, but the big speech beginning at line 46 again gives us the tormented Othello, the Othello who is so under the control of Iago that he uses Iago's animal images—"foul toads," and, in his next speech, "flies" in a slaughter—house.

4.3. Emilia thinks that Othello "looks gentler than he did," but we can guess that if Othello indeed seems calm it is probably because he has determined to kill Desdemona. The difference between Emilia and Desdemona is engagingly set forth in a bit of comic dialogue in which Emilia agrees that she would not be false "by this heavenly light," but she "might do't as well in th' dark." (The entire scene is short and acts very well, especially if one of your students can sing the willow song.)

5.1. Coleridge spoke of Iago's statements of his motives as expressions of "the motive-hunting of motiveless malignity." Early in this scene Iago, who had told us in other scenes that he feared Cassio may have cuckolded him, now gives a more plausible reason for his hatred of Cassio:

> He hath a daily beauty in his life
> That makes me ugly.

That is, Iago is someone who simply cannot bear to behold someone better than himself.

5.2. Othello's long opening speech is fairly difficult, and it probably should be read aloud a few times—straight through, then with comments (for example on his utter wrongness but also on his grandness) and then straight through again. Othello thinks he is performing a "sacrifice" (line 65) and he tries to make the execution as painless as possible:

> I that am cruel am yet merciful;
> I would not have thee linger in they pain.
> So, so.

This is *not* the man who said he will "chop her into messes." Notice, too, that in the following lines we hear the *lover* speak, not the murderer or the egotist:

> My wife! My wife! What wife? I have no wife,
> O, insupportable! O heavy hour.

Emilia disabuses Othello of the idea that Desdemona was unchaste. Her language is vigorous and not unjust ("O gull! O dolt! / As ignorant as dirt!"), but it tells only half the story. That is, Othello *has* been gulled, and he *is* ignorant—a common condition of a tragic hero—but he is also, at least at times, high-minded and well-intentioned, and he is the victim of a fiendishly clever enemy.

Presumably the news that Desdemona was chaste is both the most wonderful and the most terrifying thing that Othello can hear—wonderful because he desperately *wants* her to be chaste, wants to know that indeed her apparent heavenliness was real— but terrible because it tells him that he has destroyed this angel-like goodness. Now that he has learned he was right in his initial view of her, and wrong in the action that he took, he has reached the end of his experience:

> Here is my journey's end, here is my butt,
> And very seamark of my utmost sail.

There is nothing further to live for, especially since he feels a tremendous gulf between him and Desdemona ("This look of thine will hurl my soul from heaven").

He fails to kill Iago—thus giving some confirmation to the suggestion that Iago is indeed diabolic ("If that thou be'st the devil, I cannot kill thee") and thus also suggesting that Othello is no longer the heroic conqueror. When he characterized himself as "An honorable murderer" probably we feel that the oxymoronic characterization is just.

Almost all instructors will want to read—or to have students enact—the end of the play, perhaps beginning with Lodovico's entry (just before Othello lunges at Iago), or a little later, with Othello's big speech beginning "Soft you, a word or two before you go." Although one occasionally encounters a theologically-oriented critic who says that Othello damns himself by committing suicide, the chief attitudes toward the final action are two: (1) Othello is judging himself, and (2) Othello is cheering himself up (T. S. Eliot's position). For what it's worth, we take the first of these views. We see Othello as judging himself severely and accurately (he had judged Desdemona severely but inaccurately). He sees himself as "unlucky" and as ignorant (he threw away a rich jewel), and, perhaps most important, he compares himself to a "malignant and a turbaned Turk"—that is to an enemy of Chistendom, or (so far as the Elizabethans were concerned) an enemy to civilization, and he executes justice on himself. That is, just as once before he punished a barbaric enemy of the state, so now he again punishes one—himself. In short, he reasserts the noble values he held before Iago worked on him. In Helen Gardner's words, responding to Eliot, Othello is not cheering himself up; rather, he is cheering *us* up. We are immensely relieved that he now sees what he has done (i.e. he achieves self-knowledge), that he recovers his moral sense, and that he executes justice on himself. And surely we are immensely glad that he now understands that Desdemona was indeed what he originally had esteemed her to be.

Many instructors may feel that an introductory course is not the place to discuss textual matters, but we have found that the "base Indian" vs. "base Judean" crux *does* interest students. The footnote in the text (5.2.357) gives the gist of the problem, but a few additional comments may be useful. Most of the evidence is against the Folio reading, "Iudean," that is Judean, or Judas. First of all, in defense of the Quarto's Indean" (i.e. Indian), Shakespeare nowhere else calls Judas the Judean. Second, Indian is plausible on the grounds that many travelers reported that natives of remote places did not understand the great value of jewels. Third (still in defense of "Indian"), one may conjecture that the manuscript had "Indean" and the compositor of the Folio mistakenly inverted the *n*, producing "Iudean."

On the other hand, the Folio indisputably *does* have "Iudean," and the word makes sense. Possibly the passage draws on Matthew 13:45–46, where Jesus tells of a merchant who (correctly) bartered everything in order to obtain an unblemished pearl, the Kingdom of Heaven. Moreover, "Judean" connects the disputed passage with "tribe," a word that Shakespeare (in the *Merchant of Venice*) connects with Jews, four times. He never uses "tribe" in connection with Indians. For details about these positions, See *Shakespeare Quarterly* 19 (1968) 81–85, and 26 (Autumn 1975) 466–69.

Othello's speech during which he stabs himself is often referred to as his concluding speech, but in fact it is not. Lodovico and Gratiano utter a few words, and then Othello speaks what indeed is his last speech, a couplet:

> I kissed thee ere I kill'd thee. No way but this,
> Killing myself, to die upon a kiss.

The gulf, then, that he had envisioned a little earlier in the scene, when he imagined her in heaven and himself in hell, now is bridged, as the two bodies lie together.

Bibliographical Note: For an annotated list of material about *Othello* published between 1940 and 1985, including literary criticims, reviews, films, and suggestions about teaching, see *Othello: An Annotated Bibliography*, compiled by Margaret Lael Mikesell and Virginia Mason Vaughan (1990).

On Elizabethan attitudes toward Africans, see G. K. Hunter, *Dramatic Identities*, and Eldred Jones, *Othello's Countrymen*. For discussions of *Othello* that focus on color, see Martin Orkin, "Othello and the 'plain face' of Racism," *Shakespeare Quarterly* 38 (1987), 166–88, reprinted in Orkin's *Shakespeare against Apartheid*; Michael Neilt, "Unproper Beds: Race, Adultery, and the Hideous in *Othello*," *Shakespeare Quarterly* 40 (1989), 383–402.

There are at least two interesting feminist discussions of the play. The earlier is Carol Thomas Neely, "Women and Men in *Othello*," in *Shakespeare Studies* 10 (1977), reprinted in *The Woman's Part*, ed. Carolyn Ruth Swift Lenz et al. (1980). The other, also in *The Woman's Part*, is by Madelon Gohlke, "'I wooded thee with my sword,'" reprinted (under the name of Madelon Gohlke Sprengnether) in the revised version of the paperback Signet Classic Edition of *Othello* (1986). For a detailed discussion of the ways in which actors have interpreted the play, see Marvin Rosenberg, *The Masks of "Othello"* (1961). For a splendid short discussion of Shakespeare's tragedies, with occasional references to *Othello*, see Maynard Mack, "The Jacobean Shakespeare: Some Observations of the Construction of the Tragedies," in *Stratford-upon-Avon Studies: Jacobean Theatre*, ed. John Russell Brown and Bernard Harris (1960), reprinted in the paperback Signet Classic edition of *Othello*.

Chapter 22

Comedy

Among useful books on comedy are Louis Kronenberger, *The Thread of Laughter*; L. J. Potts, *Comedy*; Morton Gurewitch, *Comedy*; and D. H. Munro, *Argument of Laughter* (on theories of the comic). Two interesting anthologies of essays on comedy are *Comedy*, ed. Robert W. Corrigan, and *Theories of Comedy*, ed. Paul Lauter.

Wendy Wasserstein *The Man in a Case* (p. 765)

In our introductory comments about comedy we mention that comedy often shows the absurdity of ideals. The miser, the puritan, the health-faddist, and so on, are people of ideals, but their ideals are suffocating.

In his famous essay on comedy (1884) Henri Bergson suggested that an organism is comic when it behaves like a mechanism, that is when instead of responding freely, flexibly, resourcefully—one might almost say intuitively and also intelligently—to the vicissitudes of life, it responds in a predicatable, mechanical (and, given life's infinite variety, often inappropriate) way. It is not surprising that the first line in Wasserstein's comedy, spoken by a pedant to his betrothed, is "You are ten minutes late." This is not the way the Demetrius and Lysander speak in *A Midsummer Night's Dream*. True, a Shakespearean lover may fret about time when he is not in the presence of his mistress, but when he sees her, all thoughts of the clock disappear and he is nothing but lover. The Shakespearean lover is, in his way, mechanical too, but the audience feels a degree of sympathy for him that it does not feel for the pedantic clock-watcher.

The very title, *The Man in a Case*, alerts us to a man who is imprisioned—and, it turns out, a man who lives in a prison of his own making. Byelinkov says, "I don't like change very much." His words could be said by many other butts of satire— for example jealous husbands, or misers. And of course the comic writer takes such figures and puts them in a place where they will be subjected to maximum change. The dramatist puts the jealous husband or the miser, for instance, into a plot in which a stream of men visit the house, and every new visitor is (in the eyes of the comic figure) a potential seducer or a potential thief. In *The Man in a Case*, we meet a man of highly disciplined habits, who is confronted by an uninhibited woman. If you invite students to read the first two speeches—Byelinkov's one line ("You are ten minutes late") and Varinka's rambling account of "the woman who runs the grocery store," they will immediately see the comic juxtaposition.

In this play, then, we have a pedant who unaccountably has fallen

in love with a vivacious young woman. (In Chekhov's story, Byelinkov's acquaintances decided that it was time for him to get married,
so they conspired to persuade him that he was in love.) The pedant, of
course, is a stock comic character going back to the doctor (*il dottore*,
not a medical doctor but a pedant) of Renaissance Italian comedy.
Such a figure values Latin more than life. True, Byelinkov is in love,
but (as his first line shows, about Varinka being ten minutes late) he
remains the precise schoolmaster. Later, when Varinka says "It is time
for tea," he replies "It is too early for tea. Tea is at half past the hour."
Perhaps tea regularly is served at half past the hour, but, again, a lover
does not talk this way; a true lover will take every opportunity to have
tea with his mistress. Two other examples of Byelinkov's regimented
life: his belief that "heavy cream is too rich for teatime," and his need
to translate two stanzas every day because, he explains, "That is my
regular schedule." By the way, speaking of his translation, we are a bit
puzzled by the passage in which he says he is translating the *Aeneid*
"from classical Greek hexameter into Russian alexandrines." Of
course classicists sometimes did translate the *Aeneid* into Greek, as a
sort of exercise, but surely a classicist who was going to translate Virgil
into Russian alexandrines would translate from Virgil's original Latin,
not from Greek. Possibly the joke is precisely that this fool is translating from a translation, not the original; or possibly Wasserstein mistakenly thought the *Aeneid* is in Greek.

In any case, we are not surprised to hear that Byelinkov describes
his career as the teaching of "the discipline and contained beauty of
the classics." "Discipline" and containment are exactly what we expect from this sort of comic figure, a man who tells us that he smiles
three times every day, and that in 20 years of teaching he has never
been late to school. The speech that began "I don't like change very
much," went on thus: "If one works out the arithmetic the final fraction of improvement is at best less than an eighth of value over the
total damage caused by disruption."

Why, then, is this man talking to Varinka? Because he has fallen in
love. Love conquers all, even mathematicians and classicists. For the
most part, when such monomaniacs fall in love they are, as we have
said, comic objects of satire, but since audiences approve of love, these
figures—if young and genuinely in love—also can generate some
sympathy from the audience. (Toward the end of this discussion we
will talk more about two kinds of comedy, laughing *with* and laughing
at.) Thus, when Byelinkov says he will put a lilac in Varinka's hair, he
almost becomes sympathetic— but when he makes an entry in his

notebook, reminding him to do this again next year, he reverts to the pedant whom we find ridiculous.

The end of the play is fairly complex: when Varinka departs, Byelinkov takes out his pad, tears up the note about the lilac, and strews the pieces over the garden. Apparently he has had enough of her; we might almost say that he has come to his senses and has realized that a man of his temperament can not possibly live with a woman of her temperament. But then we are told that he "Carefully picks up each piece of paper and places them all in a small envelope as lights fade to black." What are we to make of this? That he retrieves the paper seems to indicate that he still loves her—or does it just mean that he is fussy enough not to litter the garden and not to leave any evidence of his folly? That is, when he retrieves the paper, is he revealing that he is still the lover, or is he revealing that he is still the pedant, the man who puts everything in its place (tea at a certain hour and at no other hour)? If the former, the audience will respond with a sympathetic chuckle; if the latter, the audience will respond with a mildly scornful laugh. Much will depend on the exact gestures that accompany tearing and strewing the note, retrieving it, and putting the pieces in an envelope. If, for instance, the pieces are fussily retrieved and prissily inserted into the envelope, we will sense the pedant, the figure we laugh *at*. If however, they are tenderly retrieved and lovingly placed into the envelope, we will sense the lover, the figure we laugh *with* as well as at. If there were a blackout while Byelinkov picked up the papers, we are inclined to think that the total effect (because sudden and surprising) would be comic, but Wasserstein's final direction ("lights fade to black") seems to us to allow for sympathy and even pathos.

We suggest that if you assign the play you ask two students to perform it, after rehearsing with a third student who serves as a director at a rehearsal or two. Our own practice—as with scenes from Shakespeare—is to photocopy the work, and to annotate it with some suggestions for stage business. For instance, we would suggest that when Byelinkov delivers his first line ("You are ten minutes late") he says it after carefully consulting a pocket watch. For that matter, you may want to gloss the initial stage direction, "Byelinkov is pacing. Enter Varinka, out of breath." The obvious (farcical?) thing to do is to have Byelinkov pace back and forth, ceremoniously take out and consult his pocket watch, replace the watch, pace back and forth again, and then to have Varinka enter at a moment when Byelinkov is pacing *away* from her. The first two speeches make evident the contrast between the uptight Byelinkov and the effusive Varinka.

Interestingly, soon after this dialogue of opposites, the two are dancing together. Byelinkov has said he is "no dancing bear," and Varinka immediately urges him to dance with her. He complies—probably she grabs him and leaves him no choice. Strangely, when they dance he apparently enjoys the activity; at least we interpret his words "And turn. And turn" to indicate that he is caught up in the dance. A moment later he stops, to place a lilac in her hair, a charming romantic touch that surely makes him sympathetic to the audience—but equally surely he loses this sympathy and becomes merely ridiculous when he takes out his notebook and pedantically writes a memorandum.

A note on Question 1 in the text (about Byelinkov on the motionless bicycle). In Bergsonian thinking, comedy mocks those whose behavior has become fixed and obsessive. What could be more fixed and obsessive than a man furiously pedaling on a bicycle that doesn't go anywhere? Of course the theory has to be modified; the behavior of a tragic hero is also obsessive. The difference, however, is that the tragic hero is obsessed about something that the audience thinks is important (e.g. Desdemona's chastity), whereas the comic hero is obsessed with trivia.

There is, naturally, a good deal more to say about the theory of comedy, but it's probably fair to say that almost all theories of comedy fit into one of two schools: (1) comedy affords the viewer a feeling of superiority (Hobbes's "sudden glory arising from some sudden conception of some eminency in ourselves, by comparison with the infirmity of others"), or (2) comedy helps the viewer to perceive universal absurdity by causing the viewer sympathetically to identify himself or herself with some absurd action. In blunt terms, (1) laughing at (derisive laughter) verses (2) laughing with (genial, affectionate laughter).

Chapter 24

Plays for Further Study

Sophocles *Oedipus the King* (p. 778)

Though interpretations are innumerable, most fall into the following categories:

1. The gods are just; Oedipus is at fault. The gods are innocent because foreknowledge is not foreordaining. (Jesus predicted that Peter would thrice deny him, but this prediction does not mean that Jesus destined Peter to deny him.) The prophecy told what Oedipus would do, but Oedipus did it because of what he was, not because the gods ordained him to do it. As we watch the play, we see a man acting freely—pursuing a course that leads to the revelation of who he is (See especially Bernard Knox, *Oedipus at Thebes*, pp. 33–41.) Though Oedipus is often praised for relentlessly pursuing a truth that ultimately destroys him, the fact is that—until very late in the play—he believes he is searching for someone other than himself, and moreover, in this search he too easily assumes that other people are subversive. Oedipus is rash and even cruel in his dealings with Teiresias, Creon, and the shepherd. His rashness is his *hamartia*, and the gods punish him for it. Given the prophecy that was given to Oedipus, a man less rash would have made it his business never to have killed anyone, and never to have married. (But he thought Polybos and Merope were his parents, and he knew that the old man [Leios] was not Polybos and that the queen in Thebes [Iocaste] was not Merope.)

2. The gods are at fault; Oedipus is innocent. When Oedipus asked the oracle who his parents were, the god answered in such a way as to cause Oedipus to leave a place of safety and to go to a tragic destination. Oedipus is a puppet of the gods; his *hamartia* is not rashness (a moral fault) but simply a mistake: He *un*intentionally killed his father and married his mother. The oracle was not conditional (it did not say, "If you do such and such, then such and such will happen"). The play is a tragedy of destiny; notice that at the end of the play no one justifies the gods; that is, no one exonerates them from forcing evil on Oedipus.

3. Oedipus is on the whole admirable (he pities his suffering kingdom; he has a keen desire to know the truth), but he is not perfect. The matter of his *intention* is irrelevant because the deeds of patricide and incest (irrespective of motive) contain pollution. The gods are mysterious, and though they sometimes shape men's

lives terribly, they are not evil because they cannot be judged by
human standards of justice or morality.
4. Sophocles is not concerned with justice; the play is an exciting
story about a man finding out something about the greatness of
humanity and about human limitations.

Walter Kaufman, *Tragedy and Philosophy*, has a long discussion of
Oedipus the King, in the course of which he finds five themes:

1. The play is about man's radical insecurity (epitomized in Oedipus's fall); Oedipus was the first of men, but he fell.
2. The play is about human blindness. Oedipus did not know who
he was (i.e., he was ignorant of his parentage); moreover, he was
blind to the honesty of Creon and Teiresias.
3. The play is about the curse of honesty. Oedipus's relentless desire
to know the truth brings him to suffering. (If one wants to hunt
for a tragic "flaw," one can see this trait as a flaw or vice, but a
more reasonable way of looking at it is to see it as a virtue. Would
we regard a less solicitous ruler as more virtuous?)
4. The play is about a tragic situation. If Oedipus abandons his
quest, he fails his people; if he pursues his quest, he ruins himself.
5. The play is about justice or, more precisely, about *in*justice, that is,
undeserved suffering. (Here we come back to Kaufmann's third
point: The reward of Oedipus's quest for truth is suffering. It is
not even clear that he is being justly punished for killing Laios, for
Oedipus belongs to the old heroic world, where killing an enemy
is celebrated.) Another point about the play as a play about justice: Sophocles talks of *human* justice too. When Oedipus curses
the unknown killer of Laios, he does not think that the killer may
have acted in self defense. And Oedipus's desire to punish Creon
and Teiresias similarly shows how wide of the mark efforts at
human justice may be.

The Norton critical edition of *Oedipus Tyrannus*, ed. L. Berkowitz
and T. F. Brunner, includes a translation, some relevant passages from
Homer, Thucydides, and Euripides, and numerous religious, psychological and critical studies, including Freud's, whose key suggestion,
in *The Interpretation of Dreams*, is that the play "moves a modern audience no less than it did the comtemporary Greek one" because there is
"voice within us ready to recognize the compelling force of destiny [in
the play] . . . . His destiny moves us only because it might have been

ours—because the oracle laid the same curse upon us before our birth as upon him. It is the fate of all of us, perhaps, to direct our first sexual impulse towards our mother and our first hatred and our first murderous wish against our father."

An instructor who uses this quotation in class may wish to call attention to the male chauvinism: Freud's "all of us" really means "all males," although he did make various efforts to account for the Oedipus complex in women. It may also be relevant to mention that if the Oedipus of the play did have an Oedipus complex, he would have wanted to go to bed with Merope (the "mother" who brought him up) rather than Iocaste. Note, too, that when he kills Laios, Laios is to him a stranger, not his father. Indeed, his flight from Corinth is a sign that he does *not* wish to sleep with his mother or to kill his father. But perhaps such a view is too literal. Perhaps this is a convenient place to mention that Oedipus's solution of the riddle of the Sphinx (man is the creature who walks on four feet in the morning, two at noon, and three in the evening) is especially applicable to Oedipus himself (the weakest of infants, the strongest of men in his maturity, and desperately in need of a staff in his blind old age), but of course it applies to all the spectators as well.

In addition to the Norton edition, the following discussions are especially interesting: Stanley Edgar Hyman, *Poetry and Criticism*; H. D. F. Kitto, *Greek Tragedy* and his *Poiesis*; Richmond Lattimore, *The Poetry of Greek Tragedy*; Cedric Whitman, *Sophocles*; Bernard Knox, *Oedipus at Thebes*; Charles Rowan Beye, *Ancient Greek Literature and Society*, especially pp. 306–312; Brian Vickers, *Toward Greek Tragedy*, Vol. I; R. P. Winnington-Ingram, *Sophocles*.

A video cassette of Sophocles's *Oedipus the King* is available from HarperCollins.

Topic for Writing

By today's standards, is Oedipus in any sense guilty, and if so, of what?

Sophocles *Antigone* (p. 821)

On *Antigone*, consult two books by H. D. F. Kitto, *Greek Tragedy*, and especially *Form and Meaning in Drama*. See also D. W. Lucas, *The Greek Tragic Poets*, Cedric H. Whitman, *Sophocles*, and R. P. Winnington-Ingram, *Sophocles*. Hegel's view, most often known though Bradley's essay on Hegel in Bradley's *Oxford Lectures* (and reprinted in *Hegel on*

Tragedy, ed. Anne and Henry Paolucci), claims that both sides are right and that both are also wrong because they assert they are exclusively right. (For a long anti-Hegelian reading, see Brian Vickers, *Towards Greek Tragedy*, which insists that Creon is brutal and Antigone is thoroughly admirable.) Bradley says, "In this catastrophe neither the right of the family nor that of the state is denied; what is denied is the absoluteness of the claim of each."

Most subsequent commentators take sides and either see Creon as a tragic hero (a headstrong girl forces him to act, and action proves ruinous, not only to her but to him), or see Antigone as a tragic heroine (a young woman does what she must and is destroyed for doing it). The critical conflict shows no sign of terminating. Mostly we get assertions, such as D. W. Lucas's "There is no doubt that in the eyes of Sophocles Creon is wrong and Antigone right," and Cedric Whitman's "Antigone's famous stubbornness, . . . the fault for which she has been so roundly reproved, is really moral fortitude." One of the most perceptive remarks on *Antigone* is by William Arrowsmith, in *Tulane Drama Review* 3 (March 1959): 135, where he says that Antigone, "trying to uphold a principle beyond her own, or human, power to uphold, gradually empties that principle in action, and then, cut off from her humanity by her dreadful heroism, rediscovers herself and love in the loneliness of her death." He suggests, too, that the play insists on "not the opposition between Antigone and Creon, but [on] the family resemblance which joins them in a common doom."

John Ferguson, in *A Companion to Greek Tragedy*, offers a fairly brief, commonsensical, scene-by-scene commentary on the play. Toward the end he argues that Hegel was utterly wrong in his view that both Creon and Antigone are right. Ferguson points out that Creon "behaves as a tyrant: and that Creon's law "is disastrous for the state." And Antigone is "wrong," Ferguson says, because although her "view of the situation is the true one," as a woman it was her duty to obey Creon. The play is about Antigone's *hubris*, and therefore it is properly titled.

Topics for Discussion and Writing

1. What stage business would you invent for Creon or Antigone at three points in the play?
2. In an essay of 500 words, compare and contrast Antigone and Ismene. In your discussion consider whether Ismene is overly cautious and whether Antigone is overly cold in her rejection of Ismene.

3. Characterize Haimon, considering not only his polite and even loving plea when he urged Creon to change his mind, but also his later despair and suicide. In what way, is he like his father and also (in other ways) like Antigone?

William Shakespeare *A Midsummer Night's Dream* (p. 853)

A video cassette of Shakespeare's *A Midsummer Night's Dream* is available from HarperCollins.

We have taught this play many times, seen a number of productions, and have read a fair amount of criticism, so we can't resist discussing the play here at some length. (No claim is made for the originality of any of the following comments; they draw on numerous published writings and productions, but we can no longer cite their sources.) We want to mention, however, that some of our best class hours have been when neither we nor the students talked about the play, but when the students acted out a scene or a portion of a scene. We usually choose a passage that will take about 10 or 15 minutes to perform, photocopy the pages, write some notes suggesting bits of business, and then put a student in charge as the director. The performers are told to study the parts individually, and then to meet at least twice to rehearse under the supervision of the director. (Of course the students are not expected to memorize the parts; they perform while reading from the text. On the day that one chooses the students for the performance, it's best to set a time for rehearsals; if the times are not set at once, it will be hard to get a time when they can agree.) On the first occasion that we set up a performance, we ask for volunteers, and we usually get some people who have had some experience performing, but for later scenes we sometimes draft students, though of course we give students the opportunity to decline if they strongly feel that they don't want to perform. We have almost never had a student refuse; and, perhaps oddly, the draftees are just about as good as the volunteers.

We have had particularly good luck with performances of 1.2 (the mechanicals meet to get parts for *Pyramus and Thisbe*) and with 4.1.49 to the end of the scene (Titania awakens, the lovers are awakened, and Bottom awakens). In the following scene-by-scene discussion, when we get to these two scenes we will talk a little about some stage business that we suggest to the students.

The title: the reference is to the summer solstice (the longest day of the year), around 23 June, but in fact the play is set in May. Still, the holiday of Midsummer Night is appropriate since this day was associated with magic (herbs gathered on this night could charm), with lover's dreams, and with madness.

1.1. In class we go over this entire scene, line by line, or, rather, speech by speech. It's our impression that our students do not find the process dull. Truth to tell, they seem to enjoy it immensely. If asked questions about some of the ways in which the lines work, they usually come up with very perceptive answers.

The play begins (and ends) in what passes for the real world, that is Athens, a city that supposedly stands for reason and law. Theseus (accent on the first syllable)—the highest ranking character—speaks first, in blank verse (the form that he and Hippolyta always use, except in the fifth act, where they sometimes speak in prose). (Shakespeare does a good deal to give different kinds of speech to the different kinds of characters. The young lovers in the wood will use rhyme, the fairies will use songs, and the mechanicals will use prose.)

In his first speech Theseus introduces the motif of marriage—and also of the moon—and though he is a mature rather than an impetuous lover, he conveys impatience at having to wait for the "nuptial hour." His comparison of himself—presumably a man of some years—to a "young man" is amusing and probably true to nature. (What older man in love thinks of himself as other than youthful? Probably also true to nature is the impatience and self-centeredness glanced at in the man's conception that the stepmother or widow is "withering out" what belongs to the young man.) We read this speech aloud, discuss it, and then ask a student to read it again, so that students can hear the tones—the affection in "fair Hippolyta," the enthusiasm in "four happy days," and the pained longing in "but, O, methinks." (Speaking of longing, notice the long vowels in "O", "methinks," "slow," "old," and "moon.") In short, this is the time when we begin to talk about the marvelous flexibility of Shakespeare's blank verse.

Hippolyta in her reply introduces the motif of dreaming, with its suggestion of unreality, reinforces the motif of the moon, and in the figure of the "silver bow" manages to suggest Diana and also to suggest her own Amazon nature. Her speech ends with a reference to "solemnities," a word which, combined with Theseus's reference (a line and a half later) to "merriments," pretty much gives us the tone of the play: marriage is both a solemn and a merry affair.

In 15–18 we learn that Theseus and Hippolyta, now representatives of maturity, law, and order, were once combatants. Theseus's "I won thy love, doing thee injuries" introduces the motif of strange transformations. The chief of these of course are the transformations that the lovers undergo, that Titania's mind undergoes, and that Bottom undergoes, but there are others; for instance Hermia's defiance of her father turns his love to hate or at least to anger. Another word about the earlier histories of Theseus and Hippolyta: we hear, in 2.1.65 that Hippolyta has had some sort of affair with Oberon, and that Theseus was once a seducer and a rapist. By the time we have finished with the play, we can reasonably feel that Shakespeare is saying something about youthful lawless passion turning into something more decorous. In any case, Theseus's war with Hippolyta has turned into love, and so too the quarreling young lovers will ultimately be reconciled.

Into this picture of loving harmony wrought out of strife, with its promise of solemn joy ("With pomp, with triumph, and with reveling"), comes Egeus (accent on the second syllable), "Full of vexation." He is almost inarticulate—comically so—with rage: "Thou, thou, Lysander, thou hast given her rhymes . . . " (28), and he too speaks of "love" (29), "moonlight" (30), and "fantasy" (32). As in much comedy descended from Greek New Comedy, he insists that a harsh law be enforced. The play ultimately, of course, will brush this law aside, and Athens will thus be transformed from a constricting place to a newly enlarged and newly happy society.

His words are harsh—"As she is mine, I may dispose of her"—but they are in accord with the law (44), and Theseus at this stage can only try to persuade Hermia to obey her father. Theseus is paternalistic but very different from the irascible and tyrannical Egeus. He speaks more gently than Egeus, and he ends by saying (one hears kindness in his tone) "Demetrius is a worthy gentleman." To Hermia's pert response ("So is Lysander") Theseus continues to try to speak in kindly fashion: "In himself he is; / But in this kind, wanting your father's voice, / The other must be held the worthier." Hermia persists ("I would my father looked but with my eyes"), and Theseus patiently tries again, picking up Hermia's words: "Rather your eyes must with his judgement look." Why is Hermia so bold? She herself does not know ("I know not by what power I am made bold"), but we do—the power of love.

Theseus at some length, and with some gentleness, sets forth the grim possibilities that await Hermia, and we feel that although he represents order and maturity, and although he is well-meaning and his speech is beautiful, the choice he now offers is monstrous. He himself is aware that it is harsh, and he urges her to "Take time to pause," and he manages to introduce a reference to his own forthcoming marriage.

Lysander makes the point that Demetrius "Made love to Nedar's daughter, Helena," and so it is appropriate that the play ends with Demetrius paired with Helena, and Lysander with Hermia. As Puck will say, "Jack shall have Jill." Theseus, that embodiment of reason and authority, confesses that he has heard of Demetrius's behavior and has been negligent in speaking to him, but notice that in line 115 he invites Egeus also to a conference, for some "private schooling." One can assume that Theseus will do what he can to persuade Egeus to relent—though we never get such a scene.

Left alone, Lysander and Hermia engage in a charming duet to the effect that "The course of true love never did run smooth"—a motif that we will see exemplified in the play. As these youthful lovers exchange their patterned lines ("O cross," "Or else," "O spite," "Or else") it is hard not to smile at them, not to think of them as charming puppets, but they are scarcely objects of severe satire. If we smile at them, we also sympathize with them, even as they talk prettily about tragic love stories. One of the things that is especially interesting here is, of course, that Shakespeare does introduce tragic motifs into this comedy. Lines 140–49 would not be out of place in *Romeo and Juliet*. Our point: *MSND* is a comedy of love, but Shakespeare gives us a glimpse of the tragedy of love—and of course later, in the story of *Pyramus and Thisbe*, he will give us a glimpse of the comedy of the tragedy of love.

And so these two eager lovers, who in line 152 talk of exhibiting "patience," immediately decide to run away from "the sharp Athenian law" (162) to the "wood" (165), the realm which Northrop Frye has called "the green world," that enchanted place that occupies the middle of so many comedies—before the lovers troop back to the ordinary world. One notices that this wood is associated (1.1.167) with an "observance to a morn of May," that is with May Day, a holiday of love. Hermia's longish speech (168–78), in which she vows true love, interestingly is filled with references to the fragility of love, notably Aeneas's betrayal of Dido.

One should notice, too, the pairs of rhyming lines in 171–78. Although for the most part the young lovers speak blank verse, we can say that couplets are one of their characteristic idioms. Notice that the couplets continue with Helena's entrance, and they go on to the end of the scene.

In Helena's long, final speech in this scene, it's worth pointing out that when she says, "Things base and vile, holding no quantity, / Love can transpose to form and dignity," Helena might almost be describing Titania's infatuation with Bottom. It's also worth pointing out—especially if you teach *Othello* in the same course—that although in *A Midsummer Night's Dream* love's obsessiveness is comic, it can be tragic elsewhere.

   1.2. If the talk of tragic love in the first scene conceivably caused a viewer to think that perhaps the play would be a tragedy, this comic scene makes it clear that the play is a comedy. Although the play of *Pyramus and Thisbe* is a tragic tale demonstrating that "the course of true love never did run smooth, "we can be assured that with these performers the play (and the larger play in which it is embedded) will afford laughter. Notice too, near the end of the scene, that Quince tells his fellows that they will meet "in the palace wood . . . by moonlight," thus assuring us that the story of these rustics will somehow be connected to that of the lovers.

   1.2 is one of the scenes (the other is 4.1) which we usually ask students to perform in class. It calls for six performers, and although the roles are all male, there is no reason not to use women. On the photocopies that we give the actors and the director, we suggest that at the beginning of the scene the performers huddle close together (they are insecure), until Bottom confidently and grandly says "Masters, spread yourselves." We also suggest that Bottom is a know-it-all, and that in his second speech ("First, good Peter Quince") his manner is somewhat that of a teacher lecturing to children. In "A very good piece of work" he sounds rather pompous. When he comes to discussing the part of the lover ("If I do it, let the audience look to their eyes") he is perhaps not so much pompous as childlishly enthusiastic and self-satisfied. (Again, our practice is to scribble suggestions of this sort on the photocopies, in order to give inexperienced readers some help, but other instructors may want to leave everything up to the students.) Presumably he recites the grotesque verse ("The raging rocks") in what he considers a lofty vein, and then, pleased with his performance, he congratulates himself ("This was lofty!") but then briskly turns back to the business at hand: "Now name the rest of the players." Still, he can't quite forget his noble performance, so he immediately adds, "This is Ercles' vein, a tyrant's vein."

   Other points about this scene: Flute's "I have a beard coming" should probably be said in a whimpering tone, perhaps while he feels his face. Bottom's "Well, proceed," may be uttered in a hurt tone, though Bottom regains his enthusiasm when he expresses the desire to play the lion too. When Quince insists that Bottom play only Pyramus, he is flattering Bottom as he describes the role ("for Pyramus, is a sweet-faced man," etc.), and Bottom accepts, but a bit unhappily ("Well, I will undertake it"). Near the very end of the scene, Bottom's "adieu" is perhaps said rather dramatically. Quince then adds a remark, but Bottom must have the last line: "Enough; hold or cut bow strings" (perhaps the "Enough" is accompanied by the gesture of raising his hand authoritatively). Bottom of course is an ass, but a likeable ass despite his bullying. One thing that makes him likeable is his utter confidence, whether among mortals or fairies.

2.1. "Puck" is not really the character's name; rather, he is "the Puck," that is, "the spook" or "the pixy" (the words probably are all related). Since he is reputed to be mischievous, he is propitiated by being called "Goodfellow," just as the Furies in Greek mythology are called the Eumenides ("the well-meaning ones"). In this play, Puck is turned into something like Cupid, that is a blind force (he errs in applying the juice of the flower) that overrides reason. One should note, however, that although Theseus describes the power of the herb in 2.1.170–173, we have already seen this power at work in Hermia, who defied her father, and we have heard how it turned Demetrius from Helena to Hermia. The herb, then, is merely a sort of concrete embodiment of what we already know exists.

This scene set in the wood—traditionally a place of unreason—makes a contrast with the Athens of the first scene, though, truth to tell, despite Theseus's attempts to reason with Hermia, Athens did not seem very reasonable. In any case, the fairys' song marks the place as something very different from the blank verse world of Theseus or the prose world of the rustics.

The fuss about the changeling (20–31) is a bit of a puzzle. Why is Oberon so eager to get the boy? Perhaps the idea is that since the child is male, he belongs ultimately in the male world, and so when Titania yields the boy we see something comparable to the proper pairing of the lovers, to Jack having Jill. That is, order is restored, things are at last in their proper places. Perhaps one can go further, and say that Oberon's triumph over Titania is the proper (in the Elizabethan view) triumph of male will over female will, something comparable to Theseus's triumph over the Amazon Hippolyta. The trouble with this reading, however, is that surely readers and viewers side with Titania, who is loyal to her dead companion, and we probably see Oberon as a sort of spoiled child who petulantly wants the toy of another child.

Titania's accusations (65–73) that Oberon has courted Phillida and has some sort of attachment to Hippolyta gives rise to Oberon's charge that Titania has favored Theseus. What is especially important here is the picture of Theseus as rapist and betrayer (78–80). The Theseus that we see in the play is well-meaning, fair-minded, and a self-restrained lover, but we are reminded that even this courtly figure has a badly tarnished history.

2.2. Again the fairies speak in a characteristic form (song). Titania is put to sleep with song, and she will be awakened by song—Bottom's raucous singing. (Later the young lovers will be put to sleep by fairy song, and will be awakened by mortal music.) If you read passages aloud in class, don't neglect the opportunity to read 34–61, in which Hermia fends off Lysander. Lysander speaks romantically ("One turf shall serve as pillow for us both, / One heart, one bed, two bosoms, and one troth") but Hermia is not taken in: "Lie further off." One further point about this scene: although in 2.1 Puck says he is mischievous (43–57), he is *not* being mischievous when he anoints the eyes of the wrong lover. Oberon has told him he will recognize the youth by his Athenian clothes, so the mistake is an honest one.

3.1. Bottom's faith that a prologue will diminish the power of the illusion that *Pyramus and Thisbe* will create allows instructors to talk about dramatic illusion, the power of art, realism versus convention, and soon we inevitably get into some of this, but we usually make a point of reading some of the scene's lines for laughs. And we always read Bottom's song, Titania's line when she awakens, and on through Bottom's "Reason and love keep little company together."

3.2. Puck's lines in 110–21 can hardly be neglected. It's worth discussing the most famous line, "Lord, what fools these mortals be." Is this Shakespeare's judgement on humanity? (No, it's the comment of one character in the play—but one feels that there certainly is *something* to it.) One can easily get into a discussion of engagement and detachment in drama, and of Horace Walpole's famous comment that life is a comedy to those who think, a tragedy to those who feel. That is, if one *feels* for the lovers (sympathizes with them), one suffers; if one *thinks* about them (i.e. if one is detached from them), they seem absurd. Also relevant is a remark (Hazlitt, if we recall) on Pope's *The Rape of the Lock*, to the effect that it is like looking through the wrong end of the telescope.

We enjoy the misunderstandings of the lovers; we can laugh at them because we scarcely *feel* their pain, and we scarcely feel their pain because Shakespeare takes care not to make their statements too powerful. The jingling couplets, for instance, help to make the lovers somewhat puppet-like.

As we mentioned a moment ago, Puck's error was innocent, not malicious. Oberon takes care to point out, when Puck talks of "damned spirits" and of those who "themselves exile from light," that "we are spirits of another sort," and he associates himself with "the Morning's love." Appropriately, then, Puck undoes his error by bringing the lovers together and by applying the juice yet again so that (in the last words of the scene) "Jack shall have Jill . . . and all shall be well."

4.1. We usually ask students to perform this scene. On the photocopies that we give the students (11 roles, plus a horn player or trumpeter) we make suggestions along the following lines.

Bottom and Titania sleep (it's ok to sit) to one side; at the other side the four lovers sleep or sit. *Then* Puck enters from one side, Oberon from the other, and they stand by Titania and Bottom. Oberon's first line is spoken enthusiastically, the second is spoken in a more thoughtful, meditative tone. Lines 74–79: recited as a spell. Titania's waking words: the first line is spoken in a voice of awe, the second perhaps in a more puzzled way. When Oberon points to Bottom, Titania says, in a tone of revulsion, "O, how mine eyes do loathe his visage now!" Line 87 ("Now, when thou wak'st") is spoken to Bottom. In the next line, be sure (following the text) to take hands. No need to dance, but if the spirit moves you . . . . Titania and Bottom go off to one side, where the sleeping lovers are *not*.

Theseus' words should be spoken authoritatively but genially. (He is confident of his authority and need not be pompous.) Egeus is still the crabby old man. His first three lines here perhaps are spoken (as the fourth line indicates) in "wonder," but also in a somewhat fussy and explosive way. Certainly in 157–59 we hear his anger: "Enough, enough, my lord; you have enough . . . They would . . . they would . . . you and me, / You . . . me." The same sputtering that we heard in the first scene of the play. Demetrius speaks 167–70 and 190–97 with puzzlement, awe. When Bottom awakens, his "Heigh-ho" is rather like an ass's braying. And when he says "methought I had," he puts his hand on top of his head, and feels to see if he has ass's ears. (Lots of opportunity for engaging in business here; with a good deal of trepidation he feels for the ears but of course doesn't find them, then checks once more, and then expresses great relief.) His last lines here are, of course, spoken with great self-satisfaction.

4.2. This scene brings an end to the complications of the play: the lovers are properly paired, and Bottom is restored to the theatrical company. Why, then, a fifth act? Because we in the audience know that there is to be a wedding, and because we want to see a performance of *Pyramus and Thisbe*. In short, what follows gives us not the pleasure of surprise but the pleasure of the fulfillment of expectation. Further, *Pyramus and Thisbe*—intended to be tragic—shows us how the lovers' story *might* have turned out but, fortunately, did not.

5.1. If one doesn't read every line of this scene aloud—and there probably isn't time to do so—one must at least read the first 26 lines, about "imaginations" and its effects on "the lunatic, the lover, and the poet." As Northrop Frye somewhere says, what ability in literary criticism there is in Athens is possessed by Hippolyta (23–27). The passage is so rich that pages can be (and have been) written on it, but here we will point out only that the confident Theseus, who dismisses "antique fables," is himself an antique fable, that is a character of legend. And if he is dismissive of "fairy toys," we have nevertheless seen fairies in this play, and we know that they attend upon his wedding. And we have seen that in dreams there is truth (e.g. Hermia's dream in 2.2 that Lysander laughed as her heart was being eaten away). Another word about Theseus: in 89–105 he sounds pretty complacent, and we probably should not try to whitewash him, but despite his self-satisfaction he makes some thoughtful points about taking a good intention for the deed.

The play-within-the-play. We have not been particularly lucky when we have had this scene performed in class. It looks easy, but it takes skillful actors to make it funny.

We can never refrain from reading Theseus's last speech, where he (presumably jocosely) acknowledges the existence of fairies ("'tis almost fairy time"), nor can we refrain from reading aloud the remainder of the play. In our general comment on the final act we mentioned that chiefly it fulfills our expectations—but now comes a surprise, for we probably did not expect to see the fairies again, although, come to think of it, we were told that they have come to Athens for the royal wedding. Further, their presence now reminds us that the mortal world—sometimes rational and sometimes irrational—is surrounded by a mysterious world that mortals can never comprehend. Puck speaks of the workaday world ("the heavy ploughman," " weary task," "a shroud," etc.), but these lines lead to an exorcism of evil spirits, and to a benediction by Oberon and Titania. The "glimmering light" perhaps put Elizabethan viewers in mind of midsummer eve revels when torches were ignited at a "blessing fire" and were brought from the woods to the hearth to promote good luck and fertility. Finally, in Puck's last lines he suggests that the audience may regard this whole performance as a mere dream—but we have seen in this play that dreams (e.g. Bottom's) are real.

Bibliographic Note: There are many valuable studies of the play, but among short introductions we especially recommend three: the chapter on the play in C. L. Barber, *Shakespeare's Festive Comedy* (1959); Frank Kermode's essay in *Stratford-upon Avon Studies 3: The Early Shakespeare* (1961), ed. John Russell Brown and Bernard Harris, reprinted in the Signet Classic Edition of *A Midsummer Night's Dream*; Alvin Kernan's discussion in *The Revels History of Drama in English*, Vol 3, ed. J. Leeds Barroll at al. (1975). For a short readable book, see David P. Young, *Something of Great Constancy: The Art of "A Midsummer Night's Dream"* (1966). Also useful is a small book by Roger Warren, *A Midsummer Night's Dream: Text and Performance* (1983). Warren devotes his first 30–odd pages to a general study of the play, and the rest of the book (again about 30 pages) to an examination of several performances, from Peter Hall's 1959 production to Elijah Moshinsky"s 1981 BBC Television production. If you have more time, you may want to read the essays collected by Harold Bloom in *William Shakespeare's A Midsummer Night's Dream* (1987), and study the Arden Edition of the play, edited by Harold F. Brooks (1979). This volume has a book-length introduction, detailed footnotes, and appendices on textual cruces and so forth.

Henrik Ibsen *A Doll's House* (p. 918)

First, it should be mentioned that the title of the play does *not* mean that Nora is the only doll, for the toy house is not merely Nora's; Torvald, as well as Nora, inhabits this unreal world, for Torvald—so concerned with appearing proper in the eyes of the world—can hardly be said to have achieved a mature personality.

A *Doll's House* (1879) today seems more "relevant" than it has seemed in decades, and yet one can put too much emphasis on its importance as a critique of male chauvinism. Although the old view that Ibsen's best-known plays are "problem plays" about remediable social problems rather than about more universal matters is still occasionally heard, Ibsen himself spoke against it. In 1898, for example, he said, "I must disclaim the honor of having consciously worked for women's rights. I am not even quite sure what women's rights really are. To me it has been a question of human rights" (quoted in Michael Meyer, *Ibsen*, II, p. 297). By now it seems pretty clear that *A Doll's House*, in Robert Martin Adams's words (in *Modern Drama*, ed. A Caputi), "represents a woman imbued with the idea of becoming a person, but it proposes nothing categorical about women becoming people; in fact, its real theme has nothing to do with the sexes. It is the irrepressible conflict of two different personalities which have founded themselves on two radically different estimates of realty." Or, as Eric Bentley puts it in *In Search of Theater* (p. 350 in the Vintage edition), "Ibsen pushes his investigation toward a further and even deeper subject [than that of a woman's place in a man's world], the tyranny of one human being over another, in this respect the play would be just as valid were Torvald the wife and Nora the husband."

Michael Meyer's biography, *Ibsen*, is good on the background (Ibsen knew a woman who forged a note to get money to aid her husband, who denounced and abandoned her when he learned of the deed), but surprisingly little has been written on the dramaturgy of the play. Notable exceptions are John Northam, "Ibsen's Dramatic Method," an essay by Northam printed in *Ibsen*, ed. Rolf Fjelde (in the Twentieth Century Views series), and Elizabeth Hardwick's chapter on the play in her *Seduction and Betrayal*. Northam calls attention to the symbolic use of properties (e.g., the Christmas tree in Act I, a symbol of a secure, happy family, is in the center of the room, but in Act II, when Nora's world has begun to crumble, it is in a corner bedraggled, and with burnt-out candles), costume (e.g., Nora's Italian costume is suggestive of pretense and is removed near the end of the play; the black shawl, symbolic of death, becomes—when worn at the end with ordinary clothes—an indication of her melancholy lonely life), and gestures (e.g., blowing out the candles, suggesting defeat; the wild dance; the final slamming of the door).

For a collection of recent essays on the play, see *Approaches to Teaching Ibsen's " A Doll's House"*, ed. Yvonne Shafer. Also of interest is Austin E. Quigley's discussion in *Modern Drama* 27 (1984): 584–603, reprinted with small changes in his *The Modern Stage and Other Worlds*. Dorothea Krook, in *Elements of Tragedy*, treats the play as a tragedy. She sets forth what she takes to be the four universal elements of the genre (the act of shame or horror, consequent intense suffering, then an increase in knowledge, and finally a reaffirmation of the value of life) and suggests that these appear in *A Doll's House*—the shameful condition being "the marriage relationship which creates Nora's doll's house' situation." Krook calls attention, too, to the "tragic irony" of Torvald's comments on Krogstad's immorality (he claims it poisons a household) and to Nora's terror, which, Krook says, "evokes the authentic Aristolelian pity."

One can even go a little further than Krook goes and make some connection between *A Doll's House* and *Oedipus the King*. Nora, during her years as a housewife, like Oedipus during his kingship, *thought* that she was happy, but finds out that she really wasn't, and at the end of the play she goes out (self-banished), leaving her children, to face an uncertain but surely difficult future. Still, although the play can be discussed as a tragedy, and cannot be reduced to a "problem play," like many of Ibsen's other plays it stimulates a discussion of the questions, What ought to be done? and What happened next? Hermann J. Weigand, in *The Modern Ibsen* (1925), offered conjectures about Nora's future actions, saying,

> But personally I am convinced that after putting Torvald through a sufficiently protracted ordeal of suspense, Nora will yield to his entreaties and return home—on her own terms. She will not bear the separation from her children very long, and her love for Torvald, which is not as dead as she thinks, will reassert itself. For a time the tables will be reversed: a meek and chastened husband will eat out of the hand of his squirrel; and Nora, hoping to make up by a sudden spurt of zeal for twenty-eight years of lost time, will be trying desperately hard to grow up. I doubt, however, whether her volatile enthusiasm will even carry her beyong the stage of resolutions. The charm of novelty worn off, she will tire of the new game very rapidly and revert, imperceptibly, to her role of songbird and charmer, as affording an unlimited range to the excercise of her inborn talents of coquetry and playacting.

Students may be invited to offer their own conjectures on the unwritten fourth act.

Another topic for class discussion or for an essay, especially relevant to question 4: Elizabeth Hardwick suggests (*Seduction and Betrayal*, p. 46.) that Ibsen failed to place enough emphasis on Nora's abandonment of the children. In putting "the leaving of her children on the same moral and emotional level as the leaving of her husband Ibsen has been too much a man in the end. He has taken the man's practice, if not his stated belief, that where self-realization is concerned children shall not be an impediment." But in a feminist reading of the play, Elaine Hoffman Baruch, in *Yale Review* 69 (Spring 1980), takes issue with Hardwick, arguing that "it is less a desire for freedom than a great sense of inferiority and the desire to find out more about the male world outside the home that drives Nora away from her children" (p.37)

Finally, one can discuss with students the comic aspects of the play—the ending (which, in a way, is happy, though of course Nora's future is left in doubt), and especially Torvald's fatuousness. The fatuousness perhaps reaches its comic height early in Act III, when, after lecturing Mrs. Linde on the importance of an impressive exit (he is telling her how, for effect, he made his "capricious little Capri girl" leave the room after her dance), he demonstrates the elegance of the motion of the hands while embroidering and the ugliness of the motions when knitting. Also comic are his ensuing fantasies, when he tells the exhausted Nora that he fantasizes that she is his "secret" love, though the comedy turns ugly when after she rejects his amorous advances ("I have desired you all evening"), he turns into a bully: "I'm your husband, aren't I?" The knock on the front door (Rank) reintroduces comedy, for it reduces the importunate husband to conventional affability ("Well! How good of you not to pass by the door"), but of course it also saves Nora from what might have been an ugly assault.

Topics for Discussion and Writing

1. To what extent is Nora a victim, and to what extent is she herself at fault for her way of life?
2. Is the play valuable only as in image of an aspect of life in the later nineteenth century, or is it still an image of an aspect of life?
3. In the earlier part of the play Nora tells Helmer, Mrs. Linde, and herself that she is happy. Is she? Explain. Why might she be happy? Why not? Can a case be made that Mrs. Linde, who must work to support herself, is happier than Nora?
4. Write a dialogue—approximately two double-spaced pages—setting forth a chance encounter when Torvald and Nora meet five years after the end of Ibsen's play.
5. Write a persuasive essay, arguing that Nora was right—or wrong—to leave her husband and children. In your essay recognize the strengths of the opposing view and try to respond to them.

Tennessee Williams *The Glass Managerie* (p. 979)

The books on Williams that have appeared so far are disappointing. The best general survey is Henry Popkin's article in *Tulane Drama Review* 4 (Spring 1960): 45–64; also useful is Gordon Rogoff, in *Tulane Drama Review* 10 (Summer 1966): 78–92. For a comparison between the play and earlier versions, see Lester A. Beaurline, *Modern Drama* 8 (1965): 142–149. For a discussion of Christian references and motifs (e.g., Amanda's candelabrum, which was damaged when lightning struck the church), see Roger B. Stein, in *Western Humanities Review* 18 (Spring 1964): 141–153, reprinted in *Tennessee Williams*, ed. Stephen S. Stanton. Stein suggests that the play shows us a world in which Christianity has been replaced by materialism.

Perhaps the two points that students find most difficult to understand are that Amanda is both tragic *and* comic (see the comments below, on the first suggested topic for writing), and that Tom's quest for reality has about it something of adolescent romanticism. Tom comes under the influence of his father (who ran away from his responsibilities), and he depends heavily on Hollywood movies. This brings up another point: It is obvious that Amanda, Laura, and Tom cherish illusions, but students sometimes do not see that Williams suggests that all members of society depended in some measure on the illusions afforded by movies, magazine fiction, liquor, dance halls, sex, and other things that "flooded the world with brief, deceptive rainbows," while the real world of Berchtesgaden, moving toward World War II, was for a while scarcely seen. If Amanda, Laura, and Tom are outsiders living partly on illusions, so is everyone else, including Jim, whose identification with the myth of science may strike most views as hopelessly out of touch with reality.

The Glass Managerie has twice been filmed, most recently in 1987, directed by Paul Newman. Newman followed Williams's sequence of scenes, and he kept almost all the dialogue, yet the film strikes us as unsuccessful. Why? Probably this "memory play" needs to be somewhat distanced, framed by a proscenium. Further, the film's abundant close-ups seem wrong; they make the play too energetic, too aggressive. Such are our impressions; instructors who rent the film (Cineplex Odeon) can ask students to set forth their own impressions—in writing.

An audio cassette of Tennessee Williams reading is available from HarperCollins.

Topics for Discussion and Writing

1. Comedy in *The Glass Managerie*. (Students should be cautioned that comedy need not be "relief". It can help to modify the tragic aspects, or rather, to define a special kind of tragedy. A few moments spent on the Porter scene in *Macbeth*—with which almost all students are familiar—will probably help to make clear the fact that comedy may be integral.)

2. Compare the function of Tom with the function of the Chorus in *Antigone*. (Williams calls his play a "memory play." What we see is supposed to be the narrator's memory—not the dramatist's representation—of what happened. Strictly speaking, the narrator is necessarily unreliable in the scene between Laura and Jim, for he was not present, but as Williams explains in the "Production Notes," what counts is not what happened but what the narrator remembers as having happened or, more exactly, the narrator's response to happenings.)

3. Cinematic techniques in *The Glass Managerie*. (Among these are fade-ins and fade-outs; projected titles, reminiscent of titles in silent films; the final "interior pantomime" of Laura and Amanda, enacted while Tom addresses the audience, resembles by its silence a scene from silent films, or a scene in a talking film in which the sound track gives a narrator's voice instead of dramatic dialogue. By the way, it should be noted that Williams, when young, like Tom, often attended movies, and that this play was adapted from Williams's rejected screen play, *The Gentleman Caller*, itself derived from one of Williams's short stories.) Topic 3 and 4 are ways of getting at the importance of *un*realistic settings and techniques in this "memory play."

4. Compare the play with the earlier Williams short story, "Portrait of a Girl in Class," in *One Arm and Other Stories*.

Arthur Miller *Death of a Salesman* (p. 1037)

(This discussion is an abbreviation of our introduction in *Types of Drama*.) The large question, of course, is whether Willy is a tragic or a pathetic figure. For the ancient Greeks, at least for Aristotle, *pathos* was the destructive or painful act common in tragedy; but in English "pathos" refers to an element in art or life that evokes tenderness or sympathetic pity. Modern English critical usage distinguishes between tragic figures and pathetic figures by recognizing some element either of strength or of regeneration in the former that is not in the latter. The tragic protagonist perhaps acts so that he brings his destruction upon himself, or if his destruction comes from outside, he resists it, and in either case he comes to at least a partial understanding of the causes of his suffering. The pathetic figure, however, is largely passive, an unknowing and unresisting innocent. In such a view Macbeth is tragic, Duncan pathetic; Lear is tragic, Cordelia pathetic; Othello is tragic, Desdemona pathetic; Hamlet is tragic (the situation is not of his making, but he does what he can to alter it), Ophelia pathetic. (Note, by the way, that of the four pathetic figures named, the first is old and the remaining three are women. Pathos is more likely to be evoked by persons assumed to be relatively defenseless than by the able-bodied.)

The guardians of critical terminology, then, have tended to insist that "tragedy" be reserved for a play showing action that leads to suffering which in turn leads to knowledge. They get very annoyed when a newspaper describes as a tragedy the death of a promising high school football player in an automobile accident, and they insist that such a death is pathetic not tragic; it is unexpected, premature, and deeply regrettable, but it does not give us a sense of human greatness achieved through understanding the sufferings that a sufferer has at least in some degree chosen. Probably critics hoard the term "tragedy" because it is also a word of praise: To call a play a comedy or a problem play is not to imply anything about its merits, but to call a play a tragedy is tantamount to calling it an important or even a great play. In most of the best-known Greek tragedies, the protagonist either does some terrible deed or resists mightily. But Greek drama has its pathetic figures too, figures who do not so much act as suffer. Euripides's *The Trojan Women* is perhaps the greatest example of a play which does not allow its heroes to choose and to act but only to undergo, to be in agony. When we think of pathetic figures in Greek drama, however, we probably think chiefly of the choruses, groups of rather commonplace persons who do not perform a tragic deed but who suffer in sympathy with the tragic hero, who lament the hardness of the times, and who draw spectators into the range of the hero's suffering.

Arthur Miller has argued that because Oedipus has given his name to a complex that the common man may have, the common man is therefore "as apt a subject for tragedy." It is not Oedipus's complex," however, but his unique importance that is the issue in the play. Moreover, even if one argues that people of no public importance may suffer as much as people of public importance (and surely no one doubts this), one may be faced with the fact that the unimportant people by their ordinances are not particularly good material for drama, and we are here concerned with drama rather than with life. In *Death of a Salesman*, Willy Loman's wife says, rightly, "A small man can be just as exhausted as a great man." Yes, but is his exhaustion itself interesting, and do his activities (and this includes the words he utters) before his exhaustion have interesting dramatic possibilities? Isn't there a colorlessness that may weaken the play, an impoverishment of what John Milton called "gorgeous tragedy"?

Miller accurately noted (*Theatre Arts*, October 1953) that American drama " has been steady year by year documentation of the frustration of man," and it is evident that Miller has set out to restore a sense of importance, if not greatness, to the individual. In "Tragedy and the Common Man," published in *The New York Times* (27 February 1949, sec. 2, pp. 1,3) in the same year that *Death of a Salesman* was produced and evidently a defense of the play, he argues on behalf of the common man as a tragic figure and he insists that tragedy and pathos are very different: "Pathos truly is the mode of the pessimist . . . The plays we revere, century after century, are the tragedies. In them, and in them alone, lies the belief—optimistic, if you will—in the perfectibility of man." Elsewhere (*Harper's* August 1958) he has said that pathos is an oversimplification and therefore is the "counterfeit of meaning." Curiously, however, many spectators and readers find that by Miller's own terms Willy Loman fails to be a tragic figure; he seems to them pathetic rather than tragic, a victim rather than a man who acts and who wins esteem. True, he is partly the victim of his own actions (although he could have chosen to be a carpenter, he chose to live by the bourgeois code that values a white collar), but he seems in larger part to be a victim of the system itself, a system of ruthless competition that has no place for the man who can no longer produce. (Here is an echo of the social-realist drama of the thirties.) Willy had believed in this system; and although his son Biff comes to the realization that Willy "had the wrong dreams," Willy himself seems not to achieve this insight. Of course he knows that he is out of a job, that the system does not value him any longer, but he still seems not to question the values he had subscribed to. Even in the last minutes of the play, when he is planning his suicide in order to provide money for his family—really for Biff—he says such things as "Can you imagine his magnificence with twenty thousand dollars in his pocket? and "When the mail comes he'll be ahead of Bernard again." In the preface to his *Collected*

Plays Miller comments on the "exultation" with which Willy faces the end, but it is questionable whether an audience shares it. Many people find that despite the gulf in rank, they can share King Lear's feelings more easily than Willy's.

Suggested references: Several reviews and essays are collected in *Two Modern American Tragedies*, ed. John D. Hurrell (1961). Among the reviews are pieces by Eleanor Clark (hostile), in *Partisan Review* 26 (June 1949): 631–635, and Harold Clurman (favorable) in Clurman's *Lies Like Truth*. Hurrell also reprints from *Tulane Drama Review* 2 [May 1958]: 63–69) an interesting discussion between Miller and several critics.

Two audio cassettes of Arthur Miller reading *Death of a Salesman* are available from HarperCollins.

Topic for Writing

Willy says Biff can't fail because "he's got spirit, personality . . . personal attractiveness . . . Personality always wins the day." In an essay of 500 to 1000 words, distinguish between "personality" and "character," and then describe each of these in Willy.

Joyce Carol Oates *Tone Clusters* (p. 1118)

In her introductory note Oates says that *Tone Clusters* is not intended to be a realistic work," and of course it is not—though many of the lines do bear an uncanny resemblance to the lines one hears on talk shows. The fatuous Voice—usually pretentious, consistently oblivious of the people he is supposedly interviewing—and the pitiful Gulicks—touchingly loyal to their son, unaware of his obvious guilt, and unaware of the way in which the interviewer is exploiting them—can be heard almost daily.

The barely hidden narrative that emerges is that Carl (a youth with severe mental problems—for one thing, he mutilates pornographic pictures of women) has killed the girl. (The play is indebted to the life of Richard Golub, who in 1990 was convicted of murdering a 13-year-old girl. Details are available by following the *New York Times Index*.) Oates's assertion (again in her initial comment) that the Gulicks' failure to perceive this "fractured narrative" is the "tragic-comedy of the piece," may shock many students. These students may feel nothing but pity for the Gulicks, and may see nothing comic (or tragi-comic) in any aspect of the play. Here is a chance to discuss the meaning(s) of "tragi-comedy," and to discuss tragedy and comedy. Oedipus's unawareness is universally agreed to be tragic; why, then, an instructor may ask, is the unawareness of the Gulicks not equally tragic? Certainly most of their lines evoke pathos, though at least occasionally their failure to understand what is happening evokes a smile. Our favorite passage of this sort occurs just after Frank complains that the neighbors "threw trash on our lawn" (surely a despicable act.) Emily says, "Oh Frank has worked so hard on that lawn, it's his pride and joy." Here we are close to the Bergsonian formula of the comic as "the mechanical encrusted on the organic." That is, in Emily's comment we get a mechanical, stock response (in effect the word "lawn" triggers the cliche,, "Frank works hard on it") which is utterly inappropriate in the context, where what is horrible is not that a carefully kept lawn has been sullied, but that neighbors instead of pitying and trying to help the Gulicks have attacked them.

Also comic, of course, are the idiocies of the Voice, especially the pretentious questions and comments about fate, "neuron discharges," and so forth, and the Voice's failure to keep the names of the characters straight. Not at all comic is Frank's pitiful recognition at the end that one day in the family is like another, "Until one day it isn't."

Luis Valdez *Los Vendidos* (p. 1164)

Students who have been told that stereotyping people is wicked, and that characters (whether in fiction or in drama) should be well-motivated, believable, and so on may find it difficult to see anything of value in a work that uses one-dimensional stock characters. Perhaps one way to help them enjoy such a work is to talk briefly about stereotypes in films that they have enjoyed and admired. The roles performed by Chaplin, the Marx Brothers, Bogart—or even some roles in soap operas—may help them to see that stereotyped characters can be powerful.

Los Vendidos is comic in the sense of having some laughs in it, and also (at least to a degree) in the more literary sense of being a play with a happy ending. If one stands at a distance, so to speak, and looks at the overall plot, one sees the good guys outwitting the bad guys (Ms. Jimenez). In the talk about going to a party, there is even a hint of the traditional *komos* or revel.

It is of course entirely appropriate that the play include amusing passages. Valdez has said that he wanted to lift the morale of his audience (chiefly striking workers), and he wrote and staged comedies—in the sense of plays with happy endings—because he wanted to help change society. He did not want, obviously, to show the tragic nature of the human condition. He makes his aims clear in his short essay, "The Actos" (see question 6). One might ask student to think especially about whether in this play he does anything to "show or hint at a solution" to the "social problem." In some *actos* the message is clear, for instance "Join the union."

It's our view that *Los Vendidos* does not at all suffer by failing to give a "solution." (Of course it's implied that Anglos should not think of Mexican-Americans as stupid and lazy, should not expect them to be subservient, and should value them as people, but Valdez does not offer a solution for Anglo prejudice.) Much of the strength of the play seems to us to lie in the wit with which the stereotypes are presented, and also in the ingenuity of the plot, when the robots come alive and thus reverse the stereotype: the Mexican-Americans are shown to be shrewd and enterprising, and Honest Sancho is shown to be lifeless.

Additional Topic for Writing or Discussion

At the end of the play the Mexican-Americans are shown as shrewd and enterprising. Has Valdez fallen into the trap of suggesting that Mexican-American culture is not distinctive but is just about the same as the Anglo imperialistic (capitalistic) culture that he has satirized earlier in the play?

August Wilson *Fences* (p. 1177)

Some background (taken from our *Types of Drama*) on the history of blacks in the American theatre may be of use. In the 1940s and 1950s black playwrights faced the difficult problem of deciding what audience they were writing for—an audience of blacks or of whites? The difficulty was compounded by the fact that although there were a number of black theatre groups—for example, the American Negro Theatre (founded by blacks in 1940)—there was not a large enough black theatre-going public to make such groups commercially successful. In fact, although the original ideal of the American Negro Theatre was "to portray Negro life . . . honestly," within a few years it was doing plays by white writers, such as Thonton Wilder's *Our Town* (not only by a white but about whites) and Philip Yordan's *Anna Lucasta* (by a white, and originally about a Polish working-class family, but transformed into a play about a black family). Further, the aim of such groups usually was in large measure to employ black actors and theater technicians; some of the most talented of these, including Harry Belafonte, Sidney Poitier, and Ruby Dee, then went on to enter the mainstream of white theatre, on Broadway, or— a short step— in Hollywood. Meanwhile, such writers as James Baldwin and Lorraine Hansberry, though writing about black life, wrote plays that were directed at least as much at whites as at blacks. That is, their plays were in large measure attempts to force whites to look at what they had done to blacks.

In the mid-1960's, however, the most talented black dramatists, including LeRoi Jones (Imamu Amiri Baraka) and Ed Bullins, largely turned their backs on white audiences and in effect wrote plays aimed at showing blacks that *they*—not their white oppressors—must change, must cease to accept the myths that whites had created. Today, however, strongly revolutionary plays by and about blacks have difficulty getting a hearing. Instead, the newest black writers seem to be concerned less with raising the consciousness of blacks than with depicting black life and with letting both blacks and whites respond aesthetically rather than politically. Baraka has attributed the change to a desire by many blacks to become assimilated in today's society, and surely there is much to his view. One might also say, however, that black dramatists may for other reasons have come to assume that the business of drama is not to preach but to show, and that a profound, honest depiction—in a traditional, realistic dramatic form—of things as they are, or in Wilson's play, things as they were in the 1950s—will touch audiences whatever their color. "Part of the reason I wrote *Fences*," Wilson has said, "was to illuminate that generation, which shielded its children from all of the indignities they went through."

This is not to say, of course, that *Fences* is a play about people who just happen to be black. The Polish family of *Anna Lucasta* could easily be converted to a black family (though perhaps blacks may feel that there is something unconvincing about this family), but Troy Maxson's family cannot be whitewashed. The play is very much about persons who are what they are because they are blacks living in an unjust society run by whites. We are not allowed to forget this. Troy is a baseball player who was too old to join a white team when the major leagues began to hire blacks. (The first black player to play in the major leagues was Jackie Robinson, whom the Brooklyn Dodgers hired in 1947. Robinson retired in 1950, a year before the time in which *Fences* is chiefly set.) For Troy's friend, Bono, "Troy just came along too early"; but Troy pungently replies, "There ought not never have been no time called too early." Blacks of Troy's day were expected to subscribe to American—ideals for instance, to serve in the army in time of war—but they were also expected to sit in the back of the bus and to accept the fact that they were barred from decent jobs. Wilson shows us the scars that such treatment left. Troy is no paragon. Although he has a deep sense of responsibility to his family, his behavior toward them is deeply flawed; he oppresses his son Cory, he is unfaithful to his wife, Rose, and he exploits his brother Gabriel.

Wilson, as we have seen, calls attention to racism in baseball, and he indicates that Troy turned to crime because he could not earn money. But Wilson does not allow *Fences* to become a prolonged protest against white oppression—though one can never quite forget that Troy insists on a high personal ideal in a world that has cheated him. The interest in the play is in Troy as a human being, or, rather, in all of the characters as human beings rather than as representatives of white victimization. As Troy sees it, by preventing Cory from engaging in athletics—the career that frustrated Troy—he is helping rather than oppressing Cory: "I don't want him to be like me. I want him to move as far from me as he can." But Wilson also makes it clear that Troy has other (very human) motives, of which Troy perhaps is unaware.

A Note on the Word *Black*: The play is set in 1957 and (the last scene) 1965, before *black* and *African-American* were the words commonly applied to persons of African descent. The blacks in the play speak of "coloreds" and of "niggers." *Black* did not become the preferred word until the late 1960s. For instance the question was still open in November 1967, when *Ebony* magazine asked its readers whether the *Negro* should be replaced by *black* or *Afro-American*. The results of polls at that time chiefly suggested that *Afro-American* was the preferred choice. Since about 1988, *African-American* seems to be the preferred choice.

A thirty-minute video cassette of Bill Moyer's 30–minute interview with August Wilson is available from HarperCollins.